653 Fast-to-Fix Recipes For the Busiest Cooks

THE TENTH EDITION in our ever-popular cookbook series, *2008 Quick Cooking Annual Recipes* will surely make you agree—this annual collection just keeps getting better and better!

From the first chapter to the last, this exciting 2008 edition is jam-packed with every speedy-yet-tasty recipe published in *Simple & Delicious* magazine during 2007. That's 653 recipes...all at your fingertips.

With hundreds of full-color photos showing the prepared recipes, this can't-miss book makes it as easy as ever for you to fix home-cooked, mouth-watering meals for your family every day of the week.

Here's what else you'll find inside:

Chapters That Meet Your Needs. We divided the 653 recipes in this book into 21 chapters that make sense for busy cooks. Simply turn to whatever chapter fits your needs, and you'll enjoy plenty of delicious options. (See page 3 for a complete list of chapters.)

For example, when you have just 10 minutes to spare in the kitchen, try Fast French Dip Sandwiches, Ham 'n' Corn Chowder, Sesame Vegetable Medley, Nutty Banana Shakes, Candy Bar Parfaits or any of the 19 other super-quick dishes in the "10 Minutes to the Table" chapter.

Or, on hectic weekdays when your family is hungry for dinner and the clock is ticking, see the "30 Minutes to Mealtime" chapter for 26 complete meals that go from start to finish in half an hour or less.

Weekly Meals Planned for You. The experts in our Test Kitchen put together 6 full weeks of Monday-through-Friday dinners, complete with a shopping list for each week. Just follow their handy meal plans to enjoy weeks of stress-free suppers. (This chapter starts on page 108.)

Contest-Winning Dishes. You get all of the rave-winning, sensational dishes that earned top honors in the six national recipe contests held last year: Slow-Cooked Favorites; Cookie Dough Creations; Easy, Breezy Berries; Fix It with 5; Last-Minute Lunches and Fuss-Free Holiday Fare. Turn to page 4 to "meet" the Grand Prize winners and see where each standout recipe is located in the book.

Easy Holiday and Party Ideas. An all-new chapter, "Plan an Instant Party," makes it a breeze to host fun-filled events for your friends and family. And in "Holiday and Seasonal Pleasers," you'll revel in festive foods for Christmas, Halloween, July Fourth and more.

Reader-Friendly Indexes. We've listed all 653 recipes in two handy indexes. (See page 316.) The general index lists every recipe by category and/or major food ingredient. The alphabetical listing is great for folks who are looking for a specific dish. In both indexes, you'll find a bold red checkmark (✓) next to the recipes that use less fat, sugar or salt and include Nutrition Facts and Diabetic Exchanges.

Every rapid recipe and helpful hint in this *2008 Quick Cooking Annual Recipes* cookbook was specially selected with busy cooks in mind. With so much fast-to-fix home cooking, you and your loved ones are sure to enjoy this indispensable treasury right away—and for years to come.

2008 Quick Cooking Annual Recipes

Editor: Michelle Bretl

Art Director: Gretchen Trautman

Vice President/Books: Heidi Reuter Lloyd

Senior Editor/Books: Mark Hagen

Associate Editor: Jean Steiner

Layout Designers: Emma Acevedo (senior), Nancy Novak, Catherine Fletcher

Proofreader: Linne Bruskewitz

Editorial Assistant: Barb Czysz

Taste of Home Books
©2008 Reiman Media Group, Inc.
5400 S. 60th St., Greendale WI 53129

International Standard Book Number (10):
0-89821-683-4
International Standard Book Number (13):
978-0-89821-683-7
International Standard Serial Number: 1522-6603

All rights reserved. Printed in U.S.A.

PICTURED ON THE FRONT COVER: Checkerboard Ice Cream Cake (p. 237), Navy Bean Tossed Salad (p. 103), Sesame Breadsticks (p. 45) and Spinach Lasagna Roll-Ups (p. 240). Cover photography by Rob Hagen. Food styled by Sarah Thompson. Set styled by Jenny Bradley Vent.

YOU COULD BE IN OUR NEXT BOOK!

Submit a recipe to *Simple & Delicious* magazine, and you could be in *Quick Cooking Annual Recipes*! We're most interested in five-ingredient, half-hour entree and slow cooker recipes. To submit, go to *www.bestsimplerecipes.com*, e-mail *editors@bestsimplerecipes.com* or mail them to *Simple & Delicious*, 5925 Country Lane, Greendale WI 53129.

TASTE OF HOME

simple&delicious

Editor: Mary Spencer
Associate Editors: Mary C. Hanson, John McMillan, Elizabeth Russell
Art Director: Nicholas Mork
Graphic Designer: Monica Bergwall
Food Director: Diane Werner RD
Food Editor: Amy Welk-Thieding RD
Recipe Editors: Mary King, Sue A. Jurack, Christine Rukavena
Test Kitchen Manager: Karen Scales
Recipe Asset System Manager: Coleen Martin
Home Economists: Tina Johnson, Kirsten Lingsweiler, Peggy Woodward RD, Marie Parker, Annie Rose, Pat Schmeling, Wendy Stenman
Test Kitchen Assistants: Rita Krajcir, Kris Lehman, Sue Megonigle, Megan Taylor
Copy Editor: S.K. Enk
Editorial Assistant: Marilyn Iczkowski
Photographers: Rob Hagen (senior), Dan Roberts, Jim Wieland, Lori Foy
Senior Food Stylist: Sarah Thompson
Set Stylists: Jenny Bradley Vent (senior), Dee Dee Jacq
Assistant Food Stylists: Kaitlyn Besasie, Alynna Malson
Studio Coordinator: Kathleen Swaney

• • •

Senior Vice President/Editor in Chief: Catherine Cassidy
Chief Marketing Officer: Lisa Karpinski
Creative Director: Ardyth Cope

• • •

President and Chief Executive Officer: Mary G. Berner
President, Food & Entertaining: Suzanne M. Grimes
Vice President, Integrated Partnerships for Taste of Home: Lora Gier
Vice President, Integrated Sales and Marketing: Mark Wildman
Executive Director, Integrated Sales and Marketing: Maureen O'Connell

For other *Taste of Home* books and products, visit *www.shoptasteofhome.com*.

⏱ Contents

Recipe Contests Yield Quick Winning Dishes

EVERY TIME *Simple & Delicious* magazine announced a national recipe contest during the past year, busy cooks from coast to coast took notice. They flipped through their recipe files and sent in their very best.

Wondering which delicious, time-saving dishes were deemed tops in one of those contests? Simply check the special section here.

On these two pages, we've featured the six talented cooks who took home the Grand Prize in a 2007 contest. We've also let you know where to find their first-place recipes in this book, so you can turn to those celebrated dishes right away...and even prepare them for your family tonight!

Plus, we've added the 11 other recipes that were honored in each contest. You get a complete listing of dishes—all 72 of them—that were judged as contest winners during the past year.

Because we've included the page numbers for all of the runners-up, too, you'll easily be able to locate each rave-winning recipe in this book. Dozens of top-honor dishes are right at your fingertips!

From Berry Treats to Merry Sweets

The contest topics during the past year yielded a wide range of reader recipes. But all of those dishes have one thing in common—they're quick-to-fix foods that suit busy cooks' lifestyles.

In the "Slow-Cooked Favorites" contest, readers eased into dinner by letting their slow cookers do most of the work. And "Cookie Dough Creations" put refrigerated dough to especially yummy uses.

Interested in pick-of-the-crop berry recipes? Glance at the desserts, salads and more in "Easy, Breezy Berries." Or turn to "Last-Minute Lunches" and put together fantastic lunch-box fillers or a can't-miss weekend meal in a snap.

When you don't have time to pull lots of items from your cupboard, look to "Fix It with 5" for tasty foods that require only a handful of ingredients. "Fuss-Free Holiday Fare" will impress your guests on special occasions without keeping you in the kitchen for hours on end.

Just choose your favorites from this array of prize-winning recipes—or plan to fit each one into an upcoming menu. Either way, you'll have standout sensations you and your family are sure to love.

Her Slow-Cooked Recipe Was a Fast Favorite

WHEN IT COMES to family meals, time and taste are the top priorities for Debbie Dunaway, Kettering, Ohio. "So I often count on slow-cooked Teriyaki Pork Roast to feed my husband, Mark, and our two children," she relates.

"It's a wonderful main dish to come home to after a busy day. The meat is moist, tender and flavorful." Our panel of judges agreed, awarding Debbie's rave-winning recipe the Grand Prize in the "Slow-Cooked Favorites" contest.

Judges Found His Convenient Dessert Delightful

SINCE he was a teen, Benjamin Clark of Warsaw, New York has been spending time in the kitchen. And when his schedule is hectic, he whips up treats such as Special Pleasure Chocolate Cheesecake—the first-place winner in our "Cookie Dough Creations" contest.

"My wife, Sue Ellen, is a fantastic cook and handles most of our meals," Benjamin says. "But I enjoy making cheesecakes. This one is a lot quicker to fix than traditional cheesecakes—yet it really does taste special."

Her "Berry" Good Blend Was the Top Pick

FOR Nancy Whitford, flavor, nutrition and easy preparation are prime considerations when cooking for herself and her son, David. That's why Special Summer Berry Medley—the top winner in our "Easy, Breezy Berries" contest—is one of her all-time favorites.

"My cousin shared the recipe years ago, and I experimented with it a bit," Nancy writes from Edwards, New York. "When I took the medley to a bridal shower and everyone loved it, I knew I had a keeper!"

Cook's Frosty Pie Recipe Is Short and Sweet

FAMILY COOK Kimberly West of Prairieville, Louisiana proves it's true—a long list of ingredients isn't necessary to prepare winning fare. Her Chocolate-Cherry Ice Cream Pie was the Grand Prize recipe in our "Fix It with 5" contest.

"This yummy, make-ahead dessert is great for special occasions or when I want to surprise my husband, John, and our two boys," Kimberly says. She suggests trying the recipe with different ice cream flavors or nut toppings for variety.

She Gives Lunchtime Dining a Quick Lift

"MY RECIPE for Onion-Beef Muffin Cups came about by accident," admits Barbara Carlucci. "I was short on time and didn't know what to make for a get-together my husband, Phil, and I were going to. I haphazardly threw these bites together, and they were a hit!"

Afterward, this Orange Park, Florida cook made sure to write down the recipe. And when she submitted it for the "Last-Minute Lunches" contest, our judges gave the cheesy muffin cups top honors.

Taste-Testers Cheered Her Holiday Fare

FRIENDS call Mary Ann Marino the "Martha Stewart of West Pittsburg, Pennsylvania." That's because she makes entertaining—even during the hustle and bustle of Christmastime—look so easy and taste so good. What's her secret?

"I try to stay organized...and I rely on easy yet tempting recipes such as Chocolate Coconut Candies," Mary Ann relates. "I was really thrilled when those goodies received the Grand Prize in the 'Fuss-Free Holiday Fare' contest."

Chapter 1

IF YOU'RE like most busy cooks around the country, you pack your daily schedule with work, school and a host of other family activities.

On most days, it probably seems that there's little extra time to prepare a wholesome, hearty dinner for your hungry bunch. But this chapter deliciously proves that memorable family meals are within reach.

Here, six fellow on-the-go cooks have shared their favorite tried-and-true menus. From Chicken a la King and Speedy Minestrone as main dishes to Blueberry Crumble and Black Forest Sundaes for dessert, these recipes are guaranteed to put dinner on the fast track.

TOP CHOICES. Broiled Sirloin Steaks and Twice-Baked Deviled Potatoes (both recipes on p. 12).

Soup and Salad Combo Is Oh-So-Easy

FOR Dona Hoffman of Addison, Illinois, planning a fast and nutritious supper for her family of four is extremely important.

"I'm a nurse and currently work part-time so that I can complete my master's degree in health care administration," Dona explains. "Often, if I'm working into the dinner hours, my husband, Doug, is in control of the kitchen, which means we need something simple yet healthy."

To keep kitchen time to a minimum, Dona plans ahead, relying on her slow cooker for stress-free but satisfying menus on the days she works. She also likes to prepare a few extra servings so that she'll be sure to have leftovers to pack for an easy work lunch the next day.

When not working, Dona loves to bake and spend time with daughters Megan and Mia. "On evenings when I'm home, I look forward to having meals with everyone gathered together around the table, just as I did with my parents when I was growing up," Dona recalls.

The Italian-inspired menu she shares here makes supper time a breeze any night of the week. And, since it serves six, Dona is guaranteed to have a few extra lunches for work.

To start the meal off right, she serves Tomato Olive Salad. "My daughters love salad," Dona notes. "Each night, I try to have a different version for them." This amazingly simple dish features a sweet three-ingredient dressing that's ready in moments. "I often top the salad with fresh mozzarella, feta or Parmesan cheese," Dona adds. "To add color, I use some red lettuce with a smaller amount of the leaf lettuce."

Speedy Minestrone makes a hearty entree on cold winter nights. Filled with veggies, sausage and beans, the flavorful soup counts on several convenience products, so it's a snap to assemble. As Dona explains, "Everything is precooked, so you're just chopping, combining and heating. To trim fat from the soup, use a reduced-fat sausage."

Ending the meal on a sweet note is easy with Mini Rum Cakes. "A good recipe for rum cake is hard to find," Dona says. "Many of them turn out dry, but these individual cakes are so moist. Plus, they use basic ingredients that are usually in your pantry. I like to serve them slightly warm with vanilla ice cream and a dollop of whipped cream."

Tomato Olive Salad

Prep/Total Time: 10 min.

    4 cups torn leaf lettuce
    1/2 cup cherry tomatoes
    1/3 cup sliced red onion
    1 can (2-1/4 ounces) sliced ripe olives, drained
DRESSING:
    2 tablespoons vegetable oil
    1 tablespoon red wine vinegar
    1 tablespoon brown sugar

In a large bowl, combine the lettuce, tomatoes, onion and olives. In a small bowl, whisk the dressing ingredients. Drizzle over salad and toss to coat. Serve immediately. **Yield:** 6 servings.

Speedy Minestrone

Prep/Total Time: 25 min.

    2 cans (14-1/2 ounces *each*) beef broth
    1 package (24 ounces) frozen vegetable and pasta medley in garlic sauce
    1 pound smoked sausage, cut into 1/2-inch slices
    1 can (16 ounces) kidney beans, rinsed and drained
    1/4 cup chopped onion
    1 teaspoon dried basil
    1 teaspoon dried parsley flakes
Shredded Parmesan cheese

In a large saucepan, combine the first seven ingredients. Bring to a boil. Reduce heat; simmer, uncovered, for 10-15 minutes or until heated through. Sprinkle with Parmesan cheese. **Yield:** 6 servings.

Mini Rum Cakes

Prep/Total Time: 10 min.

    2 cups cold milk
    1 package (3.4 ounces) instant vanilla pudding mix
    1 teaspoon rum extract
    6 individual round sponge cakes
    1-1/2 cups whipped topping
Fresh *or* frozen raspberries

In a small bowl, whisk milk and pudding mix for 2 minutes; stir in extract. Let stand for 2 minutes or until soft-set. Set cakes on plates; top with pudding. Garnish with whipped topping and berries. **Yield:** 6 servings.

Cake Creativity

WANT to get creative with your Mini Rum Cakes? Try substituting chocolate pudding for the vanilla and use almond extract in place of the rum. You could also garnish with different berries, such as strawberries.

Serve Up a Taste of the Mediterranean

FAST and simple meals are a must for Elizabeth Tomlinson of Streetsboro, Ohio. "I'm a graduate assistant who sometimes takes night classes. My husband, Ed, is a business professor who occasionally teaches night classes. So it's important for us to get supper on the table quickly," she explains.

When not working, the academic duo also has a young son, Ethan, who keeps them on their toes. "I like being able to do some food preparation while my son naps or plays," Elizabeth says, "but there are never any guarantees as to how much time I'll have—so quicker is always better!"

To make the most out of kitchen time, Elizabeth likes to plan meals in advance. "I often use side dishes from convenience items and improve them by adding additional seasonings and toppings," she notes.

To accommodate her family's hectic lifestyle, Elizabeth created this delightful menu for an easy and impressive dinner in no time.

For the main course, she serves Rosemary Lamb Chops. While the lamb chops may seem upscale, they're actually a super-fast entree. "I tend to make them for special occasions, although they are quick enough for a nice weeknight dinner," she explains.

Pair the tender lamb chops with Mediterranean Couscous. With garlic, tomatoes and Parmesan cheese, it's a great side dish for just about any main course. "It relies on a boxed item to get started; then it's just a matter of adding a few ingredients," says Elizabeth.

Finish things off with warm and inviting Blueberry Crumble. This delicious dessert features sweet blueberries with a brown sugar, almond and oat topping that's especially nice with vanilla ice cream.

Rosemary Lamb Chops

Prep/Total Time: 20 min.

    2 teaspoons dried rosemary, crushed
    1 teaspoon dried thyme
  1/2 teaspoon salt
  1/4 teaspoon pepper
  1/4 cup olive oil
    8 lamb loin chops (1 inch thick and 6 ounces each)

Combine the rosemary, thyme, salt and pepper. Brush oil over both sides of chops; rub with spice mixture. In a large skillet, cook chops over medium heat for 6-7 minutes on each side or until meat reaches desired doneness (for medium-rare, a meat thermometer should read 145°; medium, 160°; well-done, 170°). **Yield: 4 servings.**

Mediterranean Couscous

Prep/Total Time: 15 min.

      2 tablespoons chopped onion
      3 teaspoons minced garlic
      2 tablespoons olive oil, *divided*
  1-1/4 cups water
      1 package (5.6 ounces) couscous with toasted pine nuts
  1-1/2 teaspoons chicken bouillon granules
    1/2 cup cherry tomatoes, halved
      2 tablespoons grated Parmesan cheese

In a small skillet, saute onion and garlic in 1 tablespoon oil for 3-4 minutes or until tender. Meanwhile, in a large saucepan, combine the water, contents of seasoning packet from couscous mix, bouillon and remaining oil. Bring to a boil.

Stir in onion mixture and couscous. Cover and remove from heat; let stand 5 minutes. Fluff with a fork. Stir in tomatoes and Parmesan cheese. **Yield: 4 servings.**

Blueberry Crumble

Prep/Total Time: 15 min.

    3 cups fresh *or* frozen blueberries
    3 tablespoons sugar
    1 tablespoon cornstarch
  1/3 cup old-fashioned oats
  1/3 cup packed brown sugar
    3 tablespoons all-purpose flour
    2 tablespoons chopped almonds
  1/8 teaspoon ground cinnamon
    3 tablespoons cold butter
Vanilla ice cream

In a greased 9-in. microwave-safe pie plate, combine the blueberries, sugar and cornstarch. Cover and microwave on high for 7-8 minutes or until thickened, stirring twice.

Meanwhile, in a small bowl, combine the oats, brown sugar, flour, almonds and cinnamon. Cut in butter until mixture resembles coarse crumbs. Sprinkle over blueberry mixture. Microwave, uncovered, on high for 2-3 minutes or until butter is melted. Serve with ice cream. **Yield: 4 servings.**

Editor's Note: This recipe was tested in a 1,100 watt microwave.

Cooking with Lamb

DON'T BE AFRAID to use generous amounts of herbs when cooking lamb. These bold flavors will enhance any cut. For the best flavor and tenderness, serve lamb medium-rare to medium well.

Speedy Steak And Potatoes Are Pleasers

1 teaspoon fresh basil leaves, julienned
1/2 teaspoon salt
1/4 teaspoon pepper
2 medium ripe avocados, halved and pitted
2 teaspoons lime juice

In a large bowl, gently toss the tomatoes, onion, basil, salt and pepper. Spoon into avocado halves; drizzle with lime juice. Serve immediately. **Yield:** 4 servings.

Broiled Sirloin Steaks

Prep/Total Time: 20 min.

✓ Uses less fat, sugar or salt. Includes Nutrition Facts and Diabetic Exchanges.

2 tablespoons lime juice
1 teaspoon onion powder
1 teaspoon garlic powder
1/4 teaspoon ground mustard
1/4 teaspoon dried oregano
1/4 teaspoon dried thyme
4 boneless beef sirloin steaks (5 ounces *each*)
1 cup sliced fresh mushrooms

In a small bowl, combine the first six ingredients; rub over both sides of steaks. Broil 4 in. from the heat for 7 minutes. Turn steaks; top with mushrooms. Broil 7-8 minutes longer or until meat reaches desired doneness (for medium-rare, a meat thermometer should read 145°; medium, 160°; well-done, 170°) and mushrooms are tender. **Yield:** 4 servings.

Nutrition Facts: 1 steak with about 3 tablespoons mushrooms equals 187 calories, 7 g fat (3 g saturated fat), 80 mg cholesterol, 60 mg sodium, 3 g carbohydrate, trace fiber, 28 g protein. **Diabetic Exchange:** 3 lean meat.

TIME is of the essence for Karol Chandler-Ezell and her family in Nacogdoches, Texas. "I'm an anthropology professor at a local university," Karol explains. "And my husband, Alex, teaches high school science and has a long commute. I usually work late and rush to cook dinner quickly."

Besides a busy life teaching, the pair has their hands full in other arenas. "We have one child, a rambunctious baby girl named Sasha," Karol writes. In spite of their hectic schedules, Karol and her husband make family meals a priority. "We have sit-down suppers seven days a week, which is nice because Sasha's just getting the hang of eating with us."

To provide her family with fast meals, Karol relies on leftovers. "I often make extra when fixing dinner so we'll have lunches later," she says. "We also assemble the ingredients for breakfasts the night before so we can pop them in the microwave before work."

In her spare time, Karol loves to garden, read and, of course, spend time with her baby girl. She's also putting together a children's book of legends from coastal Ecuador.

For a mouth-watering menu, Karol created this dinner that's a perfect fit for on-the-go lifestyles.

She begins with tasty Tomato-Stuffed Avocados. Each attractive avocado is packed with chopped tomatoes, onion and basil for a flavorful start. Best of all, they're ready in no time.

Karol pairs the refreshing avocados with mushroom-topped Broiled Sirloin Steaks, a family favorite. "A butcher gave me great advice on cooking different types of meat," she says. "Broiling works really well on lean cuts like this."

What goes better with steak than potatoes? Twice-Baked Deviled Potatoes double the pleasure. This delicious side dish is flavored with bacon, cheddar and a hint of Dijon mustard. "The microwave makes them very quick to fix," Karol says. "Best of all, you can leave them while they're cooling if the kiddo needs your attention for a while."

Twice-Baked Deviled Potatoes

Prep/Total Time: 30 min.

4 small baking potatoes
1/4 cup butter, softened
1/4 cup milk
1 cup (4 ounces) shredded cheddar cheese
1/3 cup real bacon bits
2 green onions, chopped
1 teaspoon Dijon mustard
Dash paprika

Scrub and pierce potatoes; place on a microwave-safe plate. Microwave, uncovered, on high for 7-10 minutes or until tender, turning once. Let stand for 5 minutes. Cut a thin slice off the top of each potato and discard. Scoop out pulp, leaving thin shells.

In a large bowl, mash the pulp with butter and milk. Stir in the cheese, bacon, onions, mustard and paprika. Spoon into potato shells. Return to the microwave-safe plate. Microwave, uncovered, on high for 1-2 minutes or until cheese is melted. **Yield:** 4 servings.

Editor's Note: This recipe was tested in a 1,100-watt microwave.

Tomato-Stuffed Avocados

Prep/Total Time: 10 min.

2 plum tomatoes, seeded and chopped
3/4 cup thinly sliced red onion, quartered

Pasta Dinner Has Special Appeal

IF YOU ASK Jodi Trigg about her favorite pastime, she'll probably put cooking at the top of her list. The Toledo, Illinois reader loves to cook, and the reason is simple. "I like trying new recipes because I have a son who likes to eat," Jodi explains with a smile.

For this full-time factory worker and mom to son Wyatt, preparing dinners around a busy schedule definitely means having a plan. "I map out all of our meals a week in advance and then go grocery shopping," Jodi says. Sometimes, she cooks for as many as eight family members and friends, so preparing stress-free, delicious menus is a must.

When not at work or in the kitchen, Jodi loves to volunteer at Wyatt's school. "They often have breakfast fund-raisers," she says. "I always enjoy helping out." She also likes to read and scrapbook. On warm summer days, she makes time for several outdoor activities like softball, volleyball and riding bikes with Wyatt.

And nothing says summer to Jodi like fresh produce and festive family meals. "I use the freshest fruits and vegetables in recipes I can," she says. So it's no surprise that the menu she shares here features fresh summer produce at its peak.

With only five ingredients and water, Jodi's main course, Bow Ties with Asparagus and Prosciutto, is as easy as it is elegant. "Add a dash of nutmeg for a change of pace," Jodi suggests.

Jodi pairs this quick and tasty main dish with fanciful Triple-Berry Spinach Salad. A homemade Dijon mustard dressing flavors the summery salad, which has three kinds of berries.

Dessert is delectable when Jodi's Praline-Peach Brownie Sundaes are on the menu. She dresses up store-bought brownies and ice cream with a rich peach sauce that's absolutely wonderful. Pecans add a bit of crunch to these frosty treats that make a sweet ending to any warm summer night's supper.

Bow Ties with Asparagus And Prosciutto

Prep/Total Time: 30 min.

- 1 package (16 ounces) bow tie pasta
- 1-1/2 cups heavy whipping cream
- 1 pound fresh asparagus, trimmed and cut into 1-inch pieces
- 3 tablespoons water
- 1/2 cup shredded Parmesan cheese
- 6 ounces thinly sliced prosciutto *or* deli ham, cut into strips

Cook pasta according to package directions. Meanwhile, in a small saucepan, bring cream to a boil. Reduce heat; simmer, uncovered, for 6-7 minutes or until slightly thickened.

Place asparagus and water in a microwave-safe dish. Cover; microwave on high for 3-4 minutes or until crisp-tender. Drain.

Drain pasta and place in a large serving bowl. Add the cream, asparagus, Parmesan cheese and prosciutto; toss to coat. **Yield:** 6 servings.

Editor's Note: This recipe was tested in a 1,100-watt microwave.

Triple-Berry Spinach Salad

Prep/Total Time: 10 min.

- 1 package (6 ounces) fresh baby spinach
- 1/3 cup sliced fresh strawberries
- 1/3 cup fresh raspberries
- 1/3 cup fresh blueberries
- 1/4 cup sliced red onion

DRESSING:

- 1/4 cup vegetable oil
- 3 tablespoons raspberry lemonade concentrate
- 2 tablespoons white vinegar
- 1 to 2 tablespoons Dijon mustard
- 1 tablespoon sugar

In a large serving bowl, combine the spinach, berries and onion. In a small bowl, whisk the dressing ingredients until smooth. Drizzle over salad and toss to coat. Serve with a slotted spoon. **Yield:** 6 servings.

Praline-Peach Brownie Sundaes

Prep/Total Time: 20 min.

- 1/4 cup packed brown sugar
- 1/4 cup heavy whipping cream
- 2 tablespoons butter
- 1/4 teaspoon ground cinnamon
- 2 medium fresh peaches, peeled and sliced *or* 1 cup frozen unsweetened peach slices, thawed and patted dry
- 1/2 cup chopped pecans
- 1 teaspoon vanilla extract
- 6 prepared brownies
- 3 cups vanilla ice cream
- Additional peach slices, optional

In a large saucepan, whisk the brown sugar, cream, butter and cinnamon until smooth. Bring to a boil; cook and stir for 6-7 minutes or until thickened. Remove from the heat; stir in the peaches, pecans and vanilla. Cool for 10 minutes.

Place brownies in dessert dishes; top with ice cream and peach sauce. Garnish with additional peach slices if desired. **Yield:** 6 servings.

Weeknight Supper Is Kid-Friendly

WHEN IT COMES to quick lunches and suppers, Terri Keeney is the queen. The featured reader from Greeley, Colorado writes, "It seems like I'm always on the run, so meals need to come together in 30 minutes or less."

And she's not talking about two or three menus a week. This busy mom cooks dinners routinely for four, including husband Brad, daughter Kassi and occasionally her father-in-law. Since Brad comes home for lunch every day from his chiropractic business, Terri cooks sit-down lunches each day of the week as well.

When not preparing the next main course, Terri is very active in her community. "I volunteer and work at my husband's office. I also manage our church's bookstore, volunteer in the church office and coordinate the ministry's menus, which are taken to people recovering from illness or injury."

To save time, Terri plans menus in advance at the beginning of each week. "I keep everything simple," she says. "I try to avoid pre-packaged stuff, but I do use canned soups, veggies and fruit sometimes. The most important considerations for me are the time and ease of preparation, as well as making sure the recipes use readily available ingredients."

The dishes Terri shares here fall under all of those categories. She starts with a third-generation family favorite, the hearty Kids' Favorite Chili. This sweet and easy chili is sure to warm up the whole family on cool fall nights.

As a great side dish, she serves her speedy Cheese Quesadillas. The dippers are wonderful alongside the chili, but you can also serve them with extra salsa and sour cream for a super starter.

For dessert, Terri shares the fun Chocolate Peanut Butter Bites that her family and friends love. She writes, "These cookies are always a hit. One family even said they became a new staple in their home after I'd taken them some!" They're the perfect ending to this family-friendly meal.

Kids' Favorite Chili

Prep/Total Time: 25 min.

> 1 pound ground turkey
> 1/2 cup chopped onion
> 1 can (15-3/4 ounces) pork and beans

> 1 can (14-1/2 ounces) diced tomatoes, undrained
> 1 can (10-3/4 ounces) condensed tomato soup, undiluted
> 1 tablespoon brown sugar
> 1 tablespoon chili powder

In a large saucepan, cook turkey and onion over medium heat until meat is no longer pink; drain. Stir in the remaining ingredients. Bring to a boil. Reduce heat; cover and simmer for 15-20 minutes or until heated through. **Yield:** 4 servings.

Cheese Quesadillas

Prep/Total Time: 15 min.

> 4 flour tortillas (8 inches)
> 1-1/2 cups (6 ounces) shredded Mexican cheese blend
> 1/2 cup salsa

Place the tortillas on a greased baking sheet. Combine the cheese and salsa; spread over half of each tortilla. Fold over. Broil 4 in. from the heat for 3 minutes on each side or until golden brown. Cut quesadillas into wedges. **Yield:** 4 servings.

Chocolate Peanut Butter Bites

Prep/Total Time: 20 min.

✓ Uses less fat, sugar or salt. Includes Nutrition Facts and Diabetic Exchanges.

> 2/3 cup sweetened condensed milk
> 1/3 cup creamy peanut butter
> 1/2 teaspoon vanilla extract
> 1 cup biscuit/baking mix
> 1/3 cup semisweet chocolate chips

In a small mixing bowl, beat the milk, peanut butter and vanilla until smooth. Add biscuit mix just until blended. Fold in chocolate chips.

Drop by rounded tablespoonfuls 2 in. apart onto ungreased baking sheets. Bake at 375° for 10-12 minutes or until edges are lightly browned. Cool for 2 minutes before removing to wire racks. **Yield:** 14 cookies.

Nutrition Facts: 1 cookie equals 137 calories, 7 g fat (2 g saturated fat), 5 mg cholesterol, 155 mg sodium, 17 g carbohydrate, 1 g fiber, 3 g protein. **Diabetic Exchanges:** 1 starch, 1 fat.

Step-by-Step Plan

TO PUT this meal on the table quickly, first brown the turkey and onion for the chili. After preparing the cookie dough, stir the remaining chili ingredients into the turkey and simmer. Next, bake the cookies, then prepare and broil the quesadillas.

Simple Menu Stars Classic Comfort Food

WHETHER it's for her husband, grand-kids, children or others, Ruth Lee of Troy, Ontario has always enjoyed preparing tasty meals with a healthy twist. "Simplicity and variety are key elements in my cooking, but I always put nutrition first and use lots of fruits and vegetables," she says.

Ruth first learned to create new menus as a teenage nursing-home cook, and later honed those skills as a cook for a private school. "The diets of those at the nursing home were extremely varied due to health issues," she recalls. "At the school, we focused on creating nutrition-packed menus appealing to the eye."

These days, Ruth works part-time as a dog groomer and acts as a caregiver to her three youngest grandchildren. "I love my slow cooker because it allows me to prepare my main meal before my house fills up," she writes. "I also rely on dishes I've frozen for busy nights or to send with my husband, Doug, for work."

Besides feeding her husband and grandkids most days, Ruth has organized a group of 19 to cook meals for the local Ronald McDonald House every Friday. "To save money, I plan menus around whatever is on sale at the store," she says. "I avoid convenience products and buy most of my produce at the local outdoor market."

The supper Ruth shares here is a favorite from her days as a school cook. Comforting Chicken a la King has a thick and creamy sauce that's perfect over biscuits or rice. "I've been making this for 30 years," says Ruth. "It's a wonderful way to create a quick lunch or dinner with leftover chicken."

For an easy and colorful salad, Ruth serves Tomatoes with Feta Cheese. "I make this no-fuss dish at least once a month," she writes. "It puts fresh summer tomatoes to great use and adds zip to winter tomatoes, too."

Black Forest Sundaes make a sweet ending to the meal, and best of all, they take just 5 minutes to prepare! "My husband and grandchildren just love them," Ruth says.

Chicken a la King
Prep/Total Time: 25 min.

4 individually frozen biscuits
1-3/4 cups sliced fresh mushrooms
1/4 cup chopped onion
1/4 cup chopped celery
1/3 cup butter, cubed
1/4 cup all-purpose flour
1/8 to 1/4 teaspoon salt
  1 cup chicken broth
  1 cup milk
  2 cups cubed cooked chicken
  2 tablespoons diced pimientos

Bake biscuits according to package directions. Meanwhile, in a large skillet, saute the mushrooms, onion and celery in butter until crisp-tender. Stir in flour and salt until blended. Gradually stir in broth and milk. Bring to a boil; cook and stir for 2 minutes or until thickened.

Add chicken and pimientos. Bring to a boil. Reduce heat; simmer, uncovered, for 4-6 minutes or until heated through. Serve with biscuits. **Yield:** 4 servings.

Tomatoes with Feta Cheese
Prep/Total Time: 5 min.

✓ Uses less fat, sugar or salt. Includes Nutrition Facts and Diabetic Exchanges.

  8 slices tomato
  2 tablespoons crumbled feta cheese
  1 tablespoon balsamic vinegar
  2 tablespoons minced fresh basil
Pepper to taste

Arrange tomato slices on a serving plate. Sprinkle with feta cheese. Drizzle with vinegar; sprinkle with basil and pepper. **Yield:** 4 servings.

Nutrition Facts: 1 serving equals 20 calories, 1 g fat (trace saturated fat), 2 mg cholesterol, 38 mg sodium, 3 g carbohydrate, 1 g fiber, 1 g protein. **Diabetic Exchange:** Free food.

Black Forest Sundaes
Prep/Total Time: 5 min.

1/2 cup crushed cream-filled chocolate sandwich cookies
  4 scoops vanilla ice cream
  1 can (21 ounces) cherry pie filling
Whipped cream in a can
Chopped walnuts

Divide cookie crumbs among four dessert dishes; top each with ice cream and pie filling. Garnish with whipped cream and walnuts. Freeze until serving. **Yield:** 4 servings.

Fuss-Free Variety

FOR EXTRA COLOR and flavor, Ruth likes to add diced sweet peppers to her Chicken a la King. She also suggests replacing the feta cheese in her tomato side dish with crumbled blue cheese.

Chapter 2

SPECIAL OCCASIONS call for festive foods that add to the celebration. With the holiday and seasonal recipes in this chapter, you can serve eye-catching dishes without spending hours and hours in the kitchen.

Delight your loved ones with sweet Valentine's Day treats... sparkling extras for a patriotic picnic...frightfully fun goodies for Halloween...merry Christmas cookies and appetizers... and many more favorites that have timely flair.

Whether you want playful confections to bring to a school party or elegant hors d'oeuvres to impress guests, you'll find just the right dressed-up recipes for celebrations all year long.

FESTIVE FARE. Shrimp Cocktail (p. 39) and Beef 'n' Pepper Bread Slices (p. 38).

Valentine Sweets Spell L-O-V-E!

LOOKING for a quick way to celebrate Valentine's Day in the middle of a hectic workweek? It can be as simple as adding red napkins to the table, sprinkling candy hearts across each plate or ending the meal on a sweet note. These reader favorites should provide plenty of inspiration. Best of all, most take only a few ingredients and bake up in a heartbeat!

Strawberry Sundae Cups

(Pictured below)

Prep: 15 min. + freezing

Given to me years ago, this treat has become a favorite. It's fast to fix but looks like you fussed...and makes a Valentine's Day dessert that just melts in your mouth!
—Sandra Natera, Tucson, Arizona

4 squares (1 ounce *each*) bittersweet chocolate, *divided*
1 cup strawberry ice cream
Whipped cream in a can

In a microwave-safe bowl, melt three squares of chocolate; stir until smooth. Brush chocolate evenly on the inside of two foil muffin cup liners. Freeze for 10 minutes or until set. Repeat brushing and freezing steps two more times.

Melt remaining chocolate; transfer to a small resealable plastic bag. Cut a small hole in a corner of the bag.

Strawberry Sundae Cups

Pipe two heart shapes onto waxed paper. Freeze until set.

Just before serving, carefully peel liners off of chocolate cups and discard. Fill with ice cream. Garnish with whipped cream and chocolate hearts. **Yield:** 2 servings.

Cherry Shortbread Hearts

(Pictured at right)

Prep: 20 min. **Bake:** 20 min. + cooling

This recipe for heart-shaped cookies is one of the best I've tried. Folks always ooh and aah over the buttery taste combined with chocolate.
—Elaine Anderson
Aliquippa, Pennsylvania

1-1/4 cups all-purpose flour
    3 tablespoons sugar
1/2 cup cold butter
1/2 cup maraschino cherries, patted dry and finely chopped
    1 tablespoon cold water
1/4 teaspoon almond extract
    1 cup (6 ounces) semisweet chocolate chips
    1 tablespoon shortening

In a large bowl, combine flour and sugar; cut in butter until crumbly. Stir in the cherries, water and extract until dough forms a ball.

On a lightly floured surface, roll dough to 1/4-in. thickness. Cut with a floured 2-1/2-in. heart-shaped cookie cutter. Place 1 in. apart on ungreased baking sheets. Bake at 325° for 20-25 minutes or until edges are very lightly browned. Remove to wire racks to cool.

In a microwave-safe bowl, melt chocolate chips and shortening; stir until smooth. Dip half of each cookie into chocolate. Place on waxed paper until set. **Yield:** about 1-1/2 dozen.

Candy Bar Fudge

(Pictured above right)

Prep: 20 min. + chilling

I teach family and consumer science, and this simple but scrumptious fudge is always a hit with my high school students. Best of all, with only five ingredients, it couldn't be any easier to make!
—Bonnie Ayars
Mechanicsburg, Ohio

1 teaspoon butter
1 cup butterscotch chips
1 cup semisweet chocolate chips
1 can (16 ounces) chocolate fudge frosting
2 Snickers candy bars (2.07 ounces *each*), cut into 1/4-inch chunks, *divided*

Fruit-Filled Cupcakes
Cherry Shortbread Hearts
Candy Bar Fudge

Line a 9-in. square pan with foil and grease the foil with butter; set aside.

In a large microwave-safe bowl, melt the butterscotch and chocolate chips; stir until smooth. Stir in frosting and half of the candy bar pieces. Spread into prepared pan. Sprinkle with remaining candy bar pieces. Refrigerate for 1 hour or until set.

Cut fudge with a heart-shaped cookie cutter. Store in an airtight container in the refrigerator. **Yield:** about 1-1/2 pounds.

Fruit-Filled Cupcakes

(Pictured above)

Prep: 30 min. **Bake:** 25 min. + cooling

Kids will love the fruity surprise tucked inside these tender cupcakes. —Margaret Wilson, Hemet, California

    1 package (18-1/4 ounces) strawberry cake mix
    2 cups (16 ounces) sour cream
    2 eggs

    1/3 cup strawberry preserves
    1 can (16 ounces) vanilla frosting, *divided*
Red food coloring
Red nonpareils and pink jimmies

In a large mixing bowl, combine the dry cake mix, sour cream and eggs. Beat on low speed for 30 seconds; beat on medium for 2 minutes.

Place 27 paper or foil liners in heart-shaped or standard muffin tins. (If using standard tins, tuck a 1/2-in. foil ball or marble between each liner and cup to form a heart shape.) Fill cups half full with batter. Using the end of a wooden spoon handle, make an indentation in the center of each; fill with 1/2 teaspoon preserves. Top with remaining batter.

Bake at 350° for 22-27 minutes or until a toothpick inserted in the cake portion comes out clean. Cool for 10 minutes before removing from pans to wire racks to cool completely.

Place a third of the frosting in a bowl; tint pink with red food coloring. Frost cupcakes with white frosting; pipe edges with pink frosting. Decorate with nonpareils and jimmies. **Yield:** about 2 dozen.

Brighten Up a Spring Brunch

WHETHER you're looking for festive Easter morning fare or just something special to celebrate a feeling of spring in the air, these mouth-watering brunch dishes are just the thing. Simple and filled with flavor, they're so fast to fix that you'll be out of the kitchen with plenty of time to enjoy your day. So hop to it, and give one or more a try today!

Cinnamon Roll Bunnies

(Pictured below)

Prep/Total Time: 30 min.

A tube of purchased cinnamon roll dough and a little imagination make these adorable bunnies from our Test Kitchen staff almost too cute to eat! They're sure to appeal to "somebunny" at your house this Easter.

> 1 tube (12.4 ounces) refrigerated cinnamon roll dough
> 12 miniature M&M's baking bits
> 4 pink jelly beans
> 24 pieces black shoestring licorice (1 inch)
> 1 drop red food coloring
> Brown decorating gel *or* color of your choice

Separate dough into eight rolls. Place four rolls on a greased baking sheet. Using a 2-in. biscuit cutter, cut 3/4 in. into both sides of remaining rolls to form ears and bow ties. Place ears at the top and a bow tie below each cinnamon roll; pinch to attach. Slightly flatten rolls.

Bake at 400° for 8-10 minutes or until golden brown. Set aside 1-1/2 teaspoons icing. Spread remaining icing over bunnies. Place a baking bit in the center of each bow tie; add remaining baking bits for eyes. Place a jelly bean in each center for nose; attach licorice pieces for whiskers.

Tint reserved icing pink with red food coloring; pipe mouths and outline ears. Pipe edges of bow ties with decorating gel. **Yield:** 4 servings.

Farmer's Breakfast

(Pictured at right)

Prep/Total Time: 30 min.

I found this recipe in the newspaper several years ago and love it—especially for overnight guests. I can whip it up in no time flat, and everyone enjoys it.
—Lynn Ames, Idaho Falls, Idaho

> 3 cups finely chopped peeled potatoes (about 3 medium)
> 1/4 cup chopped green pepper
> 3 tablespoons butter
> 9 eggs
> 3 tablespoons milk
> 1/4 teaspoon pepper
> 1-1/2 cups cubed fully cooked ham
> 1 jar (4-1/2 ounces) sliced mushrooms, drained
> 1/4 cup shredded cheddar cheese

In a 2-qt. microwave-safe dish, combine the potatoes, green pepper and butter. Cover and microwave on high for 7-8 minutes or until the vegetables are tender, stirring once.

In a mixing bowl, beat the eggs, milk and pepper; stir in ham and mushrooms. Stir into potato mixture. Cover and microwave at 70% power for 8-10 minutes or until eggs are almost set, stirring every 2 minutes.

Sprinkle with cheese. Cook, uncovered, on high for 1-2 minutes or until cheese is melted and eggs are completely set. **Yield:** 6 servings.

Editor's Note: This recipe was tested in a 1,100-watt microwave.

Apricot-Coconut French Toast

(Pictured above right)

Prep: 30 min. + chilling **Bake:** 20 min.

As a busy activity director for RV parks, I was always looking for easy food to prepare for various functions. This breakfast dish brought lots of raves and recipe requests.
—Jean Groen, Apache Junction, Arizona

> 1/2 cup chopped dried apricots
> 1/2 cup water

Cinnamon Roll Bunnies

Farmer's Breakfast
Apricot-Coconut French Toast

1/4 cup butter, melted
2/3 cup flaked coconut, toasted
1/4 cup sugar
1-1/4 teaspoons ground cinnamon
7 eggs
1-3/4 cups milk
1 teaspoon vanilla extract
Pinch salt
16 slices French bread (1 inch thick)
Maple syrup

In a small microwave-safe bowl, heat apricots and water on high for 2 minutes or until mixture comes to a boil. Let stand for 5 minutes; drain.

Pour butter into a 15-in. x 10-in. x 1-in. baking pan and tilt to coat bottom. Sprinkle with coconut and apricots. Combine sugar and cinnamon; sprinkle over fruit.

In a large shallow bowl, whisk the eggs, milk, vanilla and salt. Dip bread into egg mixture; soak for 1 minute. Place slices close together over coconut mixture. Cover and refrigerate overnight.

Remove from the refrigerator 30 minutes before baking. Bake, uncovered, at 375° for 20-25 minutes or until golden brown. Serve with the syrup. **Yield:** 8 servings.

Editor's Note: A dark baking pan is not recommended for this recipe.

Morning Fruit Salad

Prep/Total Time: 25 min.

My best friend made this refreshing salad for lunch one hot summer day. It was so good, I just had to have the recipe. Now I make it every chance I get. It goes over big at picnics and church brunches.
—Nikki Gaines
Covington, Georgia

1 can (11 ounces) mandarin oranges
1/4 cup plus 2 tablespoons mayonnaise
1-1/2 cups seedless grapes, halved
2 small apples, chopped
2 small bananas, sliced
1/3 cup flaked coconut
1/3 cup chopped walnuts
1/4 cup maraschino cherries, halved
1/4 cup raisins

Drain oranges, reserving 4-1/2 teaspoons juice (discard remaining juice or save for another use). In a small bowl, combine mayonnaise and reserved juice.

In a large bowl, combine the oranges, grapes, apples, bananas, coconut, walnuts, cherries and raisins. Divide among serving dishes; drizzle with mayonnaise mixture. Serve immediately. **Yield:** 6-8 servings.

Give Summer Parties a Spark

CELEBRATE the Fourth of July or any warm-weather occasion with these effortless recipes. From a festive trifle to refreshing summer sippers, these cool treats are sure to keep your time in the kitchen short.

So go on—spend some extra moments in the sun! With these fast ideas, you won't have to miss a single parade, picnic or fireworks display.

Patriotic Trifle

(Pictured below)

Prep: 30 min. + chilling

It took only a few minutes to dream up this pretty and patriotic trifle—and not much longer to put it together!
—Sandra Brown, Independence, Iowa

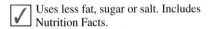

✓ Uses less fat, sugar or salt. Includes Nutrition Facts.

1 package (3 ounces) berry blue gelatin
1 package (3 ounces) strawberry gelatin
2 cups boiling water
1 cup cold water
2 cups cold milk
2 packages (3.4 ounces *each*) instant vanilla pudding mix
1 carton (8 ounces) frozen whipped topping, thawed, *divided*
1 pint fresh blueberries
1 quart fresh strawberries, quartered
1 prepared angel food cake (8 inches), cut into 1-inch cubes

In two small bowls, combine each gelatin flavor with 1 cup boiling water. Stir 1/2 cup cold water into each. Pour each into an ungreased 9-in. square pan. Refrigerate for 1 hour or until set.

In a large bowl, whisk milk and pudding mixes for 2 minutes. Let stand for 2 minutes or until soft-set. Fold in 2 cups whipped topping.

Set aside 1/4 cup blueberries and 1/2 cup strawberries for garnish. Cut the gelatin into 1-in. cubes. In a 3-qt. trifle bowl or serving dish, layer the strawberry gelatin, half of the cake cubes, the remaining blueberries and half of the pudding mixture.

Top with blue gelatin and remaining cake cubes, strawberries and pudding mixture. Garnish with reserved berries and remaining whipped topping. Serve immediately. **Yield:** 16-20 servings.

Nutrition Facts: 3/4 cup equals 189 calories, 3 g fat (2 g saturated fat), 3 mg cholesterol, 338 mg sodium, 37 g carbohydrate, 1 g fiber, 3 g protein.

Dill Bloody Marys

(Pictured at far right)

Prep/Total Time: 10 min.

With a nice level of pepper and just enough dill from the pickles, these Bloody Marys are guaranteed to be crowd-pleasing. For a Contrary Mary, simply leave out the vodka. Feel free to be creative with the garnishes you add.
—Jay Ferkovich, Green Bay, Wisconsin

1-1/2 cups Clamato juice, chilled
2 tablespoons dill pickle juice
1 tablespoon Worcestershire sauce
1/4 teaspoon celery salt
1/8 to 1/4 teaspoon pepper
1/8 teaspoon hot pepper sauce
1/4 cup vodka, optional
Ice cubes
2 celery ribs
2 pepperoni-flavored meat snack sticks
2 dill pickle spears
2 pitted ripe olives

In a small pitcher, combine the first six ingredients. Stir in vodka if desired. Pour into two glasses filled with ice; garnish with celery, snack sticks, pickles and olives. **Yield:** 2 servings.

Patriotic Trifle

Tropical Fruit Punch

(Pictured at right)

Prep/Total Time: 10 min.

This easy tropical cooler features a delicious balance of pineapple and cranberry that's great with or without the rum. —Kathy Crawford, Franklin, Wisconsin

    2 cups unsweetened pineapple juice, chilled
    2 cups cranberry-raspberry juice, chilled
    1 teaspoon lime juice
    2 cups lemon-lime soda, chilled
    1/4 cup rum, optional
Ice cubes

In a pitcher, combine the juices. Stir in soda and rum if desired. Serve immediately over ice. **Yield:** 6 servings.

Frozen Lemon-Berry Margaritas

(Pictured at right)

Prep/Total Time: 15 min.

I chill down summer months with this fantastic margarita. The nonalcoholic version will be a real hit with kids. —Julie Hieggelke, Chicago, Illinois

    6 lime wedges
    3 tablespoons coarse sugar
    2/3 cup lemonade concentrate
    1 cup frozen unsweetened raspberries
    2 cups ice cubes
    1 package (16 ounces) frozen sweetened
        sliced strawberries, thawed slightly
    1/2 cup frozen blueberries
    1 tablespoon sugar
    1/2 cup tequila, optional

Using lime wedges, moisten the rims of six glasses. Set limes aside for garnish. Sprinkle coarse sugar on a plate; hold each glass upside down and dip rim into sugar. Set aside. Discard remaining sugar on plate.

In a blender, combine the lemonade concentrate and raspberries; cover and process until smooth. Press mixture through a fine meshed sieve; discard seeds. Return raspberry mixture to blender; add ice, strawberries, blueberries, sugar and tequila if desired. Cover and process until smooth.

Pour into prepared glasses. Garnish with reserved limes. **Yield:** 6 servings.

Keeping Your Cool

BRINGING a cooler to your summer party? A full cooler stays cold longer than one that's only partially full, so pack extra ice. If you're going to be in the sun for a while or camping overnight, freeze 2-liter bottles of water for a few days before packing them in the cooler. The bottles will stay cold for several days.

Tropical Fruit Punch
Dill Bloody Marys
Frozen Lemon-Berry Margaritas

Scare Up Some Halloween Fun

YOU DON'T NEED hours of time to whip up a bewitching bash and spine-tingling party fare for your pint-sized ghouls, goblins and ghosts. With recipes this simple and quick, there's no trick to treating your gang to a night of hauntingly happy memories and food so good…it'll vanish before you can say "BOO!"

Dracula Cookies

(Pictured at far right)

Prep/Total Time: 30 min.

Come late October, friends and family can "count" on me to reintroduce them to my easily recognizable, darling Dracula Cookies. —Christy Hinrichs, Parkville, Missouri

- **6 hazelnut truffles**
- **5 ounces white candy coating, chopped**
- **1 green *or* red Fruit Roll-Up**
- **6 cream-filled chocolate sandwich cookies**
- **1 can (6.4 ounces) black decorating icing**
- **6 slivered almonds, cut in half**

Place truffles on a waxed paper-lined pan. Freeze for 10 minutes or until chilled. Meanwhile, in a small microwave-safe bowl, melt candy coating; stir until smooth. Dip truffles in coating to cover completely; return to pan. Refrigerate until hardened.

Cut roll-up into 2-1/2-in. x 1-1/2-in. strips. Reheat candy coating if necessary. Dip truffles in coating again; immediately place one on each cookie. Wrap a strip around base of each truffle for cape. Let stand until set.

Using decorating icing and a round tip, pipe hair, eyes and mouth on each. Insert almonds for fangs. Store in an airtight container. **Yield:** 6 cookies.

Editor's Note: This recipe was tested with Ferrero Rocher hazelnut truffles.

Ghoulish Caramel Apples

(Pictured at far right)

Prep/Total Time: 30 min.

Guests will have almost as much fun decorating these gooey, caramel-apple characters as they'll have biting into them. —Wilma Bailey, Sedona, Arizona

- **4 large tart apples**
- **4 Popsicle sticks**
- **4 orange candy slices**
- **1 piece black rope licorice**
- **1 piece red rope licorice**
- **1 cup flaked coconut**
- **3 drops green food coloring, optional**
- **1 package (14 ounces) caramels**
- **2 tablespoons heavy whipping cream**
- **8 Skittles bite-size candies**
- **4 gumdrops**

Line a baking sheet with waxed paper and grease the paper; set aside. Wash and thoroughly dry apples. Insert a Popsicle stick into the top of each; set aside.

For eyes, cut orange slices horizontally in half. For eyebrows, cut black licorice in half lengthwise; cut each half into four 2-in. pieces. For mouths, cut red licorice into sixteen 1/4-in. pieces. Tint coconut with food coloring if desired for hair.

In a microwave-safe bowl, heat caramels and cream, uncovered, on high for 1 minute; stir. Microwave 30-45 seconds longer or until melted; stir until smooth.

Dip one apple into caramel mixture, turning to coat. Place on prepared pan. Immediately add faces with prepared orange slices and licorice pieces. Press a Skittle below each orange slice; add a gumdrop for nose. Sprinkle coconut on top for hair. Dip and decorate remaining apples, rewarming caramel if needed. **Yield:** 4 servings.

Strawberry Ghosts

(Pictured at right)

Prep/Total Time: 30 min.

You'll hear gasps of delight at these adorable ghosts. Juicy strawberries, chocolate and a hint of almond flavor make these little bites a howling success! —Nancy Mueller, Bloomington, Minnesota

☑ Uses less fat, sugar or salt. Includes Nutrition Facts and Diabetic Exchanges.

- **30 fresh strawberries**
- **8 squares (1 ounce *each*) white baking chocolate**
- **1 teaspoon shortening**
- **1/8 teaspoon almond extract**
- **1/4 cup miniature semisweet chocolate chips**

Wash strawberries and gently pat with paper towels until completely dry. In a microwave-safe bowl, melt white chocolate and shortening at 50% power; stir until smooth. Stir in extract.

Dip strawberries in chocolate mixture; place on a waxed paper-lined baking sheet, allowing excess chocolate to form the ghosts' tails. Immediately press chocolate chips into coating for eyes. Freeze for 5 minutes.

In a microwave-safe bowl, melt remaining chips; stir until smooth. Dip a toothpick into melted chocolate; draw a mouth on each face. **Yield:** 2-1/2 dozen.

Nutrition Facts: 1 strawberry equals 54 calories, 3 g fat (2 g saturated fat), 2 mg cholesterol, 8 mg sodium, 6 g carbohydrate, trace fiber, 1 g protein. **Diabetic Exchanges:** 1/2 starch, 1/2 fat.

Ghoulish Caramel Apples
Dracula Cookies
Strawberry Ghosts

Chip 'n' Dip Bread Witch

(Pictured at right)

Prep: 40 min. + rising **Bake:** 15 min. + cooling

Who needs tricks with a treat as bewitching as this appetizer? It's sure to steal center stage on your table. Our Test Kitchen modeled this ghoulish beauty—right down to the raisin wart on her nose!

> 2 loaves (1 pound *each*) frozen bread dough, thawed
> 3 egg whites
> Black, green and red paste food coloring
> 1 sliced almond
> 1 pimiento-stuffed olive slice
> 1 raisin
> 1/4 cup shredded Parmesan cheese
> 1 to 2 jars (15-1/2 ounces *each*) salsa con queso dip
> Tortilla chips

Let dough rise according to package directions. For witch's face, on a lightly floured surface, roll one loaf into an 8-in.-high x 6-in.-wide oval. Cut a 3-in. piece off the top and set aside. Place rolled piece on a large greased baking sheet. Pull lower left side of dough down and to the left, forming a chin.

For hat, roll remaining loaf into a 9-1/2-in.-high x 6-1/2-in.-wide triangle; place above face. Divide reserved dough into thirds. Roll two pieces into 12-in.-long ropes; twist together. Place over bottom of hat for brim.

Shape two-thirds of remaining dough into a nose. Cut a 1-in. slit at an angle 1 in. below brim; insert nose. Roll remaining dough into a 4-in. piece; fold in half for lips. Cut a 2-in. slit below nose; insert lips.

Divide egg whites among three custard cups; with food coloring, tint one portion black, one green and one red. Brush black over hat. Brush green over face and nose. Brush red over lips.

For eye, place almond and olive between nose and brim. For wart, lightly press raisin into nose. Sprinkle Parmesan cheese over dough for hair.

Let rise in a warm place for 20 minutes. Bake at 350° for 15-20 minutes or until golden brown. Remove from pan to a wire rack to cool.

Hollow out center of hat; fill with dip, adding more as needed. Serve with tortilla chips. **Yield:** 1 witch (1-1/2 to 3 cups dip).

Choosing Food Coloring

USE any type of food coloring you wish to tint the frosting for Halloween Pumpkin Bars (recipe at right). But keep in mind that food coloring pastes and gels, which are a concentrated form of food color, are often best when you want to create vibrant, non-pastel colors such as deep orange or true red.

Liquid food coloring is available in supermarkets. Look for pastes and gels at cake decorating stores, at specialty kitchen supply stores and on the Internet.

Halloween Pumpkin Bars

(Pictured at far right)

Prep: 30 min. **Bake:** 20 min. + cooling

My family loves the warm pumpkin fragrance that wafts through our kitchen on brisk fall afternoons when I make these bars. Jack-o'-lantern faces only add to the festive flavor!   —Karla Johnson, East Helena, Montana

> 1-1/2 cups pumpkin pie filling
> 2 cups sugar
> 1 cup vegetable oil
> 4 eggs
> 1 teaspoon vanilla extract
> 2 cups all-purpose flour
> 2 teaspoons baking powder
> 1 teaspoon baking soda
> 1/2 teaspoon salt
> 1 cup chopped pecans
> 1 can (16 ounces) cream cheese frosting
> Yellow and red food coloring
> 70 pieces candy corn
> 1/2 cup milk chocolate chips

In a large mixing bowl, beat the pumpkin, sugar, oil, eggs and vanilla. Combine the flour, baking powder, baking soda and salt; gradually add to pumpkin mixture and mix well. Stir in pecans.

Pour into a greased 15-in. x 10-in. x 1-in. baking pan. Bake at 350° for 20-25 minutes or until a toothpick inserted near the center comes out clean. Cool on a wire rack.

Tint frosting orange with yellow and red food coloring. Frost bars; cut into 35 squares. For eyes, place two pieces of candy corn on each bar.

In a small microwave-safe bowl, melt chocolate chips; stir until smooth. Transfer to a heavy-duty resealable plastic bag; cut a small hole in a corner of the bag. Pipe dots on candy corn for pupils; decorate faces as desired. **Yield:** 35 bars.

Gummy Worm Punch

(Pictured at right)

Prep: 15 min. + freezing

I usually prepare this basic punch recipe for weddings, graduations and anniversaries. But you can easily make the tangy drink fun and festive for Halloween. Simply add gummy worms to the ice ring, and you'll have a "spooktacular" beverage.
—Kathy Kittell, Lenexa, Kansas

    4 cups unsweetened apple juice
    4 cups orange juice
  2/3 cup lemonade concentrate
    2 cups water
  20 gummy worms
4-1/3 cups lemon-lime soda, chilled

In a punch bowl, combine the apple juice, orange juice and lemonade concentrate. Pour water and 1 cup juice mixture into a 5-cup ring mold; add gummy worms. Freeze until solid. Meanwhile, refrigerate juice mixture until chilled.

Just before serving, add soda to juice mixture. Unmold ice ring by wrapping the bottom of the mold in a damp hot dishcloth; invert onto a baking sheet. Place worm side up in punch bowl. **Yield:** 3 quarts.

Eyeball Taco Salad

(Pictured at right)

Prep: 35 min. **Bake:** 25 min.

Each serving of this main-dish salad has enough beef, cheese, tomato and taco flavor to satisfy a crowd. Just add a little sour cream, olives and tomato pieces to create spooky eyeballs!   —Jolene Young, Union, Illinois

2-1/2 pounds lean ground beef
  3/4 cup water
    1 can (8 ounces) tomato sauce
    1 envelope taco seasoning
    1 package (14-1/2 ounces) nacho tortilla chips, crushed
    2 cups (8 ounces) shredded Monterey Jack cheese
    2 cups (8 ounces) shredded cheddar cheese
    4 cups torn iceberg lettuce
    1 medium red onion, finely chopped
  10 slices tomato, halved
    1 cup (8 ounces) sour cream
  10 whole pitted ripe olives, halved

In a Dutch oven, cook beef over medium heat until no longer pink; drain. Stir in the water, tomato sauce and taco seasoning. Bring to a boil. Reduce heat; simmer, un-

Gummy Worm Punch
Halloween Pumpkin Bars
Eyeball Taco Salad

covered, for 15 minutes.

Place tortilla chips in a greased 15-in. x 10-in. x 1-in. baking pan; sprinkle with Monterey Jack cheese. Spread meat mixture over top; sprinkle with cheddar cheese. Bake at 325° for 25-30 minutes or until bubbly.

Top with lettuce and onion. Cut into ten 5-in. x 3-in. pieces. On each piece, arrange two tomato slices for eyes; top each with a dollop of sour cream and an olive half. **Yield:** 10 servings.

Have a Fuss-Free Thanksgiving

MAKE your holiday dinner this year a simple one, without sacrificing taste. It's easy to do!

We've pulled together an incredibly easy Thanksgiving menu from reader recipes. Each dish has five or fewer ingredients, excluding salt, pepper and water. Having fewer ingredients means less money, and with the right ingredients, it also means full flavor.

To put a sweet ending on your simple yet satisfying Thanksgiving dinner, pick up a fresh-baked pie. It's a great complement to this meal.

Green Beans with Red Pepper

(Pictured below)

Prep/Total Time: 30 min.

This is one of our favorite in-a-snap side dishes. It's also a beautiful addition to any holiday plate.
—Tracey Medeiros, Atlanta, Georgia

  1-1/2 **pounds fresh green beans, trimmed**
    1/3 **cup water**
      6 **tablespoons butter**
    3/4 **cup sliced sweet red pepper**
      1 **tablespoon chopped shallot**
Salt and pepper to taste
    1/3 **cup sliced almonds, toasted**

Place beans and water in a 2-qt. microwave-safe dish. Cover and microwave on high for 6-8 minutes or until crisp-tender.

Meanwhile, in a large skillet, melt butter; add red pepper and shallot. Cook, uncovered, over medium heat until red pepper is crisp-tender.

Drain beans; stir into red pepper mixture. Season with salt and pepper. Transfer to a serving platter; sprinkle with the toasted almonds. **Yield:** 5 servings.

    Editor's Note: This recipe was tested in a 1,100-watt microwave.

Moist Turkey Breast

(Pictured at right)

Prep: 10 min. **Bake:** 2 hours + standing

My family always requests this turkey at family gatherings. The Italian dressing adds zip and a moistness that you don't find in other recipes. —Cindy Carlson
Ingleside, Texas

    1 **bone-in turkey breast (about 7 pounds)**
    1 **teaspoon garlic powder**
  1/2 **teaspoon onion powder**
  1/2 **teaspoon salt**
  1/4 **teaspoon pepper**
1-1/2 **cups Italian dressing**

Place turkey breast in a greased 13-in. x 9-in. x 2-in. baking dish. Combine the seasonings; sprinkle over turkey. Pour dressing over the top.

Cover and bake at 325° for 2 to 2-1/2 hours or until a meat thermometer reads 170°, basting occasionally with pan drippings. Let stand for 10 minutes before slicing. **Yield:** 12-14 servings.

Seasoned Garlic Gravy

(Pictured above right)

Prep/Total Time: 15 min.

Poultry seasoning perks up this very simple, tasty gravy that's perfect for turkey as well as mashed potatoes.
—Hannah Thompson, Scotts Valley, California

☑ Uses less fat, sugar or salt. Includes Nutrition Facts and Diabetic Exchanges.

    1 **teaspoon minced garlic**
    3 **tablespoons butter**
  1/4 **cup all-purpose flour**
  1/2 **teaspoon poultry seasoning**
  1/8 **teaspoon pepper**
    2 **cups chicken broth**

In a small saucepan, saute garlic in butter until tender. Stir in the flour, poultry seasoning and pepper; gradually add broth. Bring to a boil; cook and stir for 1-2 minutes or until thickened. **Yield:** 2 cups.

    Nutrition Facts: 2 tablespoons equals 28 calories, 2 g fat (1 g saturated fat), 6 mg cholesterol, 138 mg sodium, 2 g carbohydrate, trace fiber, trace protein. **Diabetic Exchange:** 1/2 fat.

Green Beans with Red Pepper

Dried Fruit Stuffing
Sour Cream Mashed Potatoes
Seasoned Garlic Gravy
Moist Turkey Breast

Sour Cream Mashed Potatoes

(Pictured above)

Prep/Total Time: 25 min.

I turned overcooked potatoes into a family mainstay by adding sour cream and seasonings. My boiled potatoes were too soft for seasoned potato bites, but they were perfect for mashed potatoes!
—Caroline Sperry
Shelby Township, Michigan

☑ Uses less fat, sugar or salt. Includes Nutrition Facts and Diabetic Exchanges.

> 2 pounds red potatoes, quartered
> 1 cup (8 ounces) sour cream
> 2 tablespoons minced fresh parsley
> 1 teaspoon salt
> 1/2 teaspoon garlic powder
> 1/2 teaspoon pepper

Place potatoes in a large saucepan and cover with water. Bring to a boil. Reduce heat; cover and simmer for 15-20 minutes or until tender.

Drain and transfer to a large mixing bowl. Add all of the remaining ingredients and beat until blended. **Yield:** 5 servings.

Nutrition Facts: 3/4 cup equals 229 calories, 8 g fat (6 g saturated fat), 32 mg cholesterol, 508 mg sodium, 31 g carbohydrate, 3 g fiber, 5 g protein. **Diabetic Exchanges:** 2 starch, 1-1/2 fat.

Dried Fruit Stuffing

(Pictured above)

Prep/Total Time: 20 min.

Sure, stuffing is a Thanksgiving staple. But it doesn't have to be boring. This recipe has dried fruit and almonds. It gives boxed stuffing mix a terrific twist.
—Taryn Kuebelbeck, Plymouth, Minnesota

> 1 package (6 ounces) stuffing mix
> 1/2 cup dried cranberries
> 1/2 cup chopped pitted dried plums
> 1/2 cup chopped dried apricots
> 1/3 cup slivered almonds, toasted

Prepare stuffing mix according to package directions, adding dried fruits when adding contents of stuffing mix. Just before serving, stir in almonds. **Yield:** 4 cups.

Cooking for a Crowd

ARE YOU expecting a large group at your dinner table for Thanksgiving? The Sour Cream Mashed Potatoes (recipe at left) and Green Beans with Red Pepper (recipe on p. 32) can easily be doubled to yield 10 servings instead of five. So feel free to make extra, and you'll be sure to have plenty for everyone.

'Tis the Season for Cookies!

THE HOLIDAYS just wouldn't be the same without an array of special Christmas cookies to enjoy with family and friends. This year, we've made it easy for you to share a delightful bounty of goodies without spending hours in the kitchen!

Our Test Kitchen experts developed a make-ahead cookie dough for these delicious creations. Pop the dough into the freezer until you're ready to begin baking. Then choose your favorites from the following recipes (there's even a few lighter creations).

Turn to page 37 for a Christmas Cookie Train recipe using a store-bought dough that's sure to add to family fun. No matter what you choose, these treats will definitely bring joy to you and yours!

Reindeer Bites

Holiday Cookie Dough

(Pictured at far right)

Prep: 15 min. + chilling **Bake:** 10 min./batch

Use this make-ahead dough for all of the delicious cookies that follow.

☑ Uses less fat, sugar or salt. Includes Nutrition Facts and Diabetic Exchanges.

> **2 cups butter, softened**
> **1 cup sugar**
> **1/4 cup sweetened condensed milk**
> **1 teaspoon vanilla extract**
> **4 cups all-purpose flour**
> **1/8 teaspoon salt**
> **Sprinkles, jimmies *or* colored sugar, optional**

In a large mixing bowl, cream butter and sugar until light and fluffy. Beat in milk and vanilla. Combine flour and salt; gradually add to creamed mixture and mix well.

Divide dough into five 1-cup portions; shape each into a 10-in.-long roll. Wrap individually in plastic wrap. Refrigerate for 1 hour or until easy to handle, or freeze for up to 3 months. **Yield:** 5 portions (1 cup each).

To use refrigerated cookie dough: Cut roll into 1/4-in. slices. Place 2 in. apart on ungreased baking sheets. Decorate with sprinkles, jimmies or colored sugar if desired. Bake at 350° for 7-9 minutes or until lightly browned. Cool for 2 minutes before removing to wire racks.

Or, bake according to individual directions for Reindeer Bites, Jolly Santas, Lemon Rope Trees, Strawberry Tea Cookies and Magic Stars (recipes on this page and the next two pages).

To use frozen cookie dough: Thaw in the refrigerator overnight. Bake according to recipe directions. **Yield:** 200 slice-and-bake cookies.

Nutrition Facts: 1 cookie equals 76 calories, 5 g fat (3 g saturated fat), 13 mg cholesterol, 51 mg sodium, 8 g carbohydrate, trace fiber, 1 g protein. **Diabetic Exchanges:** 1 fat, 1/2 starch.

Reindeer Bites

(Pictured at left)

Prep: 20 min.
Bake: 15 min./batch + cooling

With fruitcake flavor, these bites are sure to become much-requested favorites year after year.

☑ Uses less fat, sugar or salt. Includes Nutrition Facts and Diabetic Exchanges.

> **1/2 cup orange juice**
> **1/4 cup chopped dried apricots**

      1/4 cup dried cranberries
      1/4 cup golden raisins
      1/4 cup chopped pecans
         2 tablespoons chopped candied cherries
      1/8 teaspoon ground nutmeg
         1 cup refrigerated Holiday Cookie Dough
            (recipe at left)
ICING:
      3/4 cup confectioners' sugar
      1/8 teaspoon rum extract
         3 to 4 teaspoons orange juice
      12 candied cherries, halved

In a small saucepan, combine juice, apricots, berries and raisins. Bring to a boil. Reduce heat; simmer, uncovered, for 4-6 minutes or until liquid is absorbed. Cool to room temperature; stir in the nuts, cherries and nutmeg.

Let cookie dough stand at room temperature for 5-10 minutes to soften. In a large mixing bowl, combine dough and fruit mixture. Drop by heaping teaspoonfuls 2 in. apart onto baking sheets coated with nonstick cooking spray. Bake at 350° for 12-14 minutes or until edges are lightly browned. Cool for 2 minutes before removing to wire racks to cool completely.

For icing, combine the confectioners' sugar, extract and enough orange juice to achieve desired consistency. Spread over cookies. Top each with a candied cherry piece. **Yield:** about 1-1/2 dozen.

Nutrition Facts: 1 cookie equals 104 calories, 4 g fat (2 g saturated fat), 9 mg cholesterol, 40 mg sodium, 16 g carbohydrate, trace fiber, 1 g protein. **Diabetic Exchanges:** 1 starch, 1 fat.

Holiday Cookie Dough
Lemon Rope Trees (p. 36)
Jolly Santas
Magic Stars (p. 36)

Jolly Santas

(Pictured at right)

Prep: 30 min.
Bake: 10 min./batch + cooling

These cute cookies will bring smiles! Get kids in on the fun by letting them add the red-hots.

         1 cup refrigerated Holiday Cookie Dough
            (recipe at left)
         2 teaspoons confectioners' sugar
   1-1/4 cups vanilla frosting, *divided*
Red paste food coloring
      30 miniature semisweet chocolate chips
      15 red-hot candies

On a lightly floured surface, roll out cookie dough to 1/8-in. thickness. Cut out 15 ovals, using a 3-in. egg-shaped cookie cutter dipped in flour. Place 2 in. apart on ungreased baking sheets. Bake at 350° for 6-8 minutes or until edges are lightly browned. Cool for 2 minutes before removing to wire racks to cool completely.

Sprinkle cookies with the sugar. In a small bowl, tint 3/4 cup frosting with food coloring; frost top third of each cookie. Using a star tip and remaining vanilla frosting, pipe a pom-pom, hat brim, eyebrows, eyes, mustache and mouth on each cookie. Press on two chocolate chips and a red candy for pupils and mouth. **Yield:** 15 cookies.

Strawberry Tea Cookies

(Pictured below)

Prep: 20 min. + chilling
Bake: 10 min./batch + cooling

Using make-ahead cookie dough, these four-ingredient goodies are simply delightful. They're so easy but have that "slaved over" appearance and taste.
—Carolyn Klingensmith, Livonia, Michigan

- **1 cup refrigerated Holiday Cookie Dough (recipe on page 34)**
- **1/3 cup ground almonds**
- **1/4 cup seedless strawberry jam**
- **Confectioners' sugar**

Let cookie dough stand at room temperature for 5-10 minutes to soften. In a small mixing bowl, combine dough and almonds. Cover and refrigerate for 1 hour or until easy to handle.

On a lightly floured surface, roll dough to 1/8-in. thickness. Cut with a floured 2-1/2-in. round cookie cutter. Cut out the centers of half of the cookies with a 1-in. round cookie cutter (discard centers).

Place 2 in. apart on ungreased baking sheets. Bake at 350° for 6-8 minutes or until edges are lightly browned. Cool for 2 minutes before removing to wire racks to cool completely.

Spread each whole cookie with 1 teaspoon of jam; top with remaining cookies. Sprinkle with confectioners' sugar. **Yield:** 10 sandwich cookies.

Strawberry Tea Cookies

Lemon Rope Trees

(Pictured on page 35)

Prep: 25 min.
Bake: 10 min./batch + cooling

A holiday cookie platter just won't be complete without these scrumptious Christmas trees.

✓ Uses less fat, sugar or salt. Includes Nutrition Facts and Diabetic Exchanges.

- **1 cup refrigerated Holiday Cookie Dough (recipe on page 34)**
- **1/2 teaspoon grated lemon peel**
- **Green food coloring, optional**
- **1 cup confectioners' sugar**
- **4 to 5 teaspoons lemon juice**
- **Green sprinkles**
- **4 medium yellow spiced gumdrops**

Let the cookie dough stand at room temperature for 5-10 minutes to soften. In a small mixing bowl, combine the dough and lemon peel. Tint dough with food coloring if desired.

Divide dough into 20 pieces; shape each into an 8-in. rope. Place 2 in. apart on baking sheets coated with nonstick cooking spray; form into tree shapes.

Bake at 350° for 8-10 minutes or until firm. Cool for 2 minutes before removing the cookies to wire racks to cool completely.

For icing, combine confectioners' sugar and enough lemon juice to achieve desired consistency. Drizzle over cookies; decorate with sprinkles.

For stars, place gumdrops on a sugared work surface. With a rolling pin, roll gumdrops to 1/8-in. thickness. Using a 1/2-in. star-shaped cookie cutter, cut out five stars from each gumdrop. Gently press stars into frosting on tops of trees. **Yield:** 20 cookies.
Nutrition Facts: 1 cookie equals 86 calories, 4 g fat (2 g saturated fat), 10 mg cholesterol, 41 mg sodium, 13 g carbohydrate, trace fiber, 1 g protein. **Diabetic Exchanges:** 1 starch, 1/2 fat.

Magic Stars

(Pictured on page 35)

Prep: 20 min. + chilling
Bake: 10 min./batch + cooling

You'll love the chocolaty flavor these cookies bring, as well as how simple they are to make!

✓ Uses less fat, sugar or salt. Includes Nutrition Facts and Diabetic Exchanges.

- **1 cup refrigerated Holiday Cookie Dough (recipe on page 34)**
- **3/4 cup flaked coconut, toasted**
- **1/2 cup graham cracker crumbs**
- **1/2 cup miniature semisweet chocolate chips**
- **1/4 cup sweetened condensed milk**
- **Additional miniature semisweet chocolate chips, optional**

Let cookie dough stand at room temperature for 5-10 minutes to soften. In a large mixing bowl, combine the cookie dough, coconut, cracker crumbs, chocolate chips and milk. Cover and refrigerate dough for 1 hour or until easy to handle.

On a lightly floured surface, roll the dough to 1/8-in. thickness. Cut dough with a floured 3-in. star-shaped cookie cutter.

Place 1 in. apart on baking sheets coated with nonstick cooking spray. Bake at 350° for 8-10 minutes or until edges are lightly browned. Cool for 2 minutes before removing to wire racks.

If frosting is desired, melt additional chocolate chips; stir until smooth. Frost cooled cookies. **Yield:** about 2-1/2 dozen.

Nutrition Facts: 1 cookie (calculated without frosting) equals 71 calories, 4 g fat (3 g saturated fat), 7 mg cholesterol, 40 mg sodium, 8 g carbohydrate, trace fiber, 1 g protein. **Diabetic Exchanges:** 1 fat, 1/2 starch.

Christmas Cookie Train

(Pictured above)

Prep: 30 min. **Bake:** 10 min. + cooling

Get the entire family involved with a delightfully edible activity that's been Test Kitchen-approved! The cookies and frosting are easy to work with, letting your gang focus on having fun.

   1/2 tube refrigerated peanut butter cookie
         dough
   1/4 cup all-purpose flour
     6 tablespoons butter, softened
     3 cups confectioners' sugar
     3 tablespoons milk
     2 teaspoons vanilla extract
  Green, red, yellow and brown paste food coloring
  Assorted decorations: Peppermint candies, M&M's,
     mini vanilla wafers, animal crackers and red
     shoestring licorice

In a small mixing bowl, beat cookie dough and flour until combined. On a lightly floured surface, roll dough to 1/8-in. thickness. With a sharp knife, cut out six 4-in. x 3-in. rectangles; save the scraps.

Place rectangles 2 in. apart on ungreased baking sheets. Reroll dough scraps; cut out a 2-in. x 1-1/2-in. rectangle for engine cab, a 1-1/4-in. x 1/2-in. rectangle for smokestack and a 1-1/2-in. triangle for cowcatcher. Attach to one rectangle; gently press seams to seal.

Bake at 350° for 7-9 minutes or until edges are golden brown. Remove to wire racks to cool.

For frosting, in a small mixing bowl, beat the butter, confectioners' sugar, milk and vanilla until creamy. Set aside 1 cup. Tint 3 tablespoons frosting green, 3 tablespoons red and 1 tablespoon yellow. Tint the remaining frosting brown.

Set aside 2 tablespoons of the white frosting. Spread remaining white frosting over cookies, leaving 2-1/2-in. x 1-1/2-in. rectangles in centers of three passenger cars and 2-1/2-in. x 2-in. rectangles in the centers of the two animal cars. Frost the engine.

On a 35-in. x 8-in. covered board, attach train cars and peppermint candy wheels with a small amount of reserved frosting.

With M&M's and frosting, add a headlight above cowcatcher and couplings between the cars. Add M&M's for smoke coming out of smokestack. Use vanilla wafers for passenger faces and decorate with colored frosting. Add animal crackers and licorice bars to the animal cars. With remaining frosting, decorate train as desired. **Yield:** 6 cookies.

Serve Merry Treats in a Twinkling

WARM UP any holiday gathering with these quick party snacks. Whether you're hosting a merry get-together on Christmas Eve or a New Year's Eve bash, your guests are sure to love the cheesy bread slices, classic shrimp cocktail and more here.

Puff Pastry Holly Leaves

(Pictured below)

Prep: 30 min. **Bake:** 15 min. + cooling

These elegant appetizers look like you've slaved in the kitchen, but they can be assembled in a jiffy. They always earn raves at my office holiday party. —Angela King
Walnut Cove, North Carolina

- 1 package (17.3 ounces) frozen puff pastry, thawed
- 1 egg
- 1 tablespoon water
- 4 ounces cream cheese, softened
- 1 cup (4 ounces) crumbled feta cheese
- 1/2 cup minced fresh parsley
- 1/2 cup prepared pesto
- 24 pimiento pieces

Unfold pastry sheets onto a lightly floured surface. From each sheet, cut out 12 leaves with a floured 3-1/2-in. leaf-shaped cookie cutter. Place on ungreased baking sheets. With a toothpick, score veins in leaves. In a small bowl, beat egg and water; brush over pastry.

Bake at 400° for 12-14 minutes or until golden brown. Remove to wire racks to cool.

In a large bowl, combine the cheeses, parsley and pesto. Split pastry leaves in half. Spread 1 tablespoon cheese mixture over bottom halves; replace tops. Add a pimiento piece on each for a holly berry. Refrigerate leftovers. **Yield:** 2 dozen.

Puff Pastry Holly Leaves

Garlic-Parmesan Cheese Ball

Prep: 10 min. + chilling

This is one of our mainstays when we're entertaining, whether it's during the holiday season or another time of year. The flavorful cheese ball makes a great starter for most meals and is so easy to dress up with a variety of pretty garnishes.
—Susan Seymour, Valatie, New York

- 2 packages (one 8 ounces, one 3 ounces) cream cheese, softened
- 1/3 cup grated Parmesan cheese
- 1/4 cup mayonnaise
- 1/2 teaspoon dried oregano
- 1/4 teaspoon garlic powder *or* 1/2 to 1 teaspoon minced garlic
- 3/4 cup chopped walnuts, optional
Assorted fresh vegetables *and/or* crackers

In a large mixing bowl, combine the first five ingredients. Shape into a ball. Roll in walnuts if desired. Chill for 2 hours. Serve with vegetables and/or crackers. **Yield:** about 2 cups.

Beef 'n' Pepper Bread Slices

(Pictured above right and on page 21)

Prep/Total Time: 25 min.

My French bread slices topped with roast beef, red peppers and cheese are simple to make and easy for guests to handle. They remain a holiday hit with my family and friends year after year. —Margaret Pache, Mesa, Arizona

- 2 cups shredded cooked roast beef
- 1/2 cup mayonnaise
- 1/4 cup plain yogurt
- 2 green onions, chopped
- 1 jalapeno pepper, seeded and chopped
- 2 tablespoons prepared horseradish
- 2 teaspoons lemon juice
- 1/2 teaspoon grated lemon peel
- 1 loaf (1 pound) French bread, halved lengthwise

1 jar (7-1/4 ounces) roasted sweet red
  peppers, drained and chopped
1-1/2 cups (6 ounces) shredded pepper Jack
  cheese
1/4 cup minced fresh parsley

In a small bowl, combine the first eight ingredients. Spread the mixture over the cut sides of the French bread. Place on an ungreased baking sheet. Top with roasted red peppers; sprinkle with the pepper Jack cheese and parsley.

Bake at 450° for 8-10 minutes or until bread is golden and cheese is melted. Cut into slices. Serve warm. **Yield:** 10-12 servings.

Editor's Note: When cutting or seeding hot peppers, use rubber or plastic gloves to protect your hands. Avoid touching your face.

Shrimp Cocktail

(Pictured above and on page 20)

Prep: 30 min. + chilling

I serve this classic appetizer for every special occasion as well as for "munchie meals" on big-game day. My neighbors look for it whenever we get together. —Peggy Allen
Pasadena, California

3 quarts water
1 small onion, sliced
1/2 medium lemon, sliced
2 sprigs fresh parsley
1 tablespoon salt
5 whole peppercorns
1/4 teaspoon dried thyme
1 bay leaf
3 pounds uncooked large shrimp, peeled and
  deveined (tails on)
SAUCE:
1 cup chili sauce
2 tablespoons lemon juice
2 tablespoons prepared horseradish
4 teaspoons Worcestershire sauce
1/2 teaspoon salt
Dash cayenne pepper

In a Dutch oven, combine the water, onion, lemon, parsley, salt, peppercorns, thyme and bay leaf. Bring to a boil. Add shrimp. Reduce heat; simmer, uncovered, for 4-5 minutes or until the shrimp turn pink.

Drain shrimp and immediately rinse in cold water. Refrigerate for 2-3 hours. In a small bowl, combine the sauce ingredients. Refrigerate until serving.

Arrange shrimp on a serving platter; serve with sauce. **Yield:** about 6 dozen (1-1/4 cups sauce).

IMAGINE...putting a complete, home-cooked meal of Orange-Glazed Pork Chops, Skillet Lo Mein and Pineapple Ice Cream Topping on the table in only half an hour. With the recipes here, you can do just that!

In this big chapter, you'll see not only the scrumptious pork chop supper mentioned above, but also 25 other quick-to-fix menus. No matter which one you choose, it'll take just 30 minutes—or less—to prepare from start to finish.

Because these speedy recipes came from fellow busy cooks, you can rest assured that each delicious dish will fit right into a hectic schedule—and please your family at the same time.

DINNER IN A JIFFY. Barbecue Ham Sandwiches and Two-Bean Salad (both recipes on p. 50).

Elegant Entree And Dessert

PUT AWAY the peanut butter and plan for pizza another night. You can have all the flavor of a special restaurant-quality meal at home in just 30 minutes! Simply whip up these delightful dishes for a fast and easy supper sure to please the whole family.

Start with Dijon Chicken and Spinach from Diane Hendrixson of Wapakoneta, Ohio. "This is a quick recipe that's table-ready in very little time," Diane assures.

The tender chicken breasts are topped with a creamy Dijon sauce. Served with wilted spinach and store-bought dinner rolls on the side, it makes a complete meal in just moments.

The fresh tastes of Pound Cake with Strawberries pair perfectly with the chicken. Packaged pound cake is topped with a sweet-sour cream mixture and berries. It's a four-ingredient treat that's always a favorite with Sue Ross' family in Casa Grande, Arizona. Best of all, it comes together in a snap.

What's more, the dessert recipe makes eight servings, but it's easy to cut in half. Simply save the remaining ingredients for another night, and you can satisfy your sweet tooth yet again.

Dijon Chicken and Spinach

Prep/Total Time: 30 min.

- 1/2 cup all-purpose flour
- 1/4 teaspoon salt
- 1/4 teaspoon pepper
- 4 boneless skinless chicken breast halves (5 ounces *each*)
- 1/4 cup vegetable oil
- 1/2 cup half-and-half cream
- 2 eggs
- 1/4 cup Dijon mustard
- 1 teaspoon minced garlic
- 2 tablespoons butter
- 2 packages (9 ounces *each*) fresh baby spinach

Paprika, optional

In a shallow bowl, combine the flour, salt and pepper. Flatten chicken to 1/2-in. thickness; coat with flour mixture. In a large skillet, cook chicken in oil over medium heat for 5-6 minutes on each side or until juices run clear. Remove; keep warm.

In a bowl, whisk the cream, eggs and mustard; stir into the pan drippings. Cook and stir over medium heat until thickened and sauce reaches 160°.

Meanwhile, in another skillet, saute garlic in butter for 2-3 minutes or until tender. Add spinach; cook and stir over low heat for 3-5 minutes or until wilted. Spoon mustard sauce over chicken; sprinkle with paprika if desired. Serve with spinach. **Yield:** 4 servings.

Pound Cake with Strawberries

Prep/Total Time: 5 min.

- 1 cup (8 ounces) sour cream
- 1 teaspoon sugar
- 1 loaf (10-3/4 ounces) frozen pound cake, thawed and cut into cubes
- 1 package (10 ounces) frozen sweetened sliced strawberries, thawed

In a small bowl, combine sour cream and sugar. Place cake cubes in dessert dishes; top with strawberries and sweetened sour cream. **Yield:** 8 servings.

Pound Cake with Strawberries
Dijon Chicken and Spinach

Extra Cleaning for Eggs

WASHING EGGS at home is not necessary. Federal regulations require that eggs be cleaned before going to market. Most are cleaned with special detergents, sanitized and then sprayed with edible mineral oil.

Pizza Night Perfection

WITH ITS CRISP CRUST, gooey cheese topping and limitless ingredient variations, what's not to love about pizza? That easy family-pleaser is always welcome on busy weeknights.

Instead of heading to the grocery store or spending extra money on delivery, prepare your own at home tonight. This simple dinner features delicious individual pizzas that can be ready from start to finish in less than 30 minutes.

Start with the tangy taste of Staca Hiatt's quick-to-fix Barbecue Chicken Pita Pizzas. "I use bottled barbecue sauce, cooked chicken and cheddar cheese to create a truly Western-style pizza," writes the Twentynine Palms, California reader. "The individual servings are such a cinch to prepare."

Pair them with Almond Spinach Salad from Karena Lee of Sunland, California. The fast tossed salad is colorful and fresh, and the toasted almonds give it a pleasant crunch.

For a cool and creamy finish, serve big bowls of ice cream. Whether you prefer chocolate, vanilla, double brownie-rocky road or another flavor, you can't go wrong. Everyone will love the meal, and you'll love having time to relax at the end of the day.

Barbecue Chicken Pita Pizzas

Prep/Total Time: 25 min.

1 cup frozen diced cooked chicken, thawed
and chopped
1/2 cup barbecue sauce
4 pita breads (6 inches)
1/3 cup real bacon bits
1 small onion, halved and thinly sliced
1 small green pepper, julienned
1 can (4 ounces) chopped green chilies
1 can (4 ounces) mushroom stems and pieces,
drained
1 cup (4 ounces) shredded cheddar cheese

In a small bowl, combine chicken and barbecue sauce; spoon over pitas. Top with bacon, onion, green pepper, chilies, mushrooms and cheese.

Place on an ungreased baking sheet. Bake at 450° for 8-10 minutes or until heated through. **Yield:** 4 servings.

Almond Spinach Salad

Prep/Total Time: 15 min.

1 package (10 ounces) fresh spinach, torn
1 medium tomato, sliced
1/2 cup thinly sliced red onion
1/2 medium ripe avocado, peeled and sliced
1/4 cup sliced almonds, toasted
1/3 to 1/2 cup red wine vinaigrette

In a large salad bowl, combine the spinach, tomato, onion, avocado and almonds. Drizzle with vinaigrette and toss to coat. Serve immediately. **Yield:** 4 servings.

Mashed Potatoes with Corn and Cheese
Sweet and Tender Carrots
Pesto Halibut

Pesto Halibut

Prep/Total Time: 20 min.

        2 tablespoons olive oil
        1 envelope pesto sauce mix
        1 tablespoon lemon juice
        6 halibut fillets (4 ounces *each*)

In a small bowl, combine the oil, sauce mix and lemon juice; brush over both sides of fillets. Place in a greased 13-in. x 9-in. x 2-in. baking dish. Bake, uncovered, at 450° for 12-15 minutes or until fish flakes easily with a fork. **Yield:** 6 servings.

Sweet and Tender Carrots

Prep/Total Time: 15 min.

    1/3 cup chopped onion
        2 tablespoons butter
        5 cups frozen sliced carrots
        1 cup lemon-lime soda
        1 tablespoon sugar
    1/4 teaspoon salt
    1/8 teaspoon pepper

In a large skillet, saute onion in butter until tender. Stir in the carrots, soda, sugar, salt and pepper. Cover and cook over medium-low heat for 7-10 minutes or until carrots are crisp-tender. Serve with a slotted spoon. **Yield:** 6 servings.

Mashed Potatoes With Corn and Cheese

Prep/Total Time: 25 min.

        4 cups cubed peeled potatoes
    1-1/2 cups water
        4 to 6 tablespoons milk
        3 tablespoons butter, softened
    1/2 teaspoon salt
    1/4 teaspoon pepper
        1 cup frozen corn, thawed and warmed
    1-1/2 cups (6 ounces) shredded Colby-Monterey Jack cheese

Place potatoes and water in a microwave-safe dish. Cover and microwave on high for 12-14 minutes or until tender; drain. Place potatoes in a mixing bowl; mash with milk, butter, salt and pepper. Stir in corn and cheese. **Yield:** 6 servings.

Editor's Note: This recipe was tested in a 1,100-watt microwave.

Family-Pleasing Fish with Pesto

ON TIME-CRUNCHED WEEKNIGHTS, let the bold taste of pesto star in this easy, brightly colored supper. Besides being tasty, the whole meal uses only 13 ingredients, excluding salt, pepper and water, so it's a cinch to put together.

With just a few minutes of assembly, you can pop April Showalter's Pesto Halibut into the oven to bake. "My father-in-law took a trip to Alaska and came back with fresh halibut fillets," April notes from Milwaukee, Wisconsin. "The mildness of the fish contrasts perfectly with the pesto's deep flavor."

While the fish is baking, start on Sweet and Tender Carrots. Our home economists made Barbara Schindler's recipe even more hands-free by using frozen carrots to get you in and out of the kitchen super-quick. The Napoleon, Ohio reader uses lemon-lime soda to perk up carrots for a fast-to-fix dish.

Round out the swift supper with our Test Kitchen's Mashed Potatoes with Corn and Cheese. The microwave turns these jazzed-up potatoes into a scrumptious side dish in a flash. But if you're really tight on time, you can also use store-bought refrigerated mashed potatoes for even faster results.

Fruit Juice Clue

TO get the most juice from a lemon, orange or lime, I pop it into the microwave for a few seconds before slicing it in half to juice. It works like a charm every time!
—*Betty Kleberger, Florissant, Missouri*

Satisfying Pasta Supper

SHORT ON TIME but want to put a hot meal on the table? This quick duo makes the most of convenience products, leaving you with moments to spare.

Garlic Chicken Penne from Anne Nock of Avon Lake, Ohio requires just a few ingredients and 20 minutes of prep, so it couldn't be any easier. With pasta, snap peas and chicken, the four-ingredient main course has a garlicky sauce loaded with flavor.

"My husband and I ordered a pasta dish every time we went to a local restaurant, but they took it off the menu," Anne recalls. "So, I tried to copy it at home. My children love it!"

Serve the pasta medley with Sesame Breadsticks from our Test Kitchen. The not-too-spicy sticks have a mild herb taste that goes great with the main course or any other entree.

Round out the memorable menu with fresh fruit, such as red or green grapes. You're sure to have a meal the whole family will enjoy, and you'll love that it's ready to eat in no time flat.

Garlic Chicken Penne

Prep/Total Time: 20 min.

- 8 ounces uncooked penne pasta
- 1-1/2 cups frozen sugar snap peas
- 1 package (1.6 ounces) garlic-herb pasta sauce mix
- 1 package (6 ounces) sliced cooked chicken

In a large saucepan, cook pasta in boiling water for 6 minutes. Add peas; return to a boil. Cook for 4-5 minutes or until pasta is tender. Meanwhile, prepare sauce mix according to package directions.

Drain pasta mixture; add chicken. Drizzle with sauce and toss to coat. **Yield:** 4 servings.

Sesame Breadsticks

Prep/Total Time: 20 min.

- 1 tube (11 ounces) refrigerated breadsticks
- 1 tablespoon butter, melted
- 1 tablespoon sesame seeds, toasted
- 1 to 2 teaspoons dried basil
- 1/4 to 1/2 teaspoon cayenne pepper

Unroll and separate breadsticks. Twist each two to three times; place on an ungreased baking sheet. Brush with butter. Combine sesame seeds, basil and cayenne; sprinkle over breadsticks. Bake at 375° for 10-12 minutes or until golden brown. Serve warm. **Yield:** 1 dozen.

Sesame Breadsticks
Garlic Chicken Penne

Pork Supper In a Snap

DON'T HAVE A LOT OF TIME, but want to serve your family a hot and hearty meal? Try this incredibly easy dinner for four. There's nothing to it!

Each of these recipes has only five ingredients, not including salt and pepper, so you won't have to spend a lot of time shopping for this tasty menu that's ready in moments.

Begin with Honey Lemon Schnitzel from Carole Fraser of North York, Ontario. The succulent pork cutlets are coated in a sweet, citrusy sauce featuring honey, lemon juice and butter. They're certainly good enough for company, but perfect for a quick weeknight meal, too.

"I've served this classic entree to friends, and it is always a big hit," Carole relates. "Very seldom are there any leftovers, plus it's a breeze to double when I'm expecting a larger crowd."

Our Test Kitchen created the fresh-tasting Chive 'n' Garlic Corn to complement the lemony sweet cutlets. Just a few ingredients dress up frozen corn for this quick stovetop side dish.

Round out this simple dinner with some fun-to-eat crisp apple slices. You'll have a bright and flavorful meal the whole family will rave about.

Honey Lemon Schnitzel

Prep/Total Time: 25 min.

  2 tablespoons all-purpose flour
1/2 teaspoon salt
1/2 teaspoon pepper
  4 pork sirloin cutlets (4 ounces *each*)
  2 tablespoons butter
1/4 cup lemon juice
1/4 cup honey

In a large resealable plastic bag, combine the flour, salt and pepper. Add pork, two pieces at a time, and shake to coat. In a large skillet, cook pork in butter over medium heat for 3-4 minutes on each side or until juices run clear. Remove and keep warm.

Add lemon juice and honey to skillet; cook and stir for 3 minutes or until thickened. Return pork to pan; cook 2-3 minutes longer or until heated through. **Yield:** 4 servings.

Chive 'n' Garlic Corn

Prep/Total Time: 15 min.

  1 package (16 ounces) frozen corn, thawed
1/2 cup finely chopped onion
  2 tablespoons butter
1/4 cup minced chives
1/2 teaspoon minced garlic
1/8 teaspoon salt
Pepper to taste

In a large skillet, saute corn and onion in butter for 5-7 minutes or until tender. Stir in the chives, garlic, salt and pepper. **Yield:** 4 servings.

**Chive 'n' Garlic Corn
Honey Lemon Schnitzel**

Dressed-Up Fare for Two

NEED A SPECIAL MEAL that's just right for two people? This elegant version of pork chops and gravy with rice takes classic comfort food to new levels!

With simple, inexpensive ingredient additions, these reader recipes make down-home fare feel a bit more upscale. Plus, both of the following dishes are ready in less than 30 minutes, so you'll have a tasty meal on the table in no time flat.

For the main course, fix Judy Garvin's mouth-watering Pork Cutlet Saute. The Long Beach, California reader serves seasoned pork chops in a velvety mushroom sauce to make an impressive entree. It takes under half an hour to prepare but is sure to make someone special feel like you fussed.

Match the savory chops with the refreshing flavors found in Lemony Green Onion Rice. In Hays, Kansas, Rose Harman likes to toss rice with sauteed celery, green onions and some grated lemon peel for this attractive side dish.

The recipe pairs well with many main courses. "It's an especially good accompaniment to poultry and fish entrees," Rose relates.

For dessert, keep things on the easy side by serving your favorite ice cream. You'll have a fast and effortless menu that will prove just right for sharing with someone special.

Lemony Green Onion Rice
Pork Cutlet Saute

Pork Cutlet Saute

Prep/Total Time: 25 min.

- 3 tablespoons flour, *divided*
- 1/4 teaspoon rubbed sage
- 1/4 teaspoon pepper
- 2 boneless pork loin chops
- 1 tablespoon vegetable oil
- 1 tablespoon butter
- 8 medium fresh mushrooms, quartered
- 1 cup beef broth
- 2 tablespoons dry sherry *or* additional beef broth

In a shallow bowl, combine 1 tablespoon flour, sage and pepper. Coat pork chops with flour mixture. In a skillet, cook chops in oil and butter over medium-high heat for 5-7 minutes on each side or until juices run clear. Remove and keep warm.

In the same skillet, saute mushrooms for 2 minutes. Place remaining flour in a small bowl. Whisk in broth and sherry or additional broth until smooth; add to skillet. Bring to a boil; cook and stir for 2 minutes or until thickened. Reduce heat. Return pork to the pan; heat through. **Yield:** 2 servings.

Lemony Green Onion Rice

Prep/Total Time: 15 min.

☑ Uses less fat, sugar or salt. Includes Nutrition Facts and Diabetic Exchanges.

- 3/4 cup uncooked instant rice
- 1/3 cup chopped celery
- 1/3 cup chopped green onions
- 2 teaspoons butter
- 1/2 to 1 teaspoon grated lemon peel
- 1/4 teaspoon salt

Dash pepper

Cook rice according to package directions. In a small skillet, saute celery and onions in butter over medium heat until tender. Stir in the rice, lemon peel, salt and pepper. **Yield:** 2 servings.

Nutrition Facts: 3/4 cup equals 177 calories, 4 g fat (2 g saturated fat), 10 mg cholesterol, 356 mg sodium, 32 g carbohydrate, 1 g fiber, 3 g protein. **Diabetic Exchange:** 2 starch.

Easy Alternative

WANT to make Pork Cutlet Saute (recipe at left) but don't have any beef broth? One bouillon cube or 1 teaspoon of granules dissolved in 1 cup of boiling water may be substituted for 1 cup of broth in any recipe.

Change-of-Pace Chicken

READY to break your dinner routine? Enjoy Chicken with Leek Sauce from Vicki Atkinson of Kamas, Utah. Pair it with our Test Kitchen's Gingered Yellow Pepper 'n' Broccoli and Peanut Butter Chocolate Pie from Sara Walker, Roanoke Rapids, North Carolina.

Peanut Butter Chocolate Pie
Gingered Yellow Pepper 'n' Broccoli
Chicken with Leek Sauce

Chicken with Leek Sauce

Prep/Total Time: 25 min.

1/2 cup all-purpose flour
1/8 teaspoon paprika
1/8 teaspoon pepper
4 boneless skinless chicken breast halves
(6 ounces *each*)
2 tablespoons vegetable oil
3 tablespoons leek soup mix
1 cup water
1/2 cup sour cream
1-1/2 teaspoons minced chives

In a resealable plastic bag, combine flour, paprika and pepper. Add chicken, two pieces at a time, and shake to coat. In a large skillet, cook chicken in oil over medium heat for 6-7 minutes on each side or until juices run clear.

Meanwhile, in a small saucepan, bring soup mix and water to a boil, stirring frequently. Reduce heat; simmer, uncovered, for 5 minutes, stirring occasionally. Remove from the heat; stir in sour cream and chives. Serve with the chicken. **Yield:** 4 servings.

Gingered Yellow Pepper 'n' Broccoli

Prep/Total Time: 15 min.

 Uses less fat, sugar or salt. Includes Nutrition Facts and Diabetic Exchanges.

4 cups fresh broccoli florets
1/4 cup water
1 medium sweet yellow pepper, sliced
2 tablespoons butter
1 teaspoon minced fresh gingerroot
1/4 to 1/2 teaspoon grated orange peel
1/4 teaspoon salt
1/4 teaspoon pepper

In a microwave-safe bowl, combine the broccoli and water. Cover and microwave on high for 3 minutes. Meanwhile, in a large skillet, saute yellow pepper in butter for 3-4 minutes or until tender.

Stir broccoli; microwave 1 minute longer or until tender. Add the ginger, orange peel, salt and pepper to yellow pepper. Drain broccoli; add to pepper mixture and toss to coat. **Yield:** 4 servings.

Editor's Note: This recipe was tested in a 1,100-watt microwave.

Nutrition Facts: 3/4 cup (prepared with reduced-fat butter) equals 54 calories, 3 g fat (2 g saturated fat), 10 mg cholesterol, 202 mg sodium, 6 g carbohydrate, 2 g fiber, 3 g protein. **Diabetic Exchanges:** 1 vegetable, 1/2 fat.

Peanut Butter Chocolate Pie

Prep/Total Time: 30 min.

1 package (6 ounces) peanut butter cups
1 cup cold milk
1 package (3.9 ounces) instant chocolate pudding mix
1 carton (8 ounces) frozen whipped topping, thawed
1 chocolate crumb crust (8 inches)

Cut four cups in half; coarsely chop remaining cups and set aside. In a large bowl, whisk milk and pudding mix for 2 minutes. Fold in whipped topping until blended.

Fold in chopped peanut butter cups. Spoon into crust. Arrange halved peanut butter cups on top. Refrigerate for at least 15 minutes before cutting. **Yield:** 8 servings.

Memorable Sirloin Menu

WHETHER YOU NEED a fancy dinner for guests or just want to serve a special meal to your family, this menu is guaranteed to please. With an air of sophistication, these delectable dishes transform everyday ingredients into a restaurant-quality meal.

Begin with savory Sirloin in Wine Sauce from Barbara Kamm of Wilmington, Delaware. "This recipe is a family favorite as well as a great, easy company entree," says Barbara. The tender sirloin is coated in a hearty mushroom-wine sauce that tastes fantastic served over pasta.

Pair it with Tara Sensenbaugh's dressed-up Garlic Parmesan Asparagus for a truly succulent supper. With subtle garlic, melted butter and a hint of Parmesan cheese, this asparagus dish is a hit with guests at her Falling Waters, West Virginia kitchen.

Make the meal complete with apricot halves, another favorite fruit or a basic green salad for a menu that's sure to shine at your next dinner party.

Sirloin in Wine Sauce

Prep/Total Time: 30 min.

- 2 tablespoons all-purpose flour
- 1/8 teaspoon ground mustard
- 1 pound boneless beef top sirloin steak, thinly sliced
- 2 tablespoons butter
- 1 can (10-1/2 ounces) condensed beef consomme, undiluted
- 1/2 cup dry red wine *or* beef broth
- 1 jar (4-1/2 ounces) sliced mushrooms, drained
- 1/4 cup chopped green onions
- 1 teaspoon Worcestershire sauce

Hot cooked linguine

In a large resealable plastic bag, combine flour and mustard. Add beef, a few pieces at a time, and shake to coat. In a large skillet, brown beef in butter.

Add consomme and wine or broth. Stir in the mushrooms, onions and Worcestershire sauce. Bring to a boil. Reduce heat; simmer, uncovered, for 10-15 minutes or until sauce is thickened. Serve over linguine. **Yield:** 4 servings.

Garlic Parmesan Asparagus

Prep/Total Time: 15 min.

✓ Uses less fat, sugar or salt. Includes Nutrition Facts and Diabetic Exchanges.

- 1/2 cup water
- 1 pound fresh asparagus, trimmed
- 1 teaspoon minced garlic
- 2 tablespoons butter, melted
- 1 tablespoon grated Parmesan cheese

In a large skillet, bring water to a boil. Add asparagus and garlic. Cover and cook for 5-7 minutes or until crisp-tender, stirring occasionally; drain. Drizzle with butter. Sprinkle with Parmesan cheese; gently toss to coat. **Yield:** 4 servings.

Nutrition Facts: 1 serving (prepared with reduced-fat butter) equals 45 calories, 4 g fat (2 g saturated fat), 11 mg cholesterol, 65 mg sodium, 3 g carbohydrate, 1 g fiber, 3 g protein. **Diabetic Exchanges:** 1/2 vegetable, 1/2 fat.

Garlic Parmesan Asparagus
Sirloin in Wine Sauce

Barbecue Ham Sandwiches
Two-Bean Salad

Classic Tastes Of Summer

WHEN SUMMER IS HERE, it means swimming pools, grilling and enjoying all the foods that come with the season. Fresh corn, watermelon and ice cream shout "summer," but what could be better in warm weather than barbecue?

This summer, instead of spending hours over a hot grill or stovetop, you can have tangy barbecue flavor in under 30 minutes. Thanks to Mollie Fry of Carolina barbecue country, Raleigh, North Carolina, it's never been easier. This busy cook sends her recipe for Barbecue Ham Sandwiches, a family favorite for over 50 years.

"My mother would make a batch of the sauce on Saturday and buy the ham. After church on Sunday, our hungry family would have a fast but delicious meal," she writes. "Dill pickles served on the side are a special touch."

Beans are a natural match with barbecue, and Ann Mulford's recipe for Two-Bean Salad doesn't disappoint. The Lincolnville, Maine cook says, "This mixed salad sure is a winner.

"I make it a day or so ahead of time, and it marinates in the refrigerator. It's simple—you just stir it every 12 hours." She adds, "Any leftovers are wonderful over rice or noodles."

Barbecue Ham Sandwiches

Prep/Total Time: 25 min.

      1 cup plus 2 tablespoons chili sauce
  3/4 cup packed brown sugar
  1/2 cup plus 1 tablespoon water
  3/4 teaspoon prepared mustard
  1/4 to 1/2 teaspoon chili powder
  1/8 teaspoon ground cloves
1-1/2 pounds shaved fully cooked ham
      6 hamburger buns, split and toasted

In a large saucepan, combine the first six ingredients. Cook, uncovered, over low heat for 15 minutes. Stir in ham; heat through. Using a slotted spoon, serve on buns. **Yield:** 6 servings.

Two-Bean Salad

Prep/Total Time: 20 min.

  1 can (15 ounces) garbanzo beans *or* chickpeas, rinsed and drained
  1 can (15 ounces) black beans, rinsed and drained
2/3 cup shredded Swiss cheese
1/2 cup chopped onion
  1 can (3.8 ounces) sliced ripe olives, drained
1/4 cup chopped celery
1/4 cup *each* chopped green, sweet red and orange peppers
1/3 cup balsamic vinaigrette

In a large bowl, combine the beans, cheese, onion, olives, celery and peppers. Drizzle with vinaigrette; toss to coat. Refrigerate until serving. **Yield:** 6 servings.

Chicken Dinner On the Double

WHO SAYS you have to work hard to create a terrific meal for two tonight? With hardly any fuss at all, you can have a hot supper that's sized just right and ready to eat in 30 minutes.

Begin with Tender Chicken for Two from Rosena Vrshek of Phoenix, Arizona. Instead of tomatoes, her version of chicken cacciatore calls for ketchup, which gives the sauce a slightly sweet flavor.

"My husband always raved about this simple but tasty dish and asked for it often," she says. "You can serve it over hot rice, or try it with leftover mashed potatoes if you like."

Pair the entree with Italian Green Beans from Rudy Martino. With a few basic ingredients, the jazzed-up beans make a pleasant match for the chicken but could also be served with many other main courses. "This has been a family favorite for many years," Rudy writes from Lombard, Illinois. "It's a great treatment for a green vegetable."

Finish dinner with scoops of raspberry sherbet, strawberry sorbet or another frosty favorite. You're sure to have a meal you'll both enjoy with limited effort from the cook!

Tender Chicken for Two

Prep/Total Time: 30 min.

    1/4 cup all-purpose flour
    1/2 teaspoon salt
    1/4 teaspoon pepper
      2 boneless skinless chicken breast halves
        (6 ounces *each*)
      3 tablespoons vegetable oil
    1/2 cup chopped onion
    1/2 cup sliced mushrooms
    1/2 cup chopped green pepper
    1/2 cup ketchup
    1/4 cup water
    1/4 cup sherry *or* chicken broth
Hot cooked rice

Place the flour, salt and pepper in a large resealable plastic bag; add the chicken breast halves and shake to coat. In a large skillet, brown the chicken in the oil over medium heat for 3-1/2 to 4 minutes on each side. Remove and keep warm.

In the same skillet, saute the onion, mushrooms and green pepper until crisp-tender. Stir in the ketchup, water and sherry or broth. Add the chicken; cook, uncovered, over medium heat for 14-16 minutes or until juices run clear and sauce is thickened. Serve with rice. **Yield:** 2 servings.

Italian Green Beans

Prep/Total Time: 15 min.

☑ Uses less fat, sugar or salt. Includes Nutrition Facts and Diabetic Exchanges.

    1/2 pound fresh *or* frozen cut green beans
      2 tablespoons water
  2-1/4 teaspoons grated Parmesan cheese
  2-1/4 teaspoons seasoned bread crumbs
    1/4 teaspoon garlic salt
    1/8 teaspoon pepper
  1-1/2 teaspoons olive oil

Place beans and water in a microwave-safe dish. Cover and microwave on high for 4-5 minutes or until crisp-tender. Meanwhile, in a small bowl, combine the Parmesan cheese, bread crumbs, garlic salt and pepper. Drain beans; drizzle with olive oil. Sprinkle with cheese mixture and toss to coat. **Yield:** 2 servings.

Editor's Note: This recipe was tested in a 1,100-watt microwave.

Nutrition Facts: 3/4 cup equals 85 calories, 4 g fat (1 g saturated fat), 1 mg cholesterol, 309 mg sodium, 10 g carbohydrate, 4 g fiber, 3 g protein. **Diabetic Exchanges:** 2 vegetable, 1/2 fat.

**Tender Chicken for Two
Italian Green Beans**

Fare with Asian Flavors

YOU DON'T HAVE to order takeout from a Chinese restaurant to get the fastest food around. The entire meal here has a hands-on time of only 30 minutes!

Begin with sweet Orange-Glazed Pork Chops from Athena Russell of Florence, South Carolina. Juicy and tender, they burst with flavor and are perfect with Skillet Lo Mein from Debbie Stadtle, Fredericksburg, Virginia. "If you like it spicy, add 1/4 teaspoon of crushed red pepper with the ginger," Debbie says.

For dessert, enjoy Pineapple Ice Cream Topping from Genise Krause, Sturgeon Bay, Wisconsin.

Pineapple Ice Cream Topping
Skillet Lo Mein
Orange-Glazed Pork Chops

Orange-Glazed Pork Chops

Prep/Total Time: 25 min.

- 1/2 cup orange marmalade
- 2 tablespoons orange juice
- 2 tablespoons Dijon mustard
- 1 tablespoon reduced-sodium soy sauce
- 1/2 teaspoon minced garlic
- 1/8 to 1/4 teaspoon crushed red pepper flakes
- 4 bone-in pork loin chops (1/2 inch thick and 8 ounces *each*)
- 1 teaspoon vegetable oil
- 1/2 teaspoon salt
- 1/4 teaspoon pepper

In a small bowl, combine the marmalade, orange juice, mustard, soy sauce, garlic and pepper flakes; set aside.

In a large skillet, brown pork chops in oil on both sides over medium-high heat; sprinkle with salt and pepper. Cook, uncovered, 10 minutes longer or until a meat thermometer reads 160°. Remove and keep warm.

Add marmalade mixture to the skillet; bring to a boil. Reduce heat; simmer, uncovered, for 3-4 minutes or until thickened. Spoon over pork chops. **Yield:** 4 servings.

Skillet Lo Mein

Prep/Total Time: 20 min.

- 4 ounces uncooked spaghetti, broken into thirds
- 1 tablespoon vegetable oil
- 1 package (9 ounces) frozen Szechuan stir-fry vegetables with sauce, thawed
- 1/3 cup julienned carrot
- 1/4 cup sliced celery
- 1/4 cup sliced onion
- 2 tablespoons reduced-sodium soy sauce
- 1/8 teaspoon ground ginger

Cook spaghetti according to package directions. Meanwhile, in a large skillet, heat oil over medium-high heat; stir in the stir-fry vegetables, contents of seasoning packet, carrot, celery, onion, soy sauce and ginger. Bring to a boil.

Reduce heat; simmer, uncovered, for 3-4 minutes or until vegetables are crisp-tender. Drain spaghetti; stir into vegetable mixture. **Yield:** 4 servings.

Pineapple Ice Cream Topping

Prep/Total Time: 5 min.

- 3/4 cup pineapple preserves
- 1/2 cup pineapple tidbits
- 2 tablespoons butter
- 1/4 teaspoon ground ginger
Dash ground cinnamon
- 4 scoops vanilla ice cream

In a small microwave-safe bowl, combine the first five ingredients. Microwave, uncovered, on high for 1-2 minutes or until heated through, stirring once. Serve with ice cream. **Yield:** 4 servings.

Editor's Note: This recipe was tested in a 1,100-watt microwave.

Shrimp Salad For Supper

A REFRESHING SALAD can be perfect on hot summer nights. Instead of heating up the kitchen and stressing out the cook like other hearty entrees, a satisfying main-dish salad is a cinch to put together.

Such is the case when Avocado Shrimp Salad from Patricia Collins of Imbler, Oregon is on the menu. A homemade cilantro-lime dressing lightly coats romaine, avocado and shrimp. Feel free to cut back on the dressing's jalapeno pepper or add other ingredients to suit your family's tastes.

Serve Nutty Gouda Rolls from our Test Kitchen on the side. With just four ingredients, these speedy crescents featuring Gouda, pecans and honey come together with ease for a simple yet special side.

Round out supper by serving fresh cherries or other fruit. In no time, you'll have a wonderful meal everyone's sure to love.

Avocado Shrimp Salad

Prep/Total Time: 20 min.

1/2 cup olive oil
1/3 cup lime juice
1/3 cup finely chopped onion
3 tablespoons minced fresh cilantro
3 tablespoons white vinegar
2 tablespoons minced fresh parsley
2 tablespoons finely chopped seeded jalapeno pepper
1-1/2 teaspoons minced garlic
1 teaspoon salt
1/4 teaspoon pepper
6 cups torn romaine
1/2 pound cooked small shrimp
1 medium ripe avocado, peeled and sliced

In a jar with a tight-fitting lid, combine the first 10 ingredients; shake well. Divide romaine among four plates; top with shrimp and avocado. Drizzle with dressing. Serve immediately. **Yield:** 4 servings.

Editor's Note: When cutting or seeding hot peppers, use rubber or plastic gloves to protect your hands. Avoid touching your face.

Nutty Gouda Rolls

Prep/Total Time: 20 min.

2 ounces Gouda cheese
1 tube (8 ounces) refrigerated crescent rolls
2 tablespoons finely chopped pecans
1 tablespoon honey

Cut cheese into eight 1/2-in.-wide strips. Separate crescent dough into eight triangles; sprinkle with pecans. Place a cheese strip on the shortest side of each triangle; roll up. Pinch ends to seal.

Place on an ungreased baking sheet. Bake at 375° for 10-12 minutes or until golden brown. Immediately brush with honey. Serve warm. **Yield:** 8 servings.

Avocado Shrimp Salad
Nutty Gouda Rolls

Basil-Tomato Grilled Cheese
Strawberry Chicken Salad

Casual Salad And Sandwich

IT'S TIME to take full advantage of that outdoor picnic table or backyard patio set. With this fast and easy menu, you can enjoy the sun, family and a relaxing lunch or dinner with extra moments to savor all the warm and wonderful joys that summer brings.

The tastes of the season abound in this simple Italian-style grilled cheese sandwich from Sylvia Schmitt of Sun City, Arizona. Not only are Basil-Tomato Grilled Cheese sandwiches delicious—they're ready in a dash.

Sylvia says, "I am always busy, especially around lunchtime, so I need something that is very quick and simple to prepare. At the same time, it also has to be very tasty and satisfying as well. This recipe works on all counts."

A special salad would be just the thing to complete this warm-weather meal, and Lori Nordhoff of Boone, Iowa has the perfect complement.

Refreshing Strawberry Chicken Salad combines sweet fruit with cubed cooked chicken to create a hearty, sweet fruit salad. It's ideal for everything from casual evening picnics to fancy luncheons served outdoors. Lori likes to add a handful of chopped walnuts for extra crunch.

Basil-Tomato Grilled Cheese

Prep/Total Time: 20 min.

8 slices Italian bread (3/4 inch thick)
8 slices part-skim mozzarella cheese
2 large plum tomatoes, sliced
2 tablespoons minced fresh basil
2 teaspoons balsamic vinegar
Salt and pepper to taste
1/4 cup olive oil
3 tablespoons grated Parmesan cheese
1/4 teaspoon garlic powder

On four slices of bread, layer cheese and tomatoes; sprinkle with basil, vinegar, salt and pepper. Top with remaining bread.

In a small bowl, combine the oil, Parmesan cheese and garlic powder; brush over the outsides of each sandwich. On a griddle, cook sandwiches over medium heat until golden brown on both sides. **Yield:** 4 servings.

Strawberry Chicken Salad

Prep/Total Time: 15 min.

5 cups spring mix salad greens
2 cups cubed cooked chicken
1-1/4 cups sliced fresh strawberries
2 medium kiwifruit, peeled and chopped
1 large apple, chopped
1/4 cup crumbled blue cheese
1/3 cup poppy seed salad dressing

In a large bowl, combine the first six ingredients. Drizzle with dressing; toss to coat. Serve immediately. **Yield:** 4 servings.

Great Greek Combination

Nutrition Facts: 1 filled pita with 1/4 cup sauce equals 391 calories, 11 g fat (3 g saturated fat), 64 mg cholesterol, 774 mg sodium, 42 g carbohydrate, 2 g fiber, 30 g protein. **Diabetic Exchanges:** 3 starch, 3 lean meat, 1 fat.

MAKE IT GREEK for supper tonight with two recipes that highlight Mediterranean flavors. A warm flatbread sandwich and crunchy vegetable salad put oregano, black olives and feta cheese to terrific use. Best of all, the entire meal's so quick to fix, you'll have it on the table in less than 30 minutes!

Begin with our Test Kitchen's mouth-watering version of traditional gyros. With tender seasoned beef and sauteed onion, Beef Pitas with Yogurt Sauce is sure to be a hit. Top it with a very simple yet flavorful yogurt sauce that doubles as a dip for warmed pita chips and is also great on Greek salads.

Serve Greek Vegetable Salad with the pita sandwiches for a cool, refreshing side dish. From Rena Kilaniotou of Belleville, New Jersey, the salad can be served right away, or you can assemble it ahead to let the flavors blend overnight for added taste. Either way, these crunchy veggies with a speedy homemade dressing are delectable!

For a fresh-tasting finale, round out the meal with scoops of lemon sherbet or your favorite ice cream or sorbet.

Greek Vegetable Salad

Prep/Total Time: 15 min.

   1 medium cucumber, peeled and chopped
   1 large tomato, seeded and chopped
   1 medium green pepper, chopped
   4 green onions, chopped
  10 pitted Greek olives
 1/2 cup crumbled feta cheese
DRESSING:
 1/3 cup olive oil
   3 tablespoons cider vinegar
   1 teaspoon salt
   1 teaspoon dried oregano
 1/2 teaspoon sugar

In a serving bowl, combine the cucumber, tomato, green pepper, onions, olives and feta cheese. In a jar with a tight-fitting lid, combine the dressing ingredients; shake well. Drizzle over salad and toss to coat. Serve with a slotted spoon. **Yield:** 4 servings.

Beef Pitas with Yogurt Sauce

Prep/Total Time: 25 min.

✓ Uses less fat, sugar or salt. Includes Nutrition Facts and Diabetic Exchanges.

   1 cup (8 ounces) fat-free plain yogurt
 1/4 cup minced fresh parsley
 1/2 teaspoon minced garlic
 1/8 teaspoon salt
PITAS:
   1 teaspoon dried oregano
   1 teaspoon minced fresh rosemary
 1/2 teaspoon salt
 1/4 teaspoon pepper
   1 pound boneless beef sirloin steak, cut into thin strips
   1 large sweet onion, sliced
   4 teaspoons olive oil, *divided*
   4 whole gyro-style pitas (6 inches), warmed

For sauce, in a small bowl, combine the yogurt, parsley, garlic and salt. Refrigerate until serving.

In a large resealable plastic bag, combine the oregano, rosemary, salt and pepper; add beef. Seal bag and toss to coat. In a large nonstick skillet, saute onion in 2 teaspoons oil until golden brown. Remove and keep warm. Saute beef in remaining oil until no longer pink. Serve beef and onion on pitas with yogurt sauce. **Yield:** 4 servings.

Greek Vegetable Salad
Beef Pitas with Yogurt Sauce

Fruit Smoothies
Orange Coffee Cake Ring
Eggs with Feta and Asparagus

A Breakfast Built for Two

TIRED of the same old meat loaf and mashed potatoes? Jazz up tonight's menu by serving these cozy breakfast dishes for dinner! Or save the recipes and enjoy an eye-opening, special weekend brunch for two. No matter when you choose to serve them, we're sure you'll love these fantastic reader recipes.

Start with Carol Heine's Eggs with Feta and Asparagus. From her kitchen in New Prague, Minnesota, Carol whipped up this rise-and-shine specialty after she had an abundance of asparagus. Now it's a staple. "We always have more than enough asparagus for the two of us," she writes. "This dish is a delicious and unique way to use up extras."

Tiny Dobbin of Winchester, Virginia shares her super-easy recipe for dressed-up orange rolls. With just three ingredients, including toasted coconut and cream cheese, Orange Coffee Cake Ring turns sweet rolls from everyday to elegant.

Finish off this fancy breakfast with thick and refreshing Fruit Smoothies from Teresa Dunlap of Lima, Ohio. She says, "They're great for breakfast, and they also make a scrumptious afternoon snack with cinnamon graham crackers. My family always enjoys them whenever I serve them."

Eggs with Feta and Asparagus

Prep/Total Time: 20 min.

1 cup cut fresh asparagus (2-inch pieces)
1 tablespoon butter
4 eggs
1/8 to 1/4 teaspoon seasoned salt
4 strips ready-to-serve fully cooked bacon, crumbled
1/4 cup crumbled feta cheese

Place 1 in. of water in a saucepan; add asparagus. Bring to a boil. Reduce heat; cover and simmer for 3-5 minutes or until crisp-tender.

Meanwhile, in a large skillet, heat butter until hot. Add eggs; reduce heat to low. Cook until whites are completely set and yolks begin to thicken but are not hard. Sprinkle with seasoned salt.

Transfer eggs to serving plates; top with asparagus, bacon and feta cheese. **Yield:** 2 servings.

Orange Coffee Cake Ring

Prep/Total Time: 30 min.

1 tube (13.9 ounces) orange sweet rolls with icing
1 ounce cream cheese, softened
1/2 cup flaked coconut, toasted

Set aside icing from sweet rolls. Arrange rolls in a greased 9-in. round baking pan. Bake at 375° for 18-20 minutes or until golden brown.

In a small bowl, combine cream cheese and reserved icing. Spread over rolls. Sprinkle with coconut. Serve warm. **Yield:** 8 rolls.

Fruit Smoothies

Prep/Total Time: 5 min.

1-1/4 cups milk
1 cup frozen unsweetened strawberries
1/2 cup frozen unsweetened peach slices
1 small ripe banana, halved
3 tablespoons sugar

Place all ingredients in a blender; cover and process until smooth. Pour into chilled glasses; serve immediately. **Yield:** 2-1/2 cups.

Sensational Skillet Spread

DON'T TURN ON that hot oven tonight...let the stovetop do all the work! In just 30 minutes, a hearty and satisfying meal can be prepared on the stovetop and ready to eat.

In one skillet, prepare Bobby Taylor's Tangy Breaded Pork Chops. The Michigan City, Indiana reader gives pork chops a speedy, crisp-breaded coating starring flavorful garlic and mustard. "This has been in my recipe file for many years," Bobby says. "The chops offer lots of flavor in very little time."

In another skillet, fix Yellow Squash and Tomatoes, a surprisingly easy side dish from a reader in Pittsburgh, Pennsylvania. Kathy Smith writes, "Don't be fooled by the simplicity; this is so good. I made it at least once a week last summer when my garden was producing squash, tomatoes and basil."

Finish the meal with store-bought chocolate cake. In no time, you'll have a fantastic weeknight dinner that the whole family will adore.

Tangy Breaded Pork Chops
Prep/Total Time: 25 min.

    1 egg
1-1/2 teaspoons prepared mustard
    1 teaspoon minced garlic
    1 cup dry bread crumbs
    4 boneless pork loin chops (1/2 inch thick and 6 ounces *each*)
    2 tablespoons vegetable oil

In a shallow bowl, beat the egg, mustard and garlic. Place bread crumbs in another shallow bowl. Dip pork chops in egg mixture, then coat with crumbs.

In a large skillet, brown chops on both sides in oil. Cook, uncovered, over medium heat for 5-7 minutes on each side or until juices run clear. **Yield:** 4 servings.

Yellow Squash and Tomatoes
Prep/Total Time: 15 min.

✓ Uses less fat, sugar or salt. Includes Nutrition Facts and Diabetic Exchanges.

    2 medium yellow summer squash, coarsely chopped
    2 tablespoons olive oil
   16 cherry tomatoes, halved
    2 tablespoons minced fresh basil *or* 2 teaspoons dried basil
  1/4 teaspoon pepper
  1/8 teaspoon salt

In a large skillet, saute squash in oil until tender. Add the tomatoes, basil, pepper and salt. Reduce heat to medium; cook 1-2 minutes longer or until heated through. **Yield:** 4 servings.

Nutrition Facts: 3/4 cup equals 94 calories, 7 g fat (1 g saturated fat), 0 cholesterol, 82 mg sodium, 8 g carbohydrate, 3 g fiber, 2 g protein. **Diabetic Exchanges:** 2 vegetable, 1 fat.

Tangy Breaded Pork Chops
Yellow Squash and Tomatoes

Saucy Seafood And Sprouts

GET OUT the good plates and invite some friends or family to the table. You'll want to share this special menu with those you love. The delicate sauce and flaky salmon will definitely impress, and you'll love how little time the whole meal takes to whip up!

The key to this beautiful supper is found in Priscilla Gilbert's Salmon with Mornay Sauce. The Indian Harbour Beach, Florida cook writes, "This is a hearty salmon dish, quick and simple to prepare. My husband and I love salmon, and this is a favorite."

Serve Nutmeg Brussels Sprouts alongside the salmon for a fitting complement. Gladys De Boer of Castleford, Idaho provides this lightly spiced side dish with only a handful of ingredients for extra ease. For maximum taste, take Gladys' advice: "Try not to overcook the brussels sprouts," she says.

With a warm slice or two of your favorite bread, this dinner will have friends and family asking for more!

Salmon with Mornay Sauce

Prep/Total Time: 25 min.

1 teaspoon lemon-pepper seasoning, *divided*
4 salmon fillets (6 ounces *each*)
3 tablespoons butter, *divided*
1-1/2 teaspoons all-purpose flour
1/8 teaspoon salt
Dash pepper
Dash cayenne pepper
1/4 cup milk
1/4 cup heavy whipping cream
1/4 cup shredded Swiss cheese

Rub 1/2 teaspoon lemon-pepper seasoning over both sides of salmon. In a large skillet, cook salmon in 2 tablespoons butter for 5-6 minutes on each side or until fish flakes easily with a fork.

Meanwhile, in a small saucepan, melt remaining butter. Stir in the flour, salt, pepper, cayenne pepper and remaining lemon-pepper seasoning until blended. Gradually add milk and heavy whipping cream. Bring to a boil; cook and stir for 1-2 minutes or until thickened. Remove from the heat; stir in cheese until melted. Serve with salmon. **Yield:** 4 servings.

Nutmeg Brussels Sprouts

Prep/Total Time: 20 min.

1 pound fresh brussels sprouts, halved
1 teaspoon salt
1/8 to 1/4 teaspoon ground nutmeg
2 tablespoons butter

Place brussels sprouts and salt in a large saucepan; cover with water. Bring to a boil. Reduce heat; cover and simmer for 7-9 minutes or until crisp-tender.

Drain and return to the pan. Add nutmeg and butter; saute for 2-3 minutes or until flavors are blended. **Yield:** 4 servings.

Salmon with Mornay Sauce
Nutmeg Brussels Sprouts

Meal Made Easy as 1,2,3

Lemon Dill Couscous
Peachy Green Beans
Garlic Chicken Breasts

A HECTIC DAY calls for a no-fuss supper, and we've got just the thing! Each of the mouth-watering recipes here uses only three ingredients. So you won't have to pull a seemingly endless number of items from your pantry before you can even start cooking.

Make all three of these exceptional dishes for one fantastic meal, or pick and choose exactly what you need to round out other menus. Either way, each dish takes only a few minutes of prep, giving you plenty of time to unwind.

Our taste-testers loved the robust flavor of Garlic Chicken Breasts, shared by LaDonna Reed of Ponca City, Oklahoma. Cook up a little extra to use in a salad or sandwich for lunch the next day—you'll be glad you did!

Mary Jo Welch adds a touch of lemon and a hint of dill to dress up Lemon Dill Couscous. The Brandon, Manitoba cook enjoys serving this as a low-fat side with most any hearty entree.

Peach preserves add pleasant sweetness to Peachy Green Beans, while cayenne pepper gives them a slight kick. Lisa Ruehlow of Blaine, Minnesota shares the recipe for this winning side dish.

Garlic Chicken Breasts

Prep/Total Time: 25 min.

1/2 cup grated Parmesan cheese
 1 envelope garlic and herb *or* Italian salad
   dressing mix
 2 boneless skinless chicken breast halves
   (6 ounces *each*)

In a large resealable plastic bag, combine the Parmesan cheese and salad dressing mix. Add the chicken breast halves; shake to coat.

Place chicken in a greased 8-in. square baking dish. Bake, uncovered, at 400° for 20-25 minutes or until juices run clear. **Yield:** 2 servings.

Lemon Dill Couscous

Prep/Total Time: 10 min.

✓ Uses less fat, sugar or salt. Includes Nutrition Facts.

3/4 cup uncooked plain couscous
3-1/4 teaspoons lemon juice
1/4 to 1/2 teaspoon dill weed

Follow couscous package directions for 2 servings, adding salt to the water and omitting the oil or butter from Step 1. Stir in the couscous, lemon juice and dill. Cover and remove from the heat; let stand for 5 minutes. Fluff with a fork. **Yield:** 2 servings.

Editor's Note: This recipe was tested with Near East plain couscous.

Nutrition Facts: 1 cup equals 249 calories, 1 g fat (trace saturated fat), 0 cholesterol, 302 mg sodium, 53 g carbohydrate, 3 g fiber, 10 g protein.

Peachy Green Beans

Prep/Total Time: 20 min.

✓ Uses less fat, sugar or salt. Includes Nutrition Facts and Diabetic Exchanges.

1/2 pound fresh green beans, trimmed
 3 tablespoons peach preserves
Dash cayenne pepper

Place beans in a steamer basket; place in a large saucepan over 1 in. of water. Bring to a boil; cover and steam for 8-10 minutes or until crisp-tender.

In a small microwave-safe bowl, combine preserves and cayenne. Cook, uncovered, on high for 30 seconds or until preserves are melted. Transfer beans to a serving bowl; add the peach mixture and toss to coat. **Yield:** 2 servings.

Nutrition Facts: 3/4 cup equals 106 calories, trace fat (trace saturated fat), 0 cholesterol, 6 mg sodium, 27 g carbohydrate, 3 g fiber, 2 g protein. **Diabetic Exchanges:** 1 starch, 1 vegetable.

**Autumn Turkey Tenderloins
New England Butternut Squash**

A Perfect Fall Feast

NOTHING says fall food like a turkey dinner with apple slices, nuts and butternut squash. You'll love this fresh, flavorful menu when the weather turns cool.

Start with Brenda Sabot-Lion's Autumn Turkey Tenderloins. The busy cook from Warren, Pennsylvania shares this out-of-the-ordinary entree that's perfect for crisp evenings with family or friends.

In Coventry, Connecticut, Linda Massicotte-Black serves New England Butternut Squash, a side dish everyone likes. "It has a hint of sweetness and is a longtime family favorite. Even the pickiest eaters at the table enjoy this!" Linda writes.

Autumn Turkey Tenderloins

Prep/Total Time: 30 min.

✓ Uses less fat, sugar or salt. Includes Nutrition Facts and Diabetic Exchanges.

1-1/4 pounds turkey breast tenderloins
    1 tablespoon butter
    1 cup unsweetened apple juice
    1 medium apple, sliced
    1 tablespoon brown sugar
    2 teaspoons chicken bouillon granules
  1/4 teaspoon ground cinnamon
  1/4 teaspoon ground nutmeg

    1 tablespoon cornstarch
    2 tablespoons cold water
  1/2 cup chopped walnuts, toasted

In a large skillet, brown turkey in butter. Add the apple juice, apple, brown sugar, bouillon, cinnamon and nutmeg. Bring to a boil. Reduce heat; cover and simmer for 10-12 minutes or until turkey juices run clear.

Using a slotted spoon, remove turkey and apple slices to a serving platter; keep warm. Combine cornstarch and water until smooth; stir into pan juices. Bring to a boil; cook and stir for 2 minutes or until thickened. Spoon over turkey and apple. Sprinkle with walnuts. **Yield:** 5 servings.

Nutrition Facts: 1 serving equals 274 calories, 11 g fat (2 g saturated fat), 62 mg cholesterol, 423 mg sodium, 16 g carbohydrate, 2 g fiber, 30 g protein. **Diabetic Exchanges:** 4 very lean meat, 2 fat, 1 fruit.

New England Butternut Squash

Prep/Total Time: 30 min.

    1 medium butternut squash
  1/4 cup butter, melted
  1/4 cup maple syrup
  3/4 teaspoon ground cinnamon
  1/4 teaspoon ground nutmeg

Cut squash in half lengthwise; discard seeds. Place cut side down in a microwave-safe dish; add 1/2 in. of water. Cover and microwave on high for 15-20 minutes or until very tender; drain.

When cool enough to handle, scoop out pulp and mash. Stir in the butter, syrup, cinnamon and nutmeg. **Yield:** 5 servings.

Editor's Note: This recipe was tested in a 1,100-watt microwave.

Pork Chops With Pizzazz

1/2 pound fresh sugar snap peas
1 teaspoon cumin seeds, toasted *or* 1/4
  teaspoon ground cumin

In a large skillet, saute carrots in butter for 2 minutes. Add the broth, sugar, salt and pepper. Cover and cook for 2-5 minutes or until carrots are crisp-tender.

Add peas and cumin. Cook and stir 3-4 minutes longer or until peas are crisp-tender. **Yield:** 4 servings.

Cinnamon Apple Tartlets

Prep/Total Time: 15 min.

1 tube (8 ounces) refrigerated crescent rolls
4-1/2 teaspoons cinnamon-sugar, *divided*
1 large tart apple, thinly sliced

Separate crescent dough into four rectangles; place on an ungreased baking sheet. Seal perforations. Sprinkle with 3 teaspoons cinnamon-sugar. Bake at 375° for 5 minutes.

Arrange apple slices over dough; sprinkle with remaining cinnamon-sugar. Bake 5-8 minutes longer or until golden brown. Serve warm. **Yield:** 4 servings.

WHEN SCHOOL and schedules get in the way of meal preparation, let us do all the work. With the three simple recipes here, dinner will be on the table in no time so that you can get the kids off to soccer practice, music lessons and more!

Begin this well-rounded meal with Breaded Pork Chops from Linda Clark of Dayton, Ohio. With subtle orange flavor and right-from-the-skillet crispness, it's sure to please. She writes, "This dish came from an old orange chicken recipe my mother used to make. My family requests it often."

Give Carrots with Sugar Snap Peas a try as your side dish. With a mild hint of cumin, these veggies from Linda Foreman of Locust Grove, Oklahoma go with just about any main course. And because they're so colorful, they'll perk up any plate!

For dessert, our Test Kitchen created delectable Cinnamon Apple Tartlets. The flaky, sweet treats are a fun ending to a great weeknight meal. And they come together in just 15 minutes—who can beat that? If you don't have cinnamon-sugar on hand, combine 4 teaspoons of sugar with 1/2 teaspoon ground cinnamon.

Breaded Pork Chops

Prep/Total Time: 25 min.

2 cups orange juice
1-1/2 cups seasoned bread crumbs
2 teaspoons seasoned salt
4 boneless pork loin chops (1/2 inch thick and
  4 ounces *each*)
3 tablespoons olive oil

Place orange juice in a shallow bowl. In another shallow bowl, combine bread crumbs and seasoned salt. Dip pork chops in orange juice; coat with crumb mixture.

In a large skillet, cook pork in oil over medium heat for 7-9 minutes on each side or until juices run clear. **Yield:** 4 servings.

Carrots with Sugar Snap Peas

Prep/Total Time: 15 min.

1 package (16 ounces) frozen sliced carrots,
  thawed and patted dry
3 tablespoons butter
1/4 cup chicken broth
3 tablespoons sugar
1/4 teaspoon salt
1/4 teaspoon pepper

Cinnamon Apple Tartlets
Carrots with Sugar Snap Peas
Breaded Pork Chops

Beat-the-Clock Beef Dinner

THE KIDS will come running when you put this soon-to-be family favorite on the table. Jazzed-up shells and cheese is the cornerstone; a fantastic hot fudge sauce is the clincher. But don't let us tell you how good this dinner is; let the smiles on your family's faces do all the talking!

Of her Beefy Shells and Cheese, Louise Graybiel of Toronto, Ontario writes, "Boxed shells and cheese, store-bought salsa and canned beans make this kid-pleaser a snap to fix!" Louise sometimes adds shredded Monterey Jack or cheddar cheese for extra fun.

Pair the main dish with your family's favorite veggie for a complete meal. We chose broccoli, but green beans, asparagus or frozen peas would work equally well.

Dorothy Floyd sends her daughter's recipe for a wonderful dessert topping, Hot Fudge Sauce. While Dorothy hails from Norton, Ohio, her daughter Vicki Wolfe cooks across the state, in Cincinnati. But they're both chocoholics, and Vicki was happy to send this one to her mom.

Dorothy writes, "She has many recipes for hot fudge sauce and gave me this one because she knows I like easy recipes." We're sure you'll like it, too.

Hot Fudge Sauce
Beefy Shells and Cheese

Beefy Shells and Cheese

Prep/Total Time: 30 min.

- 1 pound ground beef
- 1 package (12 ounces) shells and cheese dinner mix
- 2 cups water
- 1-1/4 cups salsa
- 1 can (15 ounces) black beans, rinsed and drained
- 1 to 2 teaspoons chili powder
- 1/8 teaspoon salt

In a large skillet, cook beef over medium heat until no longer pink; drain. Set aside cheese sauce packet from dinner mix. Add shells and water to skillet. Bring to a boil; cover and simmer for 10-12 minutes or until pasta is tender.

Stir in the salsa, beans, chili powder, salt and contents of cheese sauce packet. Remove from the heat; cover and let stand for 5 minutes. **Yield:** 6 servings.

Hot Fudge Sauce

Prep/Total Time: 10 min.

- 1 cup miniature marshmallows
- 1 cup (6 ounces) semisweet chocolate chips
- 1 can (5 ounces) evaporated milk

Vanilla ice cream
Jimmies, optional

In a small saucepan, combine marshmallows, chocolate chips and milk. Cook and stir over low heat until smooth. Serve over ice cream. Sprinkle with jimmies if desired. **Yield:** about 1 cup.

No-Stick Solution

STORING previously opened packages of marshmallows in a warm, humid environment can cause them to become sticky. If they are not too far gone, try tossing the marshmallows in confectioners' sugar. Or prepare a pan of crispy cereal treats. Store opened packages in a tightly sealed plastic bag in the freezer.

Easy Italian Tonight!

A WARM, hearty pasta dinner can be just the thing your family's looking for on chilly fall nights. And you'll have a dinner sure to please with this simple Italian feast. It features wonderful herbs and seasonings and comes together, from start to finish, in just under 30 minutes.

Begin with Cindy Cohen's Chicken Chili Fettuccine. The classic entree is made with ingredients mild enough for kids, but flavorful enough for grownups. The dish also works well for company. The Alta Loma, California cook writes, "Not only is it tasty, but it also has a nice and colorful presentation. I often serve this with spinach fettuccine, if it's available."

Serve the chicken with Pull-Apart Herb Biscuits from Nancy Zimmerman of Cape May Court House, New Jersey. She writes, "This easy-to-prepare bread incorporates many different flavors, including garlic, cheese and various herbs. And it bakes up golden and aromatic." For a quick substitution, use a total of 3 teaspoons dried Italian seasoning for the basil, oregano and thyme.

You can serve both recipes with a quick side salad for a filling Italian meal!

Pull-Apart Herb Biscuits
Chicken Chili Fettuccine

Chicken Chili Fettuccine

Prep/Total Time: 25 min.

- 2 packages (9 ounces *each*) refrigerated fettuccine
- 1-1/2 pounds boneless skinless chicken breasts, cut into strips
- 1 tablespoon vegetable oil
- 1 jar (6 ounces) sliced mushrooms, drained
- 1 cup chopped onion
- 2 tablespoons all-purpose flour
- 2 cans (14-1/2 ounces *each*) Italian diced tomatoes, undrained
- 2 cans (4 ounces *each*) chopped green chilies
- 2 tablespoons butter
- 1 cup (4 ounces) shredded Monterey Jack cheese, optional

Cook the fettuccine according to the package directions. Meanwhile, in a large skillet, saute the chicken strips in oil until no longer pink. Add the mushrooms and onion; saute 2-3 minutes longer or until onion is tender.

Sprinkle with flour; cook and stir for 1 minute. Stir in tomatoes and chilies. Bring to a boil. Reduce heat; cover and simmer for 5-10 minutes or until thickened.

Drain the fettuccine; toss with butter. Serve with the chicken mixture; sprinkle with Monterey Jack cheese if desired. **Yield:** 5 servings.

Pull-Apart Herb Biscuits

Prep/Total Time: 20 min.

- 1 tube (12 ounces) refrigerated buttermilk biscuits
- 1/4 cup butter, melted
- 2 tablespoons grated Parmesan cheese
- 1 tablespoon sesame seeds
- 1 teaspoon minced garlic
- 1 teaspoon dried parsley flakes
- 1 teaspoon dried basil
- 1/2 teaspoon dried oregano
- 1/2 teaspoon dried thyme

Separate biscuits and cut into quarters. In an ungreased 9-in. round baking pan, combine the remaining ingredients. Add biscuits and toss to coat.

Bake at 450° for 8-12 minutes or until golden brown. Invert onto a serving platter and serve warm. **Yield:** 5 servings.

Classic Comfort Food

NOTHING warms up cold days better than bowls of hearty soup served with toasted sandwiches. Loaded with meat and veggies, Hot Italian Sausage Soup hits the spot. "I'm part owner of a tavern, and on Saturdays, we serve soup and sandwiches free of charge. Everyone loves this recipe," says Dan Bute, Ottawa, Illinois.

Scrumptious Pizza Sandwiches complement the soup's bold flavors. Mary Monaco of Columbus, Ohio shares the jazzed-up grilled cheese recipe.

Hot Italian Sausage Soup

Prep/Total Time: 25 min.

- 1 pound bulk hot Italian sausage
- 1 can (14-1/2 ounces) Italian stewed tomatoes
- 1 can (8 ounces) tomato sauce
- 1 cup frozen Italian vegetables
- 3/4 cup julienned green, sweet red *and*/*or* yellow pepper
- 1/4 cup chopped onion
- 1/4 cup white wine *or* chicken broth
- 1 teaspoon brown sugar
- 1 teaspoon minced fresh parsley
- 1/2 teaspoon Italian seasoning
- 1/8 teaspoon salt
- 1/8 teaspoon pepper

In a large skillet, cook sausage over medium heat until no longer pink. Meanwhile, in a large saucepan, combine the remaining ingredients. Bring to a boil. Reduce heat; cover and simmer for 10 minutes or until the vegetables are tender. Drain sausage; add to soup and heat through. **Yield:** 4 servings.

Pizza Sandwiches

Prep/Total Time: 20 min.

- 8 slices Italian bread (3/4 inch thick)
- 8 slices part-skim mozzarella cheese
- 8 slices tomato
- 4 teaspoons grated Parmesan cheese
- 1/4 teaspoon garlic salt
- 24 slices pepperoni
- 1/4 cup butter, softened
- Pizza sauce, warmed

On four slices of Italian bread, layer one slice of mozzarella cheese, two slices of tomato, 1 teaspoon Parmesan cheese, a dash of garlic salt and six slices pepperoni. Top with the remaining mozzarella cheese slices and Italian bread slices. Spread outside of each of the sandwiches with butter.

On a hot griddle, toast sandwiches for 3-4 minutes on each side or until golden brown. Serve with pizza sauce. **Yield:** 4 servings.

Refreshing Weekday Fare

LOOKING for a meal to give a weeknight supper a fresh twist? Look no further! Special enough for company but fitting for a family dinner too, this menu's refreshing flavors will add a springy splash to any wintry night.

Start with Cranberry-Orange Pork Chops from Margaret Wilson of Hemet, California. "My family loves the taste of these moist and spicy pork chops," she says. "In a pinch, I've substituted diced drained peaches for the mandarin oranges with equally delicious results."

The entree's colorful look and fresh flavor is a perfect match for Donna Curtis' Minted Orzo. The cook from Oakhurst, New Jersey whips up this side dish in just 15 minutes. Bright green mint leaves add a touch of elegance for a taste that can't be beat.

Cranberry-Orange Pork Chops

Prep/Total Time: 25 min.

☑ Uses less fat, sugar or salt. Includes Nutrition Facts and Diabetic Exchanges.

- 6 boneless pork loin chops (1/2 inch thick and 6 ounces *each*)
- 1/4 teaspoon salt
- 1/4 teaspoon pepper
- 1 tablespoon canola oil
- 1 can (11 ounces) mandarin oranges, drained
- 1/2 cup chicken broth
- 1/3 cup dried cranberries
- 1/4 teaspoon ground allspice
- 1/4 teaspoon paprika

Sprinkle pork chops with salt and pepper. In a large skillet, brown chops in oil on both sides.

Add the remaining ingredients. Bring to a boil. Reduce heat; cover and simmer for 8-10 minutes or until meat juices run clear. **Yield:** 6 servings.

Nutrition Facts: 1 pork chop with about 2 tablespoons cranberry mixture equals 288 calories, 12 g fat (4 g saturated fat), 82 mg cholesterol, 226 mg sodium, 11 g carbohydrate, 1 g fiber, 33 g protein. **Diabetic Exchanges:** 5 lean meat, 1/2 fruit, 1/2 fat.

Minted Orzo

Prep/Total Time: 15 min.

- 1 cup uncooked orzo pasta
- 1 teaspoon minced garlic
- 2 tablespoons olive oil
- 2 tablespoons butter
- 1/2 teaspoon salt
- 1/4 teaspoon pepper
- 3 tablespoons minced fresh mint

Cook orzo according to package directions. Meanwhile, in a large skillet, saute garlic in oil and butter for 1-2 minutes or until tender.

Drain orzo and add to the skillet. Sprinkle with salt and pepper; toss to coat. Sprinkle with mint. Serve immediately. **Yield:** 6 servings.

**Minted Orzo
Cranberry-Orange Pork Chops**

All About Orzo

MINTED ORZO (recipe above right) makes a deliciously different side dish for just about any dinner menu. Here are some fast orzo facts:

- Orzo is a type of pasta. It has a small, slender shape similar to barley and rice.
- Because of orzo's similar shape and mild flavor, it can be substituted for rice in many recipes.
- You'll find orzo alongside the other packaged dry pastas in most supermarkets.

Fast Favorites With Flair

HAVING company over? This classic duo is sure to impress...and you'll be amazed at how easy it is!

Briana Roell's Apricot Chicken has a crispy coating flecked with minced fresh parsley. The Indianapolis, Indiana cook drizzles a simple fruit sauce on top.

Snappy Pea Pods look as good as they taste. "This side dish is great and really quick," says Trisha Kruse of Eagle, Idaho. "Sesame oil enhances the flavor."

Apricot Chicken

Prep/Total Time: 30 min.

    4 boneless skinless chicken breast halves
       (6 ounces *each*)
    6 tablespoons butter, melted, *divided*
    1 cup biscuit/baking mix
    1 tablespoon minced fresh parsley
    1 tablespoon vegetable oil
1/4 cup apricot preserves
    2 tablespoons orange juice

Flatten the chicken to 1/4-in. thickness; set aside. Pour 5 tablespoons butter into a shallow bowl. In another shallow bowl, combine biscuit mix and parsley. Dip chicken in butter, then coat with biscuit mixture.

In a large skillet, cook chicken in oil and remaining butter over medium heat for 9-10 minutes on each side or until juices run clear.

Meanwhile, in a small microwave-safe bowl, combine preserves and orange juice. Cover and microwave on high for 30-40 seconds or until preserves are melted; stir until combined. Drizzle over chicken; cook for 1-2 minutes or until heated through. **Yield:** 4 servings.

Snappy Pea Pods

Prep/Total Time: 20 min.

✓ Uses less fat, sugar or salt. Includes Nutrition Facts and Diabetic Exchanges.

1/2 pound sliced fresh mushrooms
    1 small onion, thinly sliced
    1 tablespoon sesame oil
3/4 pound fresh *or* frozen sugar snap peas
1/2 cup chicken broth
1/4 teaspoon salt
1/4 teaspoon pepper

In a large skillet, saute mushrooms and onion in oil until crisp-tender. Add the remaining ingredients. Bring to a boil; cover and simmer for 2-4 minutes or until peas are crisp-tender. Serve with a slotted spoon. **Yield:** 4 servings.

Nutrition Facts: 3/4 cup equals 89 calories, 4 g fat (1 g saturated fat), 0 cholesterol, 270 mg sodium, 10 g carbohydrate, 3 g fiber, 5 g protein. **Diabetic Exchanges:** 2 vegetable, 1/2 fat.

Snappy Pea Pods
Apricot Chicken

Steak House Meal at Home

WITH A MENU as quick and delicious as this one, there's no need to go out! Parmesan Fettuccine sets the tone with its easy preparation and great taste. "It's such a simple side dish and makes a pretty presentation with many meals," writes Sundra Hauck from Bogalusa, Louisiana. With just four ingredients, it's ready in no time with a taste that's sure to please the entire family.

Dee Faulding of Santa Barbara, California brings zest to dinner with her recipe for Steaks with Peppery Onions. The name couldn't be more fitting—broiled rib eyes get a burst of flavor from caramelized onions seasoned with pepper, garlic and salt.

The tang of Sweet-Sour Spinach Salad sent in by Judith Priglmeier rounds out the menu with a splash of color. "Quick and easy is often on my mealtime agenda, so this salad is perfect," she writes from Aitkin, Minnesota. "Plus, I can make it for a few or an entire crew!"

No matter who's at the table, this medley is sure to make guests think they're dining at a fine steak house. Enjoy!

Sweet-Sour Spinach Salad
Parmesan Fettuccine
Steaks with Peppery Onions

Parmesan Fettuccine

Prep/Total Time: 20 min.

8 ounces uncooked fettuccine
1/3 cup butter, cubed
1/3 cup grated Parmesan cheese
1/8 teaspoon pepper

Cook fettuccine according to package directions; drain. In a large skillet, melt butter over low heat. Add fettuccine and stir until coated. Sprinkle with Parmesan cheese and pepper; toss to coat. **Yield:** 4 servings.

Steaks with Peppery Onions

Prep/Total Time: 25 min.

3 medium onions, sliced
1 teaspoon minced garlic
1 teaspoon salt
1 teaspoon pepper
2 tablespoons olive oil
1 tablespoon butter
4 boneless rib eye steaks (6 ounces *each*)

In a large skillet over medium heat, cook the onions, garlic, salt and pepper in oil and butter for 15-20 minutes or until the onions are golden brown, stirring frequently.

Meanwhile, broil steaks 3-4 in. from the heat for 6-8 minutes on each side or until meat reaches desired doneness (for medium-rare, a meat thermometer should read 145°; medium, 160°; well-done, 170°). Serve with onion mixture. **Yield:** 4 servings.

Sweet-Sour Spinach Salad

Prep/Total Time: 10 min.

1 package (9 ounces) fresh spinach, torn
1/4 cup dried cranberries
1/4 cup chopped green onions
1/2 cup vegetable oil
1/4 cup sugar
3 tablespoons cider vinegar
1/2 teaspoon ground mustard
1/8 to 1/4 teaspoon celery seed

In a large salad bowl, combine the spinach, cranberries and onions. In a jar with a tight-fitting lid, combine the oil, sugar, vinegar, mustard and celery seed; shake well. Drizzle over the salad and toss to coat. Serve immediately. **Yield:** 4 servings.

Chapter 4

JUST GLANCE at the shelves in your local supermarket, and you'll see an endless number of packaged mixes, canned goods, frozen foods, cooked meats and other convenience items. And all of them add up to big time-savings for busy cooks!

These handy products provide helpful shortcuts in recipes such as Sausage Spaghetti Pie, Simple Seafood Alfredo, Strawberry Fudge Torte and Lemon Crumb Bars. In fact, every dish in this chapter uses baking mix, refrigerated cookie dough or another convenience item to fast-forward your kitchen time.

But when your family tastes these scrumptious, home-style foods, no one will guess they weren't made from scratch!

SWEET CONVENIENCE. Makeover Chocolate Truffle Dessert (p. 79).

Special Pleasure Chocolate Cheesecake

(Pictured below)

Prep: 20 min. **Bake:** 40 min. + chilling

When I have time, I enjoy making cheesecakes. I like this fail-proof dessert because it's so easy to prepare and has the right mix of ingredients to make it a "special pleasure!"
—Benjamin Clark, Warsaw, New York

- 1 package (18 ounces) ready-to-bake refrigerated triple-chocolate cookie dough
- 1 package (8 ounces) milk chocolate toffee bits, *divided*
- 1 package (9-1/2 ounces) Dove dark chocolate candies
- 3 packages (8 ounces *each*) cream cheese, softened
- 1 can (14 ounces) sweetened condensed milk
- 1 carton (6 ounces) vanilla yogurt
- 4 eggs, lightly beaten
- 1 teaspoon vanilla extract

Whipped cream

Let dough stand at room temperature for 5-10 minutes to soften. Press nine portions of dough into an ungreased 13-in. x 9-in. x 2-in. baking dish (save remaining dough for another use). Set aside 2 tablespoons toffee bits; sprinkle remaining toffee bits over dough.

In a microwave-safe bowl, heat candies at 70% power for 15 seconds; stir. Microwave in 5-second intervals until melted; stir until smooth. In a mixing bowl, beat the cream cheese, milk and yogurt until smooth. Add eggs; beat on low just until combined. Fold in vanilla and melted chocolate. Pour over crust.

Bake at 350° for 40-45 minutes or until center is almost set. Cool on a wire rack. Refrigerate for 4 hours. Garnish with whipped cream and reserved toffee bits. Refrigerate leftovers. **Yield:** 24 servings.

Special Pleasure Chocolate Cheesecake

Simple Seafood Alfredo

Prep/Total Time: 20 min.

This fuss-free recipe came together because I wanted a quick-fix meal that tasted like real seafood Alfredo. After preparing the pasta, just add the seafood for a fancy supper.
—Verna Knox, Milwaukee, Wisconsin

- 1 package (4.4 ounces) quick-cooking noodles and Alfredo sauce mix
- 1 package (8 ounces) imitation lobster *or* crabmeat
- 1/2 pound frozen cooked small shrimp, thawed

Prepare the noodle mix according to the package directions. Stir in the lobster and shrimp; heat through. **Yield:** 3 servings.

Editor's Note: This recipe was tested with Lipton Alfredo mix.

Parmesan Chicken Fingers

Prep: 10 min. + marinating **Bake:** 15 min.

Buttermilk is a key ingredient in both the zesty marinade and creamy dipping sauce for this finger-lickin' favorite from our Test Kitchen.

- 1-1/4 cups buttermilk, *divided*
- 3/4 teaspoon hot pepper sauce
- 1 package (1 pound) chicken tenderloins
- 5 tablespoons grated Parmesan cheese, *divided*
- 1/4 cup mayonnaise
- 2 tablespoons sour cream
- 1 tablespoon lemon juice
- 1/2 teaspoon onion powder
- 1/4 teaspoon garlic powder
- 3/4 cup seasoned bread crumbs

In a large resealable plastic bag, combine 1/2 cup buttermilk and pepper sauce; add chicken. Seal bag and turn to coat; refrigerate for 30 minutes.

For dipping sauce, in a small bowl, combine 2 tablespoons cheese, mayonnaise, sour cream, lemon juice, onion powder, garlic powder and remaining buttermilk until blended. Cover and refrigerate until serving.

In another resealable plastic bag, combine crumbs and remaining cheese. Drain and discard marinade. Add chicken to crumb mixture; seal bag and shake to coat.

Place chicken in a greased 15-in. x 10-in. x 1-in. baking pan. Bake at 450° for 15 minutes or until juices run clear. Serve with dipping sauce. **Yield:** 4 servings.

Mayo or Salad Dressing?

MAYONNAISE and salad dressing may be used interchangeably in recipes, but keep in mind that salad dressing is sweeter. Depending on the recipe, try substituting sour cream or yogurt for some or all of the mayo if you'd prefer less sweetness.

Lemon Crumb Bars

Prep: 15 min. **Bake:** 40 min. + cooling

I like to try new cookie and bar recipes for a change of pace, but I often return to this tried-and-true favorite that starts with a convenient cake mix. My husband loves the sweet-and-salty combination of flavors.
—Anna Miller, Quaker City, Ohio

✓ Uses less fat, sugar or salt. Includes Nutrition Facts and Diabetic Exchanges.

    1 package (18-1/4 ounces) lemon cake mix
1/2 cup cold butter
    1 egg
    2 cups crushed saltines (about 60 crackers)
    3 egg yolks
    1 can (14 ounces) sweetened condensed milk
1/2 cup lemon juice

In a large mixing bowl, beat cake mix, butter and egg until crumbly. Stir in cracker crumbs; set aside 2 cups of the mixture for topping.

Press remaining mixture into a 13-in. x 9-in. x 2-in. baking dish coated with nonstick cooking spray. Bake at 350° for 18-20 minutes or until edges are lightly browned.

In a small mixing bowl, beat the egg yolks, milk and lemon juice. Pour over crust; sprinkle with reserved crumb mixture. Bake 20-25 minutes longer or until edges are lightly browned. Cool on a wire rack. Cut into bars. Store in the refrigerator. **Yield:** 2 dozen.

Nutrition Facts: 1 bar equals 153 calories, 7 g fat (3 g saturated fat), 46 mg cholesterol, 244 mg sodium, 22 g carbohydrate, 1 g fiber, 2 g protein. **Diabetic Exchanges:** 1-1/2 starch, 1 fat.

Coffee Ice Cream Cookie Cups

Prep: 30 min. **Bake:** 15 min. + freezing

My brothers, sisters and I are always looking for new ice cream recipes. I invented this for my sister's birthday party, and everyone wanted more. I've tried it with peanut butter cookie dough and different ice creams, but I like coffee best. —*Marcus Dooley, Red Oak, Texas*

    1 tube (16-1/2 ounces) refrigerated chocolate chip cookie dough
    2 cups coffee ice cream
1/3 cup English toffee bits *or* almond brickle chips
Whipped cream and chocolate syrup

Let dough stand at room temperature for 5-10 minutes to soften. Cut into 12 slices; press onto the bottoms and up the sides of greased muffin cups. Bake at 350° for 12-14 minutes or until golden brown. Cool slightly on a wire rack.

Spoon ice cream into each cup; sprinkle with toffee bits. Cover and freeze for 1-2 hours or until firm. Remove cups from pan. Garnish with whipped cream and chocolate syrup. **Yield:** 12 servings.

Sausage Spaghetti Pie

Sausage Spaghetti Pie

(Pictured above)

Prep: 20 min. **Bake:** 25 min.

I adapted this recipe to our low-fat lifestyle. It's just wonderful and has been a big hit with all who've tried it.
—*Sue Ann O'Buck, Sinking Spring, Pennsylvania*

✓ Uses less fat, sugar or salt. Includes Nutrition Facts and Diabetic Exchanges.

    4 ounces uncooked spaghetti
1/2 pound smoked turkey kielbasa, diced
    1 cup garden-style spaghetti sauce
    1 cup reduced-fat ricotta cheese
    3 egg whites
1/3 cup grated Parmesan cheese
1/4 cup shredded part-skim mozzarella cheese

Cook spaghetti according to package directions. Meanwhile, in a small nonstick skillet, saute sausage for 3-4 minutes or until browned; stir in spaghetti sauce.

In a small bowl, combine ricotta cheese and 1 egg white; set aside. Drain spaghetti; add Parmesan cheese and remaining egg whites. Press onto the bottom and up the sides of a 9-in. deep-dish pie plate coated with nonstick cooking spray. Spoon ricotta mixture into crust. Top with sausage mixture.

Bake, uncovered, at 350° for 20 minutes. Sprinkle with mozzarella cheese. Bake 5 minutes longer or until cheese is melted and filling is heated through. Let stand for 5 minutes before slicing. **Yield:** 4 servings.

Nutrition Facts: 1 piece equals 341 calories, 9 g fat (4 g saturated fat), 47 mg cholesterol, 980 mg sodium, 38 g carbohydrate, 2 g fiber, 24 g protein. **Diabetic Exchanges:** 3 lean meat, 2 starch, 1 vegetable.

Ultimate Fruit Pizza

(Pictured below)

Prep: 30 min. **Bake:** 15 min. + chilling

Here's a classic dessert that makes a refreshing snack any time of the year. We made smaller individual pizzas at school with our junior-high students. All of them enjoyed choosing their favorite fruits and eating their creations.
—Peggy Galyen, Tilden, Nebraska

   1 tube (16-1/2 ounces) refrigerated sugar
     cookie dough
   1 package (8 ounces) cream cheese, softened
 1/2 cup confectioners' sugar
   1 teaspoon lemon juice
   1 can (21 ounces) cherry pie filling
1-1/2 cups pineapple tidbits, drained
 3/4 cup mandarin oranges, drained
 3/4 cup green grapes, halved
 3/4 cup fresh strawberries, halved
GLAZE:
   1 tablespoon sugar
   2 teaspoons cornstarch
   1 can (5-1/2 ounces) unsweetened apple juice

Let dough stand at room temperature for 5-10 minutes to soften. Press onto an ungreased 12-in. pizza pan. Bake at 350° for 12-14 minutes or until set and lightly browned. Cool on a wire rack.

In a small mixing bowl, beat the cream cheese, confectioners' sugar and lemon juice. Spread over crust. Top with pie filling; arrange the pineapple, oranges, grapes and strawberries over filling.

In a small saucepan, combine sugar and cornstarch. Gradually stir in apple juice. Bring to a boil; cook and stir for 1-2 minutes or until thickened. Cool; brush over fruit. Refrigerate for at least 1 hour before serving. **Yield:** 10-12 servings.

Chicken and Rice Dish

Prep/Total Time: 20 min.

Serve this delectable main course any time you need to put something satisfying on the table in a hurry.
—Dorothy Morley, Sault Ste. Marie, Michigan

   1 package (5.7 ounces) broccoli cheddar rice
     and sauce mix
   2 cups frozen mixed vegetables
   2 cups cubed cooked chicken

Prepare the rice mix according to the package directions. Stir in the mixed vegetables and chicken; heat through. **Yield:** 3 servings.

   Editor's Note: This recipe was tested with Lipton rice mix.

Chocolate Chip Cookie Dessert

Prep: 25 min. **Bake:** 15 min. + freezing

Drizzled with melted chocolate, this frosty family favorite couldn't be much easier to prepare. My husband and three sons love it so much that we even make it on camping trips. —Carol Marnach, Sioux Falls, South Dakota

   1 tube (16-1/2 ounces) refrigerated chocolate
     chip cookie dough
 1/2 cup caramel ice cream topping
 1/2 cup cold milk
   1 package (3.4 ounces) instant vanilla pudding
     mix
   1 carton (8 ounces) frozen whipped topping,
     thawed
 3/4 cup chopped nuts
 3/4 cup English toffee bits *or* almond brickle
     chips
   3 tablespoons butter
   3 squares (1 ounce *each*) semisweet chocolate,
     chopped

Let dough stand at room temperature for 5-10 minutes to soften. Press into an ungreased 13-in. x 9-in. x 2-in. baking pan. Bake at 350° for 14-16 minutes or until golden brown. Cool completely on a wire rack.

Spread caramel topping over crust. In a bowl, whisk milk and pudding mix for 2 minutes. Let stand for 2 minutes or until soft-set. Fold in the whipped topping, nuts and toffee bits. Spread over caramel layer. Cover and freeze for 4 hours or until firm.

In a small saucepan, melt butter over medium heat. Stir in chocolate until smooth. Drizzle over pudding layer. Cut into squares. **Yield:** 16 servings.

Ultimate Fruit Pizza

Ginger Peach Upside-Down Cake

Prep: 10 min. **Bake:** 35 min. + cooling

I made this cake often when our children were young. It requires only a few ingredients, but it looks impressive and tastes so good! With red cherries and gingerbread flavor, the dessert is especially nice for Thanksgiving and Christmastime.
—June Tubb, Viroqua, Wisconsin

1/4 cup butter, melted
1/2 cup packed brown sugar
  1 can (15-1/4 ounces) sliced peaches, drained and patted dry
1/4 cup red candied cherries, halved
  1 package (14-1/2 ounces) gingerbread cake/cookie mix

In a small bowl, combine butter and brown sugar. Spoon into an ungreased 10-in. fluted tube pan. Alternately arrange peaches and cherries in pan. Prepare gingerbread batter according to package directions for cake; carefully pour over fruit.

Bake at 350° for 35-40 minutes or until a toothpick inserted near the center comes out clean. Cool for 5 minutes before inverting onto a serving plate. Cool completely before cutting. **Yield:** 12 servings.

Tropical Macadamia Custard Dessert

(Pictured at right)

Prep: 15 min. **Bake:** 40 min. + cooling

My husband's co-workers love my desserts. When they sampled this one, they raved about its unique flavor...and all asked for the recipe! Believe it or not, most of them are men. —Brenda Melancon, Baton Rouge, Louisiana

  1 package (18 ounces) ready-to-bake refrigerated white chip macadamia nut cookie dough, *divided*
  3 eggs
  1 can (20 ounces) unsweetened crushed pineapple, well drained
  1 can (12 ounces) evaporated milk
  1 package (7 ounces) dried tropical fruit bits
1/3 cup packed brown sugar
  2 tablespoons all-purpose flour
1-1/2 teaspoons rum extract
Whipped topping and maraschino cherries

Let dough stand at room temperature for 5-10 minutes to soften. Press nine portions of dough into a greased 9-in. square baking pan. Bake at 350° for 10 minutes or until set. Let stand for 2 minutes.

Meanwhile, in a bowl, combine the eggs, pineapple, milk, dried fruit, brown sugar, flour and extract. Pour over crust. Crumble the remaining dough over the filling.

Bake for 30-35 minutes or until top is golden brown. Cool on a wire rack. Cut into squares; garnish with whipped topping and cherries. Refrigerate leftovers. **Yield:** 12 servings.

Tropical Macadamia Custard Dessert

Au Gratin Pork Chops

Prep: 15 min. **Bake:** 65 min.

This cheesy pork chop bake has potatoes and good-for-you green beans. Besides the smiling faces, the best thing about this meal is that cleanup is a cinch. —Paige Austin Walkerton, Indiana

  2 packages (4.9 ounces *each*) au gratin potatoes
  1 can (10-3/4 ounces) condensed cream of mushroom soup, undiluted
  2 cups milk, *divided*
  1 package (16 ounces) frozen French-style green beans
  6 boneless pork loin chops (1/2 inch thick and 4 ounces *each*)
  1 can (10-3/4 ounces) condensed cheddar cheese soup, undiluted

Place dried potatoes in a greased 13-in. x 9-in. x 2-in. baking dish. In a small bowl, combine the mushroom soup, 1 cup milk and contents of one sauce mix packet; pour over potatoes. Top with beans and pork chops.

In a small bowl, combine the cheese soup, remaining milk and contents of remaining sauce mix packet; pour over pork chops.

Cover and bake at 350° for 45-50 minutes or until bubbly. Uncover; bake 20-25 minutes longer or until meat juices run clear. **Yield:** 6 servings.

Sausage 'n' Black Bean Pasta

(Pictured below)

Prep/Total Time: 20 min.

For a hot and hearty meal, try this super-simple pasta medley that's ready in a flash. Paired with a tossed salad and bread, this main course from our Test Kitchen becomes a swift, wholesome meal.

> 1 package (4.4 ounces) jalapeno jack pasta mix
> 1/2 pound smoked sausage, chopped
> 1 cup canned black beans, rinsed and drained

Prepare the pasta mix according to the package directions. Stir in the sausage and black beans; heat through. **Yield:** 3 servings.

Editor's Note: This recipe was tested with Lipton pasta mix.

Sombrero Bake

Prep: 10 min. **Bake:** 45 min.

Green chilies and hot pepper sauce bring a little zip to this Southwestern-style supper. It makes great use of leftover cooked chicken.
—Mary Tallman
Arbor Vitae, Wisconsin

> 2-1/2 cups cubed cooked chicken
> 1 can (4 ounces) chopped green chilies
> 1 cup (4 ounces) shredded cheddar cheese
> 1 medium tomato, chopped
> 1 can (10-3/4 ounces) condensed cream of chicken soup, undiluted
> 1/2 cup milk
> 1/2 teaspoon hot pepper sauce

Sausage 'n' Black Bean Pasta

BISCUIT TOPPING:

> 3/4 cup biscuit/baking mix
> 1/2 cup cornmeal
> 2/3 cup milk
> 1 can (2.8 ounces) french-fried onions, *divided*
> 1/2 cup shredded cheddar cheese

In a greased 13-in. x 9-in. x 2-in. baking dish, layer the chicken, chilies, cheese and tomato. In a small bowl, combine the soup, milk and hot pepper sauce. Pour over chicken mixture. Cover and bake at 375° for 20 minutes.

In a small bowl, combine the biscuit mix, cornmeal, milk and 3/4 cup onions. Drop into eight mounds over the casserole. Bake, uncovered, for 20 minutes (the topping will spread). Sprinkle with the cheese and remaining onions. Bake 5 minutes longer or until the cheese is melted. **Yield:** 6 servings.

Eggnog Over Pecan Ice Cream

Prep/Total Time: 10 min.

You're sure to get rave reviews with this delicious new take on a classic holiday beverage. The three-ingredient dessert is so easy to make, you'll have plenty of time to prepare it—even during the rush of the Christmas season.
—Amy Short
Lesage, West Virginia

> 1 quart eggnog
> 1/2 to 3/4 teaspoon rum extract
> 1/2 gallon butter pecan ice cream

In a large saucepan, heat eggnog and extract just until warmed. Serve over ice cream. **Yield:** 8-10 servings.

Editor's Note: This recipe was tested with commercially prepared eggnog.

Cherry Oatmeal Wedges

Prep/Total Time: 25 min.

Oatmeal and cherries add extra flavor and a special touch to this one-of-a-kind dessert. My kids help me make this, and it's so good! *—Richelle White, Adair, Oklahoma*

✓ Uses less fat, sugar or salt. Includes Nutrition Facts.

> 1 tube (16-1/2 ounces) refrigerated chocolate chip cookie dough
> 3/4 cup old-fashioned oats
> 1 can (21 ounces) cherry pie filling

In a large bowl, combine cookie dough and oats. Press onto an ungreased 12-in. pizza pan. Bake at 350° for 14-16 minutes or until golden brown. Cool on a wire rack for 5 minutes. Cut into wedges; top with pie filling. **Yield:** 12 servings.

Nutrition Facts: 1 wedge with about 3 tablespoons pie filling equals 264 calories, 9 g fat (3 g saturated fat), 10 mg cholesterol, 98 mg sodium, 43 g carbohydrate, 1 g fiber, 3 g protein.

Peanut Butter 'n' Jelly Bars

Peanut Butter 'n' Jelly Bars

(Pictured above)

Prep: 10 min. **Bake:** 15 min. + cooling

My two young sons are crazy about these simple, fuss-free cookie bars. And as a busy, on-the-go mom, I appreciate this scrumptious dessert because it's one I can rely on—even at the last minute. You might want to vary the jam or jelly to suit your own family's tastes.
—Carolyn Mulloy, Davison, Michigan

   1 tube (16-1/2 ounces) refrigerated peanut
     butter cookie dough
1/2 cup peanut butter chips
   1 can (16 ounces) buttercream frosting
1/4 cup creamy peanut butter
1/4 cup seedless raspberry jam *or* grape jelly

Let dough stand at room temperature for 5-10 minutes to soften. Press into an ungreased 13-in. x 9-in. x 2-in. baking dish; sprinkle with peanut butter chips. Bake at 375° for 15-18 minutes or until lightly browned and edges are firm to the touch. Cool on a wire rack.

In a small mixing bowl, beat frosting and peanut butter until smooth. Spread over bars. Drop jam by teaspoonfuls over frosting; cut through frosting with a knife to swirl the jam. **Yield:** 2 dozen.

Tuna Salad Biscuit Cups

Prep/Total Time: 25 min.

These no-hassle "boats" are filled with a tasty salad featuring water chestnuts. They're great for buffets and meals on the go. —Susan James, Cokato, Minnesota

   1 tube (12 ounces) refrigerated buttermilk
     biscuits
1/2 cup mayonnaise
   2 tablespoons sweet pickle relish
   1 tablespoon soy sauce
1/4 teaspoon dill weed
   1 can (12 ounces) tuna, drained and flaked
   1 can (8 ounces) water chestnuts, drained and
     finely chopped

Flatten each buttermilk biscuit into a 3-in. circle and press each into a greased muffin cup. Bake at 400° for 10-12 minutes or until golden brown. Cool for 5 minutes on a wire rack.

Meanwhile, in a small bowl, combine the mayonnaise, pickle relish, soy sauce and dill. Stir in the tuna and water chestnuts. Spoon into the biscuit cups. Serve immediately. **Yield:** 5 servings.

Editor's Note: Fill empty muffin cups halfway with water before baking.

Almost a Candy Bar

Prep: 15 min. **Bake:** 15 min. + chilling

I love candy bars and marshmallows, so this recipe was a delight to whip up—and I have yet to find anyone who doesn't enjoy it! The quick bars make great individually wrapped treats for picnics, lunch boxes or out-the-door snacking. And with all their different layers and flavors, these treats are sure to please just about everyone.
—Barb Wyman, Hankinson, North Dakota

   1 tube (16-1/2 ounces) refrigerated chocolate
     chip cookie dough
   4 nutty s'mores trail mix bars (1.23 ounces
     each), chopped
   1 package (11 ounces) butterscotch chips
2-1/2 cups miniature marshmallows
   1 cup chopped walnuts
1-1/2 cups miniature pretzels
   1 package (10 ounces) peanut butter chips
3/4 cup light corn syrup
1/4 cup butter, cubed
   1 package (11-1/2 ounces) milk chocolate
     chips

Let the chocolate chip cookie dough stand at room temperature for 5-10 minutes to soften. In a large bowl, combine the cookie dough and chopped trail mix bars. Press into an ungreased 13-in. x 9-in. x 2-in. baking pan. Bake, uncovered, at 350° for 10-12 minutes or until golden brown.

Sprinkle with the butterscotch chips and miniature marshmallows. Bake 3-4 minutes longer or until the marshmallows begin to brown. Sprinkle with the walnuts; arrange the pretzels over the top. In a small saucepan, melt the peanut butter chips, corn syrup and butter; spoon over the bars.

In a small microwave-safe bowl, melt chocolate chips; stir until smooth. Transfer to a small plastic bag; cut a hole in a corner of the bag. Drizzle chocolate over the bars. Refrigerate for 1 hour or until firm before cutting. **Yield:** 3 dozen.

Monterey Sausage Pie

(Pictured below)

Prep: 15 min. **Bake:** 25 min. + standing

It's a snap to make this with baking mix. I got the idea from a similar recipe that uses hamburger and cheddar cheese. It was too bland for my family, but when I made a few changes, it was a hit! —Bonnie Marlow Ottoville, Ohio

        1 pound bulk pork sausage
        1 cup chopped onion
        1 cup chopped sweet red pepper
    1/2 cup chopped fresh mushrooms
        3 teaspoons minced garlic
    2-1/2 cups (10 ounces) shredded Monterey Jack
            cheese, *divided*
    1-1/3 cups milk
        3 eggs
    3/4 cup biscuit/baking mix
    3/4 teaspoon rubbed sage
    1/4 teaspoon pepper

In a large skillet, cook the sausage, onion, red pepper, mushrooms and garlic over medium heat until meat is no longer pink; drain. Stir in 2 cups cheese. Transfer to a greased 9-in. deep-dish pie plate.

In a small bowl, combine the milk, eggs, biscuit mix, sage and pepper. Pour over sausage mixture.

Bake at 400° for 20-25 minutes or until a knife inserted near the center comes out clean. Sprinkle with the remaining cheese; bake 1-2 minutes longer or until the cheese is melted. Let stand for 10 minutes before cutting. **Yield:** 8 servings.

Monterey Sausage Pizza

Bacon-Chicken Crescent Ring

Prep: 25 min. **Bake:** 20 min.

This special-looking ring is really very easy to put together. It's so good that people always ask me for the recipe. —Michele McWhorter, Jacksonville, North Carolina

    2 tubes (8 ounces *each*) refrigerated crescent
        rolls
    1 can (10 ounces) chunk white chicken,
        drained and flaked
    1-1/2 cups (6 ounces) shredded Swiss cheese
    3/4 cup mayonnaise
    1/2 cup finely chopped sweet red pepper
    1/4 cup finely chopped onion
    6 bacon strips, cooked and crumbled
    2 tablespoons Dijon mustard
    1 tablespoon Italian salad dressing mix

Grease a 14-in. pizza pan. Unroll crescent roll dough; separate into 16 triangles. Place wide end of one triangle 3 in. from the edge of prepared pan with point overhanging the edge of pan.

Repeat with the remaining crescent dough triangles along the outer edge of the pan, overlapping the wide ends (the dough will look like a sun when complete). Lightly press the wide ends together.

In a small bowl, combine the remaining ingredients. Spoon over wide ends of dough. Fold points of triangles over filling and tuck under wide ends (filling will be visible). Bake at 375° for 20-25 minutes or until golden brown. **Yield:** 8 servings.

Peach Almond Bars

Prep: 25 min. **Bake:** 20 min. + cooling

These delicious, crisp and nutty treats have been a favorite with our family for years—and they're so pretty! When my dad retired, he took over all the baking in our home. He'd whip up a pan of these bars and say, "Put on a pot of coffee; let's invite company!" —Justine Furman-Olshan Willow Street, Pennsylvania

    1 tube (16-1/2 ounces) refrigerated sugar
        cookie dough
    1 jar (18 ounces) peach preserves
    1-1/2 cups slivered almonds, *divided*
    4 egg whites
    1/2 cup sugar

Let dough stand at room temperature for 5-10 minutes to soften. Press into an ungreased 13-in. x 9-in. x 2-in. baking pan. Bake at 350° for 12-15 minutes or until golden brown.

Spread preserves over crust. Sprinkle with 3/4 cup almonds. In a large mixing bowl, beat egg whites on medium speed until soft peaks form. Gradually beat in sugar, 1 tablespoon at a time, on high until stiff glossy peaks form and sugar is dissolved.

Spread meringue evenly over almonds. Sprinkle with remaining almonds. Bake for 20-25 minutes or until lightly browned. Cool on a wire rack. Store in the refrigerator. **Yield:** 2 dozen.

Strawberry Fudge Torte

Prep: 30 min. **Bake:** 20 min. + chilling

We love strawberries and chocolate at our house, so I developed this fudgy, fruity torte from two recipes we've enjoyed in the past. Fresh raspberries, along with raspberry cream cheese and yogurt, can also work well in this yummy dessert. —Pat Stewart, Lee's Summit, Missouri

- 1 tube (16-1/2 ounces) refrigerated chocolate chip cookie dough
- 1 carton (6 ounces) strawberry yogurt
- 1/2 cup spreadable strawberry cream cheese
- 2 teaspoons lemon juice
- 1/8 teaspoon almond extract
- 2 cups confectioners' sugar
- 2 cups whipped topping
- 1 cup hot fudge ice cream topping, warmed, *divided*
- 1-1/2 cups sliced fresh strawberries
- 1/4 cup sliced almonds

Let dough stand at room temperature for 5-10 minutes to soften. Press into an ungreased 9-in. springform pan. Bake at 350° for 18-20 minutes or until golden brown. Cool on a wire rack.

In a small mixing bowl, beat the yogurt, cream cheese, lemon juice and extract until smooth. Beat in confectioners' sugar; fold in whipped topping.

Remove sides of springform pan; place crust on a serving plate. Spread 3/4 cup fudge topping over crust to within 1/2 in. of edges; top with cream cheese mixture. Arrange strawberries on top; sprinkle with almonds. Refrigerate for 1 hour or until set.

Drizzle with remaining fudge topping. Serve immediately. **Yield:** 12 servings.

Editor's Note: Torte is best served immediately after removing from the refrigerator.

Fancy Sugar Cookie Bars

Prep: 10 min. **Bake:** 25 min. + cooling

Looking for a quick and easy way to transform plain old refrigerated cookie dough into something special enough for guests? I dress mine up with chocolate chips, coconut and pecans—or whatever nuts I have on hand. The result is an irresistible dessert in just minutes.
—Shirley Dehler, Columbus, Wisconsin

- 1 tube (16-1/2 ounces) refrigerated sugar cookie dough
- 1 cup semisweet chocolate chips
- 1/2 cup flaked coconut
- 1/4 cup chopped pecans

Let dough stand at room temperature for 5-10 minutes to soften. Press into an ungreased 13-in. x 9-in. x 2-in. baking pan. Bake at 350° for 10-12 minutes or until golden brown.

Sprinkle with chocolate chips, coconut and pecans. Bake 10-12 minutes longer or until golden brown. Cool on a wire rack. **Yield:** 2 dozen.

Giant Peanut Butter Ice Cream Sandwich

Giant Peanut Butter Ice Cream Sandwich

(Pictured above)

Prep: 30 min. **Bake:** 20 min. + freezing

I created this treat for my husband. It went over so well that I fixed it for guests, and they shrieked with delight! Since the dessert can be made ahead of time, it cuts stress for hostesses. —JoAnn Belack, Bradenton, Florida

- 2 packages (18 ounces *each*) ready-to-bake refrigerated peanut butter cup cookie dough
- 6 whole chocolate graham crackers, crushed
- 1 cup cold milk
- 1 cup heavy whipping cream
- 1 package (3.4 ounces) instant vanilla pudding mix
- 1 package (8 ounces) cream cheese, softened
- 1-1/3 cups creamy peanut butter
- 3 cups vanilla ice cream, softened
- 1/4 cup chocolate hazelnut spread

Let dough stand at room temperature for 5-10 minutes to soften. Press into two ungreased 9-in. springform pans; sprinkle with graham cracker crumbs. Bake at 350° for 20-25 minutes or until set. Cool completely.

In a bowl, whisk the milk, cream and pudding mix for 2 minutes. Let stand for 2 minutes or until soft-set. In a large mixing bowl, beat cream cheese and peanut butter until smooth. Add pudding and ice cream; beat until smooth.

Spread over one cookie crust. Remove sides of second pan; place crust, crumb side down, over filling. Cover and freeze for 4 hours or until firm.

Remove the dessert from the freezer 15 minutes before serving. Place the hazelnut spread in a small microwave-safe bowl; cover and microwave at 50% power for 1-2 minutes or until smooth, stirring twice. Remove the sides of the pan; cut the dessert into slices. Drizzle with the hazelnut spread. **Yield:** 12 servings.

Mexican Lasagna

(Pictured below)

Prep: 25 min. **Bake:** 40 min. + standing

This recipe streamlines a hearty lasagna dinner, getting it to the table fast! Using no-cook noodles and precooked chicken saves lots of time in the kitchen.
—Valonda Seward, Hanford, California

- 1 cup chopped onion
- 1 teaspoon minced garlic
- 1 tablespoon vegetable oil
- 4 cups cubed cooked chicken
- 3 cans (10 ounces *each*) enchilada sauce
- 2 eggs
- 1 carton (15 ounces) ricotta cheese
- 1/2 cup minced fresh cilantro
- 12 no-cook lasagna noodles
- 4 cups (16 ounces) shredded Mexican cheese blend

In a large skillet, cook onion and garlic in oil over medium heat until tender. Stir in chicken and enchilada sauce. Bring to a boil. Reduce heat; simmer, uncovered, for 5 minutes or until slightly thickened.

Meanwhile, in a small bowl, combine the eggs, ricotta cheese and cilantro. Spread 3/4 cup chicken mixture into a greased 13-in. x 9-in. x 2-in. baking dish. Layer with three noodles, 2/3 cup ricotta mixture, 3/4 cup chicken mixture and 1 cup shredded cheese. Repeat layers twice. Top with remaining noodles, sauce and shredded cheese.

Cover and bake at 375° for 30 minutes. Uncover; bake

Mexican Lasagna

10-15 minutes longer or until bubbly. Let stand for 10 minutes before cutting. **Yield:** 10-12 servings.

Peanut Butter S'more Bars

Prep: 10 min. **Bake:** 20 min. + chilling

I created these bars to add something new to my Christmas cookie tray. When I give them to my kids' teachers, they're gone in a flash! I make the treats ahead of time when convenient, then freeze. Use M&M's in different colors for holidays year-round.
—Julie Wischmeier
Brownstown, Indiana

- 1 tube (16-1/2 ounces) refrigerated peanut butter cookie dough
- 3-1/2 cups miniature marshmallows
- 3/4 cup milk chocolate chips
- 2 teaspoons shortening
- 1-1/2 cups milk chocolate M&M's

Let dough stand at room temperature for 5-10 minutes to soften. Cut into 24 slices; arrange side by side in an ungreased 13-in. x 9-in. x 2-in. baking pan. Pat together to close gaps.

Bake at 350° for 18-20 minutes or until lightly browned and edges are firm. Sprinkle with marshmallows; bake 2-3 minutes longer or until marshmallows are puffy.

In a small microwave-safe bowl, melt chocolate chips and shortening; stir until smooth. Sprinkle M&M's over marshmallow layer; drizzle with melted chocolate. Chill until set before cutting. **Yield:** 2 dozen.

Pumpkin Spice Layer Cake

Prep: 25 min. **Bake:** 25 min. + cooling

No one will guess this showstopper dessert with a luscious cinnamon frosting begins with a mix. It's a perennial favorite. —Linda Murray, Allenstown, New Hampshire

- 1 package (18-1/4 ounces) yellow cake mix
- 3 eggs
- 1 cup water
- 1 cup canned pumpkin
- 1-3/4 teaspoons ground cinnamon, *divided*
- 1/4 teaspoon ground ginger
- 1/4 teaspoon ground nutmeg
- 2-1/2 cups vanilla frosting
- 1-1/4 cups chopped walnuts

In a large mixing bowl, combine the cake mix, eggs, water, pumpkin, 1 teaspoon cinnamon, ginger and nutmeg. Beat on low speed for 30 seconds; beat on medium for 2 minutes.

Pour into two well-greased and floured 9-in. round baking pans. Bake at 375° for 25-30 minutes or until a toothpick inserted near the centers comes out clean. Cool for 10 minutes before removing from pans to wire racks to cool completely.

Combine frosting and remaining cinnamon; spread between the layers and over the top and sides of the cake. Press walnuts lightly into the frosting on the sides of cake. **Yield:** 10-12 servings.

Makeover Chocolate Truffle Dessert

ules. Microwave, uncovered, on high for 1 to 1-1/2 minutes or until butter is melted; stir until smooth. With food processor running, add cream mixture in a slow, steady stream. Add vanilla; cover and process until smooth.

Cut a small hole in the corner of a pastry or plastic bag. Fill with 1/4 cup chocolate mixture; set aside for the garnish. Transfer the remaining chocolate mixture to a large bowl.

Remove sides of springform pan. Spread half of the chocolate mixture over brownie layer, spreading evenly over top and sides.

In a small mixing bowl, beat remaining cream until soft peaks form; fold into remaining chocolate mixture. Spread over chocolate layer. Gently press cookies into sides of dessert. Pipe reserved chocolate mixture on top.

Cover and refrigerate for at least 4 hours or overnight. Remove from the refrigerator 5 minutes before cutting. **Yield:** 12-16 servings.

Editor's Note: This recipe was tested with Pepperidge Farm cookies in a 1,100-watt microwave. The amount of vanilla is correct.

Makeover Chocolate Truffle Dessert

(Pictured above and on page 68)

Prep: 30 min. **Bake:** 25 min. + chilling

Our Test Kitchen staff took a family-favorite dessert from Lisa Otis of New Paltz, New York and streamlined it. By utilizing the microwave and a boxed brownie mix, the team was able to cut 1 hour from Lisa's recipe without sacrificing its wonderful taste.

> 1 package fudge brownie mix
>   (8-inch-square pan size)
> 3 cups (18 ounces) semisweet chocolate chips
> 2 cups heavy whipping cream, *divided*
> 6 tablespoons butter, cubed
> 1 tablespoon instant coffee granules
> 3 tablespoons vanilla extract
> 14 to 16 Pirouette cookies, cut into 1-1/2-inch pieces

Prepare brownie batter according to package directions. Spread into a greased 9-in. springform pan. Place on a baking sheet. Bake at 350° for 25-30 minutes or until a toothpick inserted near the center comes out clean. Cool completely on a wire rack.

Place chocolate chips in a food processor. Cover; process until finely chopped. In a small microwave-safe bowl, combine 1 cup cream, butter and coffee gran-

Crescent Bundle Surprises

Prep/Total Time: 30 min.

Everyone will love discovering the delicious goodie inside these tender rolls. I tried the recipe at our teenager's New Year's Eve party—it was a hit! —Joyce Platfoot
Wapakoneta, Ohio

✓ Uses less fat, sugar or salt. Includes Nutrition Facts and Diabetic Exchanges.

> 1 tube (8 ounces) refrigerated crescent rolls
> 8 fun-size Snickers candy bars, halved
> 1/4 cup cream cheese frosting

Separate the crescent dough into eight triangles; cut each in half, forming two triangles. Place a candy bar half on each triangle. Fold the dough over the candy and pinch the corners together to seal. Place on an ungreased baking sheet.

Bake at 375° for 15-18 minutes or until golden brown. Remove to a wire rack. Cut a small hole in the corner of a resealable plastic bag. Fill bag with frosting; pipe over rolls. **Yield:** 16 servings.

Nutrition Facts: 1 bundle equals 110 calories, 6 g fat (2 g saturated fat), 1 mg cholesterol, 140 mg sodium, 13 g carbohydrate, trace fiber, 2 g protein. **Diabetic Exchanges:** 1 starch, 1 fat.

Whipping Cream Clue

BEFORE beating the cream for Makeover Chocolate Truffle Dessert (recipe at left), refrigerate the bowl and beaters for about 30 minutes. Pour the cream into a deep, chilled bowl. Then beat the cream on high until soft peaks form (when the beater is lifted from the mixture and the points of the peaks curl over).

Chapter 5

⏱ *Give Me 5 or Fewer*

SHORT AND SWEET—that's how you can describe the ingredient list for every rapid recipe in this chapter.

Page through, and you'll see that each delicious dish calls for only five ingredients (not including the basic staples of water, salt and pepper)...so you won't have to gather a grocery bag full of food items before you can start cooking.

Even restaurant-style fare that sounds complicated—such as Carribean Chutney-Crusted Chops and Pineapple-Caramel Sponge Cakes—require just a handful of ingredients.

So don't write out a lengthy shopping list. Simply turn to this chapter and take five!

GIVE ME FIVE. Mediterranean Chicken (p. 90).

Dijon-Walnut Spinach Salad

(Pictured below)

Prep/Total Time: 10 min.

This has so much flavor for so few ingredients! A family favorite of ours with great fresh taste and lots of different textures, it can be tossed together in no time. For some variety, you can change up the dressing to honey mustard or any kind you prefer.
—*Chris DeMontravel*
Mohegan Lake, New York

- 1 package (9 ounces) fresh baby spinach
- 1 package (4 ounces) crumbled feta cheese
- 1 cup dried cranberries
- 1 cup walnut halves, toasted
- 1/2 cup honey Dijon vinaigrette

In a large salad bowl, combine the spinach, feta cheese, cranberries and walnuts. Drizzle with vinaigrette; toss to coat. Serve immediately. **Yield:** 13 servings.

Dijon-Walnut Spinach Salad

Chocolate-Cherry Ice Cream Pie

Prep: 15 min. + freezing

With one bite, you'd never guess that the fancy taste and look of this yummy freezer pie comes from five simple items. The recipe makes an unbelievably easy dessert—whether for an elegant dinner party or as a cool, high-energy kids' treat on a hot day.
—*Kimberly West*
Prairieville, Louisiana

- 1 bottle (7-1/4 ounces) chocolate hard-shell ice cream topping, *divided*
- 1 graham cracker crust (9 inches)
- 1 jar (10 ounces) maraschino cherries, drained
- 1 quart vanilla ice cream, softened
- 2 packages (1-1/2 ounces *each*) peanut butter cups, chopped

Following package directions, drizzle half of the ice cream topping over the crust; gently spread to coat bottom and sides. Freeze until firm.

Set aside six cherries for garnish; chop remaining cherries. In a large bowl, combine ice cream and chopped cherries. Spread into prepared crust. Sprinkle with peanut butter cups; drizzle with remaining ice cream topping.

Garnish with reserved cherries. Cover and freeze for 2 hours or until firm. Remove from the freezer 15 minutes before serving. **Yield:** 6 servings.

Caribbean Chutney-Crusted Chops

Prep/Total Time: 30 min.

I like to impress my guests with delicious meals, and these lamb chops are one of my best entrees. It all started with a jar of chutney that I received in a gift basket and didn't know what to do with. Folks think I work all day for these sophisticated chops...but they're done in 30 minutes flat!
—*Josephine Piro, Easton, Pennsylvania*

✓ Uses less fat, sugar or salt. Includes Nutrition Facts and Diabetic Exchanges.

- 1 cup soft bread crumbs
- 1-1/2 teaspoons Caribbean jerk seasoning
- 1/4 cup mango chutney
- 1/2 teaspoon salt
- 1/2 teaspoon pepper
- 4 lamb loin chops (2 inches thick and 8 ounces *each*)

In a shallow bowl, combine bread crumbs and jerk seasoning; set aside. Combine the chutney, salt and pepper; spread over both sides of lamb chops. Coat with crumb mixture.

Place the lamb chops on a rack coated with nonstick cooking spray in a shallow baking pan. Bake at 450° for 20-25 minutes or until the meat reaches desired doneness (for medium-rare, a meat thermometer should read 145°; medium, 160°; well-done, 170°). **Yield:** 4 servings.

Nutrition Facts: 1 lamb chop equals 296 calories, 10 g fat (3 g saturated fat), 91 mg cholesterol, 711 mg sodium, 20 g carbohydrate, trace fiber, 30 g protein. **Diabetic Exchanges:** 4 lean meat, 1 starch.

Pineapple Teriyaki Chicken

(Pictured at right)

Prep: 10 min. + marinating **Grill:** 15 min.

I love to marinate this moist chicken main dish overnight, then pop it on the grill. The entree gives a taste of the islands that my family and friends really go for. Best of all, it only calls for a few kitchen staples that I always keep on hand.
—Vicki Roberts, Jacksonville, Florida

1 can (20 ounces) sliced pineapple
1/2 cup teriyaki sauce
4 boneless skinless chicken breast halves
4 slices provolone cheese

Drain pineapple, reserving juice; refrigerate pineapple. In a small bowl, combine teriyaki sauce and reserved juice. Pour 3/4 cup marinade into a large resealable plastic bag; add chicken. Seal bag and turn to coat; refrigerate for 8 hours or overnight. Cover and refrigerate remaining marinade for basting.

Drain and discard marinade. Grill chicken, covered, over medium heat or broil 4 in. from the heat for 4-6 minutes on each side or until juices run clear, basting frequently with some of the remaining marinade.

Grill eight pineapple slices for 2 minutes on each side or until lightly browned, basting with remaining marinade (save remaining pineapple for another use). Top each piece of chicken with cheese and two pineapple slices. Grill, covered, for 1-2 minutes or until cheese is melted. **Yield:** 4 servings.

Maple Balsamic Dressing

Prep/Total Time: 5 min.

This blend of maple syrup and zesty balsamic vinegar can lend bright flavor to tender grilled pork chops, a crisp summer salad or sweet strawberries. —Kim Sumrall
Aptos, California

1/3 cup balsamic vinegar
1/3 cup maple syrup
1/3 cup olive oil
FOR PORK CHOPS:
4 bone-in pork loin chops (8 ounces *each*)
FOR SALAD:
8 cups torn mixed salad greens
FOR STRAWBERRIES:
2 pounds fresh strawberries, hulled

In a blender, combine vinegar and syrup. While processing, gradually add oil in a steady stream. **Yield:** 1 cup.

For pork chops: Pour 2/3 cup dressing into a large resealable plastic bag; add pork. Seal bag and turn to coat; refrigerate for at least 30 minutes. Cover and refrigerate remaining dressing.

Drain and discard marinade. Grill pork chops, covered, over medium heat for 6-7 minutes on each side or until juices run clear, brushing with 3 tablespoons reserved dressing during the last 5 minutes. Drizzle remaining

Pineapple Teriyaki Chicken

dressing over chops before serving. **Yield:** 4 servings.

For salad: In a large bowl, toss greens with dressing. Serve immediately. **Yield:** 8 servings.

For strawberries: In a large bowl, toss berries with dressing. Chill until serving. **Yield:** 8 servings.

Tomato Salmon Bake

Prep/Total Time: 30 min.

I was looking for a healthy alternative to beef and chicken when I found this recipe and decided to personalize it. My husband doesn't usually like fish unless it's fried, but he loves the Italian flavor in this dish. Serve it with a green salad for a great meal any time of year. —Lacey Parker
Gainesville, Virginia

4 salmon fillets (6 ounces *each*)
1 can (14-1/2 ounces) diced tomatoes, drained
1/2 cup sun-dried tomato salad dressing
2 tablespoons shredded Parmesan cheese
Hot cooked rice

Place the salmon in a greased 13-in. x 9-in. x 2-in. baking dish. Combine tomatoes and salad dressing; pour over salmon. Sprinkle with Parmesan cheese.

Bake, uncovered, at 375° for 20-25 minutes or until fish flakes easily with a fork. Serve with rice. **Yield:** 4 servings.

Prosciutto Provolone Panini

(Pictured below)

Prep/Total Time: 25 min.

For a fast lunch or supper, try this take on grilled cheese sandwiches. They're quick but sophisticated enough for entertaining. I sometimes replace the fresh sage with 1 tablespoon of Italian seasoning. —Candy Summerhill
Alexander, Arkansas

    8 slices white bread
    8 slices provolone cheese
    4 thin slices prosciutto
    3 tablespoons olive oil
    3 tablespoons minced fresh sage

On four slices of bread, layer a slice of cheese, a slice of prosciutto and a second slice of cheese. Top with remaining bread.

Brush both sides of sandwiches with oil; sprinkle with sage. Cook in a panini maker or indoor grill until bread is toasted and cheese is melted. **Yield:** 4 servings.

Fiesta Corn Chowder

Prep/Total Time: 20 min.

This mouth-watering chowder will enhance any menu you add it to. The full-flavored soup with tomatoes, green chilies, Mexicorn and plenty of cheese will definitely chase away the chills each and every time you serve it. For extra flair, garnish bowls with a few tortilla chips. —Denise Hamilton, Birmingham, Alabama

    2 cans (10 ounces *each*) diced tomatoes and
      green chilies, undrained
    1 pound process cheese (Velveeta), cubed
    1 can (14-3/4 ounces) cream-style corn
    1 can (14-1/2 ounces) chicken broth
    1 can (11 ounces) Mexicorn, drained

In a large saucepan, combine all ingredients. Bring to a boil over medium-high heat, stirring frequently. Reduce heat; cover and simmer for 4-5 minutes or until cheese is melted and soup is heated through. **Yield:** 8 servings (2 quarts).

Prosciutto Provolone Panini

Smoked Chops with Cherry Sauce

(Pictured at right)

Prep/Total Time: 20 min.

Grilling out? A sweet-but-spicy sauce is the secret to these moist pork chops. With a bit of spice, they turn up the flavor on a summer night. —*Betty Kleberger Florissant, Missouri*

6 fully cooked smoked boneless pork chops (1 inch thick and 6 ounces *each*)
1 can (15 ounces) pitted dark sweet cherries, undrained
1 cup mild jalapeno pepper jelly
1/2 teaspoon ground coriander, optional

Grill pork chops, covered, over medium heat for 5-7 minutes on each side or until heated through. Meanwhile, in a small saucepan, combine the cherries, jelly and coriander if desired. Bring to a boil, stirring constantly. Serve with pork chops. **Yield:** 6 servings.

Beef Macaroni Soup

Prep/Total Time: 25 min.

This is a quick version of delicious vegetable beef soup. With beef, veggies and the addition of pasta, it's just as good as the traditional version with a lot less fuss.
—*Debra Baker, Greenville, North Carolina*

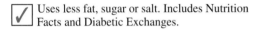 Uses less fat, sugar or salt. Includes Nutrition Facts and Diabetic Exchanges.

1 pound ground beef
1 can (14-1/2 ounces) diced tomatoes, undrained
1 can (14-1/2 ounces) beef broth
2 cups frozen mixed vegetables
1/4 teaspoon pepper
1/2 cup uncooked elbow macaroni

In a large saucepan, cook beef over medium heat until no longer pink; drain. Stir in the tomatoes, broth, vegetables and pepper. Bring to a boil; add macaroni. Reduce heat; cover and simmer for 8-10 minutes or until macaroni and vegetables are tender. **Yield:** 5 servings.
Nutrition Facts: 1 cup (prepared with reduced-sodium broth) equals 233 calories, 8 g fat (4 g saturated fat), 46 mg cholesterol, 341 mg sodium, 19 g carbohydrate, 5 g fiber, 20 g protein. **Diabetic Exchanges:** 2 lean meat, 1 starch, 1 vegetable, 1/2 fat.

Pineapple-Caramel Sponge Cakes

Prep/Total Time: 10 min.

Want the flavor of pineapple upside-down cake without the hassle and heat of turning on the oven? Whip up this delicious no-bake dessert. Only four ingredients make it a stress-free winner. —*Lynn Mahle, Quincy, Florida*

1 can (8 ounces) unsweetened crushed pineapple, drained

Smoked Chops with Cherry Sauce

1/2 cup caramel ice cream topping
4 individual round sponge cakes
1 pint vanilla ice cream

In a small saucepan, combine pineapple and caramel topping. Cook over medium heat for 2-3 minutes or until heated through, stirring occasionally.

Place sponge cakes on dessert plates. Top each with a scoop of ice cream and 1/4 cup pineapple sauce. Serve immediately. **Yield:** 4 servings.

Ham with Mustard-Cream Sauce

Prep/Total Time: 20 min.

This recipe seems too easy to taste so good! It's hard to believe that three common ingredients can turn ham into something so uncommonly special. Microwave some potatoes and open a bag of salad mix for a no-fuss meal.
—*Lisa Nelson, Broken Arrow, Oklahoma*

4 individual boneless fully cooked ham steaks (about 5 ounces *each*)
1/4 cup water
1/4 cup honey mustard
1/2 cup sour cream
1/4 cup thinly sliced green onions

Place ham steaks in a large skillet. In a small bowl, combine water and mustard; pour over ham. Bring to a boil. Reduce heat; cover and simmer for 10 minutes, turning once. Remove from the heat; stir in sour cream and onions. **Yield:** 4 servings.

Chocolate Swirl Delight

(Pictured below)

Prep: 20 min. + chilling

I made a few alterations to a great recipe and ended up with an impressive dessert. Everyone loves its light texture and chocolaty flavor. Best of all, it looks like it took hours to assemble but really comes together quite easily. —Lynne Bargar
Saegertown, Pennsylvania

- 1 package (13 ounces) Swiss cake rolls
- 2-3/4 cups cold milk
- 2 packages (3.9 ounces *each*) instant chocolate fudge pudding mix
- 2 cups whipped topping

Cut each cake roll into eight slices; set aside any chocolate coating that separates from rolls for garnish. Line a 9-in. springform pan with cake slices, completely covering the bottom and sides.

In a small bowl, whisk milk and pudding mixes for 2 minutes. Let stand for 2 minutes or until soft-set. Pour over cake. Spread with whipped topping; sprinkle with any reserved chocolate coating. Cover and refrigerate for at least 2 hours before serving. **Yield:** 12 servings.

Pina Colada Slush

Prep: 10 min. + freezing

For a special treat on a steamy day, try this fruity cooler. I first had it when I was pregnant. The tangy slush really hit the spot that summer—and ever since! I keep a batch or two in my freezer so it's always handy. —Alisa Allred
Vernal, Utah

- 3 cans (6 ounces *each*) unsweetened pineapple juice
- 2 cups water
- 1 can (10 ounces) frozen non-alcoholic pina colada mix
- 1 tablespoon lime juice
- 1 tub sugar-free lemonade soft drink mix
- 6 cups lemon-lime soda, chilled

In a large bowl, combine the pineapple juice, water, pina colada mix, lime juice and soft drink mix; stir until drink mix is dissolved. Transfer to a 2-qt. freezer container. Freeze for 6 hours or overnight.

Remove from the freezer 45 minutes before serving. For each serving, combine 1/2 cup slush mixture with 1/2 cup lemon-lime soda. **Yield:** 12 servings (3 quarts).

Editor's Note: This recipe was tested with Crystal Light lemonade soft drink mix.

Chocolate Swirl Delight

Cherry Gelatin Flowers

Prep: 15 min. + chilling

Our Test Kitchen staff had fun creating these jolly gelatin jigglers—but not as much fun as your kids will have helping to make them and cut them out!

2-1/2 cups white grape juice
4 packages (3 ounces *each*) cherry gelatin
Seedless red *or* green grapes, halved, optional

In a small saucepan, bring grape juice to a boil. Place gelatin in a bowl; stir in juice until dissolved. Pour into a 13-in. x 9-in. x 2-in. dish coated with nonstick cooking spray. Refrigerate until set.

Using cookie cutters, cut gelatin into flower shapes. Place a grape half in the center of each flower if desired. **Yield:** about 1 dozen.

Mini Chicken Loaves

Prep/Total Time: 15 min.

Have a delicious entree ready in only 15 minutes with this speedy recipe. These loaves are perfect any time of year.
—Lorraine Calandhunder, Bay, Ontario

☑ Uses less fat, sugar or salt. Includes Nutrition Facts and Diabetic Exchanges.

1 cup salsa, *divided*
3/4 cup fresh *or* frozen corn, thawed
1/3 cup dry bread crumbs
2 teaspoons chili powder
1/8 teaspoon salt
1/8 teaspoon pepper
1 pound ground chicken

In a large bowl, combine 3/4 cup salsa, corn, bread crumbs, chili powder, salt and pepper. Crumble chicken over mixture and mix well. Shape into four loaves; place in an 11-in. x 7-in. x 2-in. microwave-safe dish coated with nonstick cooking spray.

Cover and microwave on high for 5-6 minutes or until a meat thermometer reads 165°. Serve with remaining salsa. **Yield:** 4 servings.

Editor's Note: This recipe was tested in a 1,100-watt microwave.

Nutrition Facts: 1 loaf equals 235 calories, 10 g fat (3 g saturated fat), 75 mg cholesterol, 514 mg sodium, 15 g carbohydrate, 3 g fiber, 20 g protein. **Diabetic Exchanges:** 3 lean meat, 1 starch.

Jigglers Get Giggles

THE SIMPLE RECIPE for Cherry Gelatin Flowers (recipe at top) can be altered in all sorts of fun ways. For example, substitute different flavors of gelatin and use different cookie cutters, such as tree shapes for Christmas or egg shapes for Easter. Instead of decorating the jigglers with grapes, try maraschino cherries or pastel miniature marshmallows.

Peanut Butter Cereal Treats

Peanut Butter Cereal Treats

(Pictured above)

Prep/Total Time: 30 min.

Children will love these colorful, crunchy bars. They're a festive twist on traditional marshmallow crispy treats... and because they're so simple, older kids can even whip up a batch on their own!
—Christie Porter
Shipshewana, Indiana

☑ Uses less fat, sugar or salt. Includes Nutrition Facts and Diabetic Exchanges.

30 large marshmallows
3 tablespoons butter
1 tablespoon peanut butter
6 cups Peanut Butter Cap'n Crunch
1-1/2 cups milk chocolate M&M's

In a large saucepan, combine the marshmallows, butter and peanut butter. Cook and stir over medium-low heat until melted. Remove from the heat. Stir in the cereal and M&M's.

Pat into a 13-in. x 9-in. x 2-in. pan coated with nonstick cooking spray. Cool. Cut into bars. **Yield:** 2 dozen.

Nutrition Facts: 1 bar equals 147 calories, 5 g fat (3 g saturated fat), 6 mg cholesterol, 97 mg sodium, 24 g carbohydrate, 1 g fiber, 2 g protein. **Diabetic Exchanges:** 1-1/2 starch, 1 fat.

Wonton Kisses

(Pictured below)

Prep/Total Time: 25 min.

These wonderful wonton bites offer a surprise inside. Each wrapped bundle is filled with a chocolate candy kiss. They're sure to wow guests at your next party.
—Darlene Brenden, Salem, Oregon

    24 milk chocolate kisses
    24 wonton wrappers
Oil for frying
Confectioners' sugar

Place a chocolate kiss in the center of each wonton wrapper. Moisten edges with water; fold opposite corners together over candy kisses and press to seal.

    In an electric skillet, heat 1 in. of oil to 375°. Fry wontons for 2-1/2 minutes or until golden brown, turning once. Drain on paper towels. Dust with confectioners' sugar. **Yield:** 2 dozen.

    Editor's Note: Fill wonton wrappers a few at a time, keeping the others covered with a damp paper towel until ready to use.

Wonton Kisses

Baked Chicken

Prep/Total Time: 30 min.

I've been preparing this tender chicken with moist breading for years at my home. What a fuss-free way to jazz up a comforting dinner favorite!
—Shirley Smith
Yorba Linda, California

    1/3 cup mayonnaise
      1 tablespoon milk
    1/2 cup seasoned bread crumbs
    1/8 teaspoon onion powder
      2 boneless skinless chicken breast halves
        (6 ounces *each*)

In a shallow bowl, combine mayonnaise and milk. In another bowl, combine bread crumbs and onion powder. Dip chicken in mayonnaise mixture, then roll in crumb mixture.

    Place in a greased 8-in. square baking pan. Bake, uncovered, at 350° for 10 minutes. Turn chicken breasts over; bake 10-15 minutes longer or until the juices run clear. **Yield:** 2 servings.

Frosty Pineapple-Coconut Pie

Prep: 10 min. **Bake:** 15 min. + freezing

Flaked coconut forms the delightful crust for this easy-as-pie treat from our Test Kitchen. You'll love the frozen dessert's tropical flair and fresh pineapple flavor.

    3 tablespoons butter, melted
    2 cups flaked coconut
    1 pint vanilla ice cream, softened
    1 pint pineapple sherbet, softened
Fresh pineapple wedges, optional

Spread the butter over the bottom and sides of a 9-in. pie plate. Press the coconut onto the bottom and sides of the pie plate. Bake at 325° for 12-15 minutes or until the edges are golden brown. Cool crust completely on a wire rack.

    Spread ice cream into crust. Spread sherbet over ice cream. Freeze for 1 hour or until firm. Garnish with pineapple wedges if desired. **Yield:** 6-8 servings.

Pineapple Pointers

PLAN to cut fresh pineapple wedges as a garnish for your Frosty Pineapple-Coconut Pie? Here are some handy pineapple hints:

    A juicy and fibrous fruit, pineapple must be picked ripe because it will not get sweeter after it's been picked. Select pineapple that is plump and fresh looking, is slightly soft and has a sweet fragrance. Avoid fruit with dry or brown leaves, bruises and soft spots.

    Store a ripe pineapple in the refrigerator for up to 4 days. Feel free to cut it in advance—refrigerate the cut fruit in an airtight container for up to 3 days.

Sausage Manicotti

(Pictured at right)

Prep: 20 min. **Bake:** 65 min.

This classic Italian entree comes together in a snap but tastes like it took hours. It's a hearty, family-pleasing dinner that's also simple to fix. —Carolyn Henderson
Maple Plain, Minnesota

- 1 pound bulk pork sausage
- 2 cups (16 ounces) small-curd cottage cheese
- 1 package (8 ounces) uncooked manicotti shells
- 1 jar (26 ounces) Italian baking sauce
- 1 cup (4 ounces) shredded part-skim mozzarella cheese

In a large bowl, combine sausage and cottage cheese. Stuff into manicotti shells. Place in a greased 13-in. x 9-in. x 2-in. baking dish. Top with baking sauce.

Cover and bake at 350° for 55-60 minutes or until a meat thermometer inserted into the center of a shell reads 160°. Uncover; sprinkle with mozzarella cheese. Bake 8-10 minutes longer or until cheese is melted. Let stand for 5 minutes before serving. **Yield:** 7 servings.

Tangy Caesar Salad

(Pictured at right)

Prep/Total Time: 15 min.

You'll need just 15 minutes to toss together this zippy salad. I quickly jazz it up by adding a few special ingredients to prepared dressing. —Paula Stewart
Crawfordville, Georgia

- 8 cups torn romaine
- 1/4 cup Caesar salad dressing
- 1 tablespoon lemon juice
- 1/2 teaspoon pepper
- 1 cup Caesar salad croutons
- 1/3 cup grated Parmesan cheese

Place the romaine in a large salad bowl. Combine the salad dressing, lemon juice and pepper. Pour over romaine; toss to coat. Top with croutons and Parmesan cheese. Serve immediately. **Yield:** 6-8 servings.

BBQ Chip-Crusted Orange Roughy

Prep/Total Time: 25 min.

This easy and delectable entree actually converted me into a fish lover. It's frequently requested by family and friends. Even people who think they don't like seafood love this dish! —Geraldine Buba, Palos Hills, Illinois

- 4 orange roughy fillets (6 ounces *each*)
- 3 tablespoons lemon juice
- 1 tablespoon butter, melted
- 1/2 cup crushed barbecue potato chips
Tartar sauce, optional

Sausage Manicotti
Tangy Caesar Salad

Place orange roughy in a greased 13-in. x 9-in. x 2-in. baking dish. Combine lemon juice and butter; pour over fillets. Top with potato chips.

Bake, uncovered, at 400° for 20-25 minutes or until fish flakes easily with a fork. Serve with tartar sauce if desired. **Yield:** 4 servings.

Editor's Note: This recipe was tested with plain, not ridged, potato chips.

Mediterranean Chicken

(Pictured below and on page 80)

Prep/Total Time: 25 min.

As special as it is simple to prepare, this moist, flavorful chicken is dressed up with grape tomatoes, Greek olives and capers. It's really a knockout main course for guests! They can't believe how quickly and easily I can whip it together.
—Mary Relyea, Canastota, New York

4 boneless skinless chicken breast halves
   (6 ounces *each*)
1/4 teaspoon salt
1/4 teaspoon pepper
3 tablespoons olive oil
1 pint grape tomatoes
16 pitted Greek *or* ripe olives, sliced
3 tablespoons capers, drained

Sprinkle chicken with salt and pepper. In a large oven-proof skillet, cook chicken in oil over medium heat for 2-3 minutes on each side or until golden brown. Add the tomatoes, olives and capers.

Bake, uncovered, at 475° for 10-14 minutes or until chicken juices run clear. **Yield:** 4 servings.

Cherry Pie Dessert

Prep: 20 min. **Bake:** 20 min. + cooling

Cherry pie filling steals the show in this delicious dessert, which boasts a shortbread-like crust. A friend shared the recipe. It makes a simple yet satisfying treat anytime.
—Alisha Rice, Albany, Oregon

2 cups all-purpose flour
1/2 cup confectioners' sugar
1 cup cold butter
1 can (30 ounces) cherry pie filling
1 carton (12 ounces) frozen whipped topping, thawed

In a small bowl, combine the flour and confectioners' sugar. Cut in the butter until the mixture resembles coarse crumbs. Press into an ungreased 13-in. x 9-in. x 2-in. baking dish.

Bake at 350° for 18-20 minutes or until lightly browned. Cool completely on a wire rack. Spoon pie filling over crust; spread with whipped topping. Store in the refrigerator. **Yield:** 12-15 servings.

Red, White and Bleu Slaw

Prep/Total Time: 10 min.

One of my favorites, this refreshing salad is perfect for Fourth of July parties—or any occasion at all. The blend of flavors is terrific. I use the recipe as often as I can...it's simply the best! —Bonnie Hawkins, Elkhorn, Wisconsin

6 cups angel hair coleslaw
12 cherry tomatoes, halved
3/4 cup coleslaw salad dressing
3/4 cup crumbled blue cheese, *divided*
1/2 cup real bacon bits

In a large bowl, combine the coleslaw, tomatoes, salad dressing and 1/2 cup blue cheese. Cover and refrigerate until serving.

Just before serving, sprinkle the slaw with bacon bits and remaining cheese. **Yield:** 6 servings.

Mediterranean Chicken

Honeymoon Mousse

(Pictured at right)

Prep/Total Time: 20 min.

This elegant temptation is sure to delight. The chocolaty mousse is so good, I enclose the recipe with every bridal shower gift I give. The dessert is wonderful for holidays and other special celebrations, as well as for weekday surprises for my family.
—Beverly Carter, Beachwood, New Jersey

　1 cup cold evaporated milk
　3 teaspoons vanilla extract
　1 cup sugar
　4 squares (1 ounce *each*) unsweetened
　　chocolate, finely chopped
1/4 teaspoon salt
　2 cups heavy whipping cream
Chocolate curls, optional

In a blender, combine the milk, vanilla, sugar, chocolate and salt; cover and process until smooth, about 1 minute. Transfer to a large bowl.

In a small mixing bowl, beat cream until soft peaks form. Fold into chocolate mixture. Spoon into dessert dishes. Refrigerate until serving. Garnish with chocolate curls if desired. **Yield:** 6-8 servings.

Raspberry Brownie Dessert

Prep: 20 min. **Bake:** 25 min. + chilling

This is a no-stress treat that everyone lines up for. I've brought these raspberry-flavored brownies to church and work, and folks always beg for more. —Ann Vick
Rosemount, Minnesota

　1 package fudge brownie mix (13-inch x
　　9-inch pan size)
　2 cups heavy whipping cream, *divided*
　1 package (3.3 ounces) instant white
　　chocolate pudding mix
　1 can (21 ounces) raspberry pie filling

Prepare and bake brownies according to package directions, using a greased 13-in. x 9-in. x 2-in. baking pan. Cool completely on a wire rack.

In a small bowl, combine 1 cup cream and pudding mix; stir for 2 minutes or until very thick. In a small mixing bowl, beat remaining cream until stiff peaks form; fold into pudding. Carefully spread over brownies; top with pie filling. Cover and refrigerate for at least 2 hours before cutting. **Yield:** 15-18 servings.

Butterscotch Angel Cake

Prep/Total Time: 25 min.

I came across a recipe similar to this in a cookbook and made some changes. The broiled cake features an oh-so-sweet butterscotch topping that can't be beat!
—Karen Grant, Tulare, California

Honeymoon Mousse

　8 slices angel food cake
3/4 cup butter, melted, *divided*
　1 cup packed brown sugar, *divided*
　8 scoops butter brickle *or* butter pecan ice
　　cream
Butterscotch ice cream topping

Place cake slices on a greased baking sheet. Brush with 6 tablespoons butter; press 1 tablespoon brown sugar onto each slice. Broil 5-6 in. from the heat for 1-2 minutes or until bubbly.

Turn slices over; brush with remaining butter and sprinkle with remaining brown sugar. Broil 1-2 minutes longer or until bubbly. Cool for 2-3 minutes. Serve with the ice cream; drizzle with the butterscotch topping. **Yield:** 8 servings.

Mint-Chocolate Ice Cream Cake

(Pictured below)

Prep: 15 min. + freezing

Frosty and impressive, this versatile ice cream cake is pretty enough for company but simple enough for a weeknight treat. Try food coloring to tint the whipped topping, or use different flavors of ice cream, extracts and cookie or candy crumbs to suit different holidays or occasions.
—Kathy Morrow, Hubbard, Ohio

  1 package (16 ounces) Suzy Q's
  3 cups mint chocolate chip ice cream, softened
12 cream-filled chocolate sandwich cookies, crushed, *divided*
  2 cups whipped topping
1/2 teaspoon mint extract, optional

Mint-Chocolate Ice Cream Cake

Line an 8-in. x 4-in. x 2-in. loaf pan with plastic wrap. Place four Suzy Q's in pan, completely covering the bottom. Spread ice cream over Suzy Q's; sprinkle with half of the cookie crumbs. Press remaining Suzy Q's on top. Cover and freeze for at least 3 hours.

Just before serving, remove from the freezer and invert onto a serving plate. Carefully remove the pan and plastic wrap.

Combine whipped topping and extract if desired; frost top and sides of cake. Sprinkle with remaining cookie crumbs. **Yield:** 10 servings.

Rosemary Chicken

Prep/Total Time: 15 min.

You can have this zesty, five-ingredient entree ready in only 15 minutes—from start to finish! The sauce adds an elegant touch to my everyday dinner lineup. When I have extra time, I like to bake the chicken in the oven, but it's especially quick to fix in a skillet.
—Elaine Kane
Keizer, Oregon

2 boneless skinless chicken breast halves (4 ounces *each*)
2 teaspoons vegetable oil
1/4 cup prepared Italian salad dressing
1 tablespoon Dijon mustard
1/2 teaspoon dried rosemary, crushed

In a small skillet over medium heat, cook chicken in oil for 5-6 minutes on each side or until juices run clear. Remove and keep warm.

In a small bowl, whisk the salad dressing, mustard and rosemary. Pour into skillet; cook and stir for 1 minute or until mixture is heated through. Serve with chicken. **Yield:** 2 servings.

Spinach-Mushroom Beef Patties

Prep/Total Time: 25 min.

Whether grilled or broiled, these juicy, flavorful burgers flecked with spinach and cheese were always a yummy summertime favorite at our house. With or without a bun, they're sure to bring raves at your home, too!
—Jan Komarek, Friendswood, Texas

1 package (10 ounces) frozen chopped spinach, thawed and squeezed dry
1 cup (4 ounces) shredded part-skim mozzarella cheese
1 cup chopped fresh mushrooms
1 envelope onion mushroom soup mix
2 pounds ground beef

In a large bowl, combine the spinach, cheese, mushrooms and soup mix. Crumble beef over mixture and mix well.

Shape into eight patties. Grill, covered, over medium-hot heat for 5-7 minutes on each side or until no longer pink. **Yield:** 8 servings.

Bacon-Chive Potato Salad

Bacon-Chive Potato Salad

(Pictured above)

Prep: 30 min. + chilling

This creamy, colorful medley is always re-quested at our family barbecues and other get-togethers. The zippy salad is so quick to prepare and goes with almost anything. Plus, it has a crowd-pleasing taste whether it's served warm or chilled.
—*Karen White, Lawrenceburg, Tennessee*

2-1/2 **pounds small red potatoes**
 1/2 **cup real bacon bits**
 1/4 **cup minced chives**
 3/4 **cup mayonnaise**
 3/4 **teaspoon ground mustard**
 1/2 **teaspoon salt**
 1/4 **teaspoon pepper**

Place potatoes in a large saucepan and cover with water. Bring to a boil. Reduce heat; cover and cook for 15-20 minutes or until tender. Drain and cool. Cut into wedges; place in a serving bowl. Add bacon and chives.

In a small bowl, combine the mayonnaise, mustard, salt and pepper. Spoon over salad; toss to coat. Refrigerate salad for at least 1 hour before serving. **Yield:** 8 servings.

Gumbo in a Jiffy

Prep/Total Time: 20 min.

My husband loves the kick Italian sausage gives this easy gumbo. Try it with wedges of warm corn bread.
—*Amy Flack, Homer City, Pennsylvania*

✓ Uses less fat, sugar or salt. Includes Nutrition Facts and Diabetic Exchanges.

 3 **Italian sausage links, sliced**
 1 **can (14-1/2 ounces) diced tomatoes with green peppers and onions, undrained**
 1 **can (14-1/2 ounces) chicken broth**
 1/2 **cup water**
 1 **can (7 ounces) whole kernel corn, drained**
 1 **cup uncooked instant rice**

In a large saucepan, cook sausage until no longer pink; drain. Stir in the tomatoes, broth and water; bring to a boil. Stir in corn and rice; cover and remove from the heat. Let stand for 5 minutes. **Yield:** 6 servings.

Nutrition Facts: 1 cup (prepared with Italian turkey sausage and reduced-sodium broth) equals 204 calories, 6 g fat (2 g saturated fat), 30 mg cholesterol, 884 mg sodium, 23 g carbohydrate, 2 g fiber, 13 g protein. **Diabetic Exchanges:** 1-1/2 lean meat, 1-1/2 vegetable, 1 starch.

Honey Grilled Shrimp

(Pictured below)

Prep: 10 min. + marinating **Grill:** 10 min.

This has become our family's absolute favorite way to enjoy shrimp. There's no comparison! —*Lisa Blackwell Henderson, North Carolina*

✓ Uses less fat, sugar or salt. Includes Nutrition Facts and Diabetic Exchanges.

    1 bottle (8 ounces) Italian salad dressing
    1 cup honey
  1/2 teaspoon minced garlic
    2 pounds uncooked medium shrimp, peeled
      and deveined

In a small bowl, combine the salad dressing, honey and garlic; set aside 1/2 cup. Pour remaining marinade into a large resealable plastic bag; add the shrimp. Seal bag and turn to coat; refrigerate for 30 minutes. Cover and refrigerate reserved marinade for basting.

Coat grill rack with nonstick cooking spray before starting the grill. Drain and discard marinade. Thread shrimp onto eight metal or soaked wooden skewers. Grill, uncovered, over medium heat for 3 minutes, turning once. Baste with reserved marinade. Grill 3-4 minutes longer or until shrimp turn pink, turning and basting frequently. **Yield:** 8 servings.

Nutrition Facts: 1 skewer equals 175 calories, 5 g fat (1 g saturated fat), 168 mg cholesterol, 383 mg sodium, 14 g carbohydrate, trace fiber, 18 g protein. **Diabetic Exchanges:** 3 very lean meat, 1 starch, 1 fat.

Honey Grilled Shrimp

Italian Beef Hoagies

Prep/Total Time: 20 min.

These simple, hearty sandwiches require just a handful of ingredients and go together in a flash. My family thought they were wonderful, and the recipe helped me put leftover pot roast to a delicious new use. —*Annie King North Lewisburg, Ohio*

      6 hoagie buns, split
     12 slices cooked roast beef (1/4 inch thick)
    3/4 cup spaghetti sauce
  1-1/2 cups (6 ounces) shredded part-skim
        mozzarella cheese
    1/2 cup sliced banana peppers

Place buns cut side up on a baking sheet. Place beef on bottom halves; top with spaghetti sauce and cheese.

Bake at 300° for 12-15 minutes or until heated through and cheese is melted. Top with peppers. Replace bun tops. **Yield:** 6 servings.

Editor's Note: Look for banana peppers (pickled peppers) in the pickle and olive section of your grocery store.

Chocolate Peanut Butter Mousse

Prep: 15 min. + chilling

Here's a luscious way to blend milk chocolate and peanut butter. —*Maria Regakis, Somerville, Massachusetts*

    1 milk chocolate candy bar (5 ounces),
      chopped
    1 cup heavy whipping cream
    1 cup creamy peanut butter
  1/3 cup chocolate-covered peanuts, chopped

In a microwave-safe bowl, combine the candy bar, cream and peanut butter. Microwave at 50% power for 2-3 minutes or until smooth, stirring twice. Transfer to a small mixing bowl. Cover and refrigerate for 1 hour or until chilled. Beat until soft peaks form. Spoon into dessert dishes; sprinkle with chocolate-covered peanuts. **Yield:** 6 servings.

Editor's Note: This recipe was tested in a 1,100-watt microwave.

Pretzel-Crusted Chicken

(Pictured above)

Prep: 10 min. **Bake:** 40 min.

I use buttery pretzels, honey mustard and deli ham to "fancy up" this scrumptious chicken entree. This combination's a hit with my fussy family! —Marie McCarthy
Cobleskill, New York

4 boneless skinless chicken breast halves
(6 ounces *each*)
1/4 cup honey mustard
8 thin slices deli ham
1 tablespoon butter, melted
1/2 cup crushed pretzels

Cut a horizontal slit in one side of each chicken breast half to within 1/2 in. of the opposite side. Spread honey mustard inside each pocket; stuff with two ham slices.

Place in a greased 13-in. x 9-in. x 2-in. baking dish. Brush with butter; sprinkle with pretzels. Bake, uncovered, at 350° for 40-45 minutes or until chicken juices run clear. **Yield:** 4 servings.

Golden Pound Cake

Prep: 10 min. **Bake:** 45 min. + cooling

Moist, refreshing and lemon-flavored, this sunny cake just couldn't be much faster to assemble. It's a summertime favorite in our household. I sometimes use orange cake mix and a can of orange soda for a flavorful variation.
—Vicki Boyd, Newport News, Virginia

1 package (18-1/4 ounces) lemon cake mix
1 package (3.4 ounces) instant vanilla pudding mix
4 eggs
3/4 cup vegetable oil
1 can (12 ounces) Mountain Dew
Confectioners' sugar, optional

In a large mixing bowl, combine the cake mix, pudding mix, eggs, oil and soda. Beat on low speed for 30 seconds; beat on medium for 2 minutes.

Pour into a greased and floured 10-in. fluted tube pan. Bake at 350° for 45-50 minutes or until a toothpick inserted near the center comes out clean. Cool for 10 minutes before removing from pan to a wire rack to cool completely. Dust with confectioners' sugar if desired. **Yield:** 12 servings.

Citrus Torte

Prep/Total Time: 20 min.

This bright and citrusy torte is so easy to rely on because it makes the most of convenience items, such as frozen pound cake. It's a recipe I use time and again, and I always win rave reviews from those who sample it.
—Janice Prytzwrites, Murrieta, California

1 jar (10 ounces) lemon curd
1 carton (8 ounces) frozen whipped topping, thawed, *divided*
1 loaf (10-3/4 ounces) frozen pound cake, thawed
1 can (15 ounces) mandarin oranges, drained

Place the lemon curd in a large bowl; fold in half of the whipped topping until blended. Split cake horizontally into three layers. Place bottom layer on a serving plate; spread with 1/2 cup lemon curd mixture. Repeat layers; replace cake top.

Spread top with remaining lemon curd mixture. Frost sides with remaining whipped topping. Garnish with mandarin oranges. Refrigerate until serving. **Yield:** 10 servings.

Chocolate Ice Cream Pie

(Pictured below)

Prep: 15 min. + freezing

Freezer pies are great when the temperature's soaring and you don't want to turn on the oven. This take on boxed turtle candies will wow family and friends, and it's so easy to make! —Margaret Wilson, Hemet, California

- 3/4 cup pecan halves, toasted
- 6 cups chocolate ice cream, softened
- 1/2 cup caramel ice cream topping, *divided*
- 1 graham cracker crust (9 inches)
- 2/3 cup whipped topping

Set aside 12-16 pecan halves for garnish; chop the remaining pecans. In a large bowl, combine the ice cream, 1/4 cup caramel topping and chopped pecans. Spread into the pie crust. Cover and freeze for at least 2-1/2 hours.

Remove from the freezer 15 minutes before serving. Garnish with whipped topping, remaining caramel topping and reserved pecans. **Yield:** 6-8 servings.

Flounder Florentine

Prep: 10 min. **Bake:** 25 min.

A mixture of garden vegetable cream cheese and healthy chopped spinach lends rich flavor to these tender fish fillets for an elegant meal that's table-ready in just over 30 minutes. —Bobby Taylor, Michigan City, Indiana

Chocolate Ice Cream Pie

- 1 package (10 ounces) frozen chopped spinach, thawed and squeezed dry
- 1 carton (8 ounces) spreadable garden vegetable cream cheese, *divided*
- 4 flounder *or* sole fillets (3 ounces *each*)
- 2 tablespoons milk
- 1/2 teaspoon lemon juice
- 1/8 teaspoon salt
- 1/8 teaspoon pepper

In a small bowl, combine spinach and 3/4 cup cream cheese. Spoon onto each fillet; roll up. Place seam side down in a greased 8-in. square baking dish.

Bake, uncovered, at 375° for 25-30 minutes or until fish flakes easily with a fork. In a small microwave-safe bowl, combine the milk, lemon juice, salt, pepper and remaining cream cheese. Microwave on high for 30-60 seconds; stir until smooth. Spoon over fish. **Yield:** 4 servings.

Potato Flake Chicken

Prep: 10 min. **Bake:** 40 min.

Convenient potato flakes and Parmesan cheese flavor chicken breasts with a crispy golden coating in this fuss-free dish. —Jamie Saulsbery, Pittsburgh, Pennsylvania

- 2/3 cup mashed potato flakes
- 1/3 cup grated Parmesan cheese
- 1 teaspoon garlic salt
- 4 boneless skinless chicken breast halves (8 ounces *each*)
- 1/3 cup butter, melted

In a shallow bowl, combine the potato flakes, Parmesan cheese and garlic salt. Dip chicken in butter, then coat with potato flake mixture.

Place in a greased 13-in. x 9-in. x 2-in. baking pan. Bake, uncovered, at 350° for 35-40 minutes or until juices run clear. Broil 4 in. from the heat for 3-5 minutes or until lightly browned. **Yield:** 4 servings.

Potato Shrimp Chowder

Prep/Total Time: 25 min.

With only three ingredients, this recipe couldn't be simpler! I like items that get me out of the kitchen in a flash. I often serve the comforting chowder with a few crackers or hot bread and a green salad. —Martha Castille Opelousas, Louisiana

- 1 package (11 ounces) cream of potato soup mix
- 1 cup frozen mixed vegetables
- 1 pound frozen cooked small shrimp, thawed

In a large saucepan, prepare soup mix according to package directions, adding the mixed vegetables. Stir in shrimp; cook 5-6 minutes longer or until heated through. **Yield:** 12 servings (3 quarts).

Editor's Note: This recipe was tested with Bear Creek creamy potato soup mix.

Broccoli Cheese Soup

Prep/Total Time: 20 min.

I've been making this soup since a friend gave me the recipe years ago. No one can believe how fast it is to prepare. It often comes to the rescue when our children and grandchildren unexpectedly stop in for lunch.
—Janis Corkery, Independence, Iowa

- 2 cans (10-3/4 ounces *each*) condensed cheddar cheese soup, undiluted
- 3 cups milk
- 1 package (10 ounces) frozen chopped broccoli, thawed
- 1 cup frozen O'Brien hash brown potatoes, thawed
- 1/2 teaspoon salt

In a large saucepan, combine all ingredients. Bring to a boil. Reduce heat; simmer, uncovered, for 5 minutes or until heated through. **Yield:** 7 servings.

Teriyaki Salmon

Prep/Total Time: 30 min.

A time-saving marinade with maple syrup and teriyaki sauce creates a delicious sweet-and-sour glaze for my salmon entree. The fish stays extremely moist, and it is really yummy.
—Lenita Schafer
Princeton, Massachusetts

☑ Uses less fat, sugar or salt. Includes Nutrition Facts and Diabetic Exchanges.

- 3/4 cup reduced-sodium teriyaki sauce
- 1/2 cup maple syrup
- 4 salmon fillets (6 ounces *each*)

In a small bowl, combine teriyaki sauce and syrup. Set aside 1/4 cup for basting. Pour remaining marinade into a large resealable plastic bag; add salmon. Seal the bag and turn to coat; refrigerate for 15 minutes.

Drain and discard marinade. Coat grill rack or broiler pan with nonstick cooking spray. Place fillets skin side down. Grill, covered, over medium heat or broil 4 in. from the heat for 8-12 minutes or until fish flakes easily with a fork, basting frequently with reserved marinade. **Yield:** 4 servings.

Nutrition Facts: 1 fillet equals 362 calories, 18 g fat (4 g saturated fat), 100 mg cholesterol, 422 mg sodium, 12 g carbohydrate, 0 fiber, 35 g protein. **Diabetic Exchanges:** 5 lean meat, 1 fruit, 1/2 fat.

Second-Day Salmon

We grill more salmon fillets than we can eat for dinner, so we have leftovers to make salmon cakes the next day. The marinade we use lends great flavor—the cakes taste much better than those made with canned salmon. *—Bonny Salmeri, Seminole, Florida*

Chick-n-Rice Soup

Chick-n-Rice Soup

(Pictured above)
Prep/Total Time: 30 min.

The ladies of a church I attended years ago served this hearty crowd-pleaser on many occasions. It's a very satisfying soup! It also makes a family-friendly main dish for a weeknight meal. —Sara Nelson, Freeport, Michigan

- 8 cups water
- 1-1/2 cups sliced celery
- 1 cup thinly sliced fresh carrots
- 4 cups cubed cooked chicken
- 1 package (6.9 ounces) chicken-flavored rice and vermicelli mix
- 4 teaspoons chicken bouillon granules

In a large saucepan, bring water, celery and carrots to a boil. Stir in the chicken, rice mix and bouillon. Return to a boil. Reduce heat; cover and simmer for 15-20 minutes or until rice is tender. **Yield:** 10 servings.

Chapter 6

IT'S PROBABLY happened to you...your hectic day flew by, and before you knew it, dinnertime was mere moments away. You asked yourself, "How can I get a satisfying, family-pleasing meal on the table in just 10 minutes?"

It's easy—simply turn to this fast-as-can-be chapter. From mouth-watering main courses to special desserts, each home-cooked dish can be prepared from start to finish in only 10 minutes...or less!

Your hungry bunch will be amazed at how quickly you can whip up favorites such as Ham 'n' Corn Chowder, Candy Bar Parfaits, Turkey Reubens and Pears in Orange Sauce.

IN-A-SNAP SENSATIONS. Fast French Dip Sandwiches and Sesame Vegetable Medley (both recipes on p. 105).

Beer Dip

(Pictured below)

Prep/Total Time: 5 min.

Ranch dressing flavors this speedy mixture that's packed with shredded cheese. The thick dip is made to go with pretzels. Once you start eating it, you won't be able to stop!
—Michelle Long, New Castle, Colorado

> 2 packages (8 ounces *each*) cream cheese, softened
> 1/3 cup beer *or* nonalcoholic beer
> 1 envelope ranch salad dressing mix
> 2 cups (8 ounces) shredded cheddar cheese
> Pretzels

In a large mixing bowl, beat the cream cheese, beer and dressing mix until smooth. Stir in cheese. Serve with pretzels. Refrigerate leftovers. **Yield:** 3-1/2 cups.

Beer Dip
Taco Dip

Taco Dip

(Pictured below left)

Prep/Total Time: 10 min.

This timely dish is a definite family favorite. I've served it more times than I can count. It looks very colorful on a table, and it never lasts long.
—Rhonda Biancardi
Blaine, Minnesota

> 1 package (8 ounces) cream cheese, softened
> 1 cup (8 ounces) sour cream
> 1 carton (8 ounces) French onion dip
> 1 envelope taco seasoning
> 4 cups shredded lettuce
> 2 cups (8 ounces) shredded cheddar cheese
> 1-1/2 cups chopped tomatoes
> Tortilla chips

In a small mixing bowl, beat the cream cheese, sour cream, onion dip and taco seasoning until blended. Spread onto a 12-in. round serving platter. Top with lettuce, cheese and tomatoes. Serve with tortilla chips. **Yield:** 10-12 servings.

Ham 'n' Corn Chowder

Prep/Total Time: 10 min.

This soup comes together faster than you can believe! My family had a hard time finding a corn chowder we all liked, so I combined ingredients from the recipes we enjoyed most. This is the tasty result. —Danna Chambers
Topsham, Maine

> 1 can (14-1/2 ounces) diced new potatoes, drained
> 1-1/2 cups milk
> 1 can (10-3/4 ounces) condensed cheddar cheese soup, undiluted
> 1 can (8-1/2 ounces) cream-style corn
> 1 cup frozen corn, thawed
> 1 cup cubed deli ham

In a large microwave-safe bowl, combine all ingredients. Cover and microwave on high for 5-8 minutes or until heated through, stirring twice. **Yield:** 3 servings.

Editor's Note: This recipe was tested in a 1,100-watt microwave.

Is It Chowder or Soup?

A CHOWDER is defined as a thick, chunky soup or stew that typically includes seafood, onions, potatoes, salt pork or crumbled bacon. The most classic example of chowder is clam or fish chowder from New England. It's made with milk or cream, seasoned with salt pork and loaded with cubed potatoes and seafood.

Today, there are many variations of chowder, including simple-but-delicious Ham 'n' Corn Chowder (recipe above). With all of those variations, there's often a fine line between chowders and soups.

Vegetarian Hummus Wraps

(Pictured above)

Prep/Total Time: 10 min.

I created these wraps to get more veggies in my diet. I'm always on the go, like many other mothers. These sandwiches give me the energy I need and taste delicious.
—Amber Indra, Webster, New York

✓ Uses less fat, sugar or salt. Includes Nutrition Facts.

    6 tablespoons hummus
    2 flour tortillas (8 inches)
1/2 cup shredded carrots
    1 cup fresh baby spinach
    6 slices tomato
    2 tablespoons green goddess salad dressing

Spread hummus over each tortilla. Layer with carrots, spinach and tomato; drizzle with dressing. Roll up tightly. **Yield:** 2 servings.

Nutrition Facts: 1 wrap (prepared with fat-free dressing) equals 276 calories, 8 g fat (1 g saturated fat), trace cholesterol, 630 mg sodium, 43 g carbohydrate, 5 g fiber, 9 g protein.

Cottage Cheese Salad

Prep/Total Time: 10 min.

Ordinary cottage cheese gets jazzed up in this light and refreshing side dish. It's a great change-of-pace salad any time of the year.
—Lynn Penner, Prescott, Arizona

    1 cup (8 ounces) cottage cheese
    1 medium tomato, chopped
1/2 cup chopped cucumber
1/3 cup chopped green pepper
    2 tablespoons mayonnaise
    1 tablespoon sour cream
    1 tablespoon ranch salad dressing mix

In a small bowl, combine all ingredients. Serve immediately. **Yield:** 3 servings.

Country Ham Sandwiches

Prep/Total Time: 5 min.

This satisfying sandwich is ideal for lunch or a weeknight dinner when there's little time to cook. Smoked cheddar and a creamy garlic-infused spread lend special appeal to this easy handheld meal.
—Jennifer Parham
Brown Summit, North Carolina

    2 tablespoons mayonnaise
    2 tablespoons sour cream
1/8 teaspoon garlic powder
    4 slices whole wheat bread
    2 ounces smoked cheddar cheese, sliced
    4 slices tomato
    4 ounces thinly sliced deli ham
    2 lettuce leaves

In a small bowl, combine the mayonnaise, sour cream and garlic powder. Spread over two slices of bread. Layer the two bread slices with the cheddar cheese, tomato, deli ham and lettuce. Top with remaining bread slices. **Yield:** 2 servings.

Turkey Reubens
Poppy Seed Mandarin Salad

Turkey Reubens

(Pictured above)

Prep/Total Time: 10 min.

I have always enjoyed Reuben sandwiches, and I started making them with smoked turkey a few years ago. These are a favorite—especially in summer, when I don't like to heat up my kitchen. —Joann Dalrymple
Claremore, Oklahoma

    4 slices pumpernickel *or* rye bread
    2 tablespoons Thousand Island salad dressing
    6 ounces sliced deli smoked turkey
1/2 cup sauerkraut, rinsed and well drained
    2 slices Swiss cheese
    2 teaspoons butter, softened

Spread two slices of bread with salad dressing. Layer with turkey, sauerkraut and cheese; top with remaining bread. Butter the outsides of sandwiches.

In a large skillet, toast sandwiches for 3-4 minutes on each side or until heated through. **Yield:** 2 servings.

Poppy Seed Mandarin Salad

(Pictured above)

Prep/Total Time: 10 min.

Dried cranberries add color, and the cashews bring fun crunch to this pretty medley. It's nice for a covered-dish dinner, but it can also be served at luncheons with the girls. I usually pair the salad with crusty rolls.
—Darlene Hoffman, Augusta, Georgia

    1 package (10 ounces) hearts of romaine salad mix
    1 can (11 ounces) mandarin oranges, drained
    1 cup lightly salted cashews
3/4 cup shredded cheddar cheese
3/4 cup shredded smoked Swiss cheese
1/2 cup dried cranberries
3/4 cup poppy seed salad dressing

In a large salad bowl, combine the salad mix, oranges, cashews, cheeses and cranberries. Drizzle with dressing; toss to coat. Serve immediately. **Yield:** 10 servings.

Raspberry-Topped Ladyfingers

Prep/Total Time: 10 min.

This easy dessert always gets raves. I prepared it for my boyfriend and, a few days later, heard him bragging to all his friends about what a great cook I am!
—Julie Oldiges, Newport, Kentucky

> 6 ladyfingers, split
> 1/4 cup raspberry jam
> 1/2 cup vanilla yogurt
> 1/2 teaspoon vanilla extract
> 1 cup fresh raspberries

Place three ladyfinger bottoms on each of two dessert plates; spread with jam. Replace ladyfinger tops. Combine yogurt and vanilla; spoon over the top. Sprinkle with raspberries. **Yield:** 2 servings.

Navy Bean Tossed Salad

(Pictured on the front cover)

Prep/Total Time: 10 min.

Black olives, feta cheese and Caesar dressing give this salad distinctive Greek flavor. Sometimes I toast a store-bought pizza crust and cut it into cubes for croutons.
—Clara Coulston, Washington Court House, Ohio

✓ Uses less fat, sugar or salt. Includes Nutrition Facts.

> 4 cups torn romaine
> 1 can (15 ounces) navy beans, rinsed and drained
> 1 cup cherry tomatoes, halved
> 1 cup (4 ounces) crumbled reduced-fat feta cheese
> 3/4 cup sliced cucumber
> 1/2 cup red onion rings, halved
> 1/2 cup roasted sweet red peppers, chopped and patted dry
> 2 tablespoons sliced ripe olives, drained
> 1/2 cup fat-free Caesar salad dressing

In a large salad bowl, combine the first eight ingredients. Drizzle with dressing and toss to coat. Serve immediately. **Yield:** 7 servings.

Nutrition Facts: 1 cup equals 146 calories, 2 g fat (1 g saturated fat), 6 mg cholesterol, 774 mg sodium, 23 g carbohydrate, 5 g fiber, 10 g protein.

Parfait Party

WANT to serve yummy Candy Bar Parfaits (recipe above right) at a "parfait party" like Angie Cassada did? To add to the fun, offer a variety of toppings such as colored sprinkles, whipped topping, crushed sandwich cookies, maraschino cherries and fruit sauces. You could offer different flavors of ice cream, too.

Candy Bar Parfaits

(Pictured below)

Prep/Total Time: 10 min.

My kids just love making their own candy and ice cream sensations. These parfaits are such a favorite that we've featured them at build-your-own-parfait birthday parties!
—Angie Cassada, Monroe, North Carolina

> 1 cup coarsely chopped peanuts
> 1 cup coarsely crushed pretzels
> 1 milk chocolate candy bar (1.55 ounces), chopped
> 1 quart vanilla ice cream
> 1/3 cup chocolate syrup
> 2 tablespoons peanut butter

In a small bowl, combine the peanuts, pretzels and chopped candy bar; spoon 1/4 cup into each of four parfait glasses. Top each with 1/2 cup ice cream, 1/4 cup peanut mixture and another 1/2 cup ice cream.

Combine chocolate syrup and peanut butter; drizzle over ice cream. Sprinkle with remaining peanut mixture. Serve immediately. **Yield:** 4 servings.

Candy Bar Parfaits

Citrus-Apricot Vegetable Glaze

(Pictured below)

Prep/Total Time: 5 min.

For a delightful finishing touch, drizzle this refreshing citrusy glaze over carrot and zucchini strips. It's also a great way to jazz up fresh sugar snap peas. Double the glaze ingredients if you decide to serve all three veggies as shown below. —Dot Christiansen, Bettendorf, Iowa

  1/3 cup apricot preserves
     3 tablespoons butter, melted
  1/2 teaspoon grated orange peel
  1/2 teaspoon lemon juice
  1/4 teaspoon salt
  1/4 teaspoon ground nutmeg
FOR CARROTS AND ZUCCHINI:
     1 pound medium carrots
     4 medium zucchini
FOR PEAS:
     2 pounds fresh sugar snap peas

In a small bowl, combine preserves, butter, orange peel, lemon juice, salt and nutmeg. **Yield:** about 1/2 cup.

For carrots and zucchini: Trim the ends from the vegetables. With a vegetable peeler, cut very thin slices down the length of each carrot and zucchini, making long ribbons.

Place carrots in a steamer basket; place in a large saucepan over 1 in. of water. Bring to a boil; cover and steam for 2 minutes. Add zucchini; cover and steam 2-3 minutes longer or until vegetables are tender. Transfer to a serving dish. Drizzle with glaze; toss to coat. Serve with a slotted spoon. **Yield:** 8 servings.

For peas: Place peas in a steamer basket; place in a large saucepan over 1 in. of water. Bring to a boil; cover and steam for 3-5 minutes or until tender. Transfer to a serving dish. Drizzle with glaze; toss to coat. Serve with a slotted spoon. **Yield:** 8 servings.

Citrus-Apricot Vegetable Glaze

Bee My Honey Fruit Dip

Prep/Total Time: 5 min.

Orange, cinnamon and nutmeg round out this creamy appetizer dip. I like to serve the spiced spread with apples, pineapple and strawberries when they're in season.
—Carol Gillespie, Chambersburg, Pennsylvania

     1 package (8 ounces) cream cheese, softened
     1 jar (7 ounces) marshmallow creme
     1 tablespoon honey
     1 teaspoon grated orange peel
  1/4 teaspoon ground cinnamon
  1/8 teaspoon ground nutmeg
Assorted fresh fruit

In a small mixing bowl, beat the first six ingredients until smooth. Serve with fruit. Refrigerate leftovers. **Yield:** 2 cups.

Nutty Banana Shakes

Prep/Total Time: 10 min.

Children of all ages are sure to enjoy these thick shakes. Whip 'em up as a yummy and satisfying after-school snack...or sip them on the patio with a light lunch. The recipe is simple and speedy. —Maricah Le Vells
Memphis, Tennessee

     1 cup milk
     3 cups vanilla ice cream
     4 medium ripe bananas, cut into chunks
  1/2 cup chopped walnuts
     4 miniature Butterfinger candy bars

Place all ingredients in a blender; cover and process until blended. Pour into chilled glasses; serve immediately. **Yield:** 5 servings.

Yellow Squash Turkey Salad

Prep/Total Time: 10 min.

This is my favorite fast recipe. With a wonderful mix of flavors and textures, the impressive medley can be made in minutes for lunch or as a special dinner side salad.
—Mildred Sherrer, Roanoke, Texas

     4 cups spring mix salad greens
  1/4 pound thinly sliced deli smoked turkey, cut into 1-inch strips
     1 small yellow summer squash, halved lengthwise and sliced
     1 small pear, chopped
  1/2 cup dried cranberries
  1/3 cup honey-roasted sliced almonds
  1/4 cup cubed cheddar cheese
  1/3 cup red wine vinaigrette

In a large bowl, combine the first seven ingredients. Drizzle with vinaigrette and toss to coat. Serve immediately. **Yield:** 2 servings.

Fast French Dip Sandwiches
Sesame Vegetable Medley

Sesame Vegetable Medley

(Pictured above and on page 98)

Prep/Total Time: 10 min.

Here's a no-fuss dish that makes a great accompaniment to any menu. —Tanya Lamb, Talking Rock, Georgia

✓ Uses less fat, sugar or salt. Includes Nutrition Facts and Diabetic Exchanges.

> 1 cup *each* baby carrots, broccoli florets and sliced fresh mushrooms
> 1 cup sliced zucchini (1/2 inch thick)
> 1 teaspoon minced garlic
> 2 tablespoons water
> 1 tablespoon butter
> 2 teaspoons sesame seeds, toasted
> 1/8 teaspoon salt
> 1/8 teaspoon pepper

In a large microwave-safe bowl, combine the carrots, broccoli, mushrooms, zucchini, garlic and water. Cover and microwave on high for 3-5 minutes or until vegetables are tender, stirring twice; drain. Stir in the butter, sesame seeds, salt and pepper. **Yield:** 4 servings.

Editor's Note: This recipe was tested in a 1,100-watt microwave.

Nutrition Facts: 3/4 cup equals 60 calories, 4 g fat (2 g saturated fat), 8 mg cholesterol, 145 mg sodium, 6 g carbohydrate, 2 g fiber, 2 g protein. **Diabetic Exchanges:** 1 vegetable, 1/2 fat.

Fast French Dip Sandwiches

(Pictured above and on page 99)

Prep/Total Time: 10 min.

I was looking for ways to use up leftover beef when I created this tasty sandwich. I love dipping it in the onion soup. —Karrie Wagner, Barberton, Ohio

> 1 can (10-1/2 ounces) condensed French onion soup, undiluted
> 1/2 pound thinly sliced deli roast beef
> 1/3 cup water
> 4 slices provolone cheese
> 4 sandwich buns, split

In a 1-qt. microwave-safe bowl, combine the soup, beef and water. Cover and microwave on high for 3 minutes or until heated through.

Meanwhile, place a slice of cheese on each bun bottom. Broil 4-6 in. from the heat for 1 minute or until the cheese is melted. Using a slotted spoon, place the beef on buns; replace the tops. Serve with onion soup for dipping. **Yield:** 4 servings.

Editor's Note: This recipe was tested in a 1,100-watt microwave.

Raspberry Poppy Seed Dressing

(Pictured below)

Prep/Total Time: 10 min.

I simply love this creamy, fresh-tasting dressing! It's so quick to prepare in the blender and gives ordinary salads a summery gourmet touch. I often drizzle it over lettuce or fresh spinach tossed with sliced strawberries and sugared almonds. —Kendra Stoller, Kouts, Indiana

   6 tablespoons red wine vinegar
1/2 cup plus 2 tablespoons sugar
   1 teaspoon salt
   1 teaspoon ground mustard
   1 cup vegetable oil
   1 cup fresh *or* frozen raspberries, thawed
   1 teaspoon poppy seeds

In a blender, combine the vinegar, sugar, salt and mustard. While processing, gradually add oil in a steady stream. Add raspberries; cover and process until blended. Stir in poppy seeds. Serve immediately. Refrigerate leftovers. **Yield:** 2 cups.

Raspberry Poppy Seed Dressing

Garlic Butter Topping

Prep/Total Time: 5 min.

My mother gave me this microwave recipe several years ago. It's a cinch and so tasty! I use it all the time. —Marla Pinson, Granbury, Texas

   3 tablespoons butter, softened
1/2 teaspoon garlic powder
1/4 teaspoon dried thyme
FOR GARLIC BREAD:
   4 hoagie buns, split
1/4 cup grated Parmesan cheese
FOR VEGETABLES:
   3 cups fresh broccoli florets
   3 cups fresh cauliflowerets
   1 to 2 tablespoons water
1/4 cup grated Parmesan cheese

In a small microwave-safe bowl, combine the butter, garlic powder and thyme. Cover and microwave on high until butter is melted. **Yield:** 3 tablespoons.

   For garlic bread: Brush butter topping over cut sides of buns. Place cut side down on grill. Grill, uncovered, over medium heat for 1 minute or until toasted. Sprinkle with Parmesan cheese. **Yield:** 4 servings.

   For vegetables: Place broccoli, cauliflower and water in a 2-qt. microwave-safe dish. Cover and microwave on high for 5-7 minutes or until crisp-tender; drain. Drizzle with butter topping; toss to coat. Sprinkle with Parmesan cheese. Cook, uncovered, on high for 30 seconds or until heated through. **Yield:** 5 servings.

   Editor's Note: This recipe was tested in a 1,100-watt microwave.

Pears in Orange Sauce

Prep/Total Time: 10 min.

Orange juice and cream cheese perk up canned pears in this easy recipe. The cookies add a delightful crunch. —Audrey Friberg, Fridley, Minnesota

   1 can (15-1/4 ounces) pear halves
1/4 cup orange juice concentrate
   1 cinnamon stick (1 inch)
1/8 teaspoon salt
   2 ounces cream cheese, softened
1/2 teaspoon ground cinnamon
   4 Pirouette cookies *or* cookies of your choice

Drain pears, reserving liquid; set pears aside. Place liquid in a small saucepan; add the orange juice concentrate, cinnamon stick and salt. Bring to a boil, stirring occasionally. Add pears; cook, uncovered, for 2 minutes or until heated through.

   Discard cinnamon stick. Spoon pears into dessert dishes; drizzle with sauce. Dollop with the cream cheese and sprinkle with cinnamon. Serve with the cookies. **Yield:** 4 servings.

   Editor's Note: This recipe was tested with Pepperidge Farm brand cookies.

Ham and Swiss Bagels

(Pictured at right)

Prep/Total Time: 10 min.

In just 10 minutes, you can assemble these super-quick sandwiches featuring pineapple and cream cheese. The recipe never fails to get a thumbs-up...but only if the thumbs aren't wrapped around the sandwich!
—*Bev Bronleewe, Lorraine, Kansas*

- 1/4 cup whipped cream cheese
- 2 tablespoons honey mustard
- 2 whole wheat bagels, split
- 1 slice Swiss cheese, halved
- 2 slices canned pineapple
- 8 thin slices deli smoked ham
- 2 lettuce leaves

In a small bowl, combine the cream cheese and mustard until smooth; spread over the cut sides of the bagels. On the bagel bottoms, layer the Swiss cheese, pineapple slices, deli ham and lettuce leaves. Replace the bagel tops. **Yield:** 2 servings.

Green Onion Bagel Dip

Prep/Total Time: 10 min.

I've been sharing this flavor-packed dip for more than 40 years, and it is always my most popular contribution for parties. My family loves it as well, and no one suspects that the recipe takes a mere 10 minutes to whip up! —*Joy Pasby Sonora, California*

- 1 teaspoon chicken bouillon granules
- 2 tablespoons hot water
- 1 package (8 ounces) cream cheese, softened
- 1 cup mayonnaise
- 6 green onions, chopped
- 4 to 5 bagels, split and cut into bite-size pieces

In a small bowl, dissolve bouillon in water; cool slightly. In a small mixing bowl, beat cream cheese and mayonnaise until smooth. Add bouillon mixture and beat until blended. Stir in onions. Serve with bagel pieces. **Yield:** 2-1/3 cups.

Crab Salad Wraps

Prep/Total Time: 10 min.

I created this delicious recipe in my kitchen and wound up with a sandwich that adds pizzazz to any lunch or dinner menu. Each bite bursts with bacon, mustard and crab.
—*Jane Birch, Edison, New Jersey*

- 1/4 cup mayonnaise
- 2 tablespoons finely chopped onion
- 2 tablespoons sweet pickle relish
- 2 tablespoons prepared mustard
- 1 package (8 ounces) imitation crabmeat, flaked

Ham and Swiss Bagels

- 1 cup (4 ounces) shredded Swiss cheese
- 2 bacon strips, cooked and crumbled, optional
- 6 flour tortillas (6 inches), room temperature

In a small bowl, combine the mayonnaise, onion, relish and mustard. Stir in the crab, cheese and bacon if desired. Spoon about 1/2 cup down the center of each tortilla; roll up tightly. **Yield:** 6 servings.

Peach Pudding Dessert

Prep/Total Time: 10 min.

We usually have a bountiful crop of fresh peaches every summer. My family likes them just about any way they get them, but this quick recipe is a special one for us all.
—*Connie Sanborn, Lawrence, Michigan*

- 2 tablespoons brown sugar
- 2 teaspoons butter
- 2 medium fresh peaches, sliced
- 3 tablespoons sour cream
- 4 snack-size cups (3-1/2 ounces *each*) vanilla pudding
- 4 pecan shortbread cookies, coarsely crushed

In a small microwave-safe bowl, heat brown sugar and butter on high for 1 minute or until sugar is dissolved. Stir in peaches and sour cream.

Spoon pudding into dessert dishes. Top with peach mixture; sprinkle with cookie crumbs. Serve or refrigerate. **Yield:** 4 servings.

Chapter 7

FOR THE NEXT 6 weeks, leave your weekday dinner planning to this helpful chapter. All the work has been done for you!

Our Test Kitchen home economists have used some of their best recipes to put together six Monday-through-Friday supper menus. So you won't find yourself wondering, "What am I going to make tonight?"

What's more, our staff compiled a complete shopping list for each week. Just use the list, and you'll have all the ingredients needed for a whole workweek's worth of dinners.

So sit down to favorites such as Mexican-Style Ravioli, Herb Roasted Squash, Barbecue Italian Sausages and Banana Split Fruit Salad...and take the guesswork out of dinnertime!

WEEKDAY WONDERS. Salisbury Steak with Gemelli and Dressed-Up French Green Beans (both recipes on p. 127).

Week 1

Shopping List

Check for these staples:

- baking powder
- flour
- brown sugar
- dry bread crumbs
- Italian seasoning
- Greek seasoning
- dried oregano
- pepper
- salt
- butter
- egg
- milk
- minced garlic
- olive oil
- beef broth
- honey

Shop for these items:

- 4 boneless skinless chicken breast halves (6 ounces *each*)
- 1 container (18 ounces) fully cooked barbecued shredded pork
- 1-1/2 pounds ground beef
- 1 pound fresh green beans
- 2 packages (6 ounces *each*) fresh baby spinach
- 1 medium green pepper
- 1 large red onion
- 2 packages (8 ounces *each*) Monterey Jack cheese
- 1 container (6 ounces) crumbled feta cheese
- 1 package (20 ounces) refrigerated cheese ravioli
- 1 tube (13.8 ounces) refrigerated pizza crust
- 1 package (4-1/2 ounces) taco shells
- 3 cans (14-1/2 ounces *each*) diced tomatoes
- 1 can (15 ounces) black beans
- 1 jar (15 ounces) roasted sweet red peppers
- 1 can (6 ounces) tomato paste
- 2 cans (2-1/4 ounces *each*) sliced ripe olives
- 1 jar (16 ounces) salsa

Time-Saving Tips

- To ease assembly of Tuesday night's Greek Tacos, wash and dry all of the packaged spinach when you're preparing Mexican-Style Ravioli on Monday. Then refrigerate the remaining 2 cups of spinach for the next night.
- If you're particularly short on time Thursday, top the chicken with your favorite salsa, marinara sauce or diced tomatoes with Italian seasoning as a speedy alternative to the red pepper sauce.

Monday

Mexican-Style Ravioli

(Pictured above)

Prep/Total Time: 20 min.

Cheese ravioli comes alive in this tangy, slightly sweet tomato sauce. With its tasty mix of seasonings, spinach and beans, the only side to this saucy dish you'll need is an extra napkin!

- 1 package (20 ounces) refrigerated cheese ravioli
- 1 can (14-1/2 ounces) diced tomatoes, undrained
- 1 cup beef broth
- 1 can (6 ounces) tomato paste
- 1/2 cup canned black beans, rinsed and drained
- 1 tablespoon brown sugar
- 1 teaspoon dried oregano
- 1/4 teaspoon salt
- 1/4 teaspoon pepper
- 4 cups fresh baby spinach

Cook ravioli according to package directions. Meanwhile, in a large skillet, combine the tomatoes, broth, tomato paste, beans, brown sugar, oregano, salt and pepper. Bring to a boil. Reduce heat; simmer, uncovered, for 3-4 minutes or until heated through.

Drain ravioli; add to tomato mixture. Stir in spinach; cook and stir for 4-5 minutes or until spinach is wilted. **Yield:** 4 servings.

Greek Tacos

Prep/Total Time: 30 min.

Try this surprising twist on tacos that uses Greek season-ing, spinach and feta instead of taco seasoning, lettuce and cheddar. You'll truly be impressed!

☑ Uses less fat, sugar or salt. Includes Nutrition Facts and Diabetic Exchanges.

  1 pound ground beef
  1 can (14-1/2 ounces) diced tomatoes, undrained
  2 teaspoons Greek seasoning
1/2 teaspoon minced garlic
1/4 teaspoon pepper
  2 cups fresh baby spinach
  1 can (2-1/4 ounces) sliced ripe olives, drained
  1 package (4-1/2 ounces) taco shells
1/2 cup crumbled feta cheese
1/4 cup chopped red onion

In a large skillet, cook beef over medium heat until no longer pink; drain. Stir in the tomatoes, Greek season-ing, garlic and pepper. Bring to a boil. Reduce heat; sim-mer for 8-10 minutes or until thickened. Add spinach and olives; cook and stir for 2-3 minutes or until spinach is wilted.

Meanwhile, place taco shells on an ungreased baking sheet. Bake at 300° for 3-5 minutes or until heated through. Spoon about 1/4 cup beef mixture into each shell. Top with feta cheese and onion. **Yield:** 12 tacos.

Editor's Note: For a substitute for 1 tablespoon Greek seasoning, use 1/2 teaspoon each dried oregano, dried marjoram, garlic powder, lemon-pepper seasoning, ground mustard and salt. Omit the salt if the recipe calls for salt.

Nutrition Facts: 1 taco (prepared with lean ground beef and reduced-fat feta cheese) equals 130 calories, 6 g fat (2 g saturated fat), 20 mg cholesterol, 386 mg sodium, 9 g carbohydrate, 2 g fiber, 9 g protein. **Diabet-ic Exchanges:** 1 lean meat, 1 fat, 1/2 starch.

Cowboy Chili

(Pictured at right)

Prep/Total Time: 20 min.

"Sweet and chunky" describes this hearty chili that kids will love. For adults, adding a dash or two of hot sauce will make your bowlful warm up your taste buds.

1-1/2 cups cooked barbecued shredded pork
  1 can (14-1/2 ounces) diced tomatoes, undrained
  1 cup canned black beans, rinsed and drained

3/4 cup beef broth
3/4 cup chopped green pepper
1/2 teaspoon minced garlic

In a large saucepan, combine all ingredients. Bring to a boil. Reduce heat; simmer, uncovered, for 10-15 min-utes or until heated through. **Yield:** 4 servings.

Honey Biscuits

(Pictured below)

Prep/Total Time: 30 min.

These tender biscuits are a great complement to all sorts of stews, soups and chili. Monterey Jack cheese gives an extra layer of flavor to each flaky bite.

  2 cups all-purpose flour
  3 teaspoons baking powder
  1 teaspoon salt
1/2 cup plus 1 tablespoon cold butter, *divided*
3/4 cup milk
1/2 cup shredded Monterey Jack cheese
  1 tablespoon honey

In a bowl, combine the flour, baking powder and salt. Cut in 1/2 cup butter until mixture resembles coarse crumbs. Stir in milk and Monterey Jack cheese until mix-ture forms a ball.

Turn onto a lightly floured surface; knead 5-6 times. Roll out to 1/2-in. thickness; cut with a floured 2-in. bis-cuit cutter. Place on an ungreased baking sheet.

In a small microwave-safe bowl, combine honey and remaining butter. Microwave on high until melted. Brush over biscuits. Bake at 450° for 10-12 minutes or until golden brown. Serve warm. **Yield:** about 1 dozen.

Cowboy Chili
Honey Biscuits

Green Bean Side Dish
Chicken with Red Pepper Sauce

Green Bean Side Dish

(Pictured at left)
Prep/Total Time: 25 min.

Simple seasonings from your pantry perk up these fresh green beans. The versatile side dish makes a terrific partner for the chicken or any entree at all.

☑ Uses less fat, sugar or salt. Includes Nutrition Facts and Diabetic Exchanges.

> 1 pound fresh green beans, cut into 2-inch pieces
> 2 teaspoons minced garlic
> 1/2 cup water
> 2 tablespoons olive oil
> 1 teaspoon dried oregano
> 1/2 teaspoon salt
> 1/4 teaspoon pepper

In a large saucepan, bring the beans, garlic and water to a boil. Reduce heat; cover and simmer for 8-10 minutes or until tender. Drain. Stir in the oil, oregano, salt and pepper. Serve immediately. **Yield:** 4 servings.
Nutrition Facts: 3/4 cup equals 94 calories, 7 g fat (1 g saturated fat), 0 cholesterol, 301 mg sodium, 8 g carbohydrate, 4 g fiber, 2 g protein. **Diabetic Exchanges:** 1-1/2 vegetable, 1 fat.

Thursday

Chicken with Red Pepper Sauce

(Pictured above)
Prep/Total Time: 25 min.

This lightly breaded, moist and tender chicken is cooked to perfection, then topped with an Italian-seasoned red pepper puree and sprinkled with feta cheese. It's delicious!

> 1 egg
> 1/2 cup dry bread crumbs
> 1/4 teaspoon salt
> 4 boneless skinless chicken breast halves (6 ounces *each*)
> 2 tablespoons olive oil
> 1 jar (15 ounces) roasted sweet red peppers, drained
> 1 teaspoon Italian seasoning
> 3/4 cup crumbled feta cheese

In a shallow bowl, lightly beat the egg. In another shallow bowl, combine bread crumbs and salt. Dip chicken in egg, then coat with crumbs.

In a large skillet, cook chicken in oil over medium heat for 6-8 minutes on each side or until juices run clear.

Meanwhile, in a blender or food processor, combine the red peppers and Italian seasoning; cover and process until pureed. Transfer to a microwave-safe bowl. Cover and microwave on high for 1-2 minutes or until heated through, stirring once. Spoon over chicken; sprinkle with feta cheese. **Yield:** 4 servings.

Editor's Note: This recipe was tested in a 1,100-watt microwave.

Friday

Southwest Pizza

Prep/Total Time: 25 min.

Refrigerated pizza crust speeds assembly of this meat-lovers' pizza. It has a wonderful, smoky salsa taste.

> 1 tube (13.8 ounces) refrigerated pizza crust
> 1/2 pound ground beef
> 1 cup salsa
> 1/2 cup cooked barbecued shredded pork
> 1/2 cup chopped red onion
> 1 can (2-1/4 ounces) sliced ripe olives, drained
> 1-3/4 cups shredded Monterey Jack cheese

Unroll crust onto a lightly greased 12-in. pizza pan; flatten dough and build up edges slightly. Bake at 400° for 6-7 minutes or until golden brown.

Meanwhile, in a skillet, cook beef over medium heat until no longer pink; drain. Stir in salsa and pork. Spread over crust. Sprinkle with onion, olives and cheese. Bake 6-8 minutes or until cheese is melted. **Yield:** 6-8 servings.

On the Lighter Side

ARE you and your family trying to eat a little lighter? For a healthier Southwest Pizza (recipe above), try a whole wheat thin crust and use extra-lean ground turkey instead of the ground beef.

Week 2

Chicken Stew
Savory Grilled Cheese (p.114)

Shopping List

Check for these staples:

- salt
- pepper
- dried oregano
- dried parsley flakes
- dried rosemary
- dried thyme
- rubbed sage
- garlic powder
- Italian seasoning
- cornstarch
- all-purpose flour
- minced garlic
- onion
- butter
- olive oil
- lemon juice
- grated Parmesan
- instant rice

Shop for these items:

2	yellow summer squash
2	medium zucchini
1	large head romaine lettuce
2	medium tomatoes
1	bottle (16 ounces) Caesar salad dressing
1	jar (12 ounces) chicken gravy
2	cans (14 ounces *each*) chicken broth
1	can (10-3/4 ounces) condensed tomato soup
1	can (8-3/4 ounces) whole kernel corn
1	envelope spaghetti sauce mix
1	loaf (24 ounces) sliced white bread
1	package (16 ounces) wagon wheel pasta
12	ounces sliced Colby cheese
1	package (9 ounces) refrigerated cheese tortellini
2	pounds boneless skinless chicken breasts
4	boneless pork loin chops (6 ounces *each*)
1	pound ground beef
1	package (12 ounces) frozen breaded popcorn shrimp
1	package (16 ounces) frozen vegetables for stew

Time-Saving Tips

- When making the grilled cheese sandwiches on Monday, remember to save the leftover herbed butter for Wednesday's Herbed Chicken Stir-Fry (recipe on p. 114).
- Have extra time on Wednesday? Get a head start on Friday's side dish by cutting extra squash and zucchini. Store the remaining vegetables in resealable plastic bags in the refrigerator.

Monday

Chicken Stew

(Pictured above)

Prep/Total Time: 30 min.

With just chicken, veggies and a handful of other ingredients, this satisfying stew delivers old-fashioned taste.

☑ Uses less fat, sugar or salt. Includes Nutrition Facts and Diabetic Exchanges.

- 1 **pound boneless skinless chicken breasts, cut into 1-inch cubes**
- 1 **tablespoon olive oil**
- 1 **package (16 ounces) frozen vegetables for stew**
- 1 **jar (12 ounces) chicken gravy**
- 1/2 **teaspoon dried thyme**
- 1/4 **teaspoon rubbed sage**
- 1/4 **teaspoon pepper**

In a large saucepan, brown the chicken in oil over medium heat for 4-6 minutes or until no longer pink. Drain if necessary.

Stir in the remaining ingredients. Bring to a boil. Reduce heat; cover and simmer for 15 minutes or until vegetables are tender. **Yield:** 4 servings.

Nutrition Facts: 1 cup (prepared with fat-free gravy) equals 240 calories, 6 g fat (1 g saturated fat), 70 mg cholesterol, 574 mg sodium, 19 g carbohydrate, 1 g fiber, 26 g protein. **Diabetic Exchanges:** 3 very lean meat, 1 starch, 1 vegetable.

Savory Grilled Cheese

(Pictured on page 113)

Prep/Total Time: 25 min.

A fast, homemade herb butter gives these yummy sandwiches wonderful flavor.

- 1/4 cup butter, softened
- 1/2 teaspoon dried parsley flakes
- 1/2 teaspoon dried oregano
- 1/4 teaspoon garlic powder
- 8 ounces sliced Colby cheese
- 8 slices white bread

In a small bowl, combine butter, parsley, oregano and garlic powder. Cover and refrigerate 2 tablespoons for Herbed Chicken Stir-Fry (recipe below right); set aside. Place cheese on four slices of bread; top with remaining bread. Spread outside of each sandwich with 2 tablespoons butter mixture.

In a skillet over medium heat, toast sandwiches for 4-5 minutes on each side or until bread is lightly browned and cheese is melted. **Yield:** 4 servings.

Tuesday

Wagon Wheel Supper

(Pictured below)

Prep/Total Time: 25 min.

Kids will really enjoy this cheesy pasta dish "souped up" with beef, tomato soup and corn.

- 1/2 pound uncooked wagon wheel pasta
- 1 pound ground beef
- 1/2 cup chopped onion
- 1-3/4 cups water
- 1 can (10-3/4 ounces) condensed tomato soup, undiluted
- 1 can (8-3/4 ounces) whole kernel corn, drained
- 1 envelope spaghetti sauce mix

Wagon Wheel Supper

Herbed Chicken Stir-Fry

- 1/8 teaspoon pepper
- 4 ounces sliced Colby cheese, cut into strips

Cook pasta according to package directions. Meanwhile, in a large skillet, cook beef and onion over medium heat until meat is no longer pink; drain.

Stir in the water, soup, corn, spaghetti sauce mix and pepper. Bring to a boil. Reduce heat; simmer, uncovered, for 2-3 minutes or until heated through.

Drain pasta; stir into beef mixture. Top with cheese; cook and stir for 2 minutes or until cheese is melted. **Yield:** 4 servings.

Wednesday

Herbed Chicken Stir-Fry

(Pictured above)

Prep/Total Time: 25 min.

Fresh zucchini and squash brighten this chicken-and-rice dinner. Seasoned with garlic, oregano and lemon juice, it has family-pleasing taste.

- 2-3/4 cups chicken broth, *divided*
- 2 cups uncooked instant rice
- 2 teaspoons cornstarch
- 1 pound boneless skinless chicken breasts, cut into 1-inch strips
- 1 cup sliced yellow summer squash
- 1 cup sliced zucchini
- 1/2 cup chopped onion
- 1/2 teaspoon minced garlic
- 2 tablespoons prepared herb butter
- 1 teaspoon lemon juice
- 1/2 teaspoon dried oregano
- 1/4 teaspoon *each* salt and pepper

In a small saucepan, bring 2 cups broth to a boil. Stir in rice. Remove from the heat; cover and let stand for 5 minutes. In a small bowl, combine cornstarch and remaining broth until smooth; set aside.

In a large skillet or wok, stir-fry the chicken, yellow squash, zucchini, onion and garlic in herb butter for 5 minutes or until lightly browned. Stir in the lemon juice, oregano, salt and pepper. Stir cornstarch mixture and add to pan. Bring to a boil; cook and stir for 2 minutes or until thickened. Serve with rice. **Yield:** 4 servings.

**Herb Roasted Squash
Parmesan Pork Chops**

Thursday

Tortellini-Shrimp Caesar Salad

(Pictured below)

Prep/Total Time: 25 min.

This fun main dish dresses up ordinary Caesar salad with two surprise ingredients: cheese tortellini and popcorn shrimp. It makes a fantastic and filling combo.

- **2 cups frozen breaded popcorn shrimp**
- **1 package (9 ounces) refrigerated cheese tortellini**
- **8 cups torn romaine**
- **1 medium tomato, chopped**
- **1/2 cup Caesar salad dressing**

Prepare shrimp and tortellini according to package directions. In a large salad bowl, combine romaine and tomato; drizzle with dressing and toss to coat. Drain tortellini; toss with salad. Top with shrimp. **Yield:** 4 servings.

Friday

Parmesan Pork Chops

(Pictured above right)

Prep/Total Time: 25 min.

Parmesan really comes through in these moist, boneless chops that are ready in no time. The satisfying main course is ideal with veggies, rice or mashed potatoes.

Tortellini-Shrimp Caesar Salad

- **1/4 cup butter**
- **1/4 cup grated Parmesan cheese**
- **2 tablespoons all-purpose flour**
- **2 teaspoons Italian seasoning**
- **2 teaspoons dried parsley flakes**
- **1/4 teaspoon pepper**
- **4 boneless pork loin chops (3/4 inch thick and 6 ounces *each*)**
- **2 tablespoons olive oil**

In a shallow microwave-safe bowl, melt butter. In a large resealable plastic bag, combine the Parmesan cheese, flour, Italian seasoning, parsley and pepper. Dip each pork chop in butter; place in bag, one at a time, and shake to coat. In a large skillet, cook pork in oil over medium heat for 7-8 minutes on each side or until juices run clear. **Yield:** 4 servings.

Herb Roasted Squash

(Pictured above)

Prep/Total Time: 20 min.

Need a quick-to-cook side dish? This simple squash medley will do the trick. Seasoned with herbs, it enhances nearly any meal.

- **1 medium zucchini, cut into 1/4-inch slices**
- **1 yellow summer squash, cut into 1/4-inch slices**
- **1 medium tomato, seeded and chopped**
- **1/2 cup chopped onion**
- **1 teaspoon dried parsley flakes**
- **1/2 teaspoon dried rosemary, crushed**
- **1/4 teaspoon salt**
- **1/4 teaspoon pepper**
- **1 tablespoon olive oil**

In a large bowl, combine the first eight ingredients. Drizzle with oil and toss to coat.

Place vegetables in a single layer in a greased 15-in. x 10-in. x 1-in. baking pan. Bake, uncovered, at 450° for 10-15 minutes or until lightly browned and tender, stirring once. **Yield:** 4 servings.

Week 3

Shopping List

Check for these staples:

- brown sugar
- Italian seasoning
- salt
- pepper
- chili powder
- cumin
- crushed red pepper flakes
- lime juice
- Liquid Smoke
- milk
- cider vinegar
- dry red wine
- olive oil
- soy sauce
- minced garlic
- butter
- mustard
- ketchup
- cornstarch

Shop for these items:

- 1 fresh pineapple
- 2 medium green peppers
- 5 medium tomatoes
- 1 medium plum tomato
- 2 medium onions
- 2 small onions
- 1 bunch fresh cilantro
- 1 package (1-1/4 pounds) boneless beef sirloin steak
- 1 package (1/2 pound) boneless skinless chicken breasts
- 4 red snapper fillets (6 ounces *each*)
- 1 package (1 pound) Italian sausage links
- 1 package (16 ounces) California-blend vegetables
- 1 package flour tortillas (10 inches)
- 1 loaf (20 inches) French bread
- 1 package (12 ounces) hot dog buns
- 1/2 dozen eggs
- 12 ounces Havarti cheese
- 6 ounces pepper Jack cheese
- 1 package (3 ounces) cream cheese

Time-Saving Tips

- On Monday, set aside 2 cups of salsa for Wednesday's Grilled Fish with Bruschetta (recipe on p. 117). Also reserve 1 cup of pineapple for the Fajita Skillet (recipe on p. 118) on Thursday.
- Place the vegetables and sausages on the grill together for Friday's meal, and everything will be ready to eat at the same time.

Beef Quesadillas with Salsa

Monday

Beef Quesadillas with Salsa

(Pictured above)

Prep/Total Time: 30 min.

These easy, cheesy steak quesadillas are packed with beef and served with a homemade pineapple salsa. Each serving is sweet and not too spicy.

- 3/4 pound boneless beef sirloin steak, cut into thin strips
- 1/8 teaspoon salt
- 1/8 teaspoon pepper
- 2 to 3 tablespoons olive oil, *divided*
- 1-1/2 cups (6 ounces) shredded pepper Jack cheese
- 4 flour tortillas (10 inches)

SALSA:
- 4 medium tomatoes, chopped
- 1-1/2 cups cubed fresh pineapple
- 1/2 cup chopped onion
- 1/4 cup minced fresh cilantro
- 2 tablespoons lime juice
- 1 tablespoon olive oil
- 1/2 teaspoon salt
- 1/4 teaspoon crushed red pepper flakes

Sprinkle steak with salt and pepper. In a large skillet, saute steak in 1 tablespoon oil until no longer pink.

Sprinkle 1/4 cup cheese over one side of each tortilla; top with 1/3 cup beef and remaining cheese. Fold tortillas over. In another large skillet, cook two quesadillas in 1 tablespoon oil over medium heat for 1-2 minutes on each side or until cheese is melted. Repeat with remaining quesadillas and oil. Cut into wedges.

In a large bowl, combine the salsa ingredients; serve with quesadillas. Cover and refrigerate remaining salsa.
Yield: 4 servings (4-1/2 cups salsa).

California Quiche

(Pictured below)

Prep: 15 min. **Bake:** 30 min.

You can serve this refreshing dish for a simple weeknight dinner or as a hearty weekend brunch. With both Havarti and cream cheese, the quiche is rich, elegant and filling. Fresh tomato adds a splash of color.

    5 eggs
  3/4 cup milk
  1/4 teaspoon pepper
    4 ounces Havarti cheese, shredded
    1 package (3 ounces) cream cheese, cubed
  3/4 cup frozen California-blend vegetables,
        thawed and patted dry
    1 medium plum tomato, thinly sliced
  1/3 cup butter, softened
    1 teaspoon minced garlic
   12 slices French bread (1 inch thick)

In a small bowl, whisk the eggs, milk and pepper. Stir in cheeses and vegetables. Pour into a greased 9-in. pie plate. Top with tomato slices. Bake at 375° for 30-35 minutes or until a knife inserted near the center comes out clean. Let stand for 5 minutes.

Meanwhile, in a small bowl, combine butter and garlic; spread over both sides of each slice of bread. Broil 3-4 in. from the heat for 1-2 minutes on each side or until lightly browned. Serve with quiche. **Yield:** 6 servings.

Grilled Fish with Bruschetta

Grilled Fish with Bruschetta

(Pictured above)

Prep/Total Time: 30 min.

Tender red snapper is treated to a mustard-glazed onion topping in this scrumptious main dish. Paired with a dressed-up bruschetta side, the grilled fish will definitely surprise and delight everyone at the table.

    1 medium onion, thinly sliced
    6 tablespoons lime juice
    2 tablespoons brown sugar
    2 tablespoons butter
    1 tablespoon prepared mustard
    4 red snapper fillets (6 ounces *each*)
BRUSCHETTA:
  1/4 cup olive oil
    8 slices French bread (1 inch thick)
    8 ounces Havarti cheese, sliced
    2 cups salsa

In a small skillet over medium heat, cook and stir the onion, lime juice, brown sugar, butter and mustard for 4-5 minutes or until onion is tender and liquid is almost evaporated.

Place each fillet on a double thickness of heavy-duty foil (about 12 in. square). Top with onion mixture. Fold foil over fish and seal tightly. Grill, covered, over medium heat for 6-8 minutes or until fish flakes easily with a fork.

Meanwhile, brush oil over both sides of bread. Grill for 30-60 seconds on each side or until lightly browned. Top each slice of bread with a slice of cheese; grill 1 minute longer or until cheese is melted. Top with salsa.

Open foil packets carefully to allow steam to escape. Serve fish with bruschetta. **Yield:** 4 servings.

California Quiche

Fajita Skillet

Barbecue Italian Sausages

Prep/Total Time: 30 min.

Served with a tangy barbecue sauce, these sausages are fast and flavorful. They're great for special events, too, such as a Super Bowl party.

- 4 uncooked Italian sausage links
- 1/2 cup chopped green pepper
- 1/4 cup chopped onion
- 1 tablespoon olive oil
- 1/3 cup dry red wine *or* beef broth
- 1/2 cup ketchup
- 1 tablespoon cider vinegar
- 1 tablespoon soy sauce
- 1 teaspoon brown sugar
- 1/4 teaspoon ground cumin
- 1/4 teaspoon chili powder
- 1/8 teaspoon Liquid Smoke, optional
- 4 hot dog buns, split

Grill sausages, covered, over medium heat for 5-8 minutes on each side or until no longer pink. Meanwhile, in a large skillet, saute green pepper and onion in oil for 3-4 minutes or until tender. Stir in wine or broth. Bring to a boil; cook for 2 minutes or until liquid is evaporated.

Stir in the ketchup, vinegar, soy sauce, brown sugar, cumin, chili powder and Liquid Smoke if desired. Bring to a boil. Reduce heat; simmer for 2-3 minutes or until thickened. Place sausages in buns; serve with sauce. **Yield:** 4 servings.

Grilled Herb Vegetables

Prep/Total Time: 20 min.

With convenient frozen veggies and just four other ingredients, this side dish takes the worry out of dinner while offering a fresh summer taste.

> ✓ Uses less fat, sugar or salt. Includes Nutrition Facts and Diabetic Exchanges.

- 3-1/2 cups frozen California-blend vegetables, thawed
- 1 tablespoon olive oil
- 1 teaspoon Italian seasoning
- 1 teaspoon minced garlic
- 1/4 teaspoon salt

In a large bowl, combine all ingredients. Transfer to a double thickness of heavy-duty foil (about 14 in. x 12 in.). Fold foil over vegetables and seal tightly.

Grill, covered, over medium heat for 12-14 minutes or until vegetables are tender, turning once. Open foil carefully to allow steam to escape. **Yield:** 4 servings.

Nutrition Facts: 3/4 cup equals 59 calories, 3 g fat (trace saturated fat), 0 cholesterol, 180 mg sodium, 5 g carbohydrate, 2 g fiber, 2 g protein. **Diabetic Exchanges:** 1 vegetable, 1/2 fat.

Fajita Skillet

(Pictured above)

Prep/Total Time: 30 min.

Chicken, beef, vegetables and pineapple are topped with crispy tortilla strips for this mouth-watering main dish.

- 2 flour tortillas (10 inches), cut into 1/2-inch strips
- 3 tablespoons olive oil, *divided*
- 1/2 pound boneless skinless chicken breasts, cut into strips
- 1/2 pound boneless beef sirloin steak, cut into thin strips
- 1 medium green pepper, sliced
- 1 small onion, sliced
- 2 tablespoons soy sauce
- 2 teaspoons brown sugar
- 1/2 teaspoon chili powder
- 1/2 teaspoon ground cumin
- 1/4 teaspoon pepper
- 1 teaspoon cornstarch
- 2 tablespoons lime juice
- 1 cup cubed fresh pineapple
- 1 medium tomato, coarsely chopped

In a large skillet, fry tortilla strips in 2 tablespoons oil on both sides for 1 minute or until golden brown. Drain on paper towels.

In the same skillet, cook the chicken, beef, green pepper, onion, soy sauce, brown sugar, chili powder, cumin and pepper in remaining oil for 3-4 minutes or until chicken juices run clear and vegetables are crisp-tender.

In a small bowl, combine cornstarch and lime juice until smooth. Stir into skillet. Bring to a boil; cook and stir for 1 minute or until thickened. Stir in pineapple and tomato; heat through. Serve with tortilla strips. **Yield:** 4 servings.

Week 4

Focaccia Pork Salad

Shopping List

Check for these staples:

- salt
- pepper
- onion powder
- steak seasoning
- poultry seasoning
- dried tarragon
- dried thyme
- dried oregano
- minced garlic
- balsamic vinegar
- cider vinegar
- olive oil
- Dijon mustard
- butter
- mayonnaise
- chicken broth
- brown sugar
- onions

Shop for these items:

- 1 medium head romaine lettuce
- 2 medium bananas
- 1/4 medium seedless watermelon
- 2 containers (6 ounces *each*) fresh raspberries
- 2 medium sweet red peppers
- 1-1/2 pounds fresh asparagus
- 2 cups deli coleslaw
- 4 kaiser rolls
- 1 loaf (12 ounces) focaccia bread
- 1 package (8 ounces) chopped walnuts
- 1 package (16 ounces) linguine
- 1 carton (6 ounces) custard-style vanilla yogurt
- 1 package (8 ounces) provolone cheese slices
- 1 package (4 ounces) crumbled blue cheese
- 1 package (12 ounces) ready-to-serve fully cooked bacon
- 8 boneless skinless chicken breast halves (6 ounces *each*)
- 1 pound boneless beef sirloin steak
- 1 package (about 27 ounces) honey-mustard center cut pork loin filet

Time-Saving Tips

- For Wednesday's kabobs, cut the steak, bread and vegetables the same size for even grilling.
- To flatten the chicken breasts for Tuesday's main course, place them between two pieces of waxed paper. Starting in the center and working out to the edges, pound the waxed paper-covered chicken lightly with the flat side of a meat mallet.

Monday

Focaccia Pork Salad

(Pictured above)

Prep/Total Time: 25 min.

Dinner will be done in a dash with this fuss-free salad flavored with honey-mustard pork, blue cheese and a simple homemade dressing.

- 6 ounces focaccia bread, cubed
- 3/4 pound honey-mustard center cut pork loin filet, cut into 1-inch pieces
- 2 teaspoons plus 1/4 cup olive oil, *divided*
- 4 cups torn romaine
- 1/2 cup crumbled blue cheese
- 2 tablespoons balsamic vinegar
- 1/2 teaspoon dried oregano

Place bread cubes on an ungreased baking sheet. Bake at 400° for 8-10 minutes or until golden brown.

Meanwhile, in a large skillet, brown pork in 2 teaspoons oil over medium heat for 5-6 minutes or until no longer pink.

In a large bowl, combine the romaine, blue cheese, bread cubes and pork. In a small bowl, whisk the vinegar, oregano and remaining oil. Drizzle over salad and toss to coat. Serve immediately. **Yield:** 6 servings.

Editor's Note: This recipe was tested with Hormel honey-mustard center cut pork loin filet. The package weighs about 27 ounces.

Plenty of Pork

DON'T WORRY about measuring the 3/4 pound of pork loin for Focaccia Pork Salad (recipe above). Just cut the entire pork loin in half. It won't matter if there's a little extra in the salad or Thursday's pasta.

Chicken Rolls with Raspberry Sauce

(Pictured below)

Prep: 25 min. **Bake:** 35 min.

Give that weeknight menu an elegant feel with this impressive (but easy!) blue-cheese-stuffed chicken. The raspberry sauce is also great on grilled pork tenderloin.

- 4 boneless skinless chicken breast halves (6 ounces *each*)
- 1/2 cup crumbled blue cheese
- 4 strips ready-to-serve fully cooked bacon, crumbled
- 2 tablespoons butter, melted, *divided*
- Salt and pepper to taste
- 2 cups fresh raspberries
- 1/4 cup chicken broth
- 4 teaspoons brown sugar
- 1 tablespoon balsamic vinegar
- 1/2 teaspoon minced garlic
- 1/4 teaspoon dried oregano

Flatten the chicken to 1/4-in. thickness; sprinkle with the blue cheese and bacon to within 1/2 in. of edges. Roll up each jelly-roll style, starting with a short side; secure with toothpicks.

Place in a greased 8-in. square baking dish. Brush with 1 tablespoon butter; sprinkle with salt and pepper. Bake, uncovered, at 375° for 35-40 minutes or until chicken juices run clear.

Meanwhile, in a small saucepan, combine berries, broth, brown sugar, vinegar, garlic and oregano. Bring to a boil. Reduce heat; simmer, uncovered, for 5 minutes or until thickened. Press through a sieve; discard seeds. Stir in remaining butter until smooth. Discard toothpicks from chicken; serve with berry sauce. **Yield:** 4 servings.

Savory Asparagus

(Pictured below left)

Prep/Total Time: 15 min.

This fresh asparagus seasoned with aromatic tarragon can dress up just about any meal. For a twist, substitute broccoli for the asparagus.

 Uses less fat, sugar or salt. Includes Nutrition Facts and Diabetic Exchanges.

- 1 pound fresh asparagus, trimmed
- 2 tablespoons olive oil
- 1/4 to 1/2 teaspoon dried tarragon
- 1/4 teaspoon onion powder
- 1/8 teaspoon pepper

In a large skillet, bring 1/2 in. of water to a boil. Add asparagus; cover and cook for 5-7 minutes or until crisp-tender, stirring occasionally.

Meanwhile, in a small bowl, combine the oil, tarragon, onion powder and pepper until blended. Drain the asparagus; drizzle with the oil mixture and toss to coat. **Yield:** 4 servings.

Nutrition Facts: about 5 spears equals 74 calories, 7 g fat (1 g saturated fat), 0 cholesterol, 6 mg sodium, 3 g carbohydrate, 1 g fiber, 1 g protein. **Diabetic Exchanges:** 1 vegetable, 1 fat.

Steak Sandwich Kabobs

Prep/Total Time: 25 min.

Seasoned steak skewers are grilled with focaccia bread cubes and fresh vegetables and topped with provolone cheese for this fantastic main course. Deli coleslaw, spruced up with some chopped walnuts, makes an effortless side for the kabobs.

- 1 pound boneless beef sirloin steak, cut into 1-inch cubes
- 1 teaspoon steak seasoning
- 1 medium sweet red pepper, cut into 1-inch chunks
- 6 ounces focaccia bread, cut into 1-inch cubes
- 1 medium onion, cut into 1-inch chunks
- 1 tablespoon olive oil
- 3 slices provolone cheese, cut into strips
- 2 cups deli coleslaw
- 1/2 cup chopped walnuts

Sprinkle the beef with the steak seasoning. Alternately thread the beef, red pepper chunks, bread cubes and onion chunks onto four metal or soaked wooden skewers; brush with oil.

Grill, covered, over medium heat for 8-10 minutes or until meat reaches desired doneness, turning occasionally. Top with cheese; grill 1-2 minutes longer or until cheese is melted.

In a small bowl, combine the coleslaw and walnuts. Serve with kabobs. **Yield:** 4 servings.

Chicken Rolls with Raspberry Sauce
Savory Asparagus

Pork Linguine Toss

Bacon-Provolone Chicken Sandwiches

Prep/Total Time: 30 min.

Friday-night fun will get a kick-start from these delicious sandwiches...and will continue with festive Banana Split Fruit Salad (recipe below). Bacon and provolone take these hearty chicken sandwiches over the top in flavor.

>   4 boneless skinless chicken breast halves
>   (6 ounces *each*)
>   1 teaspoon poultry seasoning
>   1 tablespoon olive oil
>   4 kaiser rolls, split
>   8 strips ready-to-serve fully cooked bacon
>   4 slices provolone cheese
>   8 romaine leaves
>   1 small onion, sliced
> 1/4 cup mayonnaise

Flatten chicken to 1/4-in. thickness; sprinkle with poultry seasoning. In a large skillet, cook chicken in oil over medium heat for 4-5 minutes on each side or until juices run clear; drain.

On roll bottoms, layer the bacon, chicken and cheese. Broil 4-6 in. from the heat for 1-2 minutes or until cheese is melted. Top with romaine and onion. Spread mayonnaise over the cut side of roll tops and replace the tops. **Yield:** 4 servings.

Banana Split Fruit Salad

Prep/Total Time: 20 min.

Let these colorful, individual medleys celebrate the end of a workweek and the beginning of a wonderful weekend! Watermelon, bananas and raspberries make for a bright and healthy treat. It's a yummy alternative to high-fat, high-calorie desserts.

☑ Uses less fat, sugar or salt. Includes Nutrition Facts.

>   2 medium bananas
> 1/4 medium seedless watermelon
>   1 carton (6 ounces) custard-style vanilla yogurt
>   1 cup fresh raspberries
> 1/4 cup chopped walnuts

Cut each banana in half widthwise. Cut each half into quarters lengthwise. Using an ice cream scoop, scoop four balls from watermelon (save remaining melon for another use).

Arrange four banana quarters in each shallow dessert bowl; top with watermelon. Spoon yogurt over melon. Sprinkle with raspberries and walnuts. Serve immediately. **Yield:** 4 servings.

Nutrition Facts: 1 serving equals 248 calories, 6 g fat (1 g saturated fat), 4 mg cholesterol, 35 mg sodium, 54 g carbohydrate, 6 g fiber, 6 g protein.

Pork Linguine Toss

(Pictured above)

Prep/Total Time: 30 min.

With crisp asparagus and sweet red pepper strips, this bold dish is special enough to serve to company, but it also makes a family-pleasing weeknight meal.

>   8 ounces uncooked linguine
>   1 medium sweet red pepper, julienned
> 1/2 pound fresh asparagus, trimmed and cut
>   into 1-inch pieces
> 3/4 pound honey-mustard center cut pork loin
>   filet, cut into 1/2-inch strips
>   2 teaspoons olive oil
> DRESSING:
> 1/2 cup olive oil
> 4-1/2 teaspoons Dijon mustard
>   1 tablespoon cider vinegar
> 1/2 teaspoon minced garlic
> 1/2 teaspoon dried thyme
> 1/4 teaspoon salt
> 1/4 teaspoon pepper

Cook linguine according to package directions, stirring in red pepper during the last 6 minutes and asparagus during the last 3 minutes. Meanwhile, in a large skillet, saute pork in oil until juices run clear.

In a small bowl, combine the dressing ingredients. Drain linguine mixture; add to skillet. Add dressing and toss to coat; heat through. **Yield:** 4 servings.

Editor's Note: This recipe was tested with Hormel honey-mustard center cut pork loin filet. The package weighs about 27 ounces.

Week 5

Check for these staples:

- beef bouillon granules
- butter
- brown sugar
- chicken broth
- cider vinegar
- cornstarch
- creamy peanut butter
- garlic salt
- ground ginger
- ground mustard
- ketchup
- minced garlic
- olive oil
- onions
- pepper
- rice
- soy sauce
- Worcestershire sauce

Shop for these items:

- 1 boneless beef chuck roast (4 pounds)
- 1-1/2 pounds boneless fully cooked ham steaks
- 1-1/4 pounds boneless skinless chicken breasts
- 12 medium red potatoes
- 2 medium sweet red peppers
- 2 medium green peppers
- 1 package (3/4 ounce) chives
- 1/2 pound sliced fresh mushrooms
- 1 package (10 ounces) fresh spinach
- 1 package (16 ounces) frozen chopped broccoli
- 1 package pita breads (12 ounces)
- 1 cup pecan halves
- 1 jar (11 ounces) apple butter
- 1 can (5-1/2 ounces) apple juice
- 7 ounces shredded Swiss cheese
- 2 ounces shredded part-skim mozzarella cheese
- 1 carton (10 ounces) refrigerated Alfredo sauce
- 1 envelope brown gravy mix
- 1 envelope Italian salad dressing mix

Time-Saving Tips

- Take an extra 5 minutes on Monday and cut up some of the finished roast for Thursday's main course. Remember to save 1/4 cup Alfredo Sauce for Friday's pizza.
- Buy pre-cut vegetables from the grocery store for Wednesday's Peanut Chicken Stir-Fry (recipe on p. 123) to reduce prep time.
- Tuesday's broccoli side dish is so easy, you can make it while the ham finishes cooking. You'll have dinner on the table in under half an hour.

Italian Roast with Alfredo Potatoes

Monday

Italian Roast with Alfredo Potatoes

(Pictured above)

Prep: 20 min. **Cook:** 7 hours

This hearty main course is a great way to start the week. And since most of the work is done by your slow cooker, you'll have very little to do for a satisfying supper.

- 1 boneless beef chuck roast (4 pounds), trimmed
- 1 envelope brown gravy mix
- 1 envelope Italian salad dressing mix
- 1/2 cup water
- 1 medium sweet red pepper, cut into 1-inch pieces
- 1 cup chopped green pepper
- 2/3 cup chopped onion
- 8 medium red potatoes, quartered
- 2 tablespoons cornstarch
- 1/4 cup cold water
- 3/4 cup refrigerated Alfredo sauce
- 2 tablespoons butter
- 1/4 teaspoon pepper
- 1 tablespoon minced chives

Cut roast in half; place in a 5-qt. slow cooker. In a small bowl, combine the gravy mix, dressing mix and water; pour over roast. Top with peppers and onion. Cover and cook on low for 7-8 hours or until meat is tender.

Place potatoes in a large saucepan; cover with water. Bring to a boil. Reduce heat; cover and simmer for 15-20 minutes or until tender. Meanwhile, remove roast and cut a portion of the meat into cubes, measuring 3 cups; cover and refrigerate for Meat and Potato Soup (recipe on p. 124) or save for another use. Slice the remaining beef and keep warm.

Skim fat from cooking juices if necessary; pour into a large saucepan. Combine cornstarch and cold water until smooth; stir into cooking juices. Bring to a boil; cook and stir for 2 minutes or until thickened.

Drain potatoes; mash with Alfredo sauce, butter and pepper. Sprinkle with chives. Serve with sliced beef and gravy. **Yield:** 4 servings plus leftovers.

Tuesday

Harvest Ham Steak

(Pictured below)

Prep/Total Time: 20 min.

Sauteed onion tops this delicious ham steak. It gets autumn flavor from apple juice and apple butter.

> 1 medium onion, halved and thinly sliced
> 1/4 teaspoon pepper
> 2 tablespoons butter
> 1 boneless fully cooked ham steak (1 pound)
> 1 teaspoon cornstarch
> 1/2 cup unsweetened apple juice
> 1/2 cup apple butter

In a large skillet, saute onion and pepper in butter until crisp-tender. Remove from pan and set aside. Cut ham steak into four pieces. In the same skillet, brown ham on both sides.

Meanwhile, in a small bowl, combine cornstarch and apple juice until smooth; pour over ham. Bring to a boil; cook and stir 1-2 minutes or until slightly thickened. Reduce heat; spread apple butter over ham. Top with onion. Cover and simmer for 5-7 minutes or until heated through. **Yield:** 4 servings.

Editor's Note: This recipe was tested with commercially prepared apple butter.

Nutty Broccoli
Harvest Ham Steak

Nutty Broccoli

(Pictured below left)

Prep/Total Time: 10 min.

Tender broccoli and crunchy chopped pecans give this effortless side dish an interesting combination of textures. Your family is sure to enjoy this microwave recipe's mouthwatering taste as well.

> 1 package (16 ounces) frozen chopped broccoli, thawed
> 1/2 cup shredded Swiss cheese
> 1/2 cup chopped pecans
> 1/4 cup butter, melted
> 1/4 teaspoon garlic salt
> 1/4 teaspoon pepper

Place broccoli in a large microwave-safe bowl. Combine the remaining ingredients; pour over broccoli. Cover and microwave on high for 3-4 minutes or until tender. **Yield:** 4 servings.

Editor's Note: This recipe was tested in a 1,100-watt microwave.

Wednesday

Peanut Chicken Stir-Fry

Prep/Total Time: 30 min.

Children will dig into this stir-fry accented with soy sauce, peanut butter, ginger and garlic. And busy cooks will appreciate how fast it comes together. Just let the rice cook as you prepare the stir-fry.

> 2 teaspoons cornstarch
> 3/4 cup chicken broth
> 1/4 cup creamy peanut butter
> 3 tablespoons soy sauce
> 1 teaspoon ground ginger
> 1/4 teaspoon pepper
> 1-1/4 pounds boneless skinless chicken breasts, cut into strips
> 3 teaspoons olive oil, *divided*
> 1 cup chopped onion
> 1 cup thinly sliced green pepper
> 1 cup thinly sliced sweet red pepper
> 1-1/2 cups sliced fresh mushrooms
> 1 teaspoon minced garlic
> Hot cooked rice

In a small bowl, combine the first six ingredients until smooth; set aside.

In a large skillet or wok, stir-fry chicken in 1-1/2 teaspoons oil for 3-4 minutes or until no longer pink. Remove with a slotted spoon and keep warm.

Stir-fry onion and peppers in remaining oil for 3 minutes. Add mushrooms and garlic; stir-fry 3-4 minutes longer or until vegetables are crisp-tender.

Stir the cornstarch mixture and add to the pan. Bring to a boil; cook and stir for 2 minutes or until thickened. Add the chicken and heat through. Serve with rice. **Yield:** 4 servings.

Thursday

Meat and Potato Soup

(Pictured below)

Prep/Total Time: 30 min.

Chunks of potatoes and roast beef come together for this rich and filling soup. The result is a well-balanced, flavorful main course that's perfect for cool days.

 Uses less fat, sugar or salt. Includes Nutrition Facts and Diabetic Exchanges.

    4 cups water
    3 cups cubed cooked beef chuck roast
    4 medium red potatoes, cubed
    4 ounces sliced fresh mushrooms
1/2 cup chopped onion
1/4 cup ketchup
    2 teaspoons beef bouillon granules
    2 teaspoons cider vinegar
    1 teaspoon brown sugar
    1 teaspoon Worcestershire sauce
1/8 teaspoon ground mustard
    1 cup coarsely chopped fresh spinach

In a Dutch oven, combine the first 11 ingredients. Bring to a boil. Reduce heat; cover and simmer for 14-18 minutes or until potatoes are tender. Stir in spinach; cook 1-2 minutes longer or until tender. **Yield:** 6 servings (2 quarts).

Nutrition Facts: 1-1/3 cups equals 210 calories, 8 g fat (3 g saturated fat), 49 mg cholesterol, 431 mg sodium, 18 g carbohydrate, 2 g fiber, 17 g protein. **Diabetic Exchanges:** 2 lean meat, 1 starch.

Spinach Salad with Apple Dressing
Ham 'n' Cheese Pizzas

Friday

Ham 'n' Cheese Pizzas

(Pictured above)

Prep/Total Time: 20 min.

With leftover ham from Tuesday night's meal plus cheese and Alfredo sauce, these pizzas are sure winners.

1/4 cup refrigerated Alfredo sauce
    4 pita breads (6 inches)
    1 cup (4 ounces) shredded Swiss cheese
1-3/4 cups cubed fully cooked ham
1/2 cup shredded part-skim mozzarella cheese
    1 tablespoon minced chives

Spread Alfredo sauce over pita breads. Top with Swiss cheese, ham, mozzarella cheese and chives.

Place on an ungreased baking sheet. Bake at 350° for 10-15 minutes or until cheese is melted. **Yield:** 4 servings.

Spinach Salad with Apple Dressing

(Pictured above)

Prep/Total Time: 10 min.

Apple butter gives a delightful sweetness to this spinach salad. Pecan halves add a pleasant crunch.

1/2 cup apple butter
    3 tablespoons olive oil
    1 tablespoon cider vinegar
1/8 teaspoon pepper
    4 cups fresh spinach, torn
1/2 cup pecan halves
1/4 cup shredded Swiss cheese

For dressing, in a jar with a tight-fitting lid, combine the apple butter, oil, vinegar and pepper; shake well. Divide spinach among four plates; sprinkle with pecans and cheese. Drizzle with dressing. **Yield:** 4 servings.

Editor's Note: This recipe was tested with commercially prepared apple butter.

Meat and Potato Soup

Week 6

Shopping List

Check for these staples:

- butter
- pepper
- salt
- cayenne pepper
- chicken broth
- seafood seasoning
- Dijon mustard
- soft bread crumbs
- dill weed
- sugar
- egg
- Worcestershire sauce
- all-purpose flour
- garlic powder
- ground cinnamon
- Italian seasoning
- ketchup
- lemon juice
- maple pancake syrup
- milk
- minced garlic
- nutmeg
- olive oil
- onion
- vegetable oil

Shop for these items:

2	medium sweet red peppers
6	medium sweet potatoes
1	package (8 ounces) sliced fresh mushrooms
1	loaf white bread
1	can (16 ounces) whole-berry cranberry sauce
1	package (13.5 ounces) tortilla chips
1	package (16 ounces) gemelli pasta
1	envelope taco seasoning
1	package (8 ounces) shredded cheddar cheese
8	ounces Gouda cheese
1	package (3 ounces) cream cheese
1	package (16 ounces) frozen French-style green beans
1	package (16 ounces) frozen corn
2	packages (10 ounces *each*) frozen chopped spinach
2	pounds ground beef
1	pound orange roughy fillets
3/4	pound sliced deli turkey
1	package (2.1 ounces) ready-to-serve fully cooked bacon

Time-Saving Tips

- On Thursday, prep the green beans while the beef patties cook. Begin cooking the beans when the patties are done. To save time on Friday, crumble extra bacon from Thursday's side dish and store the bacon in a resealable plastic bag in the fridge.

Monday

Nacho Mac 'n' Cheese

(Pictured above)

Prep/Total Time: 25 min.

Creamy and comforting, this family-friendly dinner is a great way to begin the week. And since most of the ingredients are mixed in one dish, cleanup is a cinch!

- 3 cups uncooked gemelli *or* spiral pasta
- 1 pound ground beef
- 2 cups chopped sweet red peppers
- 1/4 cup butter, cubed
- 1/4 cup all-purpose flour
- 1 envelope taco seasoning
- 1/4 teaspoon pepper
- 2-1/4 cups milk
- 2 cups (8 ounces) shredded cheddar cheese
- 1 cup frozen corn, thawed
- 1 cup coarsely crushed tortilla chips

Cook gemelli according to package directions. Meanwhile, in a Dutch oven, cook beef and red peppers over medium heat until meat is no longer pink; drain.

Stir in the butter, flour, taco seasoning and pepper until blended. Gradually stir in milk. Bring to a boil; cook and stir for 2 minutes or until thickened. Remove from the heat. Stir in cheese and corn until cheese is melted.

Drain gemelli; add to beef mixture and stir to coat. Sprinkle with tortilla chips. **Yield:** 6 servings.

Just Gemelli

GEMELLI is a spiral-shaped pasta that consists of two short rods twisted together. Gemelli is an Italian word that means "twins." This type of pasta is commonly used in pastas salads and casseroles.

Skillet Fish with Spinach

Tuesday

Skillet Fish with Spinach

(Pictured above)

Prep/Total Time: 25 min.

These tender fish fillets get a burst of flavor from seafood seasoning. Paired with dressed-up spinach, this simple main course is guaranteed to impress!

    4 orange roughy fillets (4 ounces *each*)
1-1/2 teaspoons seafood seasoning
    2 tablespoons olive oil
    2 tablespoons butter
    1 cup sliced fresh mushrooms
    1 package (10 ounces) frozen chopped
       spinach, thawed and squeezed dry
  1/2 cup chicken broth
Salt and pepper to taste

Sprinkle fillets with seafood seasoning. In a large skillet, cook fillets in oil and butter over medium heat for 3-4 minutes on each side or until fish flakes easily with a fork. Remove and keep warm.

    Add mushrooms to the skillet; cook, uncovered, for 2 minutes. Add spinach and broth; cook 3-4 minutes longer or until spinach is heated through. Season with salt and pepper. Serve with fish. **Yield:** 4 servings.

Wednesday

Turkey Wafflewiches

(Pictured at right)

Prep/Total Time: 15 min.

Who knew sandwiches could be so fun? These will get lots of smiles with their great taste and whimsical touch.

    1 package (3 ounces) cream cheese, softened
  1/4 cup whole-berry cranberry sauce
    1 tablespoon maple pancake syrup
  1/4 teaspoon pepper
    8 slices white bread
  3/4 pound sliced deli turkey
    2 tablespoons butter, softened

In a small mixing bowl, beat cream cheese, cranberry sauce, syrup and pepper until combined. Spread over four slices of bread; top with turkey and remaining bread. Spread butter over both sides of sandwiches.

    Cook in a preheated waffle iron or indoor grill according to manufacturer's directions for 2-3 minutes or until golden brown. **Yield:** 4 servings.

Sweet Potato Chips

(Pictured below)

Prep: 10 min. + soaking **Cook:** 5 min./batch

These colorful chips have a balanced blend of sweet and spicy. Once you try these, you may never want to go back to the packaged variety!

    2 medium sweet potatoes, peeled
  1/2 teaspoon salt
  1/4 teaspoon ground cinnamon
  1/4 teaspoon cayenne pepper
Oil for deep-fat frying

Cut sweet potatoes into very thin slices; soak in cold water for 30 minutes.

    Drain; pat dry with paper towels. In a small bowl, combine the salt, cinnamon and cayenne; set aside.

    In an electric skillet or deep-fat fryer, heat oil to 375°. Fry potatoes in batches for 3-4 minutes or until golden brown, turning frequently. Remove with a slotted spoon; drain on paper towels. Sprinkle with seasoning mixture. Serve warm. **Yield:** 4 servings.

Turkey Wafflewiches
Sweet Potato Chips

Thursday

Salisbury Steak with Gemelli

(Pictured on page 108)

Prep/Total Time: 30 min.

This streamlined classic has plenty of appeal. Keep the recipe handy because it's ideal for busy weeknights.

- 1 egg
- 1/2 cup soft bread crumbs
- 1 teaspoon Italian seasoning
- 1/2 teaspoon pepper
- 1/2 teaspoon minced garlic
- 1 pound ground beef
- 1 tablespoon olive oil
- 1 cup sliced fresh mushrooms
- 2 tablespoons all-purpose flour
- 1 cup chicken broth
- 1 tablespoon ketchup
- 1 teaspoon Worcestershire sauce
- Hot cooked gemelli *or* spiral pasta

In a large bowl, combine the egg, bread crumbs, Italian seasoning, pepper and garlic. Crumble beef over mixture and mix well. Shape into four patties.

In a large skillet, cook patties in oil over medium-high heat for 5-7 minutes on each side or until meat is no longer pink. Remove and keep warm. Drain, reserving 2 tablespoons drippings. Saute mushrooms in drippings until tender. Stir in flour until blended. Gradually stir in the broth, ketchup and Worcestershire sauce. Bring to a boil; cook and stir for 2 minutes or until thickened.

Return patties to the skillet. Bring to a boil. Reduce heat; simmer, uncovered, for 3-4 minutes or until heated through. Serve with gemelli. **Yield:** 4 servings.

Dressed-Up French Green Beans

(Pictured on page 108)

Prep/Total Time: 20 min.

Lemon juice, bacon and Dijon mustard transform ordinary green beans into a standout partner for any entree.

✓ Uses less fat, sugar or salt. Includes Nutrition Facts and Diabetic Exchanges.

- 4 cups frozen French-style green beans
- 2 tablespoons crumbled cooked bacon
- 2 teaspoons lemon juice
- 2 teaspoons olive oil
- 2 teaspoons Dijon mustard
- 1/2 teaspoon sugar
- 1/2 teaspoon garlic powder
- 1/2 teaspoon dill weed
- 1/4 teaspoon pepper

Cook green beans according to package directions. Meanwhile, in a small bowl, combine the remaining ingredients. Drain beans; add bacon mixture and gently stir to coat. **Yield:** 4 servings.

Sweet Potato Spinach Bake

Nutrition Facts: 3/4 cup equals 67 calories, 3 g fat (1 g saturated fat), 3 mg cholesterol, 179 mg sodium, 8 g carbohydrate, 2 g fiber, 3 g protein. **Diabetic Exchanges:** 2 vegetable, 1/2 fat.

Editor's Note: This recipe was tested in a 1,100-watt microwave.

Friday

Sweet Potato Spinach Bake

(Pictured above)

Prep: 25 min. **Bake:** 10 min.

This deliciously different recipe dresses up sweet potatoes and spinach for a rich, savory meal-in-one.

- 4 medium sweet potatoes, peeled and thinly sliced
- 1/2 cup water
- 3 tablespoons finely chopped onion
- 1/4 cup butter, cubed
- 1 package (10 ounces) frozen chopped spinach, thawed and squeezed dry
- 1/4 cup all-purpose flour
- 1/4 teaspoon salt
- 1/4 teaspoon ground nutmeg
- 1/4 teaspoon pepper
- 2 cups milk
- 2 cups (8 ounces) shredded Gouda cheese
- 3 tablespoons crumbled cooked bacon

Place sweet potatoes in a 1-1/2-qt. microwave-safe dish; add water. Cover and microwave on high for 8-10 minutes or until tender.

Meanwhile, in a saucepan, saute onion in butter until tender. Add spinach. Stir in flour and seasonings until blended. Gradually stir in milk. Bring to a boil; cook and stir 2 minutes or until thickened. Remove from the heat.

Drain sweet potatoes. Spread half of the spinach mixture into a greased 11-in. x 7-in. x 2-in. baking dish. Top with half of the potatoes and cheese. Repeat layers. Sprinkle with bacon. Cover and bake at 375° for 10-15 minutes or until bubbly. **Yield:** 4 servings.

Chapter 8

Speedy Sides and Salads

TODAY, on-the-go family cooks are finding it easier than ever to round out menus and serve loved ones complete, home-cooked meals.

Thanks to convenience items and quick cooking methods, it's a cinch to whip up lip-smacking side dishes such as crisp-tender Stir-Fried Carrots and Creamy Broccoli with Cashews.

Perhaps a refreshing salad better suits your family. If so, you'll find plenty to choose from in this chapter. Consider colorful Raspberry Greek Salad or Spinach Penne Toss.

Just turn the page, and you'll discover 42 wonderful ways to complete your family's meals. Best of all, nearly all of the side dishes and salads are table-ready in just half an hour...or less!

EASY ADDITION. Veggie Spiral Salad (p. 140).

Whipped Carrots with Cranberries

1 pound fresh asparagus, trimmed
3 tablespoons unsweetened pineapple juice
1 tablespoon balsamic vinegar
1 teaspoon olive oil
1 teaspoon Dijon mustard
1/2 teaspoon minced garlic

In a large skillet, bring 1/2 in. of water to a boil. Add asparagus; cover and boil for 3 minutes; drain. When cool enough to handle, pat dry. Thread several spears onto two parallel metal or soaked wooden skewers. Repeat with remaining asparagus.

Grill, uncovered, over medium heat for 2 minutes on each side or until asparagus is crisp-tender. For vinaigrette, combine the remaining ingredients in a small bowl. Remove asparagus from skewers; drizzle with vinaigrette. **Yield:** 3 servings.

Nutrition Facts: 2/3 cup equals 46 calories, 2 g fat (trace saturated fat), 0 cholesterol, 52 mg sodium, 6 g carbohydrate, 1 g fiber, 2 g protein. **Diabetic Exchanges:** 1 vegetable, 1/2 fat.

Whipped Carrots with Cranberries

(Pictured above)

Prep/Total Time: 30 min.

This fluffy carrot dish has an autumn feel. The recipe's buttery texture, tangy cranberries and brown sugar make it a great addition to any Thanksgiving dinner.
—*Margie Haen, Menomonee Falls, Wisconsin*

1 pound sliced fresh carrots
3 tablespoons butter
1 tablespoon brown sugar
1/2 teaspoon ground ginger
1/4 teaspoon salt
1/4 cup dried cranberries

Place 2 in. of water in a small saucepan; add carrots. Bring to a boil. Reduce heat; cover and simmer for 15-20 minutes or until tender. Drain.

Place carrots in a food processor; add the butter, brown sugar, ginger and salt. Cover and process until smooth. Transfer to a serving bowl; stir in cranberries. **Yield:** 4 servings.

Asparagus with Mustard Vinaigrette

Prep/Total Time: 30 min.

Here's a special side dish to serve at a patio party or other outdoor event. The grilled asparagus gives a little color to the plate and is very tasty. —*Jo Durlam, Ames, Iowa*

✓ Uses less fat, sugar or salt. Includes Nutrition Facts and Diabetic Exchanges.

Pineapple-Orange Cranberry Sauce

Prep/Total Time: 5 min.

This delicious sauce comes together in no time at all! It's a wonderful way to dress up plain cranberries.
—*Adrienne Nicchio, North Merrick, New York*

1 can (16 ounces) whole-berry cranberry sauce
1 can (11 ounces) mandarin oranges, well drained
1 can (8 ounces) crushed pineapple, well drained
1/4 cup chopped pecans, toasted

In a small serving bowl, combine the cranberry sauce, oranges and pineapple. Stir in pecans just before serving. Refrigerate leftovers. **Yield:** 2-3/4 cups.

Speedy Side Solutions

• My wife and I enjoy steamed vegetables such as onion, peppers, zucchini, squash and broccoli, but we frequently have leftovers. I combine them with cooked rice and canned diced tomatoes. Sprinkled with grated cheese, this makes a scrumptious side dish. —*Paul Toy, Little River, South Carolina*

• I saute onion, green pepper and garlic in butter and stir it into leftover mashed potatoes. Then I sprinkle shredded cheddar or jalapeno cheese on top and bake it in the oven until it's heated through. —*Joyce Tate, Plantation, Florida*

• To create a Mediterranean-style green bean side dish quickly, I prepare a pound of frozen green beans as the package directs. I stir in a 16-ounce jar of medium salsa and a teaspoon of olive oil, then simmer it for 5-10 minutes to blend the flavors. —*Martha Blonde, Lansing, Michigan*

Mediterranean Potato Salad

(Pictured below)

Prep: 25 min. + standing

I use red onion, Greek olives and feta cheese to bring Mediterranean flavors to an all-American classic. With a few minutes of prep and time to chill, the salad makes an ideal side dish on busy summer days. Try it with grilled main courses.
—Jenny Haen, Red Wing, Minnesota

    2 pounds small red potatoes, cut into 1/4-inch
      slices
    3 cups water
    1 small red onion, thinly sliced and separated
      into rings
  1/2 cup pitted Greek olives
  1/2 cup oil-packed sun-dried tomatoes,
      undrained, chopped
  1/2 cup minced fresh parsley
  1/3 cup pine nuts, toasted
  1/8 teaspoon salt
  1/8 teaspoon pepper
  1/2 cup sun-dried tomato salad dressing
    1 package (4 ounces) crumbled tomato and
      basil feta cheese

Place potatoes in a 3-qt. microwave-safe dish; add water. Cover and microwave on high for 12-14 minutes or until tender, stirring once. Drain; rinse in cold water.

In a large bowl, combine the potatoes, onion, olives, tomatoes, parsley, pine nuts, salt and pepper. Drizzle with dressing; toss to coat. Let stand at room temperature for 1 hour before serving. Sprinkle with feta cheese. Refrigerate leftovers. **Yield:** 10 servings.

Editor's Note: This recipe was tested in a 1,100-watt microwave.

Sausage Egg Rolls

Prep: 25 min. **Cook:** 5 min./batch

These easy egg rolls are a snap to assemble with packaged coleslaw mix. Serve them alongside stir-fries or as appetizers.   *—Janet Hommes, Surprise, Arizona*

  1/2 pound bulk pork sausage
  1/4 cup chopped green pepper
    2 tablespoons plus 1-1/2 teaspoons chopped
      onion
  1/2 teaspoon minced garlic
3-3/4 cups coleslaw mix
  1/4 teaspoon pepper
  1/8 teaspoon salt
   16 egg roll wrappers
Oil for frying
Sweet-and-sour sauce

In a large skillet, cook the sausage, green pepper, onion and garlic over medium heat until meat is no longer pink; drain. In a large bowl, combine the coleslaw, pepper and salt; stir in sausage mixture.

Place 1/4 cupful in the center of each egg roll wrapper. Fold bottom corner over filling. Fold sides toward center over filling. Moisten remaining corner with water; roll up tightly to seal.

In an electric skillet or deep-fat fryer, heat 1 in. of oil to 375°. Fry egg rolls, a few at a time, for 2-3 minutes on each side or until golden brown. Drain on paper towels. Serve with sweet-and-sour sauce. **Yield:** 16 egg rolls.

Mediterranean Potato Salad

Raspberry Greek Salad

(Pictured below)

Prep/Total Time: 20 min.

An interesting combination of sweet and salty flavors gives this Greek salad a delicious twist. The tart chewiness of the dried cranberries makes a great complement to the savory feta cheese. I often take this to work for lunch.
—Carine Nadel, Laguna Hills, California

  2 packages (6 ounces *each*) ready-to-serve
     grilled chicken breast strips
  1 package (6 ounces) fresh baby spinach
1/2 pound sliced fresh mushrooms
  1 medium cucumber, peeled and sliced
  4 plum tomatoes, seeded and sliced
1/2 cup crumbled feta cheese
1/4 cup chopped Greek olives
1/4 cup dried cranberries
1/4 cup chopped red onion
1/3 cup raspberry vinaigrette
  4 whole wheat pita breads (6 inches), cut into
     quarters and warmed, optional

In a large salad bowl, toss the first nine ingredients. Just before serving, drizzle with vinaigrette. Serve with pita bread if desired. **Yield:** 8 servings.

Raspberry Greek Salad

Tossed Salad with Wonton Strips

Prep/Total Time: 30 min.

This breezy salad has it all! Fresh tomatoes and pineapple add pretty color and balance the zesty homemade dressing. Topped with golden brown, crispy wonton strips, every bite is terrific. —Bonnie Ann Bussiere-Bermeo
Sparks, Nevada

5-1/2 cups torn romaine
  2 plum tomatoes, chopped
1/2 cup diced fresh pineapple
  3 tablespoons chopped onion
  1 cup vegetable oil
  5 wonton wrappers, cut into 1/4-inch strips
VINAIGRETTE:
  3 tablespoons cider vinegar
1/2 teaspoon ground mustard
1/2 teaspoon lemon juice
1/8 teaspoon salt
Dash pepper
1/2 cup olive oil

In a large salad bowl, combine the romaine, tomatoes, pineapple and onion; set aside. In a large skillet, heat vegetable oil to 375°. Fry wonton strips, in batches, for 10-20 seconds or until lightly browned. Drain on paper towels. Sprinkle over salad.

In a blender, combine the vinegar, mustard, lemon juice, salt and pepper. While processing, gradually add olive oil in a steady stream. Transfer to a pitcher or bowl; serve with salad. **Yield:** 8 servings.

Garden Medley

Prep/Total Time: 20 min.

Not only is this veggie combo nutritious, but it has lots of eye-appeal, too. —Kim Wenzel, Jefferson, Oregon

☑ Uses less fat, sugar or salt. Includes Nutrition Facts and Diabetic Exchanges.

  1 medium carrot, cut into strips
1/2 medium sweet red pepper, cut into strips
  4 teaspoons butter
  1 large zucchini, cut into strips
  1 medium yellow summer squash, cut into
     strips
1-1/2 teaspoons minced fresh parsley
  4 teaspoons prepared Italian salad dressing
1/8 to 1/4 teaspoon pepper
1/8 teaspoon salt

In a large skillet, saute carrot and red pepper in butter for 4-6 minutes or until crisp-tender. Add the zucchini, yellow squash and parsley; saute 3-5 minutes longer or until vegetables are tender. Stir in the salad dressing, pepper and salt. **Yield:** 4 servings.

Nutrition Facts: 1 cup equals 83 calories, 6 g fat (3 g saturated fat), 10 mg cholesterol, 206 mg sodium, 7 g carbohydrate, 3 g fiber, 2 g protein. **Diabetic Exchanges:** 2 vegetable, 1 fat.

Creamy Broccoli with Cashews

6 tablespoons olive oil
1/4 cup red wine vinegar
2 tablespoons minced fresh parsley
4-1/2 teaspoons lemon juice
2 teaspoons Beau Monde seasoning
1/2 teaspoon dill weed
1/2 teaspoon grated lemon peel

Cook pasta according to package directions, adding asparagus during the last 6 minutes; drain and rinse in cold water. Transfer to a large serving bowl.

In a jar with a tight-fitting lid, combine the remaining ingredients; shake well. Pour over pasta mixture and toss to coat. Serve or refrigerate. **Yield:** 8 servings.

Avocado Chicken Salad

(Pictured below)

Prep/Total Time: 20 min.

This is the first time I've ever shared this recipe, but it's one that my family and friends request for every outing we have! I like to serve the salad with crackers...or in pita bread for a filling grab-and-go meal. —Karlene Johnson Mooresville, North Carolina

1 medium ripe avocado, peeled and cubed
2 tablespoons lemon juice, *divided*
2 cups cubed cooked chicken
2 cups seedless red grapes, halved
1 medium tart apple, chopped
1 cup chopped celery
3/4 cup mayonnaise
1/2 cup chopped walnuts, toasted
1/2 teaspoon ground ginger
Lettuce leaves, optional

In a small bowl, toss avocado with 1 tablespoon lemon juice; set aside. In a large bowl, combine the chicken, grapes, apple, celery, mayonnaise, walnuts, ginger and remaining lemon juice. Stir in avocado. Serve on lettuce-lined plates if desired. **Yield:** 5 servings.

Avocado Chicken Salad

Creamy Broccoli with Cashews

(Pictured above)

Prep/Total Time: 20 min.

Looking for a holiday side dish that's something special? The sour-cream sauce makes this broccoli a little different, and the cashews lend a nice crunch. —Karen Ann Bland Gove, Kansas

9 cups fresh broccoli florets
1/4 cup chopped onion
2 tablespoons butter
1 cup (8 ounces) sour cream
2 teaspoons honey
1 teaspoon cider vinegar
1/2 teaspoon salt
1/2 teaspoon paprika
1/2 cup coarsely chopped cashews

Place broccoli in a steamer basket; place in a large saucepan over 1 in. of water. Bring to a boil; cover and steam for 3-4 minutes or until crisp-tender.

Meanwhile, in a small skillet, saute onion in butter until tender. Remove from the heat; stir in the sour cream, honey, vinegar, salt and paprika.

Transfer broccoli to a serving bowl. Add sour cream mixture and toss to coat. Sprinkle with cashews. Serve immediately. **Yield:** 6 servings.

Asparagus Lemon Pasta

Prep/Total Time: 25 min.

Summery asparagus and citrus star in this fresh accompaniment that's ready to serve in no time flat. It's a wonderful item alongside just about any grilled meat.
—Donna Lascher, Sun Lakes, Arizona

2 cups uncooked penne pasta
1 pound fresh asparagus, trimmed and cut into 1-inch pieces

Garden Tuna Macaroni Salad

Southwestern Shell Salad

Prep/Total Time: 25 min.

You can dish up delicious Southwest flavor all year long with this bright medley. It's an excellent salad for picnics and casual gatherings. Kids usually like it with a dollop of low-fat ranch dressing. —Marguerite Shaeffer
Sewell, New Jersey

☑ Uses less fat, sugar or salt. Includes Nutrition Facts.

    8 ounces uncooked small pasta shells
    1 cup frozen corn, thawed
    1 can (15 to 16 ounces) kidney *or* black beans, rinsed and drained
    1 cup chopped sweet yellow pepper
    1 cup chopped tomatoes
    1/2 cup chopped red onion
    1/4 cup sliced pimiento-stuffed olives
    3 tablespoons lemon juice
    2 tablespoons minced fresh cilantro
    2 teaspoons ground cumin
    2 teaspoons olive oil
    1/2 teaspoon salt
    1/2 teaspoon pepper

Cook pasta according to package directions, adding corn during the last 2 minutes. Drain and rinse in cold water.

Place the pasta and corn in a large bowl; add the beans, yellow pepper, tomatoes, onion and olives. In a small bowl, whisk the lemon juice, cilantro, cumin, oil, salt and pepper. Pour over salad and toss to coat. Serve immediately. **Yield:** 10 servings.

Nutrition Facts: 3/4 cup equals 164 calories, 2 g fat (trace saturated fat), 0 cholesterol, 263 mg sodium, 30 g carbohydrate, 4 g fiber, 7 g protein.

Garden Tuna Macaroni Salad

(Pictured above)

Prep/Total Time: 30 min.

I knew this recipe was a hit the first time I served it at a barbecue. I got lovely compliments...and even received a telephone call after the party suggesting that I open a restaurant! —Scarlett Hilton, Sabina, Ohio

    2 cups uncooked elbow macaroni
    1 can (6 ounces) light water-packed tuna, drained and flaked
    2/3 cup chopped sweet yellow pepper
    2/3 cup chopped celery
    1/2 cup shredded carrot
    1/4 cup diced radishes
    2 green onions, chopped
    2 tablespoons minced fresh parsley
    3/4 cup mayonnaise
    1/2 cup ranch salad dressing
    1/4 cup grated Parmesan cheese
    2 teaspoons coarsely ground pepper

Cook macaroni according to package directions. Meanwhile, in a large bowl, combine the tuna, vegetables and parsley. Drain macaroni and rinse in cold water; add to tuna mixture.

In a small bowl, combine the mayonnaise, ranch dressing, Parmesan cheese and pepper. Pour over salad and toss to coat. Serve immediately or refrigerate. **Yield:** 6 servings.

Chicken Rice Salad

Prep: 25 min. + chilling

Dried apricots, lime juice and a hint of mint come together with conventional chicken salad ingredients in this refreshing twist on a grand classic. The idea comes from our Test Kitchen crew.

☑ Uses less fat, sugar or salt. Includes Nutrition Facts and Diabetic Exchanges.

1-1/2 cups uncooked instant rice
    2 cups cubed cooked chicken breast
    1 cup frozen peas, thawed
    1/2 cup chopped celery
    1/2 cup chopped dried apricots
    1/2 cup slivered almonds, toasted
    3 tablespoons olive oil
    1 tablespoon white wine vinegar
    1 tablespoon lime juice
    2 teaspoons minced fresh mint
    1/2 teaspoon salt
    1/4 teaspoon pepper

Cook rice according to package directions; cool. In a large bowl, combine the chicken, peas, celery, apricots and almonds. In a jar with a tight-fitting lid, combine the oil, vinegar, lime juice, mint, salt and pepper; shake well.

Stir rice into chicken mixture; drizzle with dressing and toss to coat. Chill for at least 1 hour before serving. **Yield:** 5 servings.

Nutrition Facts: 1-1/2 cups equals 386 calories, 15 g fat (2 g saturated fat), 43 mg cholesterol, 325 mg sodium, 40 g carbohydrate, 4 g fiber, 23 g protein. **Diabetic Exchanges:** 2 lean meat, 2 vegetable, 2 fat, 1 starch, 1 fruit.

Tortellini Salad

(Pictured below)

Prep/Total Time: 25 min.

This breezy, Mediterranean-style medley is hearty enough to qualify as an entree, but it could also serve as a pretty side dish. With a lip-smacking vinaigrette and bursting with pasta, zucchini, sweet pepper and onion, it's a tasty favorite. —Stacey Mofle, Universal City, Texas

  1 **package (19 ounces) frozen cheese tortellini**
1-1/2 **cups julienned zucchini**
1-1/2 **cups julienned yellow summer squash**
  1 **cup sliced fresh mushrooms**
  1 **tablespoon olive oil**
  1 **tablespoon minced garlic**
  3/4 **teaspoon Italian seasoning**
  1/4 **teaspoon pepper**
  1 **cup julienned sweet red pepper**
  1/2 **cup sliced red onion, halved**
  1 **cup balsamic vinaigrette**

Cook tortellini according to package directions. Meanwhile, in a large skillet, saute the zucchini, yellow squash and mushrooms in oil until crisp-tender. Stir in the garlic, Italian seasoning and pepper. Cook 1 minute longer

Pear Chicken Salad

or until garlic is tender.

Drain tortellini and rinse in cold water. Place in a large bowl; add the squash mixture, red pepper and onion. Drizzle with vinaigrette; toss to coat. Serve immediately or refrigerate. Serve with a slotted spoon. **Yield:** 7 servings.

Pear Chicken Salad

(Pictured above)

Prep/Total Time: 15 min.

Sprinkled with feta cheese, cranberries and walnuts, this beautiful salad is topped off with a citrusy dressing. —Rebecca Baird, Salt Lake City, Utah

✓ Uses less fat, sugar or salt. Includes Nutrition Facts and Diabetic Exchanges.

  6 **cups spring mix salad greens**
  1 **medium ripe pear, sliced**
1-1/2 **cups cooked chicken strips**
  1/4 **cup crumbled feta cheese**
  1/4 **cup dried cranberries**
  1/4 **cup chopped walnuts *or* pecans**
DRESSING:
  1/4 **cup olive oil**
  2 **tablespoons orange juice**
  2 **tablespoons white wine vinegar**
1-1/2 **teaspoons sugar**
  1/2 **teaspoon grated orange peel**
  1/8 **teaspoon salt**
Dash pepper

On four salad plates, arrange the greens, pear, chicken, feta cheese, cranberries and nuts. In a small bowl, whisk the dressing ingredients; drizzle over salads. Serve immediately. **Yield:** 4 servings.

Nutrition Facts: 2 cups equals 348 calories, 22 g fat (4 g saturated fat), 48 mg cholesterol, 203 mg sodium, 19 g carbohydrate, 4 g fiber, 21 g protein. **Diabetic Exchanges:** 3 fat, 2-1/2 lean meat, 1 vegetable, 1 fruit.

Tortellini Salad

Albacore Tuna Salad

Prep/Total Time: 15 min.

There are so many terrific things about this recipe! Sweet apple, golden raisins, celery, nuts, tuna and the tropical taste of pineapple add up to a simply wonderful salad. Leftovers are as delicious as the first bite. Sometimes I even like to substitute grapes for the raisins.
—Barbara Moravek, Jay, Florida

        2 cans (8 ounces *each*) unsweetened crushed
           pineapple, drained
        2 cans (6 ounces *each*) solid white tuna,
           drained
        1 large apple, chopped
        1 cup sliced celery
        1 cup golden raisins
      1/2 cup sliced almonds, toasted
        1 cup mayonnaise
        1 tablespoon lemon juice
    Bread slices *or* lettuce leaves

In a large bowl, combine the pineapple, tuna, apple, celery, raisins and almonds. Combine mayonnaise and lemon juice; stir into tuna mixture. Spread on bread or serve on lettuce-lined plates. **Yield:** 5 servings.

Bunny Pear Salad

(Pictured below)

Prep/Total Time: 15 min.

All dressed up for Easter, these darling bunny salads make a cute-as-can-be side dish for your family's holiday feast. Children like to help assemble them, too.
—Albertine Sperling, Abbotsford, British Columbia

    Red lettuce leaves
        1 can (15-1/4 ounces) pear halves, drained
       12 dried currants *or* raisins

Spring Greens with Berries

        8 whole almonds
        4 baby carrots
        4 parsley sprigs
    Whipped cream in a can

Arrange lettuce on four salad plates; place a pear half cut side down on each plate. For eyes, insert two currants at narrow end of pear; add one currant for nose. For ears, insert almonds upright behind eyes.

With a sharp knife, cut a small hole at one end of each carrot; insert a parsley sprig for carrot top. Place under bunny's nose. For tails, spray a small mound of whipped cream at wide end of each pear. **Yield:** 4 servings.

Spring Greens with Berries

(Pictured above)

Prep/Total Time: 15 min.

My busy sister-in-law passed along this refreshing salad recipe years ago, and it quickly became an all-time favorite with my family—just as it is with hers. It's colorful, goes together in a snap and complements a variety of entrees. Plus, the dressing can be refrigerated for several days.
—Vikki Peck Poland, Ohio

        2 packages (5 ounces *each*) spring mix salad
           greens
        1 can (11 ounces) mandarin oranges, drained
      3/4 cup sliced fresh strawberries
      3/4 cup fresh raspberries
      1/2 cup slivered almonds, toasted
    ORANGE VINAIGRETTE:
      1/4 cup vegetable oil
        1 tablespoon red wine vinegar
        1 tablespoon orange juice
        1 tablespoon honey
        1 teaspoon grated orange peel
        1 teaspoon Dijon mustard
      1/4 teaspoon salt
      1/8 teaspoon pepper

Bunny Pear Salad

In a large bowl, combine the greens, oranges, berries and almonds. In a jar with a tight-fitting lid, combine the vinaigrette ingredients; shake well. Drizzle over salad and toss to coat. Serve immediately. **Yield:** 7 servings.

Crispy Chicken Salad

Thyme Grilled Vegetables

(Pictured below)

Prep: 20 min. **Grill:** 50 min.

I love these little red garden potatoes, pepper strips and onions. They can be put in a foil pan and cooked right on the grill. Your kitchen won't get hot, and cleanup is a breeze. Best of all, I usually have all of the necessary ingredients on hand.
—Christine Wall, Bartlett, Illinois

✓ Uses less fat, sugar or salt. Includes Nutrition Facts and Diabetic Exchanges.

 16 small red potatoes (about 2 pounds), halved
1/2 cup chicken broth
1/4 cup olive oil
 2 tablespoons minced fresh thyme *or*
 2 teaspoons dried thyme
1/2 teaspoon salt
 1 *each* large green, sweet red and yellow pepper, julienned
 1 jar (15 ounces) pearl onions, drained

In an ungreased 13-in. x 9-in. x 2-in. disposable foil pan, combine the potatoes, broth, oil, thyme and salt. Grill, covered, over medium heat for 25 minutes.

Stir in peppers and onions. Grill 25-30 minutes longer or until vegetables are tender. **Yield:** 9 servings.

Nutrition Facts: 3/4 cup equals 163 calories, 6 g fat (1 g saturated fat), 0 cholesterol, 191 mg sodium, 25 g carbohydrate, 3 g fiber, 3 g protein. **Diabetic Exchanges:** 1 starch, 1 vegetable, 1 fat.

Crispy Chicken Salad

(Pictured above)

Prep/Total Time: 20 min.

Sugared almonds and chow mein noodles add fun crunch to this salad that makes the most of leftover chicken. The dish is speedy, simple and always popular at ladies' luncheons. It's a lovely change of pace. —Irene Dickhausen St. Paul, Minnesota

 1 tablespoon butter
1/4 cup sliced almonds
 3 tablespoons sugar, *divided*
1/4 cup olive oil
 2 tablespoons cider vinegar
1/2 teaspoon salt
Dash hot pepper sauce
 4 cups chopped lettuce
 2 cups cubed cooked chicken
1-1/2 cups chow mein noodles
 1 can (20 ounces) unsweetened pineapple tidbits, drained and patted dry
 1 cup chopped celery
 1 green onion, chopped

In a small skillet, melt the butter over medium heat. Add the almonds; cook and stir for 3-4 minutes or until toasted. Sprinkle with 1 tablespoon sugar; cook and stir 2-3 minutes longer or until the sugar is melted. Spread onto foil to cool.

For dressing, in a jar with a tight-fitting lid, combine the oil, vinegar, salt, hot pepper sauce and remaining sugar; shake until sugar is dissolved.

In a large bowl, combine the lettuce, chicken, noodles, pineapple, celery and onion. Shake dressing and drizzle over salad; toss to coat. Break apart sugared almonds; sprinkle over salad. **Yield:** 8 servings.

Thyme Grilled Vegetables

Grape Pasta Salad

Prep: 25 min. + chilling

Grapes and broccoli give a delightful twist to this simple crowd-pleaser. The recipe has been very popular with my family. Plus, it's super-easy and inexpensive to prepare.
—*Tia Crosson, Las Vegas, Nevada*

    1 package (16 ounces) spiral pasta
1-1/2 cups seedless red grapes, halved
1-1/2 cups fresh broccoli florets
1-1/3 cups diced fully cooked ham (1/2 pound)
    1 can (8 ounces) sliced ripe olives, drained
    1 medium red onion, diced
    1 jar (16 ounces) coleslaw dressing

Cook pasta according to package directions. Meanwhile, in a large bowl, combine the grapes, broccoli, ham, olives and onion.

Drain pasta and rinse in cold water; stir into grape mixture. Add dressing and toss to coat. Cover and refrigerate the pasta salad for at least 2 hours before serving. **Yield:** 14 servings.

Tropical Fruit Salad

(Pictured below)

Prep/Total Time: 15 min.

When I needed a speedy salad for a luncheon, I used what I had available, and everyone loved it! Light, fluffy and full of fruit, this medley could double as a healthy dessert. You can also tuck it into the kids' lunch boxes for a fun school-day treat. —*Teri Lindquist, Gurnee, Illinois*

Tropical Fruit Salad

    2 cans (15-1/4 ounces *each*) mixed tropical fruit, drained
    1 can (11 ounces) mandarin oranges, drained
    1 medium banana, sliced
    1 cup miniature marshmallows
    2 cartons (6 ounces *each*) vanilla yogurt
1/4 cup flaked coconut
1/4 cup slivered almonds, toasted

In a large salad bowl, combine the tropical fruit, oranges, banana and marshmallows. Add yogurt; toss gently to coat. Sprinkle with coconut and almonds. Refrigerate until serving. **Yield:** 6 servings.

Super Stuffed Potatoes

Prep/Total Time: 30 min.

Need a fast side dish to round out your menu? Try these mouth-watering stuffed potatoes from my kitchen.
—*Rochelle Brownlee, Big Timber, Montana*

    4 medium baking potatoes (8 to 10 ounces *each*)
    1 cup cottage cheese
1/2 cup cubed fully cooked ham
1/2 cup shredded part-skim mozzarella cheese
1/4 cup finely chopped green pepper

Scrub and pierce potatoes; place on a microwave-safe plate. Microwave, uncovered, on high for 16-18 minutes or until tender, turning once. Let stand for 5 minutes. Cut a thin slice off the top of each potato and discard. Scoop out pulp, leaving a thin shell.

In a large bowl, mash the pulp with cottage cheese. Stir in the ham, mozzarella cheese and green pepper. Spoon into potato shells (shells will be full). Return to the microwave-safe plate. Microwave, uncovered, on high for 3-5 minutes or until heated through. **Yield:** 4 servings.

Editor's Note: This recipe was tested in a 1,100-watt microwave.

Glazed Baby Carrots

Prep/Total Time: 20 min.

With only two ingredients, this side is ideal for nights when you need something extra-fast. People always want to know the secret to our wonderful carrots...here it is!
—*Linda Hoffman, Logansport, Indiana*

✓ Uses less fat, sugar or salt. Includes Nutrition Facts.

    2 packages (16 ounces *each*) baby carrots
    1 jar (12 ounces) orange marmalade

Place 1 in. of water in a large saucepan; add carrots. Bring to a boil. Reduce heat; cover and simmer for 12-15 minutes or until crisp-tender.

Drain carrots and place in a large serving bowl; stir in marmalade. Serve with a slotted spoon. **Yield:** 8 servings.

Nutrition Facts: 3/4 cup equals 144 calories, trace fat (trace saturated fat), 0 cholesterol, 112 mg sodium, 38 g carbohydrate, 2 g fiber, 1 g protein.

Apple Orchard Chicken Salad

(Pictured above)

Prep/Total Time: 20 min.

My husband and I love salads, and we especially look forward to this one as a satisfying main dish. The apple flavor really complements the chicken, Gorgonzola cheese and chopped pecans. It all comes together in only 20 minutes.
—Debbie Purdue, Westland, Michigan

- 4 boneless skinless chicken breast halves (5 ounces *each*)
- 6 tablespoons apple juice concentrate
- 1/4 cup vegetable oil
- 2 tablespoons vanilla yogurt
- 8 cups torn mixed salad greens
- 2 cups chopped apples
- 1 small red onion, cut into rings
- 1/2 cup chopped pecans
- 1/4 cup crumbled Gorgonzola cheese
- 1 package (3 ounces) dried apple chips

Grill the chicken on an indoor grill coated with nonstick cooking spray for 5-7 minutes or until the juices run clear. For the dressing, combine the apple juice concentrate, oil and vanilla yogurt in a jar with a tight-fitting lid; shake well.

On four plates, arrange the salad greens, apples, onion, pecans and cheese. Slice chicken; place over salads. Drizzle with dressing. Sprinkle with apple chips. Serve immediately. **Yield:** 4 servings.

Creamy Parmesan Spinach

Prep/Total Time: 20 min.

Fresh baby spinach meets a creamy Parmesan cheese sauce in this versatile and comforting side dish.
—Priscilla Gilbert, Indian Harbour Beach, Florida

- 2 packages (6 ounces *each*) fresh baby spinach, coarsely chopped
- 2 tablespoons water
- 2 teaspoons butter
- 1/2 cup heavy whipping cream
- 2 teaspoons grated lemon peel
- 1/2 teaspoon minced garlic
- 1/8 teaspoon crushed red pepper flakes
- 1/2 cup grated Parmesan cheese
- 2/3 cup onion and garlic salad croutons, crushed

Place spinach and water in a Dutch oven or large saucepan; cover and cook for 3 minutes or until wilted. Drain and set aside.

In the same pan, melt butter. Stir in the cream, lemon peel, garlic and pepper flakes; bring to a gentle boil. Reduce heat; simmer, uncovered, for 5 minutes or until slightly reduced. Stir in Parmesan cheese and spinach; heat through. Sprinkle with croutons. **Yield:** 3 servings.

Popcorn Chicken Salad

(Pictured below)

Prep/Total Time: 25 min.

Here's a refreshing salad that's especially nice for brown-bag lunches at work. I can mix up the simple dressing at home, then pick up enough salad ingredients at the grocery store to last for several days.
—Teresa Wilkins-Reckard, Monroe, Indiana

1 cup frozen popcorn chicken
2 tablespoons mayonnaise
4-1/2 teaspoons honey
2-1/4 teaspoons white vinegar
1-1/2 teaspoons Dijon mustard
1/8 teaspoon sesame oil
2 cups torn leaf lettuce
1/2 cup fresh snow peas
1/2 cup canned bean sprouts, drained
1/2 cup mandarin oranges, drained
1/2 cup chow mein noodles

Bake chicken according to package directions. Meanwhile, for dressing, in a small bowl, whisk the mayonnaise, honey, vinegar, mustard and oil until smooth.

Divide lettuce between two plates; top with the peas, bean sprouts, oranges, chicken and noodles. Drizzle with dressing. **Yield:** 2 servings.

Veggie Spiral Salad

Popcorn Chicken Salad

Veggie Spiral Salad

(Pictured above and on page 128)

Prep/Total Time: 20 min.

My husband and son detested pasta salad before I came up with this one. There were no leftovers the very first time I served it—now it's a summertime family favorite!
—Melody Loyd, Parowan, Utah

1 cup uncooked tricolor spiral pasta
1/2 cup chopped seeded cucumber
1/2 cup thinly sliced celery
1/2 cup chopped red onion
1/2 cup sliced radishes
1/2 cup chopped tomatoes
1/2 cup sliced ripe olives, drained
1/2 cup shredded Swiss cheese
1/8 teaspoon garlic powder
1/8 teaspoon pepper
1 tablespoon Italian salad dressing mix
2 tablespoons plus 1-1/2 teaspoons cider vinegar
2 tablespoons olive oil

Cook pasta according to package directions. Meanwhile, in a large bowl, combine the cucumber, celery, onion, radishes, tomatoes, olives, cheese, garlic powder and pepper. Drain pasta and rinse in cold water; stir into vegetable mixture.

In a jar with a tight-fitting lid, combine the Italian salad dressing mix, vinegar and oil; shake well. Drizzle over salad and toss to coat. Serve immediately or refrigerate. **Yield:** 5 servings.

Blue Cheese Tossed Salad

(Pictured below)

Prep/Total Time: 20 min.

The combination of blue cheese, tart apple and tangy lime dressing in this hearty salad keeps people asking for my secret recipe. —Heather Koetsier, Ada, Michigan

   1/2 cup sliced almonds
   1/4 teaspoon salt
   1/4 teaspoon pepper
     1 tablespoon butter
     1 package (10 ounces) hearts of romaine
       salad mix
     1 cup (4 ounces) crumbled blue cheese
     1 medium red apple, chopped
     1 teaspoon grated lime peel
DRESSING:
   1/2 cup olive oil
 1-1/2 teaspoons balsamic vinegar
   1/2 teaspoon minced garlic
   1/2 teaspoon lime juice
   1/2 teaspoon grated lime peel
   1/2 teaspoon ground cumin
   1/4 teaspoon ground coriander
   1/8 teaspoon white pepper

In a small skillet over medium heat, cook the almonds, salt and pepper in butter for 5-6 minutes or until toasted, stirring occasionally. Drain on paper towels.

In a large bowl, combine the romaine, blue cheese, apple, lime peel and almonds. In a jar with a tight-fitting lid, combine the dressing ingredients; shake well. Drizzle over salad and toss to coat. Serve immediately. **Yield:** 10-12 servings.

Stir-Fried Carrots

Stir-Fried Carrots

(Pictured above)

Prep/Total Time: 20 min.

For a colorful side dish that's as good as it is good for you, I cook up these fail-proof carrots with rosemary. —Grace Yaskovic, Branchville, New Jersey

✓ Uses less fat, sugar or salt. Includes Nutrition Facts and Diabetic Exchanges.

 1-1/2 pounds fresh carrots, julienned
     1 tablespoon olive oil
   1/2 cup chicken broth
     1 teaspoon dried rosemary, crushed
   1/4 teaspoon pepper

In a large skillet or wok, stir-fry carrots in oil until crisp-tender. Stir in the broth, rosemary and pepper. Bring to a boil. Reduce heat; simmer, uncovered, for 2-3 minutes or until liquid is reduced. **Yield:** 4 servings.

Nutrition Facts: 3/4 cup equals 106 calories, 4 g fat (1 g saturated fat), 0 cholesterol, 176 mg sodium, 18 g carbohydrate, 5 g fiber, 2 g protein. **Diabetic Exchanges:** 1 starch, 1/2 fat.

Blue Cheese Tossed Salad

Homemade Dressing Hint

THE "SHELF LIFE" of homemade salad dressings varies somewhat. Generally, vinaigrettes can be kept in your refrigerator for up to 2 weeks. Dairy-based salad dressings, such as buttermilk, and dressings made with fresh ingredients, such as chopped onion, fresh herbs, tomato sauce and chopped hard-cooked egg, generally will keep for up to 1 week.

Tomato Feta Salad

Tomato Feta Salad

(Pictured above)

Prep/Total Time: 15 min.

Light and refreshing with juicy tomatoes, feta cheese, onion and olives, this cool salad drizzled with a red wine vinaigrette is just right for hot summer days.
—Jill Bowers, Huntington, Indiana

- 5 medium tomatoes, thinly sliced
- 1 medium red onion, thinly sliced
- 1 package (6 ounces) crumbled tomato and basil feta cheese
- 1 can (2-1/4 ounces) sliced ripe olives, drained
- 1/2 cup olive oil
- 1/4 cup red wine vinegar
- 1 tablespoon dried oregano

On a serving platter, layer tomatoes and onion. Top with feta cheese and olives. In a jar with a tight-fitting lid, combine the oil, vinegar and oregano; shake well. Drizzle dressing over salad. Serve with a slotted spoon. **Yield:** 8-10 servings.

Broccoli Strawberry Salad

Prep/Total Time: 20 min.

I received this simple yet delicious recipe from a good friend of mine who frequently brings the change-of-pace salad to potlucks and cookouts. Wherever she takes it, it's almost always the very first dish to be finished! —Emily Robertson West Peoria, Illinois

- 8 cups fresh broccoli florets
- 8 ounces Colby-Monterey Jack cheese, cut into 1/2-inch cubes
- 1 cup mayonnaise

- 2 tablespoons sugar
- 1 teaspoon cider vinegar
- 2 cups fresh strawberries, quartered
- 1/4 cup sliced almonds, toasted

In a large bowl, combine broccoli and cheese. In a small bowl, whisk the mayonnaise, sugar and vinegar. Pour over broccoli mixture and toss to coat. Gently stir in strawberries; sprinkle with almonds. Serve immediately. **Yield:** 10 servings.

Parmesan Tomatoes

(Pictured below)

Prep/Total Time: 30 min.

Here's an attractive side dish that'll put your harvest of fresh, garden-grown tomatoes to mouth-watering use. The breezy four-ingredient recipe is a seasonal standard at our house and is sure to become one at yours, too. —Marcia Orlando Boyertown, Pennsylvania

✓ Uses less fat, sugar or salt. Includes Nutrition Facts and Diabetic Exchanges.

- 3 large tomatoes
- 1 tablespoon chicken bouillon granules
- 1/4 cup grated Parmesan cheese
- 1 tablespoon butter

Remove stems from tomatoes; cut in half widthwise. Place cut side up in an 11-in. x 7-in. x 2-in. baking dish coated with nonstick cooking spray. Sprinkle with bouillon and Parmesan cheese; dot with butter.

Bake, uncovered, at 400° for 20-25 minutes or until heated through. **Yield:** 6 servings.

Nutrition Facts: 1 tomato half equals 54 calories, 3 g fat (2 g saturated fat), 8 mg cholesterol, 510 mg sodium, 5 g carbohydrate, 1 g fiber, 2 g protein. **Diabetic Exchanges:** 1 vegetable, 1/2 fat.

Parmesan Tomatoes

Shrimp Salad-Stuffed Avocados

(Pictured above)

Prep/Total Time: 15 min.

This is pretty enough to serve at a ladies' luncheon. When I needed a main-dish salad for my book club, I just tripled the recipe...and got raves! Try it with imitation crabmeat, too.   —Suzanne VanAlstyne, Petoskey, Michigan

    1/2 pound deveined peeled cooked medium
         shrimp, coarsely chopped
    1/2 cup chopped celery
    1/4 cup chopped onion
      3 tablespoons mayonnaise
  4-1/2 teaspoons capers, drained
      1 tablespoon minced fresh parsley
      2 teaspoons Dijon mustard
  1-1/2 teaspoons lemon juice
    3/4 teaspoon dried tarragon
    1/4 teaspoon seasoned salt
    1/8 teaspoon pepper
      2 medium ripe avocados, halved and pitted

In a small bowl, combine the first 11 ingredients. Spoon into the avocado halves. Serve immediately. **Yield:** 4 servings.

Nectarine Pecan Salad

Prep/Total Time: 25 min.

Featuring fresh nectarines, this speedy salad is complemented by a shake-to-make dressing that comes from pantry staples.   —Marina Sanders, Altamont, Manitoba

      8 cups torn romaine
      5 medium nectarines *or* peaches, chopped
    2/3 cup chopped pecans, toasted
    1/2 cup crumbled feta cheese
  DRESSING:
      2 tablespoons plus 1-1/2 teaspoons canola oil
      2 tablespoons white vinegar
      2 tablespoons plus 1-1/2 teaspoons sugar
      1 tablespoon sesame seeds
      1 tablespoon poppy seeds
    3/4 teaspoon dried minced onion
    1/4 teaspoon Worcestershire sauce
    1/8 teaspoon paprika

In a large bowl, combine the romaine, nectarines, pecans and feta cheese. In a jar with a tight-fitting lid, combine the dressing ingredients; shake well. Pour the dressing over the salad and toss to coat. Serve immediately. **Yield:** 8 servings.

Buttermilk Salad Dressing
Avocado Salad Dressing

Buttermilk Salad Dressing

(Pictured at left)

Prep/Total Time: 10 min.

There's nothing like the taste of a homemade dressing to enhance a salad. This smooth and delectable version goes together in no time at all. We have enjoyed it for years.
—Vivian Haen, Menomonee Falls, Wisconsin

✓ Uses less fat, sugar or salt. Includes Nutrition Facts and Diabetic Exchanges.

  3/4 cup buttermilk
  1/4 cup mayonnaise
   1 tablespoon minced fresh parsley
  1/2 teaspoon sugar
  1/2 teaspoon ground mustard
  1/4 teaspoon onion powder
  1/4 teaspoon garlic powder
  1/4 teaspoon pepper

In a small bowl, whisk all ingredients until blended. Serve immediately or refrigerate. **Yield:** 1-1/2 cups.
  Nutrition Facts: 2 tablespoons equals 41 calories, 4 g fat (1 g saturated fat), 2 mg cholesterol, 41 mg sodium, 1 g carbohydrate, trace fiber, 1 g protein. **Diabetic Exchange:** 1 fat.

Avocado Salad Dressing

(Pictured above)

Prep/Total Time: 10 min.

Buttermilk and fat-free yogurt are the basis for this delicious dressing from our Test Kitchen. With avocado, parsley and dill, it's a fresh and flavorful choice for any summer pasta medley.

✓ Uses less fat, sugar or salt. Includes Nutrition Facts and Diabetic Exchanges.

   1 cup buttermilk
  1/2 cup fat-free plain yogurt
   1 ripe avocado, peeled and sliced
   2 green onions, chopped
  1/4 cup minced fresh parsley
  1/2 teaspoon salt
  1/2 teaspoon garlic powder
  1/4 teaspoon dill weed
  1/8 teaspoon pepper

In a blender, combine all ingredients; cover and process until blended. Transfer to a jar or bowl. Serve immediately or refrigerate. **Yield:** 2 cups.
  Nutrition Facts: 2 tablespoons equals 30 calories, 2 g fat (trace saturated fat), 1 mg cholesterol, 96 mg sodium, 2 g carbohydrate, 1 g fiber, 1 g protein. **Diabetic Exchange:** 1/2 fat.

Thai Chicken Salad

Prep/Total Time: 25 min.

My family can't get enough of this colorful, stir-fried salad that has spicy-sweet Asian flair. —Carrie Hickam
San Jose, California

   1 pound boneless skinless
     chicken breasts, thinly sliced
   1 tablespoon vegetable oil
   2 medium carrots, sliced
   1 medium sweet red pepper, chopped
   1 package (10 ounces) fresh spinach, torn
  1/2 cup chopped green onions
  1/2 cup minced fresh cilantro
DRESSING:
  1/3 cup creamy peanut butter
  1/4 cup water
   3 tablespoons rice wine vinegar
   2 tablespoons vegetable oil
   1 tablespoon soy sauce
   2 teaspoons sugar
 1-1/2 teaspoons minced garlic
  1/4 teaspoon salt

In a large skillet or wok, stir-fry chicken in oil until juices run clear. Remove and keep warm. In the same pan, stir-fry carrots and red pepper for 5-6 minutes or until crisp-tender. In a large serving bowl, combine the spinach, onions and cilantro; set aside.
  In a blender, combine the dressing ingredients; cover and process until blended. Add chicken, carrots, red pepper and dressing to spinach mixture; toss to coat. Serve immediately. **Yield:** 6 servings.

Summer Thyme Salad

Prep/Total Time: 15 min.

This is a quick and simple salad that's ideal for casual gatherings. It's also an excellent way to use up an abundance of garden produce. —Barbara Stewart
Portland, Connecticut

✓ Uses less fat, sugar or salt. Includes Nutrition Facts and Diabetic Exchanges.

  1 small cucumber, peeled and sliced
  1 medium tomato, chopped
  3 green onions, sliced
  1 tablespoon mayonnaise
  2 teaspoons minced fresh thyme
1/8 teaspoon salt, optional
1/8 teaspoon pepper

In a small bowl, combine all ingredients. Cover and refrigerate until serving. **Yield:** 4 servings.

Nutrition Facts: 1/2 cup (calculated without salt) equals 42 calories, 3 g fat (trace saturated fat), 1 mg cholesterol, 25 mg sodium, 4 g carbohydrate, 1 g fiber, 1 g protein. **Diabetic Exchanges:** 1 vegetable, 1/2 fat.

Buttery Sweet Potato Casserole

(Pictured below)

Prep: 15 min. **Bake:** 20 min.

Whenever we get together as a family, my kids beg me to make this dish. It goes together in minutes with canned sweet potatoes. —Sue Miller, Mars, Pennsylvania

  2 cans (15-3/4 ounces *each*) sweet potatoes, drained and mashed
1/2 cup sugar
  1 egg
1/4 cup butter, melted
1/2 teaspoon ground cinnamon
Dash salt

Buttery Sweet Potato Casserole

Spinach Penne Toss

TOPPING:
  1 cup coarsely crushed butter-flavored crackers (about 25 crackers)
1/2 cup packed brown sugar
1/4 cup butter, melted

In a large bowl, combine the first six ingredients. Transfer to a greased 8-in. square baking dish. Combine the topping ingredients; sprinkle over sweet potato mixture.

Bake, uncovered, at 350° for 20-25 minutes or until golden brown. **Yield:** 6-8 servings.

Spinach Penne Toss

(Pictured above)

Prep/Total Time: 25 min.

A good friend shared this fabulous recipe with me. The spinach-and-pasta combination is perfect for so many occasions. Plus, it's an absolute snap to prepare and marvelous to eat! —Kierste Wade, Midland, Michigan

  2 cups uncooked penne pasta
  1 medium sweet red pepper, julienned
  1 medium onion, sliced
  1 tablespoon plus 1/4 cup olive oil, *divided*
  1 package (6 ounces) fresh baby spinach
3/4 cup crumbled cooked bacon
1/2 cup crumbled feta cheese
1/2 cup oil-packed sun-dried tomatoes, chopped
  2 tablespoons cider vinegar
1/4 teaspoon pepper
1/8 teaspoon salt

Cook pasta according to package directions. Meanwhile, in a large skillet, saute red pepper and onion in 1 tablespoon oil for 3-4 minutes or until tender.

Drain pasta and place in a serving bowl. Add the red pepper mixture, spinach, bacon, feta cheese and tomatoes. In a jar with a tight-fitting lid, combine the vinegar, pepper, salt and remaining oil; shake well. Drizzle over pasta mixture and toss to coat. **Yield:** 10 servings.

Chapter 9

THINK you don't have the time to bake golden brown loaves, moist muffins, iced coffee cakes and other oven-fresh breads for your family? You'll change your mind after paging through this heartwarming chapter!

From flaky biscuits you'll be serving in just 25 minutes to tender loaves that take advantage of a bread machine, these delectable delights will let you treat loved ones to home-baked goodies in a flash.

With favorites such as Buttermilk Onion Bread, Tart Cranberry Coffee Cake, Apple Spice Muffins and Garlic Poppy Seed Spirals, the only hard part will be choosing which irresistible recipe to make!

GOLDEN GOODIES. Cinnamon Chip Scones and Chocolate-Pecan Sticky Buns (p. 152).

Hawaiian Cheese Bread

Buttermilk Onion Bread

(Pictured below)

Prep: 10 min. **Bake:** 3 hours

This oniony bread smells wonderful while it bakes. It's perfect for hearty picnic sandwiches, but it's also a great addition to a hot dinner. —Joan Powers
East Wenatchee, Washington

✓ Uses less fat, sugar or salt. Includes Nutrition Facts and Diabetic Exchanges.

1 cup plus 2 tablespoons warm buttermilk (70° to 80°)
1 tablespoon butter
2-1/2 cups bread flour
1/2 cup whole wheat flour
3 tablespoons sugar
1 tablespoon dried minced onion
1 tablespoon dried parsley flakes
1-1/2 teaspoons salt
1 teaspoon dill weed
2-1/4 teaspoons active dry yeast

In bread machine pan, place all ingredients in order suggested by manufacturer. Select basic bread setting. Choose crust color and loaf size if available. Bake according to bread machine directions (check dough after 5 minutes of mixing; add 1 to 2 tablespoons of water or flour if needed). **Yield:** 1 loaf (1-1/2 pounds, 16 slices).

Nutrition Facts: 1 slice equals 99 calories, 1 g fat (1 g saturated fat), 3 mg cholesterol, 245 mg sodium, 20 g carbohydrate, 1 g fiber, 4 g protein. **Diabetic Exchange:** 1 starch.

Hawaiian Cheese Bread

(Pictured above)

Prep: 15 min. **Bake:** 25 min.

My mother's friend brought this mouth-watering loaf to a party at work, and after one bite, Mom knew she had to have the recipe. With constant nagging, she eventually got it! —Amy McIlvain, Wilmington, Delaware

1 loaf (1 pound) Hawaiian sweet bread
1 block (8 ounces) Swiss cheese
3 slices red onion, chopped
1/2 cup butter, melted
1 tablespoon minced garlic
1 teaspoon salt

Cut the bread diagonally into 1-in. slices to within 1 in. of bottom. Repeat cuts in opposite direction. Cut Swiss cheese into 1/4-in. slices; cut slices into small pieces. Insert into bread. Combine the onion, butter, garlic and salt; spoon over bread. Wrap loaf in foil. Bake at 350° for 25-30 minutes or until the cheese is melted. Serve warm. **Yield:** 12-16 servings.

Bread Machine Basics

• For the best results, use bread flour.

• All liquid ingredients (water, milk, eggs, juice, etc.) should be at room temperature (70° to 80°) before adding to the machine.

• Recipes containing eggs, milk, sour cream and other dairy or perishable products should be baked immediately and not placed on a "time-bake" cycle.

Buttermilk Onion Bread

Garlic Parmesan Bread

(Pictured at right)

Prep: 10 min. **Bake:** 3 hours

You can rely on this loaf to round out all kinds of menus. It goes with everything from bologna sandwiches to spaghetti. —*Jami Blunt, Hardy, Arkansas*

✓ Uses less fat, sugar or salt. Includes Nutrition Facts and Diabetic Exchanges.

Garlic Parmesan Bread

  1 cup water (70° to 80°)
  2 tablespoons plus 1-1/2 teaspoons butter, softened
  1 tablespoon honey
  3 cups bread flour
 2/3 cup grated Parmesan cheese
1-1/2 teaspoons garlic powder
 3/4 teaspoon salt
2-1/4 teaspoons active dry yeast

In bread machine pan, place all ingredients in order suggested by manufacturer. Select basic bread setting. Choose crust color and loaf size if available. Bake according to bread machine directions (check dough after 5 minutes of mixing; add 1 to 2 tablespoons of water or flour if needed). **Yield:** 1 loaf (1-1/2 pounds, 16 slices).

Nutrition Facts: 1 slice equals 112 calories, 3 g fat (2 g saturated fat), 7 mg cholesterol, 191 mg sodium, 18 g carbohydrate, 1 g fiber, 5 g protein. **Diabetic Exchanges:** 1 starch, 1/2 fat.

Walnut-Cinnamon Coffee Cake

Prep: 20 min. **Bake:** 40 min. + cooling

This easy, sweet and delectable recipe is one of my favorites for coffee cake. Moist, buttery and boxed-cake-mix simple, it's also popular with my family and friends. —*Emajo Wilson, Allen, Texas*

1/2 cup butter, softened
1/2 cup vegetable oil
1/2 cup sugar
  4 eggs
  1 package (18-1/2 ounces) butter recipe golden cake mix
  1 cup (8 ounces) sour cream
FILLING:
1/2 cup chopped walnuts
1/4 cup packed brown sugar
  4 teaspoons ground cinnamon
TOPPING:
1/4 cup all-purpose flour
1/4 cup sugar
  2 teaspoons ground cinnamon
1/4 cup cold butter

In a large mixing bowl, cream butter, oil and sugar. Add eggs, one at a time, beating well after each addition. Gradually add cake mix; mix well. Beat in sour cream just until combined.

Pour half of the batter into a greased 13-in. x 9-in. x 2-in. baking pan. Combine the filling ingredients; sprinkle over batter. Top with remaining batter. Cut through with a knife to swirl.

For topping, in a small bowl, combine the flour, sugar and cinnamon. Cut in butter until mixture resembles coarse crumbs. Sprinkle over batter.

Bake at 350° for 40-45 minutes or until a toothpick inserted near the center comes out clean. Cool on a wire rack. **Yield:** 12-15 servings.

Tart Cranberry Coffee Cake

Prep: 10 min. **Bake:** 35 min.

An easy powdered-sugar glaze drizzled on top gives this tangy coffee cake homemade appeal. With festive red cranberries and a hint of orange flavor, this breakfast and brunch treat is especially nice for the Christmas holiday season. —*Karen Smeltzer, Greendale, Wisconsin*

  1 package (15.6 ounces) cranberry-orange quick bread mix
  1 carton (6 ounces) vanilla yogurt
1/3 cup milk
  1 egg
  1 cup fresh *or* frozen cranberries
GLAZE:
1/2 cup confectioners' sugar
  1 tablespoon milk
1/8 to 1/4 teaspoon vanilla extract

Place quick bread mix in a large bowl. In a small bowl, whisk the yogurt, milk and egg; stir into the bread mix just until moistened. Fold in cranberries.

Pour into a greased 9-in. deep-dish pie plate. Bake at 375° for 35-40 minutes or until golden brown. Combine glaze ingredients; drizzle over coffee cake. Serve warm if desired. **Yield:** 6-8 servings.

Apple Spice Muffins

(Pictured below)

Prep: 15 min. **Bake:** 20 min.

When I discovered that I was out of my usual muffin-making ingredients, I improvised and came up with this recipe. The results were terrific! I love the big apple flavor that's spiced with plenty of cinnamon and nutmeg. —Beckie Lapointe
Abbotsford, British Columbia

- 2 cups all-purpose flour
- 1 cup granola without raisins
- 2/3 cup sugar
- 3 teaspoons baking powder
- 1 teaspoon salt
- 1/2 teaspoon ground cinnamon
- 1/4 teaspoon ground nutmeg
- 2 eggs
- 2/3 cup unsweetened apple juice
- 1/4 cup vegetable oil
- 1-1/2 cups grated peeled apples

In a large bowl, combine the first seven ingredients. In another bowl, whisk the eggs, apple juice and oil. Stir into dry ingredients just until moistened. Fold in apples.

Fill greased or paper-lined muffin cups three-fourths full. Bake at 400° for 18-20 minutes or until a toothpick comes out clean. Cool for 5 minutes before removing from pan to a wire rack. Serve warm. **Yield:** 1 dozen.

Key Lime Bread

(Pictured below)

Prep: 15 min. **Bake:** 50 min. + cooling

I first tasted this delightfully different bread at a friend's house. The recipe is simple and absolutely yummy!
—Joan Hallford, North Richland Hills, Texas

Apple Spice Muffins
Key Lime Bread

- 2/3 cup butter, softened
- 2 cups sugar
- 4 eggs
- 2 tablespoons grated lime peel
- 2 tablespoons key lime juice
- 1 teaspoon vanilla extract
- 3 cups all-purpose flour
- 3 teaspoons baking powder
- 1 teaspoon salt
- 1 cup milk
- 1 cup chopped walnuts

GLAZE:
- 2/3 cup confectioners' sugar
- 1 to 2 tablespoons key lime juice

In a large mixing bowl, cream butter and sugar. Add eggs; mix well. Add lime peel, juice and vanilla; mix until combined. Combine the flour, baking powder and salt; add to creamed mixture alternately with milk. Fold in walnuts.

Transfer batter to two greased 9-in. x 5-in. x 3-in. loaf pans. Bake at 350° for 50-55 minutes or until a toothpick inserted near the center comes out clean. Cool for 10 minutes before removing from pans to wire racks.

Combine glaze ingredients; drizzle over warm bread. Cool completely. **Yield:** 2 loaves.

Onion-Beef Muffin Cups

Prep: 25 min. **Bake:** 15 min.

A tube of refrigerated biscuits makes these delicious bites so quick and easy. They're one of my tried-and-true lunches and always get rave reviews. In fact, I usually double the recipe just to be sure I have leftovers.
—Barbara Carlucci, Orange Park, Florida

- 3 medium onions, thinly sliced
- 1/4 cup butter
- 1 boneless beef top sirloin steak (1 inch thick and 6 ounces), cut into 1/8-inch slices
- 1 teaspoon all-purpose flour
- 1 teaspoon brown sugar
- 1/4 teaspoon salt
- 1/2 cup beef broth
- 1 tube (16.3 ounces) large refrigerated flaky biscuits
- 3/4 cup shredded part-skim mozzarella cheese
- 1/3 cup grated Parmesan cheese, *divided*

In a large skillet, cook onions in butter over medium heat for 10-12 minutes or until very tender. Remove and keep warm. In the same skillet, cook steak for 2-3 minutes or until tender.

Return the onions to the pan. Stir in the flour, brown sugar and salt until blended; gradually add the beef broth. Bring to a boil; cook and stir for 4-6 minutes or until thickened.

Separate the biscuits; split each horizontally into three portions. Press onto the bottom and up the sides of eight ungreased muffin cups, overlapping the sides and tops of biscuits. Fill each cup with about

2 tablespoons beef mixture.

Combine the mozzarella cheese and 1/4 cup Parmesan cheese; sprinkle over the filling. Fold the dough over completely to enclose filling. Sprinkle with remaining Parmesan cheese.

Bake at 375° for 12-15 minutes or until golden brown. Let stand for 2 minutes before removing from pan. Serve warm. **Yield:** 4 servings.

Carrot Bran Muffins

Prep: 20 min. **Bake:** 25 min.

With their golden brown tops, pretty flecks of orange and bursts of raisin sweetness, these bran muffins are anything but ordinary! Our home economists fine-tuned the recipe to make these treats extra moist and even more tender.

```
1-1/2 cups all-purpose flour
    1 cup wheat bran
  1/2 cup packed brown sugar
1-1/2 teaspoons ground cinnamon
1-1/4 teaspoons baking powder
  1/2 teaspoon baking soda
  1/2 teaspoon salt
    2 eggs
  3/4 cup buttermilk
  1/2 cup vegetable oil
    2 tablespoons molasses
1-1/2 cups grated carrots
    1 cup raisins
```

In a large bowl, combine the first seven ingredients. Combine the eggs, buttermilk, oil and molasses; stir into dry ingredients just until moistened. Fold in carrots and raisins.

Fill greased or paper-lined muffin cups three-fourths full. Bake at 350° for 25-30 minutes or until a toothpick comes out clean. Cool for 5 minutes before removing from pan to a wire rack. Serve warm. **Yield:** 1 dozen.

Garlic Poppy Seed Spirals

Prep/Total Time: 25 min.

This is a great way to jazz up plain rolls. Feel free to adjust the amount of seasoning to suit your family.
—*Stacey Scherer, Macomb, Michigan*

```
3 tablespoons butter, melted
1 teaspoon garlic powder
1 teaspoon dried minced onion
1/2 teaspoon poppy seeds
1 tube (8 ounces) refrigerated crescent rolls
```

In a small bowl, combine the butter, garlic powder, onion and poppy seeds; set aside. Remove crescent dough from tube; do not unroll. Cut dough into 10 slices; dip one side in butter mixture. Place buttered side up in an ungreased 9-in. round baking pan. Brush with remaining butter mixture.

Bake at 350° for 14-16 minutes or until golden brown. Serve warm. **Yield:** 10 servings.

Lemon Pull-Apart Coffee Cake

Lemon Pull-Apart Coffee Cake

(Pictured above)

Prep/Total Time: 30 min.

I found this recipe in a newspaper and make it often. The lemon cake is perfect when unexpected company stops in and I need something speedy to go with a cup of coffee.
—*Mary Tallman, Arbor Vitae, Wisconsin*

✓ Uses less fat, sugar or salt. Includes Nutrition Facts and Diabetic Exchanges.

```
1/4 cup sugar
1/4 cup chopped walnuts
1/4 cup golden raisins
  2 tablespoons butter, melted
  2 teaspoons grated lemon peel
  1 tube (12 ounces) refrigerated buttermilk
    biscuits
```
GLAZE:
```
1/2 cup confectioners' sugar
  1 tablespoon lemon juice
```

In a large bowl, combine the first five ingredients. Separate biscuits and cut each into quarters; toss with sugar mixture. Place in a greased 9-in. round baking pan.

Bake at 400° for 20-25 minutes or until golden brown. Immediately invert onto a wire rack. Combine glaze ingredients until smooth; drizzle over warm coffee cake. **Yield:** 10 servings.

Nutrition Facts: 4 pieces equals 175 calories, 5 g fat (2 g saturated fat), 6 mg cholesterol, 315 mg sodium, 31 g carbohydrate, trace fiber, 4 g protein. **Diabetic Exchanges:** 2 starch, 1/2 fat.

**Cinnamon Chip Scones
Chocolate-Pecan Sticky Buns**

Chocolate-Pecan Sticky Buns

(Pictured above and on page 146)

Prep: 10 min. **Bake:** 25 min.

You won't believe how luscious this four-ingredient recipe is. The rolls have a fun surprise inside—chocolate kisses.
—Tammy Logan, Clinton, Tennessee

    1 can (15 ounces) coconut-pecan frosting
    1 cup pecan halves
    2 tubes (12 ounces *each*) refrigerated
       buttermilk biscuits
  20 milk chocolate kisses

Spread frosting over bottom of a greased 9-in. square baking pan. Arrange pecans over frosting; set aside.

Flatten each biscuit to 1/4-in. thickness. Place a chocolate kiss on one side of each biscuit. Fold edges of dough over kiss; pinch edges to seal. Arrange biscuits, flat side down, over pecans.

Bake at 400° for 25-30 minutes or until golden brown. Cool on a wire rack for 5 minutes. Invert onto a serving plate; serve immediately. **Yield:** 20 servings.

Cinnamon Chip Scones

(Pictured above and on page 146)

Prep: 25 min. **Bake:** 10 min.

These sweet and tender scones will melt in your mouth. They're delicious hot, warm or even cold.
—Barbara Humiston, Tampa, Florida

3-1/4 cups all-purpose flour
  1/3 cup plus 2 tablespoons sugar, *divided*
2-1/2 teaspoons baking powder
  1/2 teaspoon baking soda
  1/2 teaspoon salt
  3/4 cup cold butter
    1 cup buttermilk
    1 package (10 ounces) cinnamon-flavored
      baking chips
    2 tablespoons butter, melted

In a large bowl, combine the flour, 1/3 cup sugar, baking powder, baking soda and salt. Cut in butter until mixture resembles coarse crumbs. Stir in buttermilk just until moistened. Fold in chips.

Turn onto a lightly floured surface; knead gently 10-12 times or until dough is no longer sticky. Divide in half; gently pat or roll each portion into a 7-in. circle. Brush with butter and sprinkle with remaining sugar.

Cut each circle into six wedges. Separate wedges and place on an ungreased baking sheet. Bake at 425° for 10-13 minutes or until lightly browned. Serve warm. **Yield:** 1 dozen.

Broccoli-Cheese Corn Bread

Prep: 15 min. **Bake:** 35 min.

Bright and flavorful, this bread is always a hit at church functions. One couple liked it so much, they now call it "Holly Bread!" —Holly Cummings, Baytown, Texas

  1 cup chopped onion
  1 cup butter, cubed
  2 packages (8-1/2 ounces *each*) corn
    bread/muffin mix
  2 cups (8 ounces) shredded
    cheddar-Monterey Jack cheese
  6 eggs

1-1/2 cups cottage cheese
    1 package (9 ounces) frozen broccoli cuts,
      thawed and drained
    1 cup fresh *or* frozen corn, thawed
    2 tablespoons canned jalapeno slices, chopped

In a large skillet, saute onion in butter until tender; set aside. In a large bowl, combine corn bread mix and shredded cheese. In another bowl, beat the eggs, cottage cheese and onion mixture. Stir into the corn bread mixture just until moistened. Fold in the broccoli, corn and jalapeno.

Transfer to a greased 13-in. x 9-in. x 2-in. baking pan. Bake at 400° for 35-40 minutes or until lightly browned and edges pull away from sides of pan. Serve warm. Refrigerate leftovers. **Yield:** 12-15 servings.

Editor's Note: When cutting or seeding hot peppers, use rubber or plastic gloves to protect your hands. Avoid touching your face.

Cheese Biscuits

(Pictured below)

Prep/Total Time: 25 min.

These savory biscuits couldn't be simpler to make. With from-scratch flavor and a golden brown cheese topping, they'll disappear fast at any meal. —Lynn Tice
Osage City, Kansas

    1 tube (12 ounces) refrigerated buttermilk
      biscuits
1/4 cup Italian salad dressing
1/3 cup grated Parmesan cheese
1/2 cup shredded part-skim mozzarella cheese

Separate biscuits; dip the top of each in salad dressing, then in Parmesan cheese. Place cheese side up on an ungreased baking sheet; sprinkle with mozzarella cheese. Bake at 400° for 9-11 minutes or until golden brown. Serve warm. **Yield:** 10 biscuits.

Cheese Biscuits

Pineapple-Raisin Nut Bread

Pineapple-Raisin Nut Bread

(Pictured above)

Prep: 15 min. **Bake:** 50 min. + cooling

This sweet, dark bread has a nice level of spice that makes it perfect for Christmastime. Serve slices for brunch or as an after-school snack. —Jeanne Perdu, Houston, Texas

    1 cup sugar
3/4 cup packed brown sugar
    1 cup vegetable oil
    3 eggs
    1 cup crushed pineapple, drained
    1 teaspoon rum extract
    3 cups all-purpose flour
    1 tablespoon ground cinnamon
    1 teaspoon baking soda
    1 teaspoon baking powder
    1 teaspoon salt
1/2 teaspoon ground cloves
    1 cup chopped pecans
3/4 cup raisins

In a large mixing bowl, beat the sugars, oil and eggs until smooth. Stir in pineapple and extract. Combine the flour, cinnamon, baking soda, baking powder, salt and cloves; stir into egg mixture just until moistened. Fold in pecans and raisins.

Spoon into two greased 8-in. x 4-in. x 2-in. loaf pans. Bake at 325° for 50-55 minutes or until a toothpick inserted near the center comes out clean. Cool for 10 minutes before removing from pans to wire racks. **Yield:** 2 loaves.

Banana Muffins

Prep/Total Time: 30 min.

These muffins turn out wonderful every single time. My uncle raves about them when he comes to visit.
—*Linda Heywood, Mill Bay, British Columbia*

2 cups biscuit/baking mix
1 egg, lightly beaten
1-1/3 cups mashed ripe bananas
1/2 cup packed brown sugar
3 tablespoons milk
2 tablespoons vegetable oil
1 teaspoon vanilla extract

Place biscuit mix in a large bowl. Combine egg, bananas, sugar, milk, oil and vanilla; stir into mix just until combined. Fill paper-lined muffin cups two-thirds full.

Bake at 400° for 15-20 minutes or until a toothpick comes out clean. Cool for 5 minutes before removing from pan to a wire rack. **Yield:** 1 dozen.

Sweet Potato Biscuits

(Pictured below)

Prep/Total Time: 25 min.

Only four ingredients make these moist biscuits a snap to prepare. —*Pam Bouillion, Rayne, Louisiana*

2-1/2 cups biscuit/baking mix
1-1/2 cups canned sweet potatoes
6 tablespoons milk
1/3 cup butter, melted

Place biscuit mix in a large bowl. In a small bowl, mash sweet potatoes; stir in milk and butter. Stir into biscuit mix just until moistened.

Drop by heaping tablespoonfuls 2 in. apart onto a greased baking sheet. Bake at 425° for 8-10 minutes or until golden brown. Serve warm. **Yield:** about 1 dozen.

Focaccia Bread

(Pictured below)

Prep/Total Time: 30 min.

Green olives complement this cheesy, pizza-like bread. It's a very simple recipe that's packed with flavor.
—*Ivy Laffoon, Ceres, California*

1 loaf (1 pound) frozen bread dough, thawed
1/2 cup sliced pimiento-stuffed olives
1/2 cup shredded Colby-Monterey Jack cheese
1/2 cup shredded Parmesan cheese
1 teaspoon Italian seasoning
2 tablespoons olive oil

On an ungreased baking sheet, pat dough into a 12-in. x 6-in. rectangle. Build up edges slightly. Top with olives, cheeses and Italian seasoning; press gently into dough. Drizzle with oil.

Bake at 350° for 15-20 minutes or until cheese is melted and golden brown. Let stand for 5 minutes before slicing. **Yield:** 8 servings.

Focaccia Bread
Sweet Potato Biscuits

Soft Oatmeal Bread
Pecan Raisin Bread

Pecan Raisin Bread

(Pictured above)

Prep: 10 min. **Bake:** 3 hours

We're fans of raisin bread and also enjoy the nutty flavor of pecans, so I decided to combine the two for this delectable loaf. —*Lora Sexton, Wellington, Texas*

✓ Uses less fat, sugar or salt. Includes Nutrition Facts.

    1 cup plus 2 tablespoons water (70° to 80°)
    8 teaspoons butter
    1 egg
    6 tablespoons sugar
  1/4 cup nonfat dry milk powder
    1 teaspoon salt
    4 cups bread flour
    1 tablespoon active dry yeast
    1 cup finely chopped pecans
    1 cup raisins

In bread machine pan, place the first eight ingredients in order suggested by manufacturer. Select basic bread setting. Choose crust color and loaf size if available. Bake according to bread machine directions (check dough after 5 minutes of mixing; add 1 to 2 tablespoons of water or flour if needed).

Just before the final kneading (your machine may audibly signal this), add pecans and raisins. **Yield:** 1 loaf (2-1/2 pounds, 16 slices).

Nutrition Facts: 1 slice equals 227 calories, 8 g fat (2 g saturated fat), 19 mg cholesterol, 182 mg sodium, 36 g carbohydrate, 2 g fiber, 6 g protein.

Editor's Note: If your bread machine has a time-delay feature, we recommend you do not use it for this recipe.

Soft Oatmeal Bread

(Pictured above)

Prep: 10 min. **Bake:** 3 hours

My husband loves making this tender bread. With its mild oat taste and soft texture, it's a hit with the whole family. —*Nancy Montgomery, Plainwell, Michigan*

1-1/2 cups water (70° to 80°)
  1/4 cup sugar
  1/4 cup vegetable oil
    2 teaspoons salt
    1 teaspoon lemon juice
    3 cups all-purpose flour
1-1/2 cups quick-cooking oats
2-1/2 teaspoons active dry yeast

In bread machine pan, place all ingredients in order suggested by manufacturer. Select basic bread setting. Choose crust color and loaf size if available. Bake according to bread machine directions (check dough after 5 minutes of mixing; add 1 to 2 tablespoons of water or flour if needed). **Yield:** 1 loaf (2 pounds).

Chapter 10

⏱ *Slow-Cooked Sensations*

SET THE PACE for a quick dinner by slowing down...and taking advantage of the convenience of a slow cooker.

This handy appliance lets you get supper started in the morning, then forget about it all day. When you and your family arrive home in the evening, you'll have a home-cooked meal that's hot and ready to enjoy.

Choose from a wide variety of slow-cooked meals in this chapter, including Cajun-Style Pot Roast, Greek Garlic Chicken, Zippy Spaghetti Sauce and Tender Spareribs.

You can even round out your menus with terrific accompaniments—Nacho Salsa Dip and Creamy Hash Brown Potatoes.

SLOW AND SPECIAL. Turkey Leg Pot Roast (p. 168).

Bavarian Meatballs

Tender Chicken Dinner

(Pictured below)

Prep: 10 min. **Cook:** 5-1/4 hours

With potatoes, carrots, green beans and gravy, this all-in-one poultry dinner provides lots of family appeal. I appreciate the fact that it can be put together quickly in the morning before you leave for work, errands or other activities.

—Wanda Sanner, Amarillo, Texas

4 boneless skinless chicken breast halves (4 ounces *each*)
1 can (14-1/2 ounces) chicken broth
1 can (14-1/2 ounces) chicken gravy
2 cups sliced peeled potatoes
1 package (16 ounces) frozen sliced carrots, thawed
1 package (16 ounces) frozen cut green beans, thawed
1 teaspoon pepper
2 tablespoons cornstarch
1/3 cup cold water
1 cup french-fried onions

Place chicken in a 5-qt. slow cooker. Add the broth, gravy, potatoes, carrots, beans and pepper. Cover and cook on low for 5 to 5-1/2 hours or until chicken juices run clear.

In a small bowl, combine cornstarch and water; stir into cooking juices. Sprinkle with onions. Cover and cook on high for 15 minutes or until thickened. **Yield:** 4 servings.

Bavarian Meatballs

(Pictured above)

Prep: 15 min. **Cook:** 3-1/2 hours

I use my slow cooker so much, and these mouth-watering bites are one reason why. Serve them in sandwiches or as an appetizer. —Peggy Rios, Mechanicsville, Virginia

1 package (38 ounces) frozen cooked Italian meatballs
1/2 cup chopped onion
1/4 cup packed brown sugar
1 envelope onion soup mix
1 can (12 ounces) beer *or* nonalcoholic beer
12 hoagie buns, split
3 cups (12 ounces) shredded Swiss cheese

In a 3-qt. slow cooker, combine the meatballs, onion, brown sugar, soup mix and beer. Cover and cook on low for 3-1/2 to 4-1/2 hours or until heated through.

Serve with toothpicks for an appetizer. Or for sandwiches, place six meatballs on each bun bottom. Sprinkle each sandwich with 1/4 cup cheese. Place on baking sheets. Broil 4-6 in. from the heat for 2-3 minutes or until cheese is melted. Replace bun tops. **Yield:** 12 servings.

Slow Going

To transport my slow cooker to a potluck, I use a clean milk crate. I just line it with a towel and set the cooker right inside. The crate keeps the cooker from tipping, so I arrive at the potluck with no problem.
—Helen Phillips, Horseheads, New York

Tender Chicken Dinner

Satisfying Chicken And Veggies

Prep: 20 min. **Cook:** 4 hours

This complete, home-style supper with chicken and vegetables is seasoned with plenty of herbs. —Kat Sadi
San Luis Obispo, California

   2 medium potatoes, peeled and cut into 1-inch pieces (about 1-1/2 cups)
   1 cup thickly sliced onion
1/2 cup sliced celery
   1 medium carrot, cut into 1-inch pieces
   1 medium sweet yellow pepper, cut into 1-inch pieces
   1 broiler/fryer chicken (3 to 4 pounds), cut up and skin removed
   1 jar (26 ounces) meatless spaghetti sauce
   1 cup water
1-1/2 teaspoons minced garlic
1/4 teaspoon salt
1/4 teaspoon dried oregano
1/4 teaspoon dried basil
1/4 teaspoon pepper

Place the potatoes, onion, celery, carrot and yellow pepper in a 5-qt. slow cooker. Top with chicken. Combine the remaining ingredients; pour over chicken.

Cover and cook on low for 4 to 4-1/2 hours or until chicken juices run clear and vegetables are tender. **Yield:** 6 servings.

Thai-Style Pork

Prep: 15 min. **Cook:** 6 hours

A creamy peanut butter sauce coats moist slices of pork in this delectable dish. —Amy Van Orman
Rockford, Michigan

   2 pounds boneless pork loin chops
1/4 cup teriyaki sauce
   2 tablespoons rice wine vinegar
   1 teaspoon crushed red pepper flakes
   1 teaspoon minced garlic
   1 tablespoon cornstarch
1/4 cup cold water
1/4 cup creamy peanut butter
Hot cooked rice
1/2 cup chopped green onions
1/2 cup dry roasted peanuts
Lime juice, optional

Place chops in a 3-qt. slow cooker. Combine teriyaki sauce, vinegar, pepper flakes and garlic; pour over meat. Cover; cook on low for 6 hours or until meat is tender.

Remove pork and cut into bite-size pieces; keep warm. Strain cooking juices into a large saucepan. Combine cornstarch and water until smooth; stir into juices. Bring to a boil; cook and stir for 2 minutes or until thickened. Stir in peanut butter; add meat.

Serve with rice. Sprinkle with onions and peanuts. Drizzle with lime juice if desired. **Yield:** 6 servings.

Beef Burgundy

Beef Burgundy

(Pictured above)

Prep: 10 min. **Cook:** 5-1/2 hours

The night before I serve this satisfying entree, I trim the meat, cut up the vegetables and store them in the fridge in separate containers. That way, prep takes only minutes the next morning. At night, I simply cook the noodles and bake some cheesy garlic toast for a warm, wonderful meal.
—Mary Jo Nikolaus, Mansfield, Ohio

1-1/2 pounds beef stew meat, cut into 1-inch cubes
1/2 pound whole fresh mushrooms, halved
   4 medium carrots, chopped
   1 can (10-3/4 ounces) condensed golden mushroom soup, undiluted
   1 large onion, cut into thin wedges
1/2 cup Burgundy wine *or* beef broth
1/4 cup quick-cooking tapioca
1/2 teaspoon salt
1/4 teaspoon dried thyme
1/4 teaspoon pepper
Hot cooked egg noodles

In a 5-qt. slow cooker, combine the first 10 ingredients. Cover and cook on low for 5-1/2 to 6-1/2 hours or until meat is tender. Serve over noodles. **Yield:** 6 servings.

Teriyaki Pork Roast

(Pictured below)

Prep: 10 min. **Cook:** 6 hours + standing

This is the only kind of meat my kids will eat and enjoy—other than hot dogs! The recipe was given to me by my mother. I can put it together in the morning and have a moist, tender roast ready at the end of the day. We like it best with mashed potatoes.
—Debbie Dunaway
Kettering, Ohio

>   1 boneless pork shoulder roast (3 to 4
>   pounds), trimmed
>   1 cup packed brown sugar
> 1/3 cup unsweetened apple juice
> 1/3 cup soy sauce
> 1/2 teaspoon salt
> 1/4 teaspoon pepper
>   2 tablespoons cornstarch
>   3 tablespoons cold water

Cut roast in half; rub with brown sugar. Place in a 5-qt. slow cooker. Pour apple juice and soy sauce over roast. Sprinkle with salt and pepper. Cover and cook on low for 6 to 6-1/2 hours or until meat is tender.

Remove roast; cover and let stand for 15 minutes.

Meanwhile, strain cooking juices and return to slow cooker. Combine cornstarch and cold water until smooth; gradually stir into juices. Cover and cook on high for 15 minutes or until thickened. Slice pork; serve with gravy. **Yield:** 6-8 servings.

Tender Spareribs

Prep: 10 min. **Cook:** 5-1/2 hours

Even my three little ones love this easy, delicious meal. After slow cooking, the succulent meat falls right off the bone.   —Julie Czmer, West Bloomfield, Michigan

>   4 pounds pork spareribs
> 1/4 cup soy sauce
> 1/4 cup prepared mustard
> 1/4 cup molasses
>   3 tablespoons cider vinegar
>   2 tablespoons Worcestershire sauce
>   1 to 2 teaspoons hot pepper sauce

Place ribs in a 5-qt. slow cooker. Combine the remaining ingredients; pour over ribs. Cover and cook on low for 5-1/2 to 6 hours or until meat is tender. Serve with a slotted spoon. **Yield:** 8 servings.

Teriyaki Pork Roast

Greek Garlic Chicken

Prep: 20 min. **Cook:** 3-1/2 hours

The lively flavors of the Greek Isles come through in this mouth-watering chicken entree. I created it so my husband and I could have a nice, home-cooked dinner after a busy day out and about. This definitely fills the bill. —Margee Berry
Trout Lake, Washington

1/2 cup chopped onion
  3 tablespoons minced garlic
  1 tablespoon plus 1 teaspoon olive oil, *divided*
2-1/2 cups chicken broth, *divided*
1/4 cup pitted Greek olives, chopped
  3 tablespoons chopped sun-dried tomatoes
    (not packed in oil)
  1 tablespoon quick-cooking tapioca
  2 teaspoons grated lemon peel
  1 teaspoon dried oregano
  6 boneless skinless chicken breast halves
    (6 ounces *each*)
1-3/4 cups uncooked couscous
1/2 cup crumbled feta cheese

In a small skillet, saute onion and garlic in 1 tablespoon oil. Transfer to a 5-qt. slow cooker. Stir in 3/4 cup broth, olives, tomatoes, tapioca, lemon peel and oregano. Add chicken. Cover and cook on low for 3-1/2 to 4 hours or until a meat thermometer reads 170°.

In a saucepan, bring remaining oil and broth to a boil. Stir in couscous. Cover and remove from the heat; let stand for 5 minutes or until broth is absorbed. Serve with chicken; sprinkle with feta cheese. **Yield:** 6 servings.

Beef Tips

Prep: 20 min. **Cook:** 6-1/4 hours

When I was growing up, my mother made this recipe. I have my own family now, and we've reduced the amount of red meat we eat. But this beef is so good, I still fix it!
—Diane Benskin, Lewisville, Texas

  1 pound beef sirloin tips, cut into 1-inch cubes
  2 to 3 medium carrots, chopped
  1 to 1-1/2 cups chopped celery
  1 cup chopped onion
  1 can (10-3/4 ounces) condensed golden
    mushroom soup, undiluted
1/2 to 1 cup white wine *or* beef broth
  2 teaspoons cornstarch
1/4 cup cold water
Hot cooked egg noodles

In a 3-qt. slow cooker, combine the beef, carrots, celery, onion, soup and wine or broth. Cover and cook on low for 6-7 hours or until meat is tender.

Combine cornstarch and water until smooth; gradually stir into cooking juices. Cover and cook on high for 15 minutes or until thickened. Serve with noodles. **Yield:** 4 servings.

Cajun-Style Pot Roast

Cajun-Style Pot Roast

(Pictured above)

Prep: 15 min. **Cook:** 6 hours

I often make this zippy roast for guests. It gives me time to visit, and everyone likes it—even my friend who's a chef. —Ginger Menzies, Steamboat Springs, Colorado

  1 boneless beef chuck roast (2 to 3 pounds)
  2 tablespoons Cajun seasoning
  1 tablespoon olive oil
  2 cans (10 ounces *each*) diced tomatoes and
    green chilies
  1 medium sweet red pepper, chopped
1-1/2 cups chopped celery
3/4 cup chopped onion
1/4 cup quick-cooking tapioca
1-1/2 teaspoons minced garlic
  1 teaspoon salt
Hot cooked rice

Cut roast in half; sprinkle with Cajun seasoning. In a large skillet, brown roast in oil on all sides; drain. Transfer to a 5-qt. slow cooker.

Combine the tomatoes, red pepper, celery, onion, tapioca, garlic and salt; pour over roast. Cover and cook on low for 6-8 hours or until meat is tender. Slice and serve with rice. **Yield:** 6 servings.

Cajun Clue

CAJUN SEASONING is available in the spice section of most grocery stores. You can also easily make your own Cajun seasoning. Although it comes in many different blends, a typical blend includes salt, onion powder, garlic powder, cayenne pepper, ground mustard, celery seed and pepper.

Slow 'n' Easy Barbecued Chicken

minutes. Remove from the heat.

Place the chicken in a 3-qt. slow cooker. Top with sauce. Cover and cook on low for 3-4 hours or until chicken juices run clear.

Remove the chicken to a serving platter and keep warm. Strain the cooking juices and skim the fat; transfer to a saucepan. Combine the cornstarch and water until smooth; stir into juices. Bring to a boil; cook and stir for 2 minutes or until thickened. Spoon some of the sauce over chicken and serve the remaining sauce on the side. **Yield:** 4 servings.

Sweet 'n' Sour Pork Chops

Prep: 5 min. **Cook:** 4-1/4 hours

With only five ingredients, these tender and tangy pork chops couldn't be much simpler to put together. Barbecue sauce, chili sauce, crushed pineapple and chopped onion make them lip-smacking good every time.
—Laurie Stafford, Waterville, New York

   1 can (8 ounces) crushed pineapple, undrained
   1 cup honey barbecue sauce
1/3 cup finely chopped onion
   2 tablespoons chili sauce
   4 bone-in pork loin chops (3/4 inch thick and 8 ounces *each*)

In a small bowl, combine the pineapple, barbecue sauce, onion and chili sauce. Pour half into a greased 3-qt. slow cooker. Top with pork chops and remaining sauce. Cover and cook on low for 4-1/4 to 5-1/4 hours or until meat is tender. **Yield:** 4 servings.

Slow 'n' Easy Barbecued Chicken

(Pictured above)

Prep: 20 min. **Cook:** 3 hours

I turn to this dinner on warmer days when I have a lot of yard work to do. Just pair the chicken with a side vegetable and salad, and supper is served! The recipe is also great with pork or beef...and is easy to double for a crowd.
—Dreama Hughes, London, Kentucky

1/4 cup water
   3 tablespoons brown sugar
   3 tablespoons white vinegar
   3 tablespoons ketchup
   2 tablespoons butter
   2 tablespoons Worcestershire sauce
   1 tablespoon lemon juice
   1 teaspoon salt
   1 teaspoon paprika
   1 teaspoon ground mustard
1/2 teaspoon cayenne pepper
   1 broiler/fryer chicken (2-1/2 to 3 pounds), cut up and skin removed
   4 teaspoons cornstarch
   1 tablespoon cold water

In a small saucepan, combine the first 11 ingredients. Bring to a boil. Reduce heat; simmer, uncovered, for 5

Chicken with Mushroom Gravy

Prep: 10 min. **Cook:** 4-1/4 hours

This delicious chicken is a longtime favorite with my family because it's so comforting, rich and filling, especially served over hot rice. A friend shared the recipe years ago, and I adapted it by adding a few new ingredients. The green chilies and Italian salad dressing provide a nice flavor boost.
—Darolyn Jones, Fishers, Indiana

   4 boneless skinless chicken breast halves (6 ounces *each*)
   1 can (12 ounces) mushroom gravy
   1 cup milk
   1 can (8 ounces) mushroom stems and pieces, drained
   1 can (4 ounces) chopped green chilies
   1 envelope Italian salad dressing mix
   1 package (8 ounces) cream cheese, cubed

In a 3-qt. slow cooker, combine the chicken, gravy, milk, mushrooms, chilies and dressing mix. Cover and cook on low for 4 to 4-1/2 hours or until chicken juices run clear.

Stir in cream cheese; cover and cook 15 minutes longer or until cheese is melted. **Yield:** 4 servings.

Hearty Jambalaya

(Pictured below)

Prep: 15 min. **Cook:** 6-1/4 hours

I love anything with Cajun spices, so I came up with this slow cooker jambalaya that's just as good as versions I've had in restaurants. If you can't find andouille sausage, hot links, smoked sausage or chorizo will also work. I like to pair each bowl with warm corn bread and to garnish with green onions.
—Jennifer Fulk
Moreno Valley, California

  1 can (28 ounces) diced tomatoes, undrained
  1 pound fully cooked andouille sausage links, cubed
1/2 pound boneless skinless chicken breasts, cut into 1-inch cubes
  1 can (8 ounces) tomato sauce
  1 cup diced onion
  1 small sweet red pepper, diced
  1 small green pepper, diced
  1 cup chicken broth
  1 celery rib with leaves, chopped
  2 tablespoons tomato paste
  2 teaspoons dried oregano
  2 teaspoons Cajun seasoning
1-1/2 teaspoons minced garlic
  2 bay leaves
  1 teaspoon Louisiana-style hot sauce
1/2 teaspoon dried thyme
  1 pound cooked medium shrimp, peeled and deveined
Hot cooked rice

Melt-in-Your-Mouth Pot Roast

In a 5-qt. slow cooker, combine the first 16 ingredients. Cover and cook on low for 6-7 hours or until chicken juices run clear.

Stir in shrimp. Cover and cook 15 minutes longer or until heated through. Discard bay leaves. Serve with rice. **Yield:** 8 servings.

Melt-in-Your-Mouth Pot Roast

(Pictured above)

Prep: 10 min. **Cook:** 6 hours

Slow-simmered and seasoned with rosemary, mustard and thyme, this mouth-watering pot roast is always a hit. I sometimes substitute Burgundy wine or brandy plus a half cup of water for the broth...and the aroma is wonderful!
—Jeannie Klugh, Lancaster, Pennsylvania

  1 pound medium red potatoes, quartered
  1 cup fresh baby carrots
  1 boneless beef chuck roast (3 to 4 pounds)
1/4 cup Dijon mustard
  2 teaspoons dried rosemary, crushed
  1 teaspoon garlic salt
1/2 teaspoon dried thyme
1/2 teaspoon pepper
1/3 cup chopped onion
1-1/2 cups beef broth

Place potatoes and carrots in a 5-qt. slow cooker. Cut roast in half. In a small bowl, combine the mustard, rosemary, garlic salt, thyme and pepper; rub over roast. Place in slow cooker; top with onion and broth. Cover and cook on low for 6-8 hours or until meat and vegetables are tender. **Yield:** 6-8 servings.

Hearty Jambalaya

Creamy Hash Brown Potatoes
Polynesian Roast Beef

Creamy Hash Brown Potatoes

(Pictured at left)

Prep: 5 min. **Cook:** 3-1/2 hours

Convenient frozen hash browns are the secret behind the cheesy slow cooker potatoes I make for potlucks and big-group gatherings. —Julianne Brown, Springfield, Illinois

>   1 package (32 ounces) frozen Southern-style
>   hash brown potatoes
>   1 can (10-3/4 ounces) condensed cream of
>   potato soup, undiluted
>   2 cups (8 ounces) shredded Colby-Monterey
>   Jack cheese
>   1 cup (8 ounces) sour cream
> 1/4 teaspoon pepper
> 1/8 teaspoon salt
>   1 carton (8 ounces) spreadable chive and
>   onion cream cheese

Place potatoes in a lightly greased 3-qt. slow cooker. In a small bowl, combine the soup, cheese, sour cream, pepper and salt. Pour over potatoes and mix well. Cover and cook on low for 3-1/2 to 4 hours or until potatoes are tender. Stir in cream cheese. **Yield:** 12-14 servings.

Polynesian Roast Beef

(Pictured at left)

Prep: 15 min. **Cook:** 8 hours

This simple and delicious recipe was shared by my sister and has been a family favorite for years. Pineapple and green pepper add color and taste. —Annette Mosbarger
Peyton, Colorado

>   1 boneless beef top round roast (3-1/4 pounds)
>   2 tablespoons browning sauce, optional
> 1/4 cup all-purpose flour
>   1 teaspoon salt
> 1/4 teaspoon pepper
>   1 medium onion, sliced
>   1 can (8 ounces) unsweetened sliced
>   pineapple
> 1/4 cup packed brown sugar
>   2 tablespoons cornstarch
> 1/4 teaspoon ground ginger
> 1/2 cup beef broth
> 1/4 cup soy sauce
> 1/2 teaspoon minced garlic
>   1 medium green pepper, sliced

Cut roast in half; brush with browning sauce if desired. Combine the flour, salt and pepper; rub over meat. Place onion in a 3-qt. slow cooker; top with roast.

Drain pineapple, reserving juice; refrigerate the pineapple. In a small bowl, combine the brown sugar, cornstarch and ginger; whisk in the broth, soy sauce, garlic and reserved pineapple juice until smooth. Pour over meat. Cover and cook on low for 7-8 hours. Add pineapple and green pepper. Cook 1 hour longer or until meat and green pepper are tender. **Yield:** 10-11 servings.

Sweet-and-Sour Chicken Wings

Prep: 15 min. **Cook:** 3 hours

For a great appetizer at your next get-together, try these saucy, sweet and tangy wings. They can also be served over rice for a main dish.
—June Eberhardt
Marysville, California

  1 cup sugar
  1 cup cider vinegar
1/2 cup ketchup
  2 tablespoons reduced-sodium soy sauce
  1 teaspoon chicken bouillon granules
16 chicken wings
  6 tablespoons cornstarch
1/2 cup cold water

In a small saucepan, combine the first five ingredients. Bring to a boil; cook and stir until sugar is dissolved. Place chicken wings in a 3-qt. slow cooker; add vinegar mixture. Cover and cook on low for 3 to 3-1/2 hours or until chicken juices run clear.

Transfer chicken wings to a serving dish and keep warm. Pour cooking juices into a small saucepan. Combine cornstarch and the cold water until smooth; stir into juices. Bring to a boil; cook and stir for 2 minutes or until thickened. Spoon over chicken wings. Serve with a slotted spoon. **Yield:** 4 servings.

Zippy Spaghetti Sauce

Prep: 20 min. **Cook:** 6 hours

This thick and hearty sauce goes a long way toward filling up a hungry family! We all enjoy the leftovers ladled over thick grilled slices of garlic bread. To be sure I have the ingredients on hand, I keep chopped green pepper in my freezer and minced garlic in my fridge.
—Elaine Priest, Dover, Pennsylvania

  2 pounds ground beef
  1 cup chopped onion
1/2 cup chopped green pepper
  2 cans (15 ounces *each*) tomato sauce
  1 can (28 ounces) diced tomatoes, undrained
  1 can (12 ounces) tomato paste
1/2 pound sliced fresh mushrooms
  1 cup grated Parmesan cheese
1/2 to 3/4 cup dry red wine *or* beef broth
1/2 cup sliced pimiento-stuffed olives
1/4 cup dried parsley flakes
  1 to 2 tablespoons dried oregano
  2 teaspoons Italian seasoning
  2 teaspoons minced garlic
  1 teaspoon salt
  1 teaspoon pepper
Hot cooked spaghetti

In a large skillet, cook the beef, onion and green pepper over medium heat until meat is no longer pink; drain. Transfer to a 5-qt. slow cooker.

Stir in the tomato sauce, tomatoes, tomato paste, mushrooms, Parmesan cheese, wine or broth, olives,

Saucy Pork Chops

parsley, oregano, Italian seasoning, garlic, salt and pepper. Cover and cook on low for 6-8 hours. Serve with spaghetti. **Yield:** about 3 quarts.

Saucy Pork Chops

(Pictured above)

Prep: 15 min. **Cook:** 4-1/4 hours

I don't always have time in the evening to fix the home-cooked meals my family loves, so I've come to rely on my slow cooker. I serve these tongue-tingling chops at least once a week—the meat's so tender you can cut it with a fork.
—Jennifer Ruberg, Two Harbors, Minnesota

  4 bone-in pork loin chops (8 ounces *each*)
  1 teaspoon garlic powder
1/2 teaspoon salt
1/4 teaspoon pepper
  2 tablespoons vegetable oil
  2 cups ketchup
1/2 cup packed brown sugar
  1 teaspoon hickory-flavored Liquid Smoke

Sprinkle the pork chops with the garlic powder, salt and pepper. In a large skillet, brown pork chops in oil on both sides; drain.

In a bowl, combine the ketchup, brown sugar and Liquid Smoke. Pour half of the sauce into a 3-qt. slow cooker. Top with pork chops and remaining sauce. Cover and cook on low for 4-1/4 to 5-1/4 hours or until meat is tender. **Yield:** 4 servings.

Rosemary Chicken with White Beans

Nacho Salsa Dip

Prep: 15 min. **Cook:** 3 hours

This zesty dip is great for any get-together and allows me to spend more time with my guests. I always have requests to bring it when my husband and I attend parties.
—Sally Hull, Homestead, Florida

> 1 pound ground beef
> 1/3 cup chopped onion
> 2 pounds process cheese (Velveeta), cubed
> 1 jar (16 ounces) chunky salsa
> 1/4 teaspoon garlic powder
> **Tortilla chips** *or* **cubed French bread**

In a large skillet, cook the beef and onion over medium heat until the meat is no longer pink; drain well. Transfer to a greased 3-qt. slow cooker; stir in the process cheese, salsa and garlic powder. Cover and cook on low for 3 hours. Stir; serve with the tortilla chips or cubed French bread. **Yield:** 7 cups.

Country-Style Pork Loin

Prep: 20 min. **Cook:** 5 hours

So moist and tender, this pork roast absolutely melts in your mouth. It ranks high on my son's list of favorites. We often enjoy it with a side of mashed potatoes.
—Corina Flansberg, Carson City, Nevada

✓ Uses less fat, sugar or salt. Includes Nutrition Facts and Diabetic Exchanges.

> 1 boneless whole pork loin roast (3 pounds)
> 1/2 cup all-purpose flour
> 1 teaspoon onion powder
> 1 teaspoon ground mustard
> 2 tablespoons canola oil
> 2 cups chicken broth
> 1/4 cup cornstarch
> 1/4 cup cold water
> **Hot mashed potatoes, optional**

Cut pork roast in half. In a large resealable plastic bag, combine the flour, onion powder and mustard. Add pork, one piece at a time, and shake to coat.

In a large skillet, brown the pork in oil over medium-high heat. Transfer to a 5-qt. slow cooker. Pour the chicken broth over the pork. Cover and cook on low for 5-6 hours or until tender.

Remove pork and keep warm. For gravy, pour 2-1/2 cups cooking juices into a large saucepan. Combine cornstarch and water until smooth; stir into juices. Bring to a boil; cook and stir for 2 minutes or until thickened. Slice pork; serve with gravy and mashed potatoes if desired. **Yield:** 8 servings.

Nutrition Facts: 3 ounces cooked meat with 1/4 cup gravy (prepared with reduced-sodium broth; calculated without potatoes) equals 291 calories, 11 g fat (3 g saturated fat), 85 mg cholesterol, 204 mg sodium, 10 g carbohydrate, trace fiber, 34 g protein. **Diabetic Exchanges:** 3 lean meat, 2 fat, 1/2 starch.

Rosemary Chicken With White Beans

(Pictured above)

Prep: 15 min. **Cook:** 3 hours

With a full-time job and active 5-year-old, I have little time for cooking when I get home. I use my slow cookers at least twice a week...I've even been known to have two or three going at once! I've made this chicken for years and, after a few tweaks, it's become a treasured recipe.
—Sharon Johannes, Ashley, Illinois

> 6 boneless skinless chicken breast halves
>   (6 ounces *each*)
> 1 tablespoon vegetable oil
> 2 cans (15-1/2 ounces *each*) great northern beans, rinsed and drained
> 1 cup sliced fresh carrots
> 1/2 cup sliced celery
> 2/3 cup Italian salad dressing
> 2 teaspoons dried rosemary, crushed
> 1/2 teaspoon salt
> 1 teaspoon pepper

In a skillet, brown chicken in oil in batches on both sides. Place the beans, carrots and celery in a 5-qt. slow cooker; top with chicken.

Combine the Italian salad dressing, rosemary, salt and pepper; pour over the chicken. Cover and cook on low for 3-4 hours or until the chicken juices run clear. **Yield:** 6 servings.

Round Steak Italiano

(Pictured below)

Prep: 20 min. **Cook:** 7 hours

My mother used to serve this delicious Italian-style beef, and it's still one of my top choices for dinner. I like to have lots of the thick gravy draping over both the meat and potatoes. —Deanne Stephens, McMinnville, Oregon

✓ Uses less fat, sugar or salt. Includes Nutrition Facts and Diabetic Exchanges.

    2 pounds boneless beef top round steak
    1 can (8 ounces) tomato sauce
    2 tablespoons onion soup mix
    2 tablespoons canola oil
    2 tablespoons red wine vinegar
    1 teaspoon ground oregano
 1/2 teaspoon garlic powder
 1/4 teaspoon pepper
    8 medium potatoes (7 to 8 ounces *each*)
    1 tablespoon cornstarch
    1 tablespoon cold water

Cut steak into serving-size pieces; place in a 5-qt. slow cooker. In a large bowl, combine the tomato sauce, soup mix, oil, vinegar, oregano, garlic powder and pepper; pour over meat.

Scrub and pierce potatoes; place over meat. Cover; cook on low for 7 to 7-1/2 hours or until meat and potatoes are tender.

Remove meat and potatoes and keep warm. For gravy, pour cooking juices into a small saucepan; skim fat. Combine cornstarch and water until smooth; gradually stir into juices. Bring to a boil; cook and stir for 2 minutes or until thickened. Serve with meat and potatoes. **Yield:** 8 servings.

Nutrition Facts: 3 ounces cooked beef with 1 potato and 3 tablespoons gravy equals 357 calories, 7 g fat (2 g saturated fat), 64 mg cholesterol, 329 mg sodium, 42 g carbohydrate, 4 g fiber, 31 g protein. **Diabetic Exchanges:** 3 lean meat, 2-1/2 starch, 1/2 fat.

Round Steak Italiano

Beef Brisket in Beer

Prep: 15 min. **Cook:** 8 hours

One bite of this brisket, and you'll want to savor it for the whole evening! Prep takes just 15 minutes before the slow cooker takes over. —Eunice Stoen, Decorah, Iowa

    1 fresh beef brisket (2-1/2 to 3 pounds)
    2 teaspoons Liquid Smoke, optional
    1 teaspoon celery salt
 1/2 teaspoon pepper
 1/4 teaspoon salt
    1 large onion, sliced
    1 can (12 ounces) beer *or* nonalcoholic beer
    2 teaspoons Worcestershire sauce
    2 tablespoons cornstarch
 1/4 cup cold water

Cut brisket in half; rub with Liquid Smoke if desired, celery salt, pepper and salt. Place in a 3-qt. slow cooker. Top with onion. Combine beer and Worcestershire sauce; pour over meat. Cover and cook on low for 8-9 hours or until tender.

Remove the brisket and keep warm. Strain the cooking juices; transfer to a small saucepan. Combine the cornstarch and water until smooth; stir into the juices. Bring to a boil; cook and stir for 2 minutes or until thickened. Thinly slice the beef across the grain; serve with gravy. **Yield:** 6 servings.

Editor's Note: This is a fresh beef brisket, not corned beef. The meat comes from the first cut of the brisket.

Tender Pork Chops

Prep: 20 min. **Cook:** 6 hours

My family has enjoyed these flavorful pork chops for years. They're cooked to perfection—the meat falls right off the bone. —Patricia Dick, Anderson, Indiana

 1/2 cup all-purpose flour
 1-1/2 teaspoons ground mustard
    1 teaspoon seasoned salt
 1/2 teaspoon garlic powder
    6 bone-in pork loin chops (1 inch thick)
    2 tablespoons vegetable oil
    1 can (10-1/2 ounces) condensed chicken with rice soup, undiluted

In a large resealable plastic bag, combine the flour, mustard, seasoned salt and garlic powder. Add pork chops, one at a time, and shake to coat.

In a large skillet, brown pork chops on both sides in oil. Place in a 3-qt. slow cooker. Pour soup over pork. Cover and cook on low for 6-7 hours or until tender. **Yield:** 6 servings.

Turkey Leg Pot Roast

(Pictured below and on page 156)

Prep: 15 min. **Cook:** 5 hours

Well-seasoned turkey legs and tender veggies make this meal ideal for a crisp fall day. Old-fashioned and wholesome, the recipe couldn't be more comforting.
—Rick and Vegas Pearson, Cadillac, Michigan

> 3 medium potatoes, peeled and quartered
> 2 cups fresh baby carrots
> 2 celery ribs, cut into 2-1/2-inch pieces
> 1 medium onion, peeled and quartered
> 3 garlic cloves, peeled and quartered
> 1/2 cup chicken broth
> 3 turkey drumsticks (about 1/2 pound *each*)
> 2 teaspoons seasoned salt
> 1 teaspoon dried thyme
> 1 teaspoon dried parsley flakes
> 1/4 teaspoon pepper

In a greased oval 5- or 6-qt. slow cooker, combine the first six ingredients. Place drumsticks over vegetables. Sprinkle with seasoned salt, thyme, parsley and pepper. Cover; cook on low for 5 to 5-1/2 hours or until a meat thermometer reads 180°. **Yield:** 3 servings.

Turkey Leg Pot Roast

Zesty Beef Stew

Prep: 10 min. **Cook:** 3-1/2 hours

I came up with this recipe one day when I didn't have some of the usual ingredients for vegetable beef soup on hand. My husband says it's the best stew I've ever made! Pizza sauce and pinto beans give it an interesting taste twist.
—Margaret Turza, South Bend, Indiana

> 1 pound beef stew meat, cut into 1-inch cubes
> 1 package (16 ounces) frozen mixed vegetables, thawed
> 1 can (16 ounces) pinto beans, rinsed and drained
> 1-1/2 cups water
> 1 can (8 ounces) pizza sauce
> 2 tablespoons medium pearl barley
> 1 tablespoon dried minced onion
> 2 teaspoons beef bouillon granules
> 1/4 teaspoon crushed red pepper flakes

In a 3-qt. slow cooker, combine all ingredients. Cover and cook on low for 3-1/2 to 4-1/2 hours or until meat is tender. **Yield:** 6 servings.

Seasoned Pork Sandwiches

Prep: 20 min. **Cook:** 5 hours

This is one of those recipes that my husband never seems to get tired of. And I never tire of making it! That's because the delicious shredded pork sandwiches are quick, are a snap to prepare and have even easier cleanup.
—Jacque Thompson Houston, Texas

> 1 boneless whole pork loin roast (2 to 3 pounds)
> 1 tablespoon fajita seasoning mix
> 1/4 teaspoon garlic powder
> 1/2 cup Italian salad dressing
> 1/4 cup Worcestershire sauce
> 8 sandwich rolls, split

Cut roast in half; place in a 5-qt. slow cooker. Sprinkle with fajita seasoning and garlic powder. Pour salad dressing and Worcestershire sauce over meat. Cover and cook on low for 5-6 hours or until tender.

Remove roast; shred meat with two forks. Return to cooking juices; heat through. Using a slotted spoon, serve pork on rolls. **Yield:** 8 servings.

Pork Possibilities

CRAVING something other than a sandwich? Serve the pulled pork from Seasoned Pork Sandwiches (recipe above) without the bun and include a side of mashed potatoes or egg noodles.

Italian Sausage and Vegetables

(Pictured below)

Prep: 20 min. **Cook:** 5-1/2 hours

Here's a complete meal-in-a-pot. Each helping is wonderful served with a slice of Italian or garlic bread. I found the recipe in a magazine and made a few adjustments.
—Ginny Stuby, Altoona, Pennsylvania

> 1-1/4 pounds sweet *or* hot Italian turkey sausage links
>   1 can (28 ounces) diced tomatoes, undrained
>   2 medium potatoes, cut into 1-inch pieces
>   4 small zucchini, cut into 1-inch slices
>   1 medium onion, cut into wedges
> 1/2 teaspoon garlic powder
> 1/4 teaspoon crushed red pepper flakes
> 1/4 teaspoon dried oregano
> 1/4 teaspoon dried basil
>   1 tablespoon dry bread crumbs
> 3/4 cup shredded pepper Jack cheese

In a nonstick skillet, cook sausages over medium heat until no longer pink; drain. Place in a 5-qt. slow cooker. Add vegetables and seasonings. Cover and cook on low for 5-1/2 to 6-1/2 hours or until vegetables are tender.

Remove sausages and cut into 1-in. pieces; return to slow cooker. Stir in bread crumbs. Serve in bowls; sprinkle with cheese. **Yield:** 6 servings.

Lazy Man's Ribs

Lazy Man's Ribs

(Pictured above)

Prep: 20 min. **Cook:** 6 hours

These ribs are finger-lickin' good and fall-off-the-bone tender. I've prepared them for my buddies, and they have suggested that I try bottling my sauce and selling it!
—Allan Stackhouse, Jennings, Louisiana

> 2-1/2 pounds pork baby back ribs, cut into eight pieces
>   2 teaspoons Cajun seasoning
>   1 medium onion, sliced
>   1 cup ketchup
> 1/2 cup packed brown sugar
> 1/3 cup orange juice
> 1/3 cup cider vinegar
> 1/4 cup molasses
>   2 tablespoons Worcestershire sauce
>   1 tablespoon barbecue sauce
>   1 teaspoon stone-ground mustard
>   1 teaspoon paprika
> 1/2 teaspoon garlic powder
> 1/2 teaspoon Liquid Smoke, optional
> Dash salt
>   5 teaspoons cornstarch
>   1 tablespoon cold water

Rub ribs with Cajun seasoning. Layer ribs and onion in a 5-qt. slow cooker. In a bowl, combine the next 12 ingredients. Pour over ribs. Cover and cook on low for 6 hours or until meat is tender.

Remove ribs and keep warm. Strain cooking juices and skim fat; transfer to a saucepan. Combine cornstarch and water until smooth; stir into juices. Bring to a boil; cook and stir for 2 minutes or until thickened. Serve with ribs. **Yield:** 4 servings.

Italian Sausage and Vegetables

Oriental-Style Round Steak

(Pictured below)

Prep: 20 min. **Cook:** 7 hours

I have long relied on this hearty dinner, chock-full of wholesome vegetables, to please my family. My friend gave me the recipe more than 2 decades ago, and I tossed in a little more round steak, the celery and the mushrooms.
—Marilyn Wolfe, Des Moines, Iowa

2 pounds boneless beef top round steak, cut into 3-inch strips
2 tablespoons vegetable oil
1 cup chopped onion
3 celery ribs, chopped
1/4 cup soy sauce
1 teaspoon sugar
1/2 teaspoon salt
1/2 teaspoon minced garlic
1/4 teaspoon ground ginger
1/4 teaspoon pepper
2 medium green peppers, julienned
1 can (15 ounces) tomato sauce
1 can (14 ounces) bean sprouts, rinsed and drained
1 can (8 ounces) sliced water chestnuts, drained
1 jar (4-1/2 ounces) sliced mushrooms, drained
1 tablespoon cornstarch
1/2 cup cold water
Hot cooked rice

In a large skillet, brown the steak strips in oil on all sides. Transfer the steak strips and drippings to a 5-qt. slow cooker. Combine the onion, celery, soy sauce, sugar, salt, garlic, ginger and pepper; pour over the steak strips. Cover and cook on low for 5-1/2 to 6 hours or until the meat is tender.

Add the green peppers, tomato sauce, bean sprouts, water chestnuts and mushrooms; cover and cook on low 1 hour longer.

In a small bowl, combine cornstarch and water until smooth; stir into beef mixture. Cover and cook on high for 30 minutes or until gravy is thickened. Serve with rice. **Yield:** 8 servings.

Italian Chicken Chili

Prep: 20 min. **Cook:** 6-3/4 hours

Though the list of ingredients may seem long, this recipe takes just 20 minutes of prep before it simmers into a heartwarming main course. Each bite brings a variety of textures, not to mention loads of Italian flavor.
—Genise Krause, Sturgeon Bay, Wisconsin

✓ Uses less fat, sugar or salt. Includes Nutrition Facts and Diabetic Exchanges.

1/2 pound bulk Italian sausage
1 teaspoon olive oil
1 pound boneless skinless chicken breasts, cut into 1-inch cubes
1 can (28 ounces) crushed tomatoes
1 can (28 ounces) diced tomatoes, undrained
1 can (15 ounces) white kidney *or* cannellini beans, rinsed and drained
2 celery ribs, chopped
1 cup chopped onion
1 small sweet red pepper, chopped
1/2 cup dry red wine *or* chicken broth
2 tablespoons chili powder
2 teaspoons dried oregano
2 teaspoons minced garlic
1 teaspoon dried thyme
1 medium zucchini, diced
1 cup sliced fresh mushrooms
1/4 cup minced fresh parsley
Shredded Italian cheese blend, optional

In a large skillet, cook sausage in oil over medium heat until no longer pink; drain. Transfer to a 5-qt. slow cooker. Stir in the chicken, tomatoes, beans, celery, onion, red pepper, wine or broth, chili powder, oregano, garlic and thyme. Cover and cook on low for 6 hours or until chicken juices run clear.

Stir in the zucchini and mushrooms. Cover and cook on high for 45 minutes or until vegetables are tender. Sprinkle with parsley. Serve with cheese if desired. **Yield:** 8 servings (2-3/4 quarts).

Nutrition Facts: 1-1/3 cups (calculated without cheese) equals 243 calories, 7 g fat (2 g saturated fat), 43 mg cholesterol, 516 mg sodium, 25 g carbohydrate, 8 g fiber, 20 g protein. **Diabetic Exchanges:** 2 lean meat, 1-1/2 starch.

Oriental-Style Round Steak

Slow-Cooked Taco Meat Loaf

Prep: 20 min. **Cook:** 3 hours + standing

This main dish is guaranteed to get your family to the dinner table fast. My three sons eat two pieces each—which is incredible, considering that they are very picky toddlers! The Southwestern-style loaf is topped with a sweet and tangy sauce. —Lacey Kirsch, Thornton, Colorado

- 2 cups crushed tortilla chips
- 1 cup (4 ounces) shredded cheddar cheese
- 1 cup salsa
- 1/2 cup egg substitute
- 1/4 cup sliced ripe olives
- 1 envelope taco seasoning
- 2 pounds lean ground beef
- 1/2 cup ketchup
- 1/4 cup packed brown sugar
- 2 tablespoons Louisiana-style hot sauce

In a large bowl, combine the first six ingredients. Crumble the ground beef over the mixture; mix well. Shape into a round loaf.

Cut three 20-in. x 3-in. strips of heavy-duty aluminum foil. Crisscross the strips so they resemble the spokes of a wheel. Place meat loaf in the center; pull the strips up and bend the edges to form handles. Grasp the foil handles to transfer loaf to a 3-qt. slow cooker. (Leave the foil in during cooking time.)

Cover and cook on low for 3-4 hours or until no pink remains and a meat thermometer reads 160°. Combine the ketchup, brown sugar and hot sauce; pour over meat loaf during the last hour of cooking. Let stand for 10 minutes. Use foil strips to lift loaf out of slow cooker. **Yield:** 8 servings.

Slow Cooker Beef Stew

Prep: 20 min. **Cook:** 6 hours

Because I work long hours, I try to find recipes for hearty meals like this that'll be ready when I arrive home. —Donna Wenger, Little Rock, Arkansas

- 2 pounds boneless beef top round steak, cut into 1-inch cubes
- 8 medium carrots, cut into 1-inch pieces
- 1 pound small red potatoes, quartered
- 1/2 pound sliced fresh mushrooms
- 1 medium sweet red pepper, chopped
- 1 can (14-1/2 ounces) diced tomatoes, undrained
- 1/4 cup all-purpose flour
- 1 can (6 ounces) tomato paste
- 3/4 cup beef broth
- 1/3 cup dry red wine *or* additional beef broth
- 1-1/2 teaspoons salt
- 1 teaspoon *each* minced garlic and pepper
- 1/2 teaspoon dried thyme

In a large skillet, brown beef on all sides. In a 5-qt. slow cooker, combine the carrots, potatoes, mushrooms and red pepper. Pour tomatoes over the top.

In a small bowl, whisk the flour, tomato paste and

Moist Drumsticks

broth until smooth. Stir in the wine or additional broth, salt, garlic, pepper and thyme; pour into slow cooker. Top with beef. Cover and cook on low for 6-8 hours or until meat is tender. **Yield:** 6 servings.

Moist Drumsticks

(Pictured above)

Prep: 10 min. **Cook:** 5 hours

I found this in my mother's recipe box years ago. It's extremely quick to prepare and makes the whole house smell wonderful while it's cooking. Plus, my daughter just loves it! —Lianne Felton, Riverside, California

- 3 pounds skinless chicken drumsticks
- 1 can (8 ounces) tomato sauce
- 1/2 cup soy sauce
- 1/4 cup packed brown sugar
- 1 teaspoon minced garlic
- 3 tablespoons cornstarch
- 1/4 cup cold water

Place drumsticks in a 5-qt. slow cooker. In a small bowl, combine the tomato sauce, soy sauce, brown sugar and garlic; pour over chicken. Cover and cook on low for 5-6 hours or until chicken juices run clear.

Remove chicken and keep warm. Strain cooking juices. In a small saucepan, combine cornstarch and cold water until smooth; stir in juices. Bring to a boil; cook and stir for 2 minutes or until thickened. Serve with chicken. **Yield:** 6 servings.

Chapter 11

Breakfast & Brunch Favorites

RISE AND SHINE! With recipes such as Hash Brown Sausage Bake, Cherry-Granola French Toast Sticks, Puff Pancake with Blueberry Sauce, Minty Mocha and Spicy Scrambled Egg Sandwiches, you'll look forward to waking up your taste buds each and every morning of the week.

Not only are these sunny selections delicious, but they also come together in a snap. So you and your family can enjoy a home-cooked breakfast and still get out the door exactly when you need to.

Instead of stopping at a fast food restaurant—or settling for only a morning cup of coffee—turn to this chapter and start off your day in a sensational way.

DAYBREAK DELIGHTS. Chocolate Chip Pumpkin Muffins, Kiwi Fruit Salad and Zippy Egg Casserole (all recipes on p. 178).

Hash Brown Sausage Bake

Spicy Scrambled Egg Sandwiches

(Pictured below)

Prep/Total Time: 30 min.

A little hot sauce gives a nice kick to these energy-building English muffins. Each satisfying sandwich is packed with veggies, good taste and easy-to-eat nutrition!
—Helen Vail, Glenside, Pennsylvania

✓ Uses less fat, sugar or salt. Includes Nutrition Facts and Diabetic Exchanges.

    1/3 cup chopped green pepper
    1/4 cup chopped onion
      3 eggs
      4 egg whites
      1 tablespoon water
    1/4 teaspoon salt
    1/4 teaspoon ground mustard
    1/8 teaspoon pepper
    1/8 teaspoon hot pepper sauce
    1/3 cup fresh *or* frozen corn, thawed
    1/4 cup real bacon bits
      4 English muffins, split and toasted

In a 10-in. skillet coated with nonstick cooking spray, cook green pepper and onion over medium heat until tender, about 8 minutes.

In a large bowl, whisk the eggs, egg whites, water, salt, mustard, pepper and hot pepper sauce. Pour into skillet. Add corn and bacon; cook and stir until the eggs are completely set. Spoon onto English muffin bottoms; replace tops. Serve immediately. **Yield:** 4 servings.

Nutrition Facts: 1 sandwich equals 248 calories, 6 g fat (2 g saturated fat), 164 mg cholesterol, 739 mg sodium, 31 g carbohydrate, 2 g fiber, 16 g protein. **Diabetic Exchanges:** 2 starch, 2 lean meat.

Hash Brown Sausage Bake

(Pictured above)

Prep: 30 min. **Bake:** 40 min.

This is one of my son's all-time favorites. Buttered hash browns form a savory crust for the yummy sausage-and-cheese filling. It's sure to please your family at breakfast, brunch or even lunch.
—Vicky Dempsey
Louisville, Mississippi

      1 package (20 ounces) refrigerated shredded hash brown potatoes
    1/3 cup butter, melted
      1 teaspoon beef bouillon granules
      1 pound bulk pork sausage
    1/3 cup chopped onion
      1 cup (8 ounces) small-curd cottage cheese
      3 eggs, lightly beaten
      4 slices process American cheese, chopped

In a large bowl, combine the hash browns, butter and bouillon. Press onto the bottom and up the sides of a greased 10-in. pie plate. Bake at 350° for 25-30 minutes or until edges are lightly browned.

Meanwhile, in a large skillet, cook sausage and onion over medium heat until meat is no longer pink; drain. In a large bowl, combine the sausage mixture, cottage cheese, eggs and American cheese.

Pour the filling into the crust. Bake at 350° for 40-45 minutes or until a knife inserted near the center comes out clean. Let stand for 5 minutes before cutting. **Yield:** 6-8 servings.

Spicy Scrambled Egg Sandwiches

Fruity Baked Oatmeal

Prep: 15 min. **Bake:** 35 min.

This is always my husband's first choice for breakfast. It's the ultimate comfort food because it's warm and filling.
—Karen Schroeder, Kankakee, Illinois

✓ Uses less fat, sugar or salt. Includes Nutrition Facts.

    3 cups quick-cooking oats
    1 cup packed brown sugar
    2 teaspoons baking powder
    1 teaspoon salt
  1/2 teaspoon ground cinnamon
    2 eggs, lightly beaten
    1 cup fat-free milk
  1/2 cup butter, melted
  3/4 cup chopped peeled tart apple
  1/3 cup chopped fresh *or* frozen peaches
  1/3 cup fresh *or* frozen blueberries
Additional fat-free milk, optional

In a large bowl, combine the oats, brown sugar, baking powder, salt and cinnamon. Combine the eggs, milk and butter; add to the dry ingredients. Stir in the apple, peaches and blueberries.

Pour into an 8-in. square baking dish coated with nonstick cooking spray. Bake, uncovered, at 350° for 35-40 minutes or until a knife inserted near the center comes out clean. Cut into squares. Serve with milk if desired. **Yield:** 9 servings.

Editor's Note: If using frozen blueberries, do not thaw before adding to batter.

Nutrition Facts: 1 piece (calculated without additional milk) equals 322 calories, 13 g fat (7 g saturated fat), 75 mg cholesterol, 492 mg sodium, 46 g carbohydrate, 3 g fiber, 7 g protein.

Minty Mocha

Prep/Total Time: 15 min.

I've had this recipe for more than 20 years and serve it during the Christmas season, but the creamy beverage is delightful any time of the year. I think whipped topping and chocolate curls make the perfect garnish.
—Sharon Haswell
Cheshire, Massachusetts

    1 cup water
  1/3 cup sugar
    6 mint Andes candies
  3/4 cup half-and-half cream
  3/4 cup milk
    2 cups hot brewed coffee
Whipped topping and chocolate curls, optional

In a large saucepan, combine the water, sugar and candies. Cook and stir until sugar is dissolved and candies are melted. Stir in cream and milk; heat through. Stir in coffee. Ladle into mugs. Garnish with whipped topping and chocolate curls if desired. **Yield:** 4-5 servings.

Sunshine Crepes

Sunshine Crepes

(Pictured above)

Prep: 15 min. + chilling **Cook:** 15 min.

My family wanted a light brunch and coffee last year for Christmas morning, so I whipped up these sweet and fruity crepes. —Mary Hobbs, Campbell, Missouri

✓ Uses less fat, sugar or salt. Includes Nutrition Facts and Diabetic Exchanges.

  2/3 cup milk
    2 eggs
    1 tablespoon canola oil
  1/2 cup all-purpose flour
    1 teaspoon sugar
  1/4 teaspoon salt
FILLING:
    1 can (20 ounces) crushed pineapple, drained
    1 can (11 ounces) mandarin oranges, drained
    1 teaspoon vanilla extract
    1 carton (8 ounces) frozen whipped topping, thawed
Confectioners' sugar

In a large mixing bowl, beat the milk, eggs and oil. Combine the flour, sugar and salt; add to milk mixture and mix well. Cover and refrigerate for 1 hour.

Coat an 8-in. nonstick skillet with nonstick cooking spray; heat over medium heat. Stir crepe batter; pour 2 tablespoons into center of skillet. Lift and tilt pan to coat bottom evenly. Cook until top appears dry; turn and cook 15-20 seconds longer. Remove to a wire rack. Repeat with remaining batter, coating skillet as needed. When cool, stack crepes with waxed paper or paper towels in between.

For filling, in a large bowl, combine the pineapple, oranges and vanilla; fold in whipped topping. Spoon 1/3 cup down the center of each crepe; roll up. Dust with confectioners' sugar. **Yield:** 6 servings.

Nutrition Facts: 2 crepes equals 302 calories, 11 g fat (8 g saturated fat), 75 mg cholesterol, 136 mg sodium, 43 g carbohydrate, 1 g fiber, 5 g protein. **Diabetic Exchanges:** 2 starch, 2 fat, 1 fruit.

Greatest Granola

Puff Pancake with Blueberry Sauce

Prep/Total Time: 30 min.

I'm a cookbook collector and discovered this recipe while I was in Texas on vacation. The light and puffy pancake really does melt in your mouth, and it's irresistible with the homemade sauce. It's a definite crowd-pleaser that's as impressive served for dessert as it is at breakfast.
—Barbara Mohr, Millington, Michigan

 2 tablespoons butter
 2 eggs
 1/2 cup milk
 1/2 cup all-purpose flour
 2 tablespoons sugar
 1/8 teaspoon ground cinnamon
BLUEBERRY SAUCE:
 1/4 cup packed brown sugar
 1 tablespoon cornstarch
 1/4 cup orange juice
 1 cup fresh *or* frozen blueberries
 1/4 teaspoon vanilla extract

Place the butter in a 9-in. pie plate; bake in a 425° oven for 4-5 minutes or until melted. Meanwhile, in a small bowl, whisk eggs and milk. In another small bowl, combine the flour, sugar and cinnamon; whisk in egg mixture until smooth. Pour into prepared pie plate. Bake for 18-22 minutes or until sides are crisp and golden brown.

Meanwhile, in a small saucepan, combine the brown sugar and cornstarch. Gradually whisk in the orange juice until smooth. Stir in the blueberries. Bring to a boil over medium heat, stirring constantly. Cook and stir 1-2 minutes longer or until thickened. Remove from the heat; stir in the vanilla extract. Serve the blueberry sauce with pancake. **Yield:** 4 servings.

Greatest Granola

(Pictured above)

Prep: 15 min. **Bake:** 25 min. + cooling

I call this tasty granola "the greatest." Try it, and you'll likely agree! —Jonie Daigle, Greensburg, Pennsylvania

 2 cups old-fashioned oats
 1 cup Grape-Nuts
 1/2 cup sliced almonds
 1/2 cup honey
 1/3 cup vegetable oil
 1/4 cup packed brown sugar
 1-1/2 teaspoons vanilla extract
 1/4 teaspoon ground cinnamon
 1 cup crisp rice cereal
 1/2 cup toasted wheat germ
 1/2 cup chopped dried apricots
 1/2 cup dried cranberries, chopped
Yogurt flavor of your choice, optional

In a large bowl, combine oats, Grape-Nuts and almonds. Spread onto a greased, foil-lined 15-in. x 10-in. x 1-in. baking pan. Coat mixture with nonstick cooking spray. Bake, uncovered, at 300° for 20 minutes, stirring once.

Meanwhile, in a small saucepan, combine the honey, oil and brown sugar. Cook and stir over low heat until heated through. Remove from the heat; add vanilla and cinnamon.

Stir cereal and wheat germ into oat mixture. Drizzle with honey mixture; stir to coat. Bake 5-10 minutes longer or until golden brown. Cool on a wire rack.

Break granola into pieces. Sprinkle with apricots and cranberries; mix well. Store in an airtight container. Serve with yogurt if desired. **Yield:** about 8 cups.

Cranberry Chip Pancakes

Prep/Total Time: 25 min.

These simple flapjacks are so good, you don't even need syrup! To make them, I add cranberries, orange juice, orange peel and vanilla chips to a classic pancake batter.
—Aris Gonzalez, Deltona, Florida

 1/2 cup fresh *or* frozen cranberries
 1 cup water, *divided*
 1 cup complete pancake mix
 1/4 cup orange juice
 1 teaspoon grated orange peel
 1/4 cup vanilla *or* white chips

In a small saucepan over medium heat, cook the cranberries and 1/2 cup water until berries pop, about 10 minutes. Meanwhile, in a large bowl, combine the pancake mix, orange juice, orange peel and remaining water just until moistened. Fold in chips. Drain cranberries; fold into batter.

Pour by 1/4 cupfuls onto a greased hot griddle; turn when bubbles form on top. Cook until second side is golden brown. **Yield:** 6 pancakes.

Eggs to Go

Prep/Total Time: 25 min.

My handy ham- and cheese-packed egg "muffins" are extremely kid-friendly. My children would always grab one of these on the way out the door to catch the bus.
—Christine Smoot, Childress, Texas

  6 eggs, lightly beaten
  3 tablespoons butter, melted
1-1/2 cups chopped deli ham
1/2 cup dry bread crumbs
1/4 cup shredded cheddar cheese
  1 tablespoon minced chives

In a large bowl, combine all ingredients. Fill greased muffin cups three-fourths full. Bake at 375° for 15-20 minutes or until a knife inserted near the center comes out clean. Serve warm. **Yield:** 12 servings.

Gingerbread Pancakes

(Pictured below)

Prep/Total Time: 20 min.

I wake 'em up Christmas morning with the warm aroma of these fluffy pancakes. They've got a great gingerbread flavor and a refreshing fruit topping. —Michelle Smith Sykesville, Maryland

  1 cup all-purpose flour
  2 tablespoons sugar
  1 teaspoon baking powder
1/2 teaspoon ground cinnamon
1/4 teaspoon ground ginger
1/4 teaspoon ground allspice
  1 egg
3/4 cup milk
  2 tablespoons molasses
  1 tablespoon vegetable oil
  6 tablespoons maple pancake syrup

Hearty Brunch Pockets

3/4 cup apple pie filling, warmed
  3 tablespoons dried cranberries

In a large bowl, combine the first six ingredients. Combine the egg, milk, molasses and oil; stir into dry ingredients just until moistened.

Pour batter by 1/4 cupfuls onto a greased hot griddle; turn when bubbles form on top. Cook until the second side is golden brown.

To serve, place two pancakes on each plate; drizzle with 2 tablespoons syrup. Top with 1/4 cup apple pie filling; sprinkle with cranberries. **Yield:** 3 servings.

Hearty Brunch Pockets

(Pictured above)

Prep/Total Time: 25 min.

I created this recipe one night when I was looking for a quick and delicious meal for my family. It was an instant hit! —Meredith Beyl, Stillwater, Oklahoma

  6 brown-and-serve sausage links, sliced
  6 ready-to-serve fully cooked bacon strips, diced
  6 eggs
  2 tablespoons milk
  1 teaspoon salt
1/4 teaspoon pepper
  1 cup (4 ounces) shredded Colby-Monterey Jack cheese
  3 pita breads (6 inches), halved

In a nonstick skillet, cook sausage for 2 minutes. Add bacon; cook 4 minutes longer or until sausage is heated through and bacon is crisp. Remove and keep warm.

In a small bowl, whisk the eggs, milk, salt and pepper. Pour into the skillet; cook and stir over medium heat until eggs are almost set. Add sausage mixture and cheese. Cook and stir for 2 minutes or until eggs are completely set and cheese is melted. Spoon into pita halves. **Yield:** 6 servings.

Gingerbread Pancakes

**Chocolate Chip Pumpkin Muffins
Kiwi Fruit Salad
Zippy Egg Casserole**

a knife inserted near the center comes out clean. Let stand for 10 minutes before serving. **Yield:** 8-10 servings.

Kiwi Fruit Salad

(Pictured at left and on page 172)
Prep/Total Time: 15 min.

This simple combination of fruits and ginger ale creates a colorful, refreshing winter salad. Both kids and adults enjoy it. —*Linda Muir, Big Lake, Minnesota*

✓ Uses less fat, sugar or salt. Includes Nutrition Facts and Diabetic Exchange.

2 large kiwifruit, peeled and sliced
1 large pear, peeled and sliced
1 medium navel orange, peeled and sectioned
1 cup seedless red grapes, halved
1/2 cup ginger ale
1/2 teaspoon grated orange peel

In a large bowl, combine all ingredients. Serve with a slotted spoon. **Yield:** 4 servings.
Nutrition Facts: 3/4 cup equals 114 calories, 1 g fat (trace saturated fat), 0 cholesterol, 6 mg sodium, 29 g carbohydrate, 4 g fiber, 1 g protein. **Diabetic Exchange:** 1-1/2 fruit.

Zippy Egg Casserole

(Pictured above and on page 172)
Prep: 20 min. + chilling **Bake:** 40 min. + standing

With three kinds of cheese and seasoned croutons, this easy overnight casserole fills you up with heartwarming flavor. The recipe makes a big batch, so it's perfect for sharing with family and friends. —*Anita Jones Raytown, Missouri*

1 pound bulk pork sausage
1 package (5-1/2 ounces) seasoned salad croutons
1-1/2 cups (6 ounces) shredded cheddar cheese
1 cup (4 ounces) shredded Swiss cheese
1 cup (4 ounces) shredded pepper Jack cheese
8 eggs
2 cups half-and-half cream
1-1/2 cups milk
1 tablespoon finely chopped onion
1-1/2 teaspoons ground mustard
1/4 teaspoon salt
1/4 teaspoon pepper

In a large skillet, cook sausage over medium heat until no longer pink; drain. Place the croutons in a greased 13-in. x 9-in. x 2-in. baking dish. Sprinkle with cheeses and sausage.

In a large bowl, whisk the remaining ingredients; pour over the casserole. Cover and refrigerate overnight.

Remove from the refrigerator 30 minutes before baking. Bake, uncovered, at 350° for 40-45 minutes or until

Chocolate Chip Pumpkin Muffins

(Pictured above left and on page 172)
Prep: 15 min. **Bake:** 20 min.

Here's a muffin recipe you'll truly love! The ginger really comes through in these special goodies. If you prefer a milder ginger taste, just halve the amount. —*Jennifer Jackson, Charlottesville, Virginia*

2 cups all-purpose flour
2-1/2 teaspoons baking powder
1 teaspoon ground ginger
1 teaspoon ground cinnamon
3/4 teaspoon salt
1/4 teaspoon baking soda
Dash ground allspice
1 egg
3/4 cup packed brown sugar
3/4 cup canned pumpkin
2/3 cup milk
3 tablespoons butter, melted
1 teaspoon vanilla extract
1/2 cup miniature semisweet chocolate chips

In a large bowl, combine the first seven ingredients. Combine the egg, brown sugar, pumpkin, milk, butter and vanilla; stir into dry ingredients just until moistened. Stir in chocolate chips.

Fill greased or paper-lined muffin cups three-fourths full. Bake at 375° for 18-22 minutes or until a toothpick comes out clean. Cool for 5 minutes before removing from the pan to a wire rack. **Yield:** 1 dozen.

Breakfast Crepes with Berries

(Pictured below)

Prep/Total Time: 20 min.

After a long day of blackberry picking, I used my harvest to whip up a sauce and dressed up some crepes I had on hand. This dessert-like dish really hit the spot and tied everything together beautifully. The sauce is delectable over warm waffles, too.
—Jennifer Weisbrodt
Oconomowoc, Wisconsin

✓ Uses less fat, sugar or salt. Includes Nutrition Facts and Diabetic Exchanges.

- 1-1/2 cups fresh raspberries
- 1-1/2 cups fresh blackberries
- 1 cup (8 ounces) sour cream
- 1/2 cup confectioners' sugar
- 1 carton (6 ounces) orange creme yogurt
- 1 tablespoon lime juice
- 1-1/2 teaspoons grated lime peel
- 1/2 teaspoon vanilla extract
- 1/8 teaspoon salt
- 8 prepared crepes (9 inches)

In a large bowl, combine the raspberries and blackberries; set aside. In a small bowl, combine sour cream and confectioners' sugar until smooth. Stir in the yogurt, lime juice, lime peel, vanilla and salt.

Spread 2 tablespoons sour cream mixture over each crepe; top with about 1/3 cup berries. Roll up; drizzle with remaining sour cream mixture. Serve immediately. **Yield:** 8 servings.

Nutrition Facts: 1 crepe equals 182 calories, 7 g fat (4 g saturated fat), 27 mg cholesterol, 144 mg sodium, 27 g carbohydrate, 3 g fiber, 3 g protein. **Diabetic Exchanges:** 1-1/2 starch, 1-1/2 fat.

Breakfast Crepes with Berries

Roasted Veggie Omelets

Prep: 20 min. **Bake:** 20 min.

Roast some veggies and put on that first pot of coffee in the morning. As soon as the vegetables are done, this standout omelet from our Test Kitchen staff will be ready in minutes. It's great for a weekend breakfast.

- 2 medium red potatoes, diced
- 1 cup whole fresh mushrooms, quartered
- 1/3 cup chopped zucchini
- 1/4 cup chopped sweet red pepper
- 1/4 cup chopped green pepper
- 3 tablespoons butter, *divided*
- 1/2 teaspoon dill weed
- 1/4 teaspoon salt
- 1/4 teaspoon pepper
- 6 eggs
- 6 tablespoons water
- 6 tablespoons shredded Swiss cheese

Place the potatoes, mushrooms, zucchini and peppers in a greased 15-in. x 10-in. x 1-in. baking pan. Melt 2 tablespoons butter; add dill, salt and pepper. Drizzle over vegetables; toss gently to coat. Bake, uncovered, at 450° for 20-25 minutes or until tender.

In a small skillet, melt 1 teaspoon butter over medium-high heat. In a small bowl, whisk eggs and water. Pour 1/2 cup egg mixture into skillet (mixture should set immediately at edges). As eggs set, push cooked edges toward the center, letting uncooked portion flow underneath.

When the eggs are set, spoon about 3/4 cup vegetable mixture over one side and sprinkle with 2 tablespoons cheese; fold other side over filling. Invert omelet onto a plate to serve. Repeat with remaining butter, egg mixture, vegetables and cheese. **Yield:** 3 servings.

Creamy Ham 'n' Egg Casserole

Prep: 15 min. **Bake:** 20 min.

Have leftover cooked potatoes or eggs on hand? Here's a terrific way to use them up. This breakfast main dish is guaranteed to fill up family members before they head out for work, school or wherever they need to be.
—Dixie Terry, Goreville, Illinois

- 2 medium cooked potatoes, peeled and sliced
- 4 hard-cooked eggs, chopped
- 1 cup diced fully cooked ham
- 1/2 teaspoon salt
- 1/4 teaspoon pepper
- 1 egg
- 1-1/2 cups (12 ounces) sour cream
- 1/4 cup dry bread crumbs
- 1 tablespoon butter, melted

In a large bowl, combine the potatoes, eggs, ham, salt and pepper. Combine the egg and sour cream; add to potato mixture and gently toss to coat. Transfer to a greased 11-in. x 7-in. x 2-in. baking dish.

Toss bread crumbs and butter; sprinkle over casserole. Bake, uncovered, at 350° for 20 minutes or until mixture reaches 160°. **Yield:** 6 servings.

Strawberries 'n' Cream French Toast Sticks
Cherry-Granola French Toast Sticks

Strawberries 'n' Cream French Toast Sticks

(Pictured at left)

Prep/Total Time: 15 min.

I open my family's eyes in the morning with this luscious French toast breakfast. It tastes like a dessert.
—Taryn Kuebelbeck, Plymouth, Minnesota

    1 container (16 ounces) frozen sweetened
       sliced strawberries, thawed
1/4 to 1/2 teaspoon ground cinnamon
    1 teaspoon cornstarch
    2 teaspoons water
    1 package (12.7 ounces) frozen French toaster
       sticks
    2 ounces cream cheese, softened
1-1/2 teaspoons brown sugar
    1 square (1 ounce) white baking chocolate,
       melted and cooled

In a small saucepan, combine strawberries and cinnamon. Combine cornstarch and water until smooth; stir into berries. Bring to a boil; cook and stir for 2 minutes or until thickened.

Prepare French toast sticks according to package directions. Meanwhile, in a small mixing bowl, beat cream cheese and brown sugar until light and fluffy. Stir in chocolate. Serve berry mixture over French toast; dollop with cream cheese topping. **Yield:** 4 servings.

Editor's Note: This recipe was tested with Eggo French Toaster Sticks.

Cherry-Granola French Toast Sticks

(Pictured at left)

Prep/Total Time: 20 min.

These convenient toast sticks topped with granola, banana and cherry syrup will carry you through busy days.
—Terri McKitrick, Delafield, Wisconsin

1/4 cup heavy whipping cream
    3 tablespoons brown sugar
    2 tablespoons butter
    1 tablespoon dried cherries
1/4 teaspoon ground cinnamon
1/4 teaspoon vanilla extract
    1 package (12.7 ounces) frozen French toaster
       sticks
    1 medium banana, sliced
1/4 cup granola without raisins

For syrup, in a small saucepan, combine the cream, brown sugar, butter, cherries and cinnamon. Bring to a boil over medium heat, stirring constantly. Cook and stir for 2 minutes. Remove from the heat; stir in vanilla. Prepare French toast sticks according to package directions. Serve with banana, granola and syrup. **Yield:** 4 servings.

Editor's Note: This recipe was tested with Eggo French Toaster Sticks.

Asparagus on Toast Points

Prep: 30 min. **Bake:** 10 min.

I rely on this springtime specialty when I want to treat family and friends. It's a cinch to make, delightful to present and absolutely scrumptious to eat! Plus, I can easily double the recipe if I'm serving a crowd.
— *Wendy Prevost, Cody, Wyoming*

1-1/4 pounds fresh asparagus, trimmed
  2 tablespoons finely chopped onion
  2 tablespoons plus 4 teaspoons butter, *divided*
  2 tablespoons all-purpose flour
1/8 teaspoon pepper
Dash ground nutmeg
2/3 cup chicken broth
1/3 cup half-and-half cream
  4 slices bread, toasted
1/2 cup shredded cheddar cheese

In a large skillet, bring 1/2 in. of water to a boil. Add asparagus. Reduce heat; cover and simmer for 3-5 minutes or until crisp-tender. Drain well; set aside.

In a small saucepan, saute onion in 2 tablespoons butter. Stir in the flour, pepper and nutmeg. Gradually add broth and cream. Bring to a boil; cook and stir for 2 minutes or until thickened and bubbly.

Melt remaining butter; spread over one side of each slice of toast. Cut each slice into four triangles; arrange in an ungreased 13-in. x 9-in. x 2-in. baking dish. Top with asparagus and white sauce. Sprinkle with cheese. Bake, uncovered, at 400° for 8-10 minutes or until cheese is melted. **Yield:** 4 servings.

Leek 'n' Brie Omelet

Prep/Total Time: 20 min.

This simple-but-special omelet from our Test Kitchen staff is so unusual and delicious, it will surely impress your breakfast or brunch guests.

  1 small leek (white portion only), chopped
1/4 teaspoon minced garlic
  1 teaspoon olive oil
  2 teaspoons butter
  2 eggs
  2 tablespoons water
1/8 teaspoon salt
1/8 teaspoon pepper
  1 ounce Brie cheese, diced

In a small nonstick skillet, cook leek and garlic in oil over medium heat for 5 minutes or until tender; remove and set aside.

In the same skillet, melt butter over medium-high heat. In a small bowl, whisk the eggs, water, salt and pepper. Pour into skillet (mixture should set immediately at edges). As eggs set, push cooked edges toward the center, letting uncooked portion flow underneath.

When the eggs are set, spoon leek mixture over one side and sprinkle with cheese; fold other side over filling. Slide omelet onto a plate. **Yield:** 1 serving.

Eggs Benedict

Eggs Benedict

(Pictured above)

Prep/Total Time: 30 min.

Tomato and asparagus dress up this traditional egg dish, which my family loves. The Gouda cheese gives it great smoky flavor. — *Marla Clark, Moriarty, New Mexico*

  8 fresh asparagus spears, trimmed and halved
  4 eggs
3-1/2 teaspoons butter
1-1/2 teaspoons all-purpose flour
1/2 cup milk
  2 ounces smoked Gouda cheese, shredded
  2 English muffins, split and toasted
  4 slices tomato
  4 slices Canadian bacon
1/8 teaspoon pepper

Place asparagus in a steamer basket; place in a large saucepan over 1 in. of water. Bring to a boil; cover and steam for 8-10 minutes or until crisp-tender.

In a large skillet, bring 2-3 in. of water to a boil. Reduce heat; simmer gently. Break cold eggs, one at a time, into a custard cup. Holding the cup close to the surface of the water, slip eggs into simmering water. Cook, uncovered, for 3-5 minutes or until whites are completely set and yolks begin to thicken.

Meanwhile, in a large saucepan, melt butter. Stir in flour until smooth; gradually add milk. Bring to a boil; cook and stir for 1-2 minutes or until thickened. Remove from the heat; stir in cheese until melted.

With a slotted spoon, lift the poached eggs out of the water. On each English muffin half, place a slice of tomato, a slice of Canadian bacon, a poached egg and four pieces of asparagus. Top each with about 3 tablespoons cheese sauce. Sprinkle with pepper. Serve immediately. **Yield:** 4 servings.

Chapter 12

⏱ *Snappy Soups & Sandwiches*

WHEN IT COMES to casual comfort food, nothing beats a bowl of piping-hot soup served alongside a chock-full sandwich. And that heartwarming fare will get to the table in a snap when you choose from the rapid recipes in this chapter.

Simmer up a pot of Mushroom Chicken Soup, done in a mere 30 minutes. Fix Southwestern Panini sandwiches in a flash on the grill...use convenient frozen meatballs to make saucy Meatball Pizza Subs...the list of speedy selections goes on and on.

Whether you want a satisfying lunch or quick weeknight dinner, you'll find plenty of family-pleasing favorites here.

ON-A-ROLL RECIPE. Steak Veggie Wraps (p. 192).

Dilled Cajun Chicken Sandwiches
BLTs with Raisin-Avocado Spread

Dilled Cajun Chicken Sandwiches

(Pictured above)

Prep/Total Time: 25 min.

I came up with this recipe when my husband and I were looking for something quick. We both love Cajun seasoning, and the same goes for garlic and dill. We combined them in these delicious sandwiches that even my 4-year-old loves. —Abby Teel, Kuna, Idaho

- 4 boneless skinless chicken breast halves (4 ounces *each*)
- 3 tablespoons olive oil
- 2 tablespoons Cajun seasoning
- 1/4 cup mayonnaise
- 2 teaspoons dill weed
- 1 teaspoon minced garlic
- 4 sandwich rolls, split
- 4 lettuce leaves
- 4 slices tomato
- 4 slices provolone cheese

Flatten the chicken to 1/4-in. thickness. In a large skillet, combine the olive oil and Cajun seasoning; add the chicken and turn to coat. Cook, uncovered, over medium heat for 5-6 minutes on each side or until the juices run clear.

Meanwhile, in a small bowl, combine the mayonnaise, dill and garlic. Spread over cut sides of rolls. On roll bottoms, layer lettuce, tomato, cheese and chicken; replace roll tops. **Yield:** 4 servings.

BLTs with Raisin-Avocado Spread

(Pictured above)

Prep/Total Time: 20 min.

If you're looking to dress up a bacon, lettuce and tomato sandwich, try spreading on a blend of cream cheese, avocado and raisins instead of mayonnaise. —Veronica Callaghan, Glastonbury, Connecticut

- 1 medium ripe avocado, peeled and cubed
- 4 ounces cream cheese, cubed
- 1/2 cup golden raisins
- 1/4 cup pine nuts
- 1/4 cup minced fresh parsley
- 1/2 teaspoon salt
- 1/4 teaspoon pepper
- 12 slices sourdough bread, toasted
- 12 bacon strips, cooked and halved
- 12 romaine leaves
- 6 slices tomato

In a food processor, combine the first seven ingredients; cover and process until blended. Spread evenly over six slices of toast. Layer with bacon, lettuce and tomato. Top with remaining toast. **Yield:** 6 servings.

Steak 'n' Cheese Subs

Prep/Total Time: 15 min.

These easy subs call for flank steak, but you could use any kind of leftover steak. I serve them with extra ketchup for dipping. —Debbie Stadtler, Fredericksburg, Virginia

- 1/2 pound cooked beef flank steak, cut into thin strips
- 1 small onion, thinly sliced
- 1 tablespoon Worcestershire sauce
- 2 French rolls, split
- 1/3 cup shredded part-skim mozzarella cheese
- 2 tablespoons ketchup

In a large skillet, saute the steak, onion and Worcestershire sauce for 4-6 minutes or until onion is tender. Spoon onto roll bottoms; sprinkle with cheese.

Place on a baking sheet. Broil 3-4 in. from the heat for 5-8 minutes or until cheese is melted. Drizzle with ketchup. Replace roll tops. **Yield:** 2 servings.

Roast Beef Roll-Ups

(Pictured below)

Prep/Total Time: 15 min.

This lunch favorite can also be cut into thin slices for appetizers, or "Reubenized": Substitute corned beef, sauerkraut, caraway seeds and Thousand Island dressing. —Clarissa Jo Seeger, Columbiana, Ohio

- 1 package (16 ounces) coleslaw mix
- 3/4 cup coleslaw salad dressing
- 1/2 cup mayonnaise
- 1/4 cup Dijon mustard
- 2 tablespoons cider vinegar
- 2 teaspoons sugar
- 1/2 teaspoon celery seed
- 1 pound thinly sliced deli roast beef
- 4 Italian herb flatbread wraps
- 1/2 pound Swiss cheese, thinly sliced

In a small bowl, combine the first seven ingredients. Divide roast beef among flatbread wraps. Top with cheese and coleslaw mixture; roll up tightly. **Yield:** 4 servings.

Roast Beef Roll-Ups

Tomato-Basil Orzo Soup

Tomato-Basil Orzo Soup

(Pictured above)

Prep/Total Time: 30 min.

With tender pasta, sauteed veggies and lots of flavor, this tasty soup comes really close to the tomato rosamarina soup I've had at great Greek restaurants in Chicago. I like it with a small Greek salad and pita chips. —Mary Lu Wasniewski, Orland Park, Illinois

- 1/2 cup *each* chopped carrot, celery and onion
- 1/8 teaspoon *each* dried basil, oregano and thyme
- 2 tablespoons olive oil
- 1 can (19 ounces) ready-to-serve tomato basil *or* hearty tomato soup
- 1 cup chicken broth
- 1/3 cup uncooked orzo pasta

In a small saucepan, saute the carrot, celery and onion with basil, oregano and thyme in oil for 8-10 minutes or until crisp-tender.

Add soup and broth. Bring to a boil. Stir in orzo. Reduce heat; simmer, uncovered, for 10-12 minutes or until orzo and vegetables are tender. **Yield:** 2 servings.

Editor's Note: This recipe was tested with ready-to-serve Progresso Tomato Basil soup.

Mom's Egg Salad Sandwiches

(Pictured below)

Prep/Total Time: 15 min.

Green pepper and celery add crunch to this flavorful and creamy classic. —Tirzah Lujan, Wichita Falls, Texas

   1 package (3 ounces) cream cheese, softened
 1/4 cup mayonnaise
   1 tablespoon chili sauce
 1/2 teaspoon salt
 1/8 teaspoon pepper
   8 hard-cooked eggs, chopped
 1/4 cup chopped green pepper
 1/4 cup chopped celery
   2 tablespoons finely chopped onion
   2 tablespoons diced pimientos, drained
   1 tablespoon minced fresh parsley
 12 slices white bread
   6 lettuce leaves
   6 slices tomato

In a small mixing bowl, beat the cream cheese, mayonnaise, chili sauce, salt and pepper. Stir in eggs, green pepper, celery, onion, pimientos and parsley.

On six slices of bread, layer lettuce, tomato and 1/2 cup egg salad. Top with remaining bread. **Yield:** 6 servings.

Meatball Pizza Subs

Prep/Total Time: 25 min.

On a busy weekday, I created these satisfying sandwiches. Using frozen meatballs and canned pizza sauce makes them a snap to prepare. My family requests these simple subs all the time, and I'm happy to oblige! —Ann Nolte
Elmendorf Air Force Base, Alaska

1-1/3 cups pizza sauce
   4 submarine buns, split and toasted
1-1/3 cups shredded part-skim mozzarella cheese
 20 slices pepperoni
   1 package (12 ounces) frozen fully cooked
     meatballs, thawed
Italian seasoning to taste

Spread 1/3 cup pizza sauce on the bottom of each bun. Top each with 1/3 cup cheese, five slices of pepperoni and three meatballs; sprinkle with Italian seasoning. Replace tops.

Wrap each sandwich in foil. Bake at 400° for 10-12 minutes or until heated through. **Yield:** 4 servings.

Ham 'n' Cabbage Soup

Prep: 15 min. **Cook:** 25 min.

I sampled a cabbage soup in a restaurant and liked it so much that I spent the next week trying to duplicate it. This is the tasty result. —Carolyn Bixenmann
Grand Island, Nebraska

   1 small head cabbage, quartered
   2 medium carrots, halved
 2/3 cup butter
   7 cups milk, *divided*
   1 can (10-1/2 ounces) condensed chicken
     broth, undiluted
 2/3 cup all-purpose flour
 3/4 teaspoon salt
1-1/2 cups cubed fully cooked ham
   2 teaspoons Liquid Smoke, optional

In a food processor, shred the cabbage. Transfer to a bowl. Shred the carrots; add to cabbage. Return half of the mixture to the food processor; cover and process until finely chopped.

In a Dutch oven, saute all of the cabbage and carrots in butter for 3-4 minutes or until tender. Stir in 5 cups milk and the chicken broth. Bring to a boil. Reduce heat; simmer, uncovered, for 5-6 minutes or until heated through.

Combine the flour, salt and remaining milk until smooth. Gradually stir into soup. Bring to a boil; cook and stir for 2 minutes or until thickened. Add ham and Liquid Smoke if desired. Reduce heat; simmer, uncovered, for 3-4 minutes or until heated through. **Yield:** 8 servings (3 quarts).

Egg Ease

TO EASILY PEEL hard-cooked eggs, refrigerate the fresh eggs 7-10 days before hard-cooking. To cook, put a single layer of eggs in a saucepan and add enough water to cover them by 1 inch. Cover the pan and bring the water to a boil, then turn off the heat, remove the pan from the burner and let it stand 15 minutes (for large eggs). Rinse with cold water and cover with ice water until completely cool.

Mom's Egg Salad Sandwiches

Baked Deli Focaccia Sandwich

Baked Deli Focaccia Sandwich

(Pictured above)

Prep: 10 min. **Bake:** 20 min. + standing

Pesto and focaccia bread combine to make this pretty sandwich deliciously different from most deli sandwiches. It's a fantastic choice for Super Bowl parties and other group gatherings.
—Mary Humeniuk-Smith
Perry Hall, Maryland

  1 loaf (12 ounces) focaccia bread
1/4 cup prepared pesto
1/4 pound sliced deli ham
1/4 pound sliced deli smoked turkey
1/4 pound sliced deli pastrami
  5 slices process American cheese
1/3 cup thinly sliced onion
  1 small tomato, sliced
1/4 teaspoon Italian seasoning

Cut focaccia horizontally in half; spread pesto over cut sides. On bread bottom, layer the ham, turkey, pastrami, cheese, onion and tomato. Sprinkle with Italian seasoning. Replace bread top; wrap in foil.

Place on a baking sheet. Bake at 350° for 20-25 minutes or until heated through. Let stand for 10 minutes. Cut into wedges. **Yield:** 8 servings.

Avocado Smoked Turkey Wraps

Prep/Total Time: 20 min.

Crisp veggies and seasoned cream cheese come together for this summery sandwich. It's so easy to assemble and is perfect for last-minute lunches on the go.
—Shawndell Atkinson, Provo, Utah

  1 package (8 ounces) cream cheese, softened
  2 tablespoons chopped jalapeno peppers
  1 teaspoon pepper
1/4 teaspoon salt
  4 flour tortillas (8 inches)
3/4 cup shredded lettuce
1/2 cup chopped tomato
 10 ounces sliced deli smoked turkey
  1 medium ripe avocado, peeled and chopped
1/4 cup chopped red onion

In a small bowl, combine the cream cheese, jalapenos, pepper and salt until blended; spread over one side of each tortilla. Layer with lettuce, tomato, turkey, avocado and onion. Roll up tightly. Serve immediately. **Yield:** 4 servings.

Editor's Note: When cutting or seeding hot peppers, use rubber or plastic gloves to protect your hands. Avoid touching your face.

Flavorful Onion Burgers

Flavorful Onion Burgers

(Pictured above)

Prep: 20 min. **Grill:** 25 min.

Cheddar cheese, green pepper and Thousand Island salad dressing make this juicy sandwich a real treat. You may never want any other type of burger again!
—Dave Bremson, Plantation, Florida

    1 large onion
    1 to 2 tablespoons olive oil
Salt and pepper to taste, optional
    1/2 cup chopped green pepper
    1/2 cup shredded cheddar cheese
    2 tablespoons minced fresh parsley
    1 tablespoon Worcestershire sauce
1-1/2 pounds ground beef
    6 whole wheat hamburger buns, split
    6 tablespoons Thousand Island salad dressing
    6 lettuce leaves
    6 slices tomato

Slice onion into 1/2-in.-thick rings; thread onto metal or soaked wooden skewers. Brush with oil. Season with salt and pepper if desired. Grill, covered, over medium-hot heat for 8-10 minutes on each side.

Meanwhile, in a large bowl, combine green pepper, cheese, parsley and Worcestershire sauce. Crumble beef over mixture; mix well. Shape into six patties.

Move onion to indirect heat. Place burgers over direct heat. Grill, covered, for 5-7 minutes on each side or until meat is no longer pink. Cook onion 10 minutes longer or until tender.

Spread bun bottoms with dressing; top each with lettuce, tomato, onion and a burger. Replace bun tops. **Yield:** 6 servings.

Flutter-By Franks

(Pictured below)

Prep/Total Time: 30 min.

Easy, fun and adorable all describe Flutter-By Franks! My daughter loves them. —*Lois Lewis, Bartlett, Illinois*

    1 tube (8 ounces) refrigerated crescent rolls
    4 hot dogs
Ketchup and mustard

Unroll dough and separate into eight triangles; cut each triangle in half. Roll each piece into a ball; flatten to 1/2-in. thickness. For wings, place dough balls in a square shape 2 in. apart on an ungreased baking sheet. Cut each hot dog lengthwise to within 3 in. of the opposite end. Press a hot dog between each set of dough wings.

Bake at 375° for 14-16 minutes or until golden brown. Place drops of ketchup and mustard below cut edge of each hot dog for eyes and mouth. **Yield:** 4 servings.

Brats in Beer

Prep: 10 min. + marinating **Grill:** 15 min.

With just a few minutes of preparation and a short time on the grill, these jazzed-up brats will be a hit at your next outdoor event. —*Jill Hazelton, Hamlet, Indiana*

  1 can (12 ounces) beer *or* nonalcoholic beer
  2 tablespoons brown sugar
  2 tablespoons soy sauce
  1 tablespoon chili powder
  1 tablespoon prepared mustard
1/8 teaspoon garlic powder
  8 uncooked bratwurst links
  1 large onion, thinly sliced
  8 brat *or* hot dog buns, split

In a small bowl, combine the first six ingredients. Pour 1-3/4 cups into a large resealable plastic bag; add the bratwurst. Seal the bag and turn to coat; refrigerate for 4 hours or overnight. Cover and refrigerate the remaining marinade.

Add onion to remaining marinade; toss to coat. Place on a double thickness of heavy-duty foil (about 18 in. square). Fold foil around onion mixture and seal tightly. Drain and discard marinade from bratwurst.

Grill bratwurst and onion, covered, over medium heat or broil 4 in. from the heat for 15-20 minutes or until meat is no longer pink and onion is tender, turning frequently. Open foil carefully to allow steam to escape. Serve brats in buns with onion mixture. **Yield:** 8 servings.

Chicken Bagel Melts

Prep/Total Time: 15 min.

These tasty melts use up leftover chicken. Deli chicken works well, too, when you don't have rotisserie on hand. —*Shannon Brown, Omaha, Nebraska*

1/2 cup mayonnaise
  4 Asiago cheese bagels, split
1/2 pound sliced cooked rotisserie chicken
  8 strips ready-to-serve fully cooked bacon
1/2 medium sweet red pepper, sliced
  4 slices cheddar cheese
1/4 cup chipotle mustard

Spread mayonnaise over bagel bottoms; layer with chicken, bacon, red pepper and cheese. Place on an ungreased baking sheet.

Broil 2-4 in. from the heat for 2-3 minutes or until cheese is melted. Spread mustard over bagel tops; place over cheese. Serve immediately. **Yield:** 4 servings.

Refried Bean Soup

(Pictured below)

Prep/Total Time: 25 min.

This fast favorite combines the ease of soup with the heartiness of chili. It's a perfect filler-upper on nippy afternoons or cool evenings. If you like your food on the spicy side, use medium or hot green chilies rather than mild ones. —*Darlene Brenden, Salem, Oregon*

1 can (16 ounces) spicy fat-free refried beans
1 can (15-1/4 ounces) whole kernel corn, drained
1 can (15 ounces) black beans, rinsed and drained
1 can (14-1/2 ounces) chicken broth
1 can (14-1/2 ounces) stewed tomatoes, cut up
1/2 cup water
1 can (4 ounces) chopped green chilies
1/4 cup salsa
Tortilla chips

In a large saucepan, combine the first eight ingredients. Bring to a boil. Reduce heat; simmer, uncovered, for 8-10 minutes or until heated through. Serve with tortilla chips. **Yield:** 8 servings (2 quarts).

Refried Bean Soup

Best Brats

BRATS (bratwurst) are a spicy German sausage. If they're overcooked, the casings can split, allowing the juices to escape. Pricking the casing before or during cooking can also release the juices, causing the sausage to dry out. During grilling, watch brats carefully and turn them frequently with tongs to avoid overcooking. Avoid pricking them with a fork.

Tuna Melt on Corn Bread

(Pictured below)

Prep/Total Time: 30 min.

For a new twist on open-faced tuna melts, try this scrumptious version served on corn bread. Our Test Kitchen created this quick variation that's just right for lunch.

- 1 package (8-1/2 ounces) corn bread/muffin mix
- 2 cans (6 ounces *each*) light water-packed tuna, drained and flaked
- 1/3 cup mayonnaise
- 1/3 cup chopped celery
- 2 tablespoons finely chopped onion
- 1 hard-cooked egg, chopped
- 1 teaspoon dill weed
- 1/4 teaspoon salt
- 1/8 teaspoon pepper
- 6 slices cheddar cheese
- 1 medium tomato, sliced
- 1 medium ripe avocado, peeled and sliced

Prepare and bake corn bread according to package directions, using a greased 8-in. square baking pan. Cool on a wire rack.

In a small bowl, combine the tuna, mayonnaise, celery, onion, egg, dill, salt and pepper. Cut corn bread into six pieces; place on an ungreased baking sheet. Top each with 1/4 cup tuna mixture and a slice of cheese. Broil 4-6 in. from the heat for 2-3 minutes or until cheese is melted. Top with tomato and avocado. **Yield:** 6 servings.

Tuna Melt on Corn Bread

Tangy Sloppy Joes

Prep/Total Time: 30 min.

I first tasted this recipe at a rehearsal dinner for a church Christmas program, about 20 years ago. The sloppy joes are the best I've ever had! When I bring them to get-togethers, I always receive many compliments and recipe requests.
—Sharon De Roos, Elgin, Illinois

- 1 pound ground beef
- 1/2 cup chopped celery
- 1/3 cup chopped onion
- 2 tablespoons chopped green pepper
- 1 cup ketchup
- 1/2 cup chili sauce
- 1 tablespoon sugar
- 1 tablespoon brown sugar
- 1 tablespoon cider vinegar
- 2 teaspoons ground mustard
- 1/4 teaspoon salt
- 1/8 teaspoon pepper
- 6 hamburger buns, split

In a large skillet, cook the beef, celery, onion and green pepper over medium heat until meat is no longer pink and vegetables are tender; drain.

Stir in the ketchup, chili sauce, sugars, vinegar, mustard, salt and pepper. Bring to a boil. Reduce heat; simmer, uncovered, for 15 minutes. Serve on buns. **Yield:** 6 servings.

Tuscan Turkey Soup

Prep/Total Time: 30 min.

You'll love dishing up this quick, creamy soup full of leftover Thanksgiving turkey, pumpkin and beans to family and friends. It's fabulous!
—Marie McConnell
Las Cruces, New Mexico

- 1 cup chopped onion
- 1 cup chopped celery
- 1 teaspoon minced garlic
- 2 tablespoons olive oil
- 2 cans (14-1/2 ounces *each*) chicken broth
- 2 cups cubed cooked turkey
- 1 can (15 ounces) solid-pack pumpkin
- 1 can (15 ounces) white kidney *or* cannellini beans, rinsed and drained
- 1/2 teaspoon salt
- 1/2 teaspoon dried basil
- 1/4 teaspoon pepper
Grated Parmesan cheese, optional

In a large saucepan, saute the onion, celery and garlic in oil until tender. Stir in the broth, turkey, pumpkin, beans, salt, basil and pepper. Bring to a boil. Reduce heat; simmer, uncovered, for 10-15 minutes or until heated through, stirring occasionally. Serve with Parmesan cheese if desired. **Yield:** 8 servings (2 quarts).

Hot Turkey Bunwiches

Hot Turkey Bunwiches

(Pictured above)

Prep/Total Time: 30 min.

Put extra turkey and hard-cooked eggs to tasty use in these warm, buttery sandwiches. Everyone in our family looks forward to them after holiday meals. I just mix the salad ingredients, spread it on the buns and bake. —Patty Costantino
Canonsburg, Pennsylvania

1-1/2 cups chopped cooked turkey
   2 hard-cooked eggs, chopped
  1/3 cup chopped onion
  1/2 cup chopped celery
  1/2 cup cubed sharp cheddar cheese
  1/2 cup mayonnaise
  1/8 teaspoon salt
  1/8 teaspoon pepper
   4 teaspoons butter, softened
   4 sandwich buns, split

In a large bowl, combine the first eight ingredients. Spread butter over cut sides of each bun. Spread about 2/3 cup turkey salad over each bun bottom; replace tops. Wrap individually in foil.

Place the wrapped sandwiches on a baking sheet. Bake at 375° for 15-20 minutes or until the cheese is melted. **Yield:** 4 servings.

Mexican Chicken Sandwiches

Prep/Total Time: 25 min.

These lively sandwiches with grilled bread seem special. But they come together in less than 30 minutes!
—Samantha Anhalt, Redford Township, Michigan

   3 tablespoons olive oil
   4 teaspoons chili powder
  1/2 teaspoon garlic powder
  1/4 to 1/2 teaspoon cayenne pepper
   4 boneless skinless chicken breast halves
     (4 ounces *each*)
1-1/2 cups (6 ounces) shredded taco *or* Mexican
     blend cheese, *divided*
  1/3 cup mayonnaise
   8 slices sourdough bread
  1/2 cup salsa

In a small bowl, combine the oil and seasonings. Brush over both sides of chicken. Grill, covered, over medium heat for 6-8 minutes on each side or until juices run clear.

Meanwhile, combine 1 cup cheese and mayonnaise; set aside. Grill bread slices on one side until lightly browned. Spread with cheese mixture; grill until cheese is melted.

Place chicken on four slices of bread; top with salsa, remaining cheese and remaining bread, cheese side down. **Yield:** 4 servings.

Editor's Note: Reduced-fat or fat-free mayonnaise is not recommended for this recipe.

Beefy Bean Soup

Steak Veggie Wraps

(Pictured below and on page 182)

Prep: 25 min. **Cook:** 15 min.

You'll rave about the fresh flavor of these healthy and delicious wraps! They're a family favorite. I often add a sprinkle of parsley for extra flair. —Jennifer Wilksin
Thornton, Colorado

✓ Uses less fat, sugar or salt. Includes Nutrition Facts and Diabetic Exchanges.

- 1/2 teaspoon minced garlic
- 1/4 teaspoon Italian seasoning
- 1/4 teaspoon ground cumin
- 2 tablespoons olive oil, *divided*
- 1-1/4 cups chopped yellow summer squash
- 1 medium sweet red pepper, cut into strips
- 3/4 cup julienned carrot
- 1/2 cup sliced onion
- 1 jalapeno pepper, chopped
- 15 ounces boneless beef sirloin steak, cut into thin strips
- 1/3 cup fat-free ranch salad dressing
- 1/3 cup salsa
- 2/3 cup shredded reduced-fat Mexican cheese blend
- 1/3 cup minced fresh cilantro
- 1 large tomato, chopped
- 5 whole wheat tortillas (8 inches), warmed

In a large bowl, combine the garlic, Italian seasoning, cumin and 1 tablespoon oil. Add summer squash, red pepper, carrot, onion and jalapeno; toss to coat. Place in a single layer in an ungreased 15-in. x 10-in. x 1-in. baking pan. Broil 4-6 in. from the heat for 10-15 minutes or until tender and lightly browned, stirring once.

Meanwhile, in a large skillet, saute steak in remaining oil for 4-6 minutes or until no longer pink. Combine the salad dressing and salsa. Sprinkle cheese, cilantro and tomato over each tortilla; drizzle with dressing mixture. Top with vegetables and steak. Roll up tightly. **Yield:** 5 servings.

Editor's Note: When cutting or seeding hot pep-

Beefy Bean Soup

(Pictured above)

Prep/Total Time: 30 min.

This quick and hearty recipe makes a big batch, and the leftover soup is even better the next day. I love it because we get two filling meals out of one short cooking session.
—Carolyn Burbidge, Bountiful, Utah

- 1 can (29 ounces) tomato puree
- 1 can (14-1/2 ounces) diced tomatoes, undrained
- 1 cup water
- 1 cup beef broth
- 4-1/2 teaspoons chicken bouillon granules
- 3/4 teaspoon salt
- 3/4 teaspoon dried basil
- 3/4 teaspoon dried oregano
- 3/4 cup uncooked elbow macaroni
- 1/2 pound ground beef
- 1 cup chopped celery
- 1/2 cup chopped onion
- 1/2 teaspoon dried minced garlic
- 1 can (16 ounces) kidney beans, rinsed and drained
- 1 can (15-1/2 ounces) great northern beans, rinsed and drained

In a Dutch oven, combine the first eight ingredients. Bring to a boil. Stir in the macaroni. Reduce the heat; simmer, uncovered, for 10-15 minutes or until the macaroni is tender.

Meanwhile, in a large skillet, cook the beef, celery, onion and garlic over medium heat until meat is no longer pink and vegetables are tender; drain. Add to the tomato mixture. Stir in beans; heat through. **Yield:** 8 servings (3 quarts).

Steak Veggie Wraps

pers, use rubber or plastic gloves to protect your hands. Avoid touching your face.

Nutrition Facts: 1 wrap equals 334 calories, 13 g fat (4 g saturated fat), 59 mg cholesterol, 588 mg sodium, 34 g carbohydrate, 4 g fiber, 25 g protein. **Diabetic Exchanges:** 3 lean meat, 2 starch, 1 vegetable.

Sesame Hot Dogs

Prep/Total Time: 30 min.

Kids of all ages love these cute, cheese-stuffed hot dogs wrapped in sesame-seed biscuits, which require just five basic ingredients. I've served the dogs with bowls of chili, mustard, ketchup...even bean dip and salsa for tasty dipping!
—Sue Mackey, Galesburg, Illinois

8 hot dogs
1/4 cup sharp American cheese spread
1 tube (16.3 ounces) large refrigerated buttermilk biscuits
2 tablespoons butter, melted
1/4 cup sesame seeds

Make a lengthwise slit three-fourths of the way through each hot dog to within 1/2 in. of each end. Spread cheese into pockets. Roll each biscuit into a 5-in. circle; wrap one around each hot dog. Brush with butter and roll in sesame seeds.

Place on a lightly greased baking sheet. Bake at 425° for 11-13 minutes or until golden brown. **Yield:** 8 servings.

Mushroom Chicken Soup

Prep/Total Time: 30 min.

This creamy soup makes fantastic use of extra cooked chicken. Tarragon really brightens up the flavor. I pair each big bowlful with a side of crusty bread.
—Joan Anderson, West Covina, California

✓ Uses less fat, sugar or salt. Includes Nutrition Facts and Diabetic Exchanges.

1/4 cup chopped onion
1/4 cup sliced carrot
1 tablespoon canola oil
2 tablespoons all-purpose flour
1/4 teaspoon dried tarragon
1/4 teaspoon pepper
4 cups chicken broth
1-1/2 cups diced cooked chicken
1 can (8 ounces) mushroom stems and pieces, drained
1 cup evaporated milk

In a large saucepan, saute onion and carrot in oil until tender. Stir in flour, tarragon and pepper until blended. Gradually add broth. Bring to a boil over medium heat; cook and stir for 2 minutes or until slightly thickened.

Reduce heat; stir in chicken, mushrooms and milk. Cover and simmer for 10-15 minutes or until heated

Southwestern Panini

through (do not boil). **Yield:** 5 servings.

Nutrition Facts: 1 cup (prepared with reduced-sodium broth and fat-free evaporated milk) equals 185 calories, 6 g fat (1 g saturated fat), 39 mg cholesterol, 760 mg sodium, 12 g carbohydrate, 1 g fiber, 20 g protein. **Diabetic Exchanges:** 2 lean meat, 1 starch.

Southwestern Panini

(Pictured above)

Prep/Total Time: 20 min.

I'm a busy wife, mother, grandmother and great-grandmother who loves to cook. This simple grilled sandwich is a convenient way for me to serve a complete meal that tastes great. Crunchy carrot sticks make a nice accompaniment.
—Janet Miller, Midland, Texas

1 medium ripe avocado, peeled
1/2 teaspoon sugar
1/2 teaspoon garlic salt
1/2 teaspoon lemon juice
8 slices oat bread
1/2 pound thinly sliced deli ham
4 slices Swiss cheese
2 tablespoons butter

In a small bowl, mash the avocado with sugar, garlic salt and lemon juice. Spread over four slices of bread; layer with ham and cheese. Top with remaining bread.

Spread butter over both sides of sandwiches. Cook on an indoor grill for 2-3 minutes or until bread is browned and cheese is melted. **Yield:** 4 servings.

Tortilla Turkey Sandwiches

Prep/Total Time: 20 min.

When my kids were learning how to cook, this was one of their favorite lunches to fix. We all like the creamy blend of flavors. The original recipe came from my husband, but I tweaked it a bit to make it even easier.
—Leslie Heath, Salt Lake City, Utah

    4 ounces cream cheese, softened
    2 tablespoons mayonnaise
1-1/2 teaspoons prepared pesto
    4 flour tortillas (8 inches), room temperature
    1 cup shredded lettuce
1/2 pound sliced deli smoked turkey
3/4 cup chopped tomato
    1 can (2-1/4 ounces) sliced ripe olives, drained
    1 cup (4 ounces) shredded Colby-Monterey Jack cheese

In a small mixing bowl, beat the cream cheese, mayonnaise and pesto until blended. Spread about 2 tablespoons over each tortilla. Layer with lettuce, turkey, tomato, olives and cheese; roll up. Secure with toothpicks. **Yield:** 4 servings.

Muffuletta Subs

(Pictured below)

Prep/Total Time: 25 min.

I love the taste and no-fuss preparation of these Italian sandwiches. They're a snap to fix and can be kept warm in an insulated carrier for handy transporting.
—Joan Hallford, North Richland Hills, Texas

    1 cup pimiento-stuffed olives
    1 cup pitted ripe olives
    1 jar (7-1/2 ounces) marinated artichoke hearts, drained
1/2 cup mayonnaise
    1 tablespoon capers, drained
1/2 teaspoon garlic salt
    6 submarine buns, split
    1 pound sliced deli ham
1/2 pound thinly sliced hard salami
  12 slices process American cheese

In a food processor, finely chop olives and artichokes. Add mayonnaise, capers and garlic salt; cover and process until blended. Spread over cut sides of buns. Layer ham, salami and cheese on bun bottoms; replace tops.

Wrap each sandwich in foil; place on an ungreased baking sheet. Bake at 350° for 10-15 minutes or until cheese is melted. **Yield:** 6 servings.

Honeydew Soup

Prep: 15 min. + chilling

Crisp and refreshing, this sweet melon soup is sure to cool you off on warm spring or summer days.
—Mrs. Earle Davis, Pittsburgh, Pennsylvania

☑ Uses less fat, sugar or salt. Includes Nutrition Facts and Diabetic Exchanges.

1-1/2 cups diced cantaloupe, *divided*
1-1/4 cups diced honeydew
4-1/2 teaspoons sugar
    1 teaspoon minced fresh mint
1/4 cup white wine *or* white grape juice
    3 tablespoons plain yogurt

Muffuletta Subs

1 tablespoon half-and-half cream
Mint sprigs, optional

In a blender, combine 1-1/4 cups cantaloupe, honey-dew, sugar and mint; cover and process for 1 minute. Add the wine or grape juice, yogurt and cream; cover and process for 1-2 minutes or until smooth. Refrigerate for at least 2 hours.

Pour into soup bowls. Garnish with remaining cantaloupe and mint if desired. **Yield:** 2 servings.

Nutrition Facts: 1 cup equals 160 calories, 2 g fat (1 g saturated fat), 7 mg cholesterol, 37 mg sodium, 31 g carbohydrate, 2 g fiber, 3 g protein. **Diabetic Exchanges:** 1-1/2 fruit, 1 starch.

Chicken Tortilla Soup

Prep: 25 min. **Cook:** 15 min.

After I sampled a delicious tortilla soup at a restaurant, I decided to try to duplicate that Southwestern specialty in my own kitchen. With a little trial and error, I came up with this easy recipe that lets me enjoy the wonderful taste at home any time I want to. —Kim Seeger
Brooklyn Park, Minnesota

☑ Uses less fat, sugar or salt. Includes Nutrition Facts and Diabetic Exchanges.

1-1/4 pounds boneless skinless chicken breasts
  1 cup chopped onion
  1 teaspoon minced garlic
  2 cans (14-1/2 ounces *each*) reduced-sodium chicken broth
  1 can (28 ounces) crushed tomatoes
  1 can (16 ounces) kidney beans, rinsed and drained
  1 can (8 ounces) tomato sauce
  1 can (6 ounces) tomato paste
  1 can (4 ounces) chopped green chilies
  2 teaspoons chili powder
  1 teaspoon ground cumin
  3/4 teaspoon dried oregano
  1/2 teaspoon sugar
  1/4 teaspoon salt
  1/4 teaspoon pepper
  3 corn tortillas (6 inches), cut into 1/2-inch strips

Broil the chicken 3-4 in. from the heat for 5-6 minutes on each side or until juices run clear.

In a Dutch oven coated with nonstick cooking spray, cook the onion and garlic until tender. Stir in the chicken broth, tomatoes, beans, tomato sauce, tomato paste, chilies and seasonings. Shred chicken with two forks; add to soup. Bring to a boil. Reduce heat; simmer, uncovered, for 10-15 minutes.

Meanwhile, place tortilla strips on an ungreased baking sheet. Bake at 350° for 12-15 minutes or until crisp. Serve with soup. **Yield:** 8 servings (3 quarts).

Nutrition Facts: 1-1/2 cups equals 227 calories, 2 g fat (1 g saturated fat), 39 mg cholesterol, 818 mg sodium, 30 g carbohydrate, 8 g fiber, 23 g protein. **Diabetic Exchanges:** 2-1/2 very lean meat, 2 starch.

Eggplant-Portobello Sandwich Loaf

Eggplant-Portobello Sandwich Loaf

(Pictured above)
Prep: 25 min. **Grill:** 20 min.

Our Test Kitchen staff used fresh eggplant and marinara sauce to make these hearty dinner sandwiches for four. If you can't find smoked mozzarella, regular mozzarella will work just as well.

  1 loaf (1 pound) Italian bread
1/2 cup olive oil
  2 teaspoons minced garlic
  1 teaspoon Italian seasoning
1/2 teaspoon salt
1/4 teaspoon pepper
  1 large eggplant (1 pound), cut into 1/2-inch slices
  1 package (6 ounces) sliced portobello mushrooms
  1 cup marinara sauce
  2 tablespoons minced fresh basil
  4 ounces smoked fresh mozzarella cheese, cut into 1/4-inch slices

Cut bread lengthwise in half. Carefully hollow out top and bottom, leaving a 1/2-in. shell; set aside. In a small bowl, combine the oil, garlic, Italian seasoning, salt and pepper. Brush over eggplant and mushrooms. Grill, covered, over medium heat for 3-5 minutes on each side or until tender.

Spread half of the marinara sauce over bottom of bread. Top with eggplant and mushrooms. Spread with remaining sauce; top with basil and cheese. Replace bread top.

Wrap loaf in a large piece of heavy-duty foil (about 28 in. x 18 in.); seal tightly. Grill, covered, over medium heat for 8-10 minutes, turning once. **Yield:** 4 servings.

Chapter 13

CREAMY Marinara Tortellini… Asparagus Steak Oscar…Sugar 'n' Spice Salmon…who knew that 30-minute main courses could look and taste so special? Busy cooks from around the country, that's who!

Here, they've shared their favorite family-pleasing entrees for time-crunched nights. Every exceptional dish has so much eye-appeal and flavor, it's hard to believe that they require just half an hour—or less—to fix from start to finish.

With a whopping 54 recipes to choose from in this chapter, you're sure to find many that suit your family's schedules and tastes. So go ahead—count on a 30-minute entree tonight!

THINK 30. Turkey Portobello Pasta (recipe on p. 201).

Pork Kiev

Pesto Turkey Pasta

Prep/Total Time: 25 min.

Give this family-friendly dish from our Test Kitchen a try tonight. With its simple ingredients and short start-to-finish time, it's sure to become a supper standby.

- 3 cups uncooked tricolor rotini
- 1 package (17.6 ounces) turkey breast slices, cut into thin strips
- 3 tablespoons prepared Italian salad dressing
- 1 jar (12 ounces) roasted sweet red peppers, drained and cut into thin strips
- 1/2 cup prepared pesto
- 1/2 teaspoon salt
- 1/4 teaspoon pepper
- 3 tablespoons pine nuts, toasted
- Shredded Parmesan cheese, optional

Cook pasta according to package directions. Meanwhile, in a large skillet, saute turkey in Italian dressing for 5 minutes or until no longer pink.

Drain pasta; add to the skillet. Stir in the roasted peppers, pesto, salt and pepper; heat through. Sprinkle with pine nuts and Parmesan cheese if desired. **Yield:** 6 servings.

Pork Kiev

(Pictured above)

Prep/Total Time: 25 min.

With this recipe, you simply slice a pocket into the chop and fill it with a garlic-herb butter. It's easy and always a hit.   —Jeanne Barney, Saratoga Springs, New York

- 4 teaspoons butter, softened
- 2 teaspoons minced chives
- 2 teaspoons dried parsley flakes
- 1 teaspoon minced garlic
- 1/2 teaspoon pepper
- 4 boneless pork loin chops (4 ounces *each*)
- 1 egg
- 1 teaspoon water
- 1/2 cup all-purpose flour
- 1/2 cup dry bread crumbs
- 2 tablespoons vegetable oil

In a small bowl, combine the butter, chives, parsley, garlic and pepper. Cut a pocket in each pork chop. Fill with butter mixture; secure with toothpicks.

In a shallow bowl, beat egg and water. Place flour and bread crumbs in separate shallow bowls. Dip chops in flour, then in egg mixture; coat with bread crumbs.

In a large skillet over medium heat, cook chops in oil for 6-8 minutes on each side or until juices run clear. **Yield:** 4 servings.

Thai Beef Stir-Fry

Prep/Total Time: 25 min.

One day, I wanted to spice up stir-fry with a little peanut sauce, so I added chunky peanut butter. This dinner is now a menu staple.   —Janet Lowe, Kennewick, Washington

- 2 tablespoons cornstarch
- 3/4 cup water
- 2 tablespoons plus 1-1/2 teaspoons chunky peanut butter
- 4 tablespoons soy sauce, *divided*
- 1-1/2 pounds boneless beef top sirloin steak, thinly sliced
- 1-1/2 teaspoons minced garlic
- 1/4 teaspoon pepper
- 2 tablespoons olive oil
- 1 *each* medium green, sweet red and yellow pepper, julienned
- 1 can (8 ounces) bamboo shoots, drained
- 1/2 cup julienned carrot
- 1/2 teaspoon crushed red pepper flakes
- Hot cooked rice

In a small bowl, combine cornstarch and water until smooth. Stir in peanut butter and 3 tablespoons soy sauce; set aside.

In a large skillet or wok, stir-fry the beef, garlic, pepper and remaining soy sauce in oil until meat is no longer pink; remove and keep warm. Add the peppers, bamboo shoots, carrot and pepper flakes; stir-fry for 2-3 minutes or until tender.

Stir cornstarch mixture; add to the pan. Bring to a boil; cook and stir for 1 minute or until thickened. Return beef mixture to the pan. Serve with rice. **Yield:** 6 servings.

Perfect Pasta

FOR DISHES such as Pesto Turkey Pasta (recipe above right), cook the pasta in a large kettle or Dutch oven until the pasta is "al dente," or firm but tender. Al dente is an Italian term meaning "to the tooth."

Smoked Salmon Pizza

Prep/Total Time: 20 min.

Need a special meal in a hurry? This dressed-up entree is not only impressive, but it's also a snap to prepare.
—Monica Woods, Springfield, Missouri

- 1 prebaked Italian bread shell crust (14 ounces)
- 1/4 cup ranch salad dressing
- 1/4 teaspoon lemon juice
- 6 ounces fully cooked smoked salmon fillets, flaked
- 3/4 cup thinly sliced cucumber
- 1/4 cup chopped red onion
- 1 tablespoon capers

Place crust on an ungreased 12-in. pizza pan. Bake at 450° for 5-7 minutes or until golden brown. Cool for 5 minutes.

In a small bowl, combine dressing and lemon juice; spread over crust. Top with salmon, cucumber, onion and capers. **Yield:** 10 slices.

Company Chicken with Artichokes

Prep/Total Time: 30 min.

My son shared this recipe, which is now a family favorite. The speedy chicken dish is elegant and great for last-minute guests. *—Shirley Lough, Northglenn, Colorado*

✓ Uses less fat, sugar or salt. Includes Nutrition Facts and Diabetic Exchanges.

- 1/4 cup all-purpose flour
- 1/2 teaspoon salt
- 1/2 teaspoon rubbed sage
- 1/4 teaspoon pepper
- 4 boneless skinless chicken breast halves (4 ounces *each*)
- 2 tablespoons canola oil
- 1 can (14 ounces) water-packed artichoke hearts, rinsed and drained
- 1 jar (4-1/2 ounces) sliced mushrooms, drained
- 3 tablespoons chicken broth
- 1/4 cup white wine *or* additional chicken broth
- 2 tablespoons grated Parmesan cheese
- 2 tablespoons minced fresh parsley

In a large resealable plastic bag, combine the flour, salt, sage and pepper. Remove 1 tablespoon to a small bowl and set aside. Add chicken to bag, two pieces at a time, and shake to coat.

In a large skillet, cook chicken in oil over medium heat for 6-7 minutes on each side or until juices run clear; drain. Remove and keep warm.

In the same skillet, combine the artichokes, mushrooms and broth. Add wine or additional broth to reserved flour mixture until smooth; gradually stir into skillet. Bring to a boil; cook and stir for 2 minutes or until thickened. Serve with chicken. Sprinkle with Parmesan cheese and parsley. **Yield:** 4 servings.

Nutrition Facts: 1 chicken breast half with 1/2 cup sauce equals 278 calories, 10 g fat (2 g saturated fat), 65 mg cholesterol, 825 mg sodium, 14 g carbohydrate, 1 g fiber, 28 g protein. **Diabetic Exchanges:** 3 lean meat, 1 starch, 1 fat.

Christmas Eve Confetti Pasta

(Pictured below)

Prep/Total Time: 25 min.

This pasta is a holiday tradition. The prep is done before we attend Christmas Eve services. On returning, I just boil water and saute. *—Ellen Fiore, Ridgewood, New Jersey*

- 1 package (16 ounces) linguine
- 1 cup chopped sweet red pepper
- 1 cup chopped green pepper
- 1/3 cup chopped onion
- 3 garlic cloves, peeled and thinly sliced
- 1/4 teaspoon salt
- 1/4 teaspoon dried oregano
- 1/8 teaspoon crushed red pepper flakes
- 1/8 teaspoon pepper
- 1/4 cup olive oil
- 1 package (2 pounds) frozen cooked small shrimp, thawed
- 1/2 cup shredded Parmesan cheese

Cook linguine according to package directions. Meanwhile, in a Dutch oven, saute the peppers, onion, garlic and seasonings in oil until vegetables are tender.

Add the shrimp; cook and stir 2-3 minutes longer or until heated through. Drain linguine; toss with shrimp mixture. Sprinkle with Parmesan cheese. **Yield:** 8 servings.

Christmas Eve Confetti Pasta

Smoked Sausage Primavera

Creamy Marinara Tortellini

Prep/Total Time: 25 min.

Visit Italy without leaving your kitchen by making this simple pasta combination. I add artichoke hearts and heavy cream to regular marinara to create a special sauce. Round out the menu with a garden salad and garlic bread. —Sarah Vasques
Milford, New Hampshire

    2 packages (9 ounces *each*) refrigerated cheese tortellini
    2 cups marinara sauce
    1 cup heavy whipping cream
    2 tablespoons all-purpose flour
 1/2 cup cold water
    1 can (14 ounces) water-packed artichoke hearts, rinsed, drained and chopped
    2 tablespoons minced fresh thyme *or* 2 teaspoons dried thyme
    2 tablespoons olive oil
 1/2 cup shredded Parmesan cheese
    1 tablespoon minced fresh parsley
 1/4 teaspoon pepper

Cook the cheese tortellini according to the package directions. Meanwhile, in a large saucepan, combine the marinara sauce and heavy whipping cream. Combine the flour and water until smooth; gradually add to the sauce. Bring to a boil; cook and stir for 2 minutes or until thickened.

    Add the artichokes, thyme and oil. Reduce heat; simmer, uncovered, for 3-4 minutes or until heated through. Drain tortellini; toss with sauce. Sprinkle with Parmesan cheese, parsley and pepper. **Yield:** 6 servings.

Smoked Sausage Primavera

(Pictured above)

Prep/Total Time: 25 min.

My family loves Italian food, and this delicious, creamy sauce is a nice change of pace from tomato-based dishes.
—Misty Church, St. Petersburg, Florida

    8 ounces uncooked spaghetti
1-1/2 cups frozen broccoli cuts
 1/2 cup julienned sweet red, yellow *and/or* green pepper
 1/4 cup coarsely chopped onion
 1/2 pound smoked sausage, cut into 1/2-inch slices
 1/4 cup water
 3/4 cup evaporated milk
    2 tablespoons butter
 1/2 teaspoon Italian seasoning
 1/4 cup grated Parmesan cheese

In a Dutch oven, cook spaghetti according to package directions, adding vegetables during the last 4 minutes.

    Meanwhile, in a large skillet, bring sausage and water to a boil. Reduce heat; cover and simmer for 7-8 minutes or until heated through. Add milk, butter and Italian seasoning; cook and stir until butter is melted. Drain spaghetti and vegetables; return to the pan. Add Parmesan cheese and sausage mixture; toss to coat. **Yield:** 4 servings.

Salmon with Pecan-Honey Sauce

Prep/Total Time: 20 min.

If you're looking for an effortless dish to serve to company, try this elegant entree. The flaky salmon fillets are draped with a sweet pecan glaze. —Buffy Sias
Whitehorse, Yukon Territory

    6 salmon fillets (6 ounces *each*)
 1/4 teaspoon salt
 1/4 teaspoon pepper
 1/4 cup vegetable oil
 3/4 cup butter, *divided*
    1 cup coarsely chopped pecans, toasted
    1 cup honey

Sprinkle the salmon fillets with the salt and pepper. In a large skillet, cook salmon fillets in oil and 6 tablespoons butter for 10-12 minutes or until the fish flakes easily with a fork.

    Meanwhile, in a small saucepan, cook the pecans and honey in the remaining butter over medium-low heat for 8-10 minutes or until bubbly. Serve with the salmon. **Yield:** 6 servings.

Turkey Portobello Pasta

(Pictured below and on page 196)

Prep/Total Time: 25 min.

With mushrooms and a host of seasonings, this entree is truly special...and a great solution for leftover holiday turkey. —Heather Fergeson, Idaho Springs, Colorado

✓ Uses less fat, sugar or salt. Includes Nutrition Facts.

    6 ounces uncooked spaghetti
    2 cups cubed cooked turkey breast
    1 can (10-3/4 ounces) reduced-fat
      reduced-sodium condensed cream of
      mushroom soup, undiluted
    1 cup water
  3/4 cup sliced baby portobello mushrooms
    1 teaspoon dried rosemary, crushed
    1 teaspoon Italian seasoning
  1/2 teaspoon onion powder
  1/2 teaspoon garlic powder
  1/2 cup shredded Italian cheese blend
  1/2 cup reduced-fat sour cream
    2 tablespoons shredded Parmesan cheese
    1 tablespoon dried parsley flakes

Cook the spaghetti according to the package directions. Meanwhile, in a large saucepan, combine the turkey, cream of mushroom soup, water, portobella mushrooms, rosemary, Italian seasoning, onion powder and garlic powder. Bring to a boil. Reduce heat; simmer, uncovered, for 5-7 minutes or until heated through and mushrooms are tender.

Remove from the heat. Whisk in Italian cheese and sour cream until smooth. Drain spaghetti; place in a serving bowl. Top with turkey mixture, Parmesan cheese and parsley. **Yield:** 4 servings.

Nutrition Facts: 1 cup turkey mixture with 3/4 cup spaghetti equals 416 calories, 12 g fat (6 g saturated fat), 81 mg cholesterol, 502 mg sodium, 42 g carbohydrate, 2 g fiber, 33 g protein.

Best Chicken 'n' Biscuits

Prep/Total Time: 30 min.

Quick and comforting, this home-style dish is filled with chunky chicken, colorful veggies and spoonfuls of creamy flavor—all served over golden, flaky biscuits.
—Judith Whitford, East Aurora, New York

✓ Uses less fat, sugar or salt. Includes Nutrition Facts.

      6 individually frozen biscuits
      1 can (49-1/2 ounces) chicken broth, *divided*
  1-1/2 pounds boneless skinless chicken breasts,
        cubed
      5 medium carrots, coarsely chopped
      2 celery ribs, chopped
    1/2 cup chopped onion
    1/2 cup frozen corn
      3 teaspoons dried basil
    1/4 teaspoon pepper
      1 cup all-purpose flour
    3/4 teaspoon browning sauce, optional

Bake biscuits according to package directions. Meanwhile, in a Dutch oven, combine 4 cups broth, chicken, carrots, celery, onion, corn, basil and pepper. Bring to a boil. Reduce heat. Cover; simmer for 7-10 minutes or until vegetables are tender.

In a bowl, combine flour and remaining broth until smooth. Stir into chicken mixture. Bring to a boil; cook and stir for 2 minutes or until thickened. Stir in browning sauce if desired. Split biscuits; top with chicken mixture. **Yield:** 6 servings.

Nutrition Facts: 1-2/3 cups chicken mixture with 1 biscuit (prepared with reduced-sodium chicken broth) equals 460 calories, 14 g fat (4 g saturated fat), 63 mg cholesterol, 1,353 mg sodium, 51 g carbohydrate, 4 g fiber, 33 g protein.

Turkey Portobello Pasta

More Leftover Turkey

When I have leftover cooked turkey from Thanksgiving, I put the turkey in a slow cooker and add some minced garlic, our favorite barbecue sauce and a dash of hot sauce. When the meat mixture is heated through, I serve it on warmed hamburger buns. My family looks forward to these sandwiches every year.
—Stacy Anderson, Twin Falls, Idaho

Chicken with Florentine Sauce

(Pictured below)

Prep/Total Time: 30 min.

This is the best chicken-and-spinach combination I've ever had. A creamy topping and pretty presentation make it elegant enough for company, but it's also fast enough for busy weeknights. —Julie Fitzgerald, St. Louis, Missouri

- 6 boneless skinless chicken breast halves (4 ounces *each*)
- 1/2 cup grated Parmesan cheese
- 1/2 teaspoon dried basil
- 1/2 teaspoon dried oregano
- 3 tablespoons butter, *divided*
- 2 green onions, chopped
- 1 teaspoon minced garlic
- 1 tablespoon all-purpose flour
- 1/4 teaspoon salt
- 1/2 cup milk
- 1 tablespoon sherry *or* chicken broth
- 1 package (10 ounces) frozen chopped spinach, thawed and squeezed dry
- 2 tablespoons diced pimientos
- 1/2 cup sour cream
- 1 cup (4 ounces) shredded part-skim mozzarella cheese

Flatten chicken to 1/2-in. thickness. In a large resealable plastic bag, combine the Parmesan cheese, basil and oregano. Add chicken, a few pieces at a time, and shake to coat.

In a large skillet over medium heat, cook chicken in 2 tablespoons butter for 4-5 minutes on each side or until juices run clear. Remove and keep warm.

In the same skillet, saute onions and garlic in remaining butter for 2-3 minutes or until tender. Add flour and salt; stir in milk and sherry or chicken broth until blended. Bring to a boil. Reduce heat; cook and stir for 1-2 minutes or until thickened. Stir in spinach and pimientos; heat through.

Remove from the heat. Stir in sour cream until blended. Spoon over chicken; sprinkle with mozzarella cheese. **Yield:** 6 servings.

Shrimp 'n' Chicken Noodle Soup

Prep/Total Time: 25 min.

Dinner will have a Thai twist when you serve this out-of-the-ordinary soup. With ramen noodles, shrimp and chicken, it's a special meal anytime. —Todd Schaal Colorado Springs, Colorado

- 1/4 cup chopped sweet onion
- 3 green onions, sliced
- 2 teaspoons minced garlic
- 1 can (4 ounces) mushroom stems and pieces, drained
- 2 teaspoons olive oil
- 3/4 cup frozen cooked salad shrimp, thawed
- 1 teaspoon dried rosemary, crushed
- 1/4 teaspoon lemon-pepper seasoning
- 2 cans (14-1/2 ounces *each*) chicken broth
- 1 cup cubed cooked chicken
- 1 package (3 ounces) chicken ramen noodles
- 2 tablespoons crumbled cooked bacon, optional

In a large saucepan, saute the onions, garlic and mushrooms in oil. Add the shrimp, rosemary and lemon-pepper. Cook for 3-4 minutes or until vegetables are tender.

Stir in the broth, chicken, ramen noodles and contents of seasoning packet if desired. Bring to a boil. Reduce heat; cover and simmer for 6-8 minutes or until noodles are tender. Garnish with bacon if desired. **Yield:** 4 servings.

Tasty Tuna Turnovers

Prep/Total Time: 25 min.

You'll have both kids and adults gobbling up these easy tuna pockets, which use refrigerated crescent roll dough. —Brenda Rohlman, Kingman, Kansas

- 1 can (7 ounces) tuna, drained and flaked
- 1 hard-cooked egg, chopped
- 1/4 cup chopped celery
- 1/4 cup mayonnaise
- 2 tubes (8 ounces *each*) refrigerated crescent rolls
- 1-1/2 cups (6 ounces) shredded cheddar cheese

In a small bowl, combine the tuna, egg, celery and mayonnaise; set aside. Separate crescent dough into eight rectangles; seal perforations. Top each with tuna mixture and cheese. Fold each in half; pinch edges to seal.

Place on an ungreased baking sheet. Bake at 425° for 10-15 minutes or until golden brown. **Yield:** 8 servings.

Chicken with Florentine Sauce

Turkey Tostadas

(Pictured above)

Prep/Total Time: 25 min.

Made with tostadas, but just as tasty with tortillas, this Southwestern classic will be requested by your family time and again. —Liz Raisig, New York, New York

 1 package (20 ounces) lean ground turkey
 1/2 cup chopped onion
 1/2 cup chopped green pepper
 1 teaspoon vegetable oil
 3/4 cup water
 1 envelope taco seasoning
 1 can (15-1/2 ounces) hominy, rinsed and drained
 12 tostada shells
 3 cups shredded lettuce
 1 cup (4 ounces) shredded Mexican cheese blend
 1 cup chopped tomato
 1 cup cubed avocado

In a large skillet, cook the ground turkey, onion and green pepper in the oil over medium heat for 5 minutes or until the meat is no longer pink; drain. Stir in the water, taco seasoning and hominy. Bring to a boil. Reduce the heat; simmer, uncovered, for 5 minutes or until heated through.

On each tostada shell, layer lettuce, about 1/3 cup turkey mixture, cheese, tomato and avocado. Serve immediately. **Yield:** 6 servings.

Hamburger Stroganoff

Prep/Total Time: 25 min.

This recipe was a winner in a local contest, and it's one of my favorite quick dinners. It's rich, creamy and so simple. Best of all, it tastes great. —Sally Lilja, Plains, Montana

 4 cups uncooked wide egg noodles
 1 pound ground beef
 1/2 cup chopped onion
 1/2 pound sliced fresh mushrooms
 2 tablespoons all-purpose flour
 2 teaspoons paprika
 1 teaspoon salt
 1/8 teaspoon garlic powder
Dash cayenne pepper
 1/2 teaspoon beef bouillon granules
 1/2 cup boiling water
 1 cup (8 ounces) sour cream
 4 green onions, sliced

Cook noodles according to package directions. Meanwhile, in a large skillet, cook beef and onion over medium heat until meat is no longer pink; drain. Stir in the mushrooms, flour, paprika, salt, garlic powder and cayenne pepper.

Dissolve bouillon in boiling water; add to beef mixture. Bring to a boil. Reduce heat; cook, uncovered, for 5-7 minutes or until mushrooms are tender. Remove from heat; stir in sour cream. Drain noodles; top with beef mixture and green onions. **Yield:** 4 servings.

Asparagus Steak Oscar

(Pictured above)

Prep/Total Time: 30 min.

Asparagus is my favorite vegetable. This recipe combines the delicious taste of asparagus with tenderloin steaks. I love to serve it for special occasions. —Cindy Dorsett
Lubbock, Texas

　1 envelope bearnaise sauce
　1 pound fresh asparagus, trimmed
1/4 pound fresh crabmeat
1/2 teaspoon minced garlic
　2 tablespoons butter
　1 tablespoon lemon juice
　4 beef tenderloin steaks (1 inch thick and
　　3 ounces *each*)
1/8 teaspoon paprika

Prepare the bearnaise sauce according to the package directions. Meanwhile, place the asparagus in a steamer basket; place in a large saucepan over 1 in. of water. Bring to a boil; cover and steam for 8-10 minutes or until crisp-tender.

In a large skillet, saute crab and garlic in butter for 3-4 minutes or until heated through. Stir in lemon juice; keep warm.

Grill steaks, covered, over medium heat or broil 4 in. from the heat for 6-8 minutes on each side or until meat reaches desired doneness (for medium-rare, a meat thermometer should read 145°; medium, 160°; well-done, 170°). Top with crab mixture, asparagus and bearnaise sauce. Sprinkle with paprika. **Yield:** 4 servings.

Vegetable Beef Casserole

Prep/Total Time: 30 min.

My sister fixed this ground beef entree often as a newlywed, and she shared the recipe with me when I got married. The biscuit-topped dish has a heartwarming flavor, and canned veggies make preparation a breeze. —Andrea Hickerson
Trenton, Tennessee

1-1/2 pounds ground beef
　2 cups frozen cut green beans, thawed
　1 can (10-3/4 ounces) condensed tomato
　　soup, undiluted
　1 can (15-1/4 ounces) whole kernel corn,
　　drained
3/4 cup water
　1 teaspoon Worcestershire sauce
　1 tube (12 ounces) refrigerated buttermilk
　　biscuits
　1 cup (4 ounces) shredded cheddar cheese

In a large skillet, cook beef over medium heat until no longer pink; drain. Stir in the beans, soup, corn, water and Worcestershire sauce. Bring to a boil; cook and stir for 2-3 minutes or until heated through. Keep warm.

Separate biscuits and cut into quarters; place on an ungreased baking sheet. Bake at 400° for 5 minutes.

Transfer beef mixture to a greased 13-in. x 9-in. x 2-in. baking dish. Top with biscuits and cheese. Bake for 8-10 minutes or until biscuits are golden brown. **Yield:** 6 servings.

Mango Couscous with Salmon

(Pictured below)

Prep/Total Time: 30 min.

This elegant meal-in-one features a hearty portion of salmon served with couscous and an amazing mango sauce. —Tammy Strange, Statham, Georgia

　　1/4 cup vegetable oil
2-1/2 teaspoons minced garlic
　　1/4 teaspoon salt
　　1/4 teaspoon pepper
　　1/4 cup minced fresh parsley, *divided*
　　　4 salmon fillets (6 ounces *each*)
　　　2 cups chicken broth
　　　1 tablespoon butter
　　　1 package (10 ounces) plain couscous
　　　2 medium tomatoes, chopped
　　　1 medium mango, peeled and chopped
MANGO SAUCE:
　　　1 medium mango, peeled and cut into chunks
　　　2 tablespoons lemon juice
　　　2 tablespoons honey
　　　2 fresh basil leaves
　　　1 tablespoon minced fresh parsley
　　　1 tablespoon water
　　　1 tablespoon Dijon mustard

In a small bowl, combine the oil, garlic, salt, pepper and 2 tablespoons parsley. Rub over salmon. Broil 4 in. from the heat for 6-8 minutes on each side or until fish flakes easily with a fork.

Meanwhile, in a large saucepan, bring broth and butter to a boil. Stir in couscous. Cover and remove from the heat; let stand for 5 minutes. Stir in the tomatoes, mango and remaining parsley.

In a blender, combine the sauce ingredients; cover and puree for 1-2 minutes or until smooth. Serve with salmon and couscous. **Yield:** 4 servings.

Biscuit Nugget Chicken Bake

Biscuit Nugget Chicken Bake

(Pictured above)

Prep/Total Time: 30 min.

Topped with seasoned golden biscuits, this yummy casserole will fill up a family in no time. As a beginning cook, I really enjoy trying new recipes, and this is one of the best I've found. —Kayla Dempsey, O'Fallon, Illinois

　　　3 cups cubed cooked chicken
　　　1 can (10-3/4 ounces) condensed cream of chicken soup, undiluted
　　　1 cup milk
　　　1 jar (4-1/2 ounces) sliced mushrooms, drained
　　1/2 teaspoon dill weed
　　1/2 teaspoon paprika
TOPPING:
　　1/4 cup grated Parmesan cheese
　　　1 tablespoon dried minced onion
　　　1 teaspoon dried parsley flakes
　　1/2 teaspoon paprika
　　　1 tube (12 ounces) refrigerated buttermilk biscuits

In a large saucepan, combine the first six ingredients. Cook and stir over medium heat for 5-7 minutes or until heated through; keep warm.

In a large resealable plastic bag, combine the Parmesan cheese, onion, parsley and paprika. Separate the biscuits and cut into quarters; add to the bag and shake to coat. Place on an ungreased baking sheet. Bake at 400° for 5 minutes.

Transfer chicken mixture to a greased 8-in. square baking dish; top with biscuits. Bake, uncovered, for 10-13 minutes or until bubbly and biscuits are golden brown. **Yield:** 4-6 servings.

Mango Couscous with Salmon

Baked Tilapia

(Pictured below)

Prep/Total Time: 20 min.

I've decided to cook healthier for my family, and that includes eating more fish at home. I found this recipe, changed the ingredients slightly, and it was a success!
—Hope Stewart, Raleigh, North Carolina

- 4 tilapia fillets (6 ounces *each*)
- 3 tablespoons butter, melted
- 3 tablespoons lemon juice
- 1-1/2 teaspoons garlic powder
- 1/8 teaspoon salt
- 2 tablespoons capers, drained
- 1/2 teaspoon dried oregano
- 1/8 teaspoon paprika

Place tilapia in an ungreased 13-in. x 9-in. x 2-in. baking dish. In a small bowl, combine the butter, lemon juice, garlic powder and salt; pour over the fillets. Sprinkle with the capers, oregano and paprika.

Bake, uncovered, at 425° for 10-15 minutes or until fish flakes easily with a fork. **Yield:** 4 servings.

Baked Tilapia

Rotisserie Chicken Ragout

Prep/Total Time: 25 min.

Deli-roasted chicken is the secret to my fast skillet dinner. I appreciate this recipe most after a long day of shopping, on rushed weeknights...any time I'm tired! It's a quick, home-cooked meal—what could be better? —*Paula Marchesi*
Lenhartsville, Pennsylvania

- 1 cup chopped yellow summer squash
- 1 cup chopped zucchini
- 1/2 cup chopped onion
- 1-1/2 teaspoons minced garlic
- 2 tablespoons olive oil
- 2 cups cubed cooked rotisserie chicken
- 1 can (15 ounces) white kidney *or* cannellini beans, rinsed and drained
- 1 tablespoon heavy whipping cream
- 1 tablespoon minced fresh thyme
- 1/8 teaspoon salt
- 1/8 teaspoon pepper
- 1/2 cup shredded Parmesan cheese

In a large skillet, saute the yellow squash, zucchini, onion and garlic in oil for 4-6 minutes or until tender.

Add the chicken, beans, heavy whipping cream, thyme, salt and pepper. Cook and stir 3-4 minutes longer or until heated through. Sprinkle with Parmesan cheese. **Yield:** 5 servings.

Microwave Meatballs and Rice

Prep/Total Time: 25 min.

On blustery autumn or winter days, I often rely on this satisfying dinner made in the microwave. The savory meatballs and rice really warm up my family and friends. I received the recipe from my mother. —*Loni Fancher*
Corfu, New York

- 1 egg
- 1-1/2 teaspoons chili powder
- 1 teaspoon salt
- 1/4 teaspoon pepper
- 1 pound ground beef
- 1 can (14-1/2 ounces) stewed tomatoes, undrained
- 1 cup uncooked instant rice
- 1 cup sliced onion
- 1 cup chopped green pepper

In a large bowl, whisk the egg, chili powder, salt and pepper. Crumble beef over mixture and mix well. Shape into 1-1/2-in. balls. Place in a 2-qt. microwave-safe dish. Cover and microwave on high for 4-5 minutes or until meat is no longer pink; drain.

Stir in the tomatoes, rice, onion and green pepper. Cover and microwave on high for 5-7 minutes or until rice and vegetables are tender. **Yield:** 3-4 servings.

Editor's Note: This recipe was tested in a 1,100-watt microwave.

Peach-Topped Pork Chops

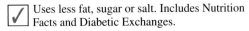

(Pictured below)

Prep/Total Time: 25 min.

Even finicky eaters like these pork chops. Served with fresh peach slices and sweet caramelized onions, they're sure to be a hit with folks of all ages. —Frankie Allen Mann
Warrior, Alabama

✓ Uses less fat, sugar or salt. Includes Nutrition Facts and Diabetic Exchanges.

    1 cup chopped onion
    1 tablespoon canola oil
    4 pork rib chops (1/2 inch thick and 6 ounces *each*)
  1/2 teaspoon salt
  1/2 teaspoon dried thyme
  1/2 cup chopped peeled fresh peach *or* frozen unsweetened peach slices, chopped
  1/4 cup sugar
    2 tablespoons white vinegar
  1/4 teaspoon pepper

In a large skillet, saute onion in oil for 4-5 minutes or until crisp-tender. Remove and keep warm. Sprinkle both sides of pork chops with salt and thyme; add to skillet. Cover and cook for 6-7 minutes on each side or until juices run clear. Remove and keep warm.

In the same skillet, combine the peach, sugar, vine-

Peach-Topped Pork Chops

Chicken Taco Fettuccine

gar and pepper. Bring to a boil. Reduce heat; cook and stir for 2-3 minutes or until thickened. Return pork and onion to the pan; heat through. **Yield:** 4 servings.

Nutrition Facts: 1 pork chop with about 1/4 cup peach mixture equals 261 calories, 11 g fat (3 g saturated fat), 54 mg cholesterol, 328 mg sodium, 19 g carbohydrate, 1 g fiber, 22 g protein. **Diabetic Exchanges:** 3 lean meat, 1 starch, 1/2 fat.

Chicken Taco Fettuccine

(Pictured above)

Prep/Total Time: 20 min.

There are never any leftovers when I whip up this creamy noodle entree, which I adapted from a cookbook.
—Carey Judy, Paris, Tennessee

      8 ounces uncooked fettuccine
      2 cups cubed cooked chicken
    1/2 teaspoon minced garlic
  1-1/2 teaspoons olive oil
    1/2 cup heavy whipping cream
      3 to 4-1/2 teaspoons taco seasoning
      2 tablespoons shredded Parmesan cheese

Cook fettuccine according to package directions. Meanwhile, in a large skillet over medium heat, cook the chicken and garlic in oil for 4-5 minutes or until heated through.

Whisk in cream and taco seasoning until blended. Cook and stir until heated through (do not boil). Stir in Parmesan cheese. Drain fettuccine; toss with chicken mixture. **Yield:** 4 servings.

Pasta Primavera with Shrimp

Chili Pockets

Prep/Total Time: 25 min.

You'll bring some fun to the dinner table with this scrumptious twist on canned chili. I stuff it into triangular pockets made with convenient refrigerated pizza crust. We like them best served with salsa and sour cream on the side.
—*Diane Angell, Rockford, Illinois*

> 1 can (15 ounces) chili with beans
> 1/2 cup shredded cheddar cheese
> 2 tablespoons minced fresh cilantro
> 1 can (13.8 ounces) refrigerated pizza crust
> 4-1/2 teaspoons cornmeal, *divided*
> Sour cream and salsa

In a small bowl, combine the chili, cheese and cilantro. Roll pizza dough into a 12-in. square; cut into four 6-in. squares. Spoon 1/2 cup chili mixture onto the center of each square; brush edges of dough with water. Fold one corner of each square over filling to the opposite corner, forming a triangle. Using a fork, crimp edges to seal.

Sprinkle 1-1/2 teaspoons cornmeal over a greased 15-in. x 10-in. x 1-in. baking pan. Place pockets in pan; prick tops with a fork. Sprinkle with remaining cornmeal. Bake at 425° for 10-12 minutes or until golden brown. Serve with sour cream and salsa. **Yield:** 4 servings.

Pasta Primavera with Shrimp

(Pictured above)

Prep/Total Time: 30 min.

This restaurant-style supper bursts with fresh flavor in every bite. —*Kimberly Wagner, Castle Rock, Colorado*

> 1 package (1 pound) linguine
> 1 pound uncooked medium shrimp, peeled and deveined
> 2 cups chopped fresh broccoli
> 1 cup sliced fresh carrots
> 1 cup fresh green beans, cut into 2-inch pieces
> 1 medium zucchini, cut into 1/4-inch slices
> 1 medium sweet red pepper, julienned
> 2 tablespoons all-purpose flour
> 1-1/4 cups heavy whipping cream
> 3/4 cup chicken broth
> 1/4 cup grated Parmesan cheese
> 3/4 teaspoon salt
> 1/2 teaspoon pepper

In a Dutch oven, cook linguine according to package directions, adding shrimp and vegetables during the last 4 minutes.

Meanwhile, in a small saucepan, combine the flour, cream and broth until smooth. Add the Parmesan cheese, salt and pepper. Bring to a boil over medium heat; cook and stir for 2 minutes or until thickened. Drain linguine mixture and return to the pan. Add cream sauce and toss to coat. **Yield:** 6 servings.

Southwestern Frittata

Prep/Total Time: 25 min.

This skillet dish makes a memorable breakfast entree, but it could also be served for lunch or dinner. Eggs are jazzed up with fresh vegetables, then treated to a topping of melted mozzarella cheese.
—*Mary Relyea*
Canastota, New York

> 4 eggs
> 1 tablespoon milk
> 1/4 teaspoon salt
> 1/4 teaspoon ground mustard
> 1/4 teaspoon pepper
> Dash to 1/8 teaspoon cayenne pepper
> 1/2 cup chopped onion
> 1/2 cup chopped green pepper
> 1/2 teaspoon minced garlic
> 1 teaspoon olive oil
> 1 large tomato, chopped
> 2 tablespoons sliced ripe olives, drained
> 1/2 cup shredded part-skim mozzarella cheese

In a small bowl, whisk the eggs, milk, salt, mustard, pepper and cayenne; set aside. In a large skillet over medium heat, cook the onion, green pepper and garlic in oil until tender. Add tomato and olives; heat through.

Pour egg mixture over vegetables. As eggs set, lift edges, letting uncooked portion flow underneath. When eggs are set, sprinkle with cheese. Remove from the heat. Cover and let stand for 1-2 minutes or until cheese is melted. Cut into four wedges. **Yield:** 4 servings.

Roast Beef Chimichangas

Prep/Total Time: 30 min.

You and your family are sure to enjoy this fabulous home-made take on a restaurant favorite. The chimichangas are a terrific way to use up your leftover roast beef, and they make a complete meal all by themselves.
—Delia Kennedy, Deer Park, Washington

  1/2 cup chopped onion
  1/2 teaspoon minced garlic
    1 tablespoon vegetable oil
1-1/2 cups shredded cooked roast beef
    1 can (2-1/4 ounces) sliced ripe olives, drained
  1/2 cup salsa
  1/4 teaspoon ground cumin
  1/2 cup shredded cheddar cheese
    6 flour tortillas (10 inches)
Oil for deep-fat frying

In a large skillet, saute onion and garlic in oil for 1-2 minutes or until tender. Add the roast beef, olives, salsa and cumin. Cook and stir over medium heat for 4-6 minutes or until heated through. Stir in cheese. Remove from the heat.

Spoon about 1/3 cup meat mixture off-center on each tortilla. Fold sides and ends over filling and roll up; secure with a toothpick. Repeat.

In an electric skillet or deep-fat fryer, heat oil to 375°. Fry chimichangas for 2-3 minutes on each side or until lightly browned. Drain on paper towels. Discard toothpicks. **Yield:** 6 servings.

Beef 'n' Cheese French Bread

Prep/Total Time: 30 min.

This open-faced sandwich is guaranteed to be a winner with people of all ages. In fact, my family hurries to the table whenever my menu features the beefy, cheesy slices of French bread. And we eat up every last crumb almost as quickly!
—Becky Stubbs, Larned, Kansas

    1 pound ground beef
  1/2 cup chopped onion
    1 jar (8 ounces) salsa
    1 medium green pepper, chopped
    2 cans (2-1/4 ounces *each*) sliced ripe olives, drained
    1 teaspoon salt
    1 teaspoon chili powder
    1 teaspoon minced garlic
  1/2 teaspoon ground cumin
    1 loaf (1 pound) unsliced French bread
    2 cups (8 ounces) shredded sharp cheddar cheese

In a large skillet, cook beef and onion over medium heat until meat is no longer pink; drain. Stir in the salsa, green pepper, olives, salt, chili powder, garlic and cumin. Remove from the heat.

Cut the bread in half lengthwise; place on a baking sheet. Spread meat mixture over cut sides; sprinkle with cheese. Bake at 450° for 10-15 minutes or until cheese is melted. **Yield:** 8 servings.

Crab Cakes with Lime Sauce

(Pictured below)

Prep/Total Time: 25 min.

Reel in a breezy taste of the sea with these delectable, crispy-coated crab cakes. The refreshing, lip-smacking lime sauce adds a delightful summery tang to this traditional favorite. —Marjie Gaspar, Oxford, Pennsylvania

    2 cans (6 ounces *each*) crabmeat, drained, flaked and cartilage removed
    1 green onion, chopped
    1 tablespoon Dijon mustard
    1 teaspoon Italian salad dressing mix
1-1/2 cups crushed butter-flavored crackers (about 37), *divided*
    1 cup mayonnaise, *divided*
    2 tablespoons lime juice, *divided*
  1/4 cup vegetable oil
  1/4 cup sour cream
1-1/2 teaspoons grated lime peel

In a small bowl, combine the crab, onion, mustard, dressing mix, 1 cup cracker crumbs, 1/2 cup mayonnaise and 1 tablespoon lime juice. Shape into six patties; coat with remaining cracker crumbs.

In a large skillet, heat the oil over medium heat. Cook the crab cakes for 3-4 minutes on each side or until lightly browned.

For sauce, in a small bowl, combine the sour cream, lime peel, and remaining mayonnaise and lime juice until blended. Serve with crab cakes. **Yield:** 3 servings.

Crab Cakes with Lime Sauce

Italian Sausage with Bow Ties

(Pictured below)

Prep/Total Time: 25 min.

Here's a family favorite that's requested monthly at our house. The Italian sausage paired with creamy tomato sauce is out of this world. Not only is this dish simple to make, it tastes like you slaved over a hot stove for hours!
—*Janelle Moore, Federal Way, Washington*

- 1 package (16 ounces) bow tie pasta
- 1 pound bulk Italian sausage
- 1/2 cup chopped onion
- 1-1/2 teaspoons minced garlic
- 1/2 teaspoon crushed red pepper flakes
- 2 cans (14-1/2 ounces *each*) Italian stewed tomatoes, drained and chopped
- 1-1/2 cups heavy whipping cream
- 1/2 teaspoon salt
- 1/4 teaspoon dried basil
- Shredded Parmesan cheese

Cook pasta according to package directions. Meanwhile, in a Dutch oven, cook the sausage, onion, garlic and pepper flakes over medium heat for 4-5 minutes or until meat is no longer pink; drain.

Stir in the tomatoes, cream, salt and basil. Bring to a boil over medium heat. Reduce heat; simmer, uncovered, for 6-8 minutes or until thickened, stirring occasionally. Drain pasta; toss with sausage mixture. Garnish with Parmesan cheese. **Yield:** 5 servings.

Italian Sausage with Bow Ties

Antipasto Wraps

Prep/Total Time: 25 min.

On hurried weeknights, I make short work of family suppers with these hearty, colorful and easy-to-handle wraps. They're so moist and chock-full of flavor, and they're ready to eat in minutes.
—*Amanda Lanuto*
Forked River, New Jersey

- 6 sun-dried tomato basil tortillas (8 inches)
- 6 slices deli ham
- 6 slices deli turkey
- 6 slices provolone cheese, halved
- 1 jar (6-1/2 ounces) marinated artichoke hearts, drained and sliced
- 2 cans (2-1/4 ounces *each*) sliced ripe olives, drained
- 1/2 cup chopped pitted green olives, drained
- 6 roasted sweet red peppers, drained and cut into 1-inch strips
- 3/4 cup chopped tomatoes
- 3/4 cup red wine vinaigrette
- 6 romaine leaves

On each tortilla, layer the ham, turkey, provolone cheese, artichokes, ripe olives, green olives, red peppers and tomatoes. Drizzle each with 2 tablespoons red wine vinaigrette. Top with the lettuce leaves and roll up the tortillas. **Yield:** 6 servings.

Bow Tie Beef Soup

Prep/Total Time: 30 min.

Though this soup's ingredient list may seem longer, it's actually a quick, simple recipe. I think it's among the best one-dish meals I've made.
—*Lee Anne McBride*
Austin, Texas

- 2 cups sliced zucchini
- 1 can (14-1/2 ounces) beef broth
- 1 cup uncooked bow tie pasta
- 3/4 cup water
- 1/2 teaspoon dried oregano
- 1/4 to 1/2 teaspoon dried thyme
- 1/4 to 1/2 teaspoon crushed red pepper flakes
- 1-1/2 pounds ground beef
- 1 cup chopped onion
- 2 teaspoons minced garlic
- 4 plum tomatoes, cut into chunks
- 1/4 cup minced fresh basil
- 1/2 cup shredded Parmesan cheese

In a Dutch oven, combine the first seven ingredients. Bring to a boil. With a spoon, press pasta into broth mixture. Reduce heat; cover and simmer for 15 minutes or until pasta is tender, stirring once.

Meanwhile, in a large skillet, cook the beef, onion and garlic over medium heat until meat is no longer pink; drain.

Add the beef mixture, tomatoes and basil to the broth mixture; heat through. Garnish with Parmesan cheese. **Yield:** 8 servings (about 2 quarts).

Herbed Chicken Breasts

Prep/Total Time: 30 min.

I love this chicken because it's quick and looks so attractive on the table. I have a large pot of herbs in my kitchen, and just a few snips here and there turn an ordinary dinner dish into something extraordinary.
—Mary Kay Dixson, Catlin, Illinois

    4 boneless skinless chicken breast halves
      (5 ounces *each*)
1/2 teaspoon lemon-pepper seasoning
    2 tablespoons olive oil, *divided*
    2 tablespoons butter, *divided*
    1 tablespoon lemon juice
    2 teaspoons Dijon mustard
1/4 cup chicken broth
1/2 cup minced fresh parsley
    3 tablespoons minced chives
    1 tablespoon minced fresh thyme *or*
      1 teaspoon dried thyme
    1 tablespoon minced fresh basil *or* 1 teaspoon
      dried basil
1/2 teaspoon minced garlic
1/2 teaspoon salt

Flatten chicken to 1/4-in. thickness; sprinkle with lemon-pepper. In a large skillet, saute chicken in 1 tablespoon each oil and butter for 6-7 minutes on each side or until juices run clear. Remove and keep warm.

Add lemon juice and mustard to the skillet; whisk until smooth. Whisk in broth, herbs, garlic, salt, and remaining oil and butter; simmer for 1 minute. Spoon over chicken. **Yield:** 4 servings.

Sausage Apple Supper

Prep/Total Time: 30 min.

Smoked sausage, tangy sauerkraut, tender potatoes and apple wedges come together in this hearty, home-style main course. I think it's especially good in the winter after a day of work or playing in the snow or on the ice.
—Gladys De Boer, Castleford, Idaho

    1 pound smoked sausage, cut into 2-inch pieces
    1 medium onion, coarsely chopped
    1 teaspoon butter
    1 can (27 ounces) sauerkraut, rinsed and well
      drained
    4 medium red potatoes, cut into 1-1/2-inch
      pieces
    3 medium Cortland apples, peeled and cut
      into thick wedges
    1 cup apple juice
1/4 teaspoon salt
1/4 teaspoon pepper

In a large skillet, saute sausage and onion in butter. Top with the sauerkraut, potatoes and apples. Add the apple juice, salt and pepper.

Bring to a boil. Reduce heat; cover and simmer for 18-20 minutes or until potatoes are tender. **Yield:** 4 servings.

Cabbage Kielbasa Skillet

Cabbage Kielbasa Skillet

(Pictured above)

Prep/Total Time: 25 min.

I can assemble this colorful medley in mere moments with sausage and a packaged coleslaw mix. It makes a lot and is very filling. Plus, it's great for potlucks because it travels well. —Shona Germino, Casa Grande, Arizona

    1 large red onion, sliced
    1 large green pepper, julienned
    1 large sweet red pepper, julienned
    2 tablespoons butter
    1 pound smoked kielbasa *or* Polish sausage,
      cut into 1-inch slices
    1 package (16 ounces) coleslaw mix
1/2 cup reduced-sodium chicken broth
    1 teaspoon garlic powder
1/2 teaspoon pepper

In a large skillet, saute the onion and peppers in the butter until tender. Add the remaining ingredients. Cook and stir for 6-8 minutes or until heated through. **Yield:** 4 servings.

Ham 'n' Salami Jambalaya

(Pictured below)

Prep/Total Time: 30 min.

Here's an all-in-one entree that's packed with flavor. With onion, celery, tomatoes and two types of meat, the hearty dish will please the whole family. —Carol Gawronski
Lake Wales, Florida

```
2-1/2 cups water
    2 cups sliced celery
    2 cups cubed fully cooked ham
    1 can (14-1/2 ounces) diced tomatoes,
      undrained
    1 cup uncooked long grain rice
  1/4 pound thinly sliced hard salami, julienned
  3/4 cup chopped onion
    2 tablespoons butter
  1/2 teaspoon dried parsley flakes
  1/2 teaspoon dried thyme
  1/2 teaspoon minced garlic
  1/4 teaspoon pepper
    2 bay leaves
```

In a Dutch oven, combine all ingredients. Bring to a boil. Reduce heat; cover and simmer for 15-20 minutes or until rice and vegetables are tender. Discard bay leaves before serving. **Yield:** 8 servings.

Ham 'n' Salami Jambalaya

Potato Soup in Bread Bowls

Prep/Total Time: 20 min.

This satisfying main course helps my husband get a swift yet filling meal on the table while I'm at work. He loves clam chowder, and he can prepare this simple recipe in 20 minutes. Dinner's done when I get home—you can't beat that! —Cheryl Cor, Auburn, Washington

```
    2 cans (18.8 ounces each) ready-to-serve
      chunky baked potato with cheddar and
      bacon bits soup
    2 cans (6-1/2 ounces each) chopped clams,
      drained
    1 bacon strip, cooked and crumbled
    1 teaspoon minced chives
    1 teaspoon dried parsley flakes
    1 teaspoon dried rosemary
  1/4 teaspoon pepper
    5 round loaves (8 ounces each) sourdough
      bread
```

In a large saucepan, combine the first seven ingredients; heat through. Meanwhile, cut a thin slice off the top of each bread loaf; set aside. Hollow out the loaves, leaving 3/4-in. shells (discard the removed bread or save for another use). Ladle the soup into the bread bowls; replace the tops. **Yield:** 5 servings.

Classic Sweet-and-Sour Chicken

Prep/Total Time: 30 min.

Purchased sweet-and-sour sauce takes the work out of preparing this traditional dish, which tastes very much like the take-out version. —Holly Tittel, Great Bend, Kansas

```
1-1/4 cups all-purpose flour
    1 cup water
    1 egg
    2 teaspoons baking powder
    1 teaspoon sugar
    1 teaspoon salt
    1 teaspoon white pepper
Oil for frying
    1 pound boneless skinless chicken breasts, cut
      into 1-inch cubes
SWEET-AND-SOUR SAUCE:
    2 jars (10 ounces each) sweet-and-sour sauce
    2 medium carrots, chopped
    1 medium green pepper, chopped
  1/2 cup chopped onion
    1 can (8 ounces) unsweetened pineapple
      chunks, drained
Hot cooked rice
```

In a large bowl, combine the flour, water, egg, baking powder, sugar, salt and pepper. In an electric skillet, heat 1/4 in. of oil to 375°. Dip chicken into batter. Fry in oil, a few pieces at a time, for 1 to 1-1/2 minutes on each side or until golden brown. Drain on paper towels.

In a large microwave-safe bowl, combine the sweet-and-sour sauce, carrots, green pepper, onion and pineapple. Cover and microwave on high for 4-6 minutes or until vegetables are tender. Serve chicken and sauce with rice. **Yield:** 4 servings.

Editor's Note: This recipe was tested in a 1,100-watt microwave.

Colorful Mac 'n' Cheese

Prep/Total Time: 25 min.

My family loves this rich macaroni and cheese. And as long as the kids don't realize it has zucchini, they'll keep on eating it! —Debbie Amacher, Amherst, New York

1-1/2 cups uncooked elbow macaroni
    2 cups chopped zucchini
1/2 cup chopped onion
    2 tablespoons vegetable oil
    1 can (14-1/2 ounces) diced tomatoes, drained
    1 can (10-3/4 ounces) condensed cheddar
      cheese soup, undiluted
    2 cups (8 ounces) shredded cheddar cheese
1/2 cup milk
1/2 teaspoon dried basil
1/2 teaspoon prepared mustard

Cook macaroni according to package directions. Meanwhile, in a large saucepan, saute zucchini and onion in oil until tender. Stir in the tomatoes, soup, cheese, milk, basil and mustard.

Cook, uncovered, over medium heat for 6-7 minutes or until cheese is melted, stirring often. Drain macaroni; toss with vegetable cheese sauce. **Yield:** 4 servings.

Tangy Turkey Saute

Prep/Total Time: 30 min.

Topped with garlic, thyme and mushrooms, this dish has plenty of flavor. —Amy Wenger, Severance, Colorado

1/4 cup all-purpose flour
    8 turkey breast slices (2 ounces *each*)
    3 tablespoons olive oil, *divided*
    2 cups sliced fresh mushrooms
1/2 cup thinly sliced green onions
1/2 teaspoon minced garlic
1/2 cup chicken broth
    1 cup marsala wine *or* additional chicken broth
1/2 teaspoon salt
1/4 teaspoon dried thyme
    1 tablespoon minced fresh parsley

Place flour in a large resealable plastic bag. Add turkey, a few pieces at a time, and shake to coat. In a large skillet, saute turkey in 2 tablespoons oil in batches for 2 minutes on each side or until no longer pink; drain. Remove and keep warm.

In the same skillet, saute the mushrooms, onions and garlic in remaining oil for 3 minutes or until crisp-tender. Stir in the broth, wine or additional broth, salt and thyme. Bring to a boil; cook and stir for 3 minutes or until slightly thickened. Stir in parsley. Serve over turkey. **Yield:** 4 servings.

Mandarin Pork and Wild Rice

Mandarin Pork and Wild Rice

(Pictured above)

Prep/Total Time: 25 min.

Mandarin oranges add a splash of color and citrus flavor to this tasty entree. With just a few minutes of prep, it makes a fast, easy and complete meal. —Melanie Gable
Roseville, Michigan

    4 boneless pork loin chops (3/4 inch thick and
      5 ounces *each*), cut into strips
1/4 teaspoon pepper
1/8 teaspoon salt
    1 tablespoon vegetable oil
    1 can (11 ounces) mandarin oranges
1-1/2 cups water
    1 package (6.2 ounces) fast-cooking long grain
      and wild rice mix
1/4 cup thinly sliced green onions

Sprinkle pork with pepper and salt. In a large skillet, brown pork in oil. Meanwhile, drain oranges, reserving juice; set oranges aside.

Add water, rice mix with contents of seasoning packet, onions and reserved juice to the skillet. Bring to a boil. Reduce heat; cover and simmer for 10-12 minutes or until liquid is absorbed. Stir in oranges; heat through. **Yield:** 4 servings.

Onions in a Snip

TO QUICKLY and easily cut green onions for Mandarin Pork and Wild Rice (recipe above), try using a kitchen scissors. You can snip several onions at once, and you won't have to wash a cutting board later.

Sausage Macaroni Supper

(Pictured below)

Prep/Total Time: 25 min.

I mix tomato bisque, milk and cheese to create a creamy sauce for macaroni, Italian sausage and broccoli. It's a recipe your family is sure to love. —Margie Haen
Menomonee Falls, Wisconsin

- 2 cups uncooked elbow macaroni
- 1 pound bulk Italian sausage
- 1 cup chopped onion
- 2 teaspoons vegetable oil
- 1 can (11 ounces) condensed cream of tomato bisque soup, undiluted
- 1/2 cup milk
- 1/2 cup shredded Parmesan cheese
- 2 teaspoons Italian seasoning
- 1 package (10 ounces) frozen broccoli florets, thawed

Cook macaroni according to package directions. Meanwhile, in a Dutch oven, cook sausage and onion in oil over medium heat until meat is no longer pink; drain.

Stir in the soup, milk, Parmesan cheese and Italian seasoning. Bring to a boil; reduce heat. Drain macaroni; add to sausage mixture. Stir in broccoli; heat through. **Yield:** 6 servings.

Sausage Macaroni Supper

Spicy Shrimp 'n' Scallop Skewers

Prep/Total Time: 30 min.

I absolutely love shrimp. Throw in some scallops, and I'm in heaven! I put both on these spiced-up skewers, which we serve with grilled steaks and a fresh garden salad. When it comes to great summertime meals, this one's hard to beat.
—Traci Wynne, Bear, Delaware

✓ Uses less fat, sugar or salt. Includes Nutrition Facts and Diabetic Exchanges.

- 2 tablespoons butter
- 1/2 teaspoon chili powder
- 1/4 teaspoon dried oregano
- 1/4 teaspoon ground cumin
- 1/8 teaspoon dried thyme
- 1/8 teaspoon *each* white pepper, cayenne pepper and black pepper
- 18 uncooked large shrimp (about 3/4 pound)
- 12 sea scallops (1-1/2 pounds)

In a small saucepan or microwave-safe bowl, melt butter. Stir in seasonings; set aside and keep warm.

Coat grill rack with nonstick cooking spray before starting the grill. Peel and devein shrimp, leaving tails on. On six metal or soaked wooden skewers, alternately thread shrimp and scallops.

Grill, covered, over medium heat for 3-5 minutes on each side or until shrimp turn pink and scallops are firm and opaque, basting occasionally with butter mixture. **Yield:** 6 servings.

Nutrition Facts: 1 skewer equals 176 calories, 5 g fat (3 g saturated fat), 128 mg cholesterol, 316 mg sodium, 3 g carbohydrate, trace fiber, 28 g protein. **Diabetic Exchanges:** 4 very lean meat, 1 fat.

Breaded Italian Pork Chops

Prep/Total Time: 25 min.

Italian salad dressing and seasoned bread crumbs add a touch of Italian flavor to these nicely coated, tender pork chops. Baking mix and vegetable oil are the only other ingredients you'll need for this easy-as-can-be main course.
—Joan Lockwood, San Jose, California

- 1/2 cup biscuit/baking mix
- 1/3 cup prepared Italian salad dressing
- 1/2 cup seasoned bread crumbs
- 4 bone-in pork loin chops (1/2 inch thick and 7 ounces *each*)
- 2 tablespoons vegetable oil

Place biscuit mix, dressing and crumbs in separate shallow bowls. Coat chops in biscuit mix, then dip in dressing and coat with crumbs. In a large skillet, brown chops in oil over medium-high heat for 2-3 minutes on each side. Reduce heat; cook, uncovered, for 10-15 minutes or until juices run clear. **Yield:** 4 servings.

Pasta with Flavorful Veggies

Prep/Total Time: 25 min.

Italian-seasoned veggies are served with pasta and topped with two types of cheese in this meal-in-one. It's so quick to prepare and so flavorful, but lighter, too.
—Rachel Schmeckenbecher, Whitehall, Pennsylvania

✓ Uses less fat, sugar or salt. Includes Nutrition Facts.

8 ounces uncooked whole wheat spaghetti
2 medium zucchini, halved and sliced
1/3 cup chopped onion
2 tablespoons Italian seasoning
2 teaspoons minced garlic
1/2 teaspoon salt
1/2 teaspoon pepper
2 tablespoons olive oil
2 tablespoons butter
4 medium tomatoes, quartered
1 cup (4 ounces) shredded part-skim mozzarella cheese
1/2 cup shredded Parmesan cheese

Cook spaghetti according to package directions. Meanwhile, in a large skillet, saute the zucchini, onion, Italian seasoning, garlic, salt and pepper in oil and butter for 4-5 minutes or until tender.

Add the tomatoes. Bring to a boil. Reduce the heat; cook and stir for 2 minutes or until heated through. Sprinkle with the mozzarella cheese and Parmesan cheese; cover and simmer for 2-3 minutes or until cheese is melted. Drain the spaghetti; serve with the vegetable mixture. **Yield:** 4 servings.

Nutrition Facts: 1-1/4 cups sauce over 3/4 cup spaghetti equals 478 calories, 21 g fat (9 g saturated fat), 39 mg cholesterol, 676 mg sodium, 56 g carbohydrate, 11 g fiber, 22 g protein.

Italian Beef Patties

Prep/Total Time: 25 min.

Make these pizza-flavored patties, then watch the kids devour them! Serve them in buns for pizza-like cheeseburgers...or over rice or with a side of deli pasta salad for a speedy weeknight dinner. —*Deanna Maciejewski*
Bridgeton, Missouri

2/3 cup pizza sauce, *divided*
1 egg, beaten
1/3 cup dry bread crumbs
2 teaspoons dried minced onion
1/2 teaspoon dried oregano
1/4 teaspoon salt
1/8 teaspoon pepper
1-1/2 pounds ground beef
3 slices part-skim mozzarella cheese, halved

In a large bowl, combine 1/3 cup pizza sauce and the egg, dry bread crumbs, onion, oregano, salt and pepper. Crumble the ground beef over the mixture and mix well. Shape into six patties. Place on a broiler pan

Barbecue Chicken Burritos

coated with nonstick cooking spray.

Broil 6 in. from the heat for 5-6 minutes on each side or until juices run clear, basting frequently with remaining pizza sauce. Top with cheese. **Yield:** 6 servings.

Barbecue Chicken Burritos

(Pictured above)

Prep/Total Time: 30 min.

We always have the ingredients for these fast burritos on hand. My husband came up with the rave-winning recipe.
—Amy Dando, Apalachin, New York

1/2 pound boneless skinless chicken breasts, cut into 1/2-inch cubes
1-1/2 cups julienned green peppers
1 cup chopped onion
4 tablespoons vegetable oil, *divided*
1/2 cup barbecue sauce
1-1/2 cups (6 ounces) shredded Mexican cheese blend
4 flour tortillas (10 inches), warmed
Lime wedges, sour cream, shredded lettuce and chopped tomatoes, optional

In a large skillet over medium heat, cook the chicken, green peppers and onion in 2 tablespoons oil for 6-8 minutes or until chicken juices run clear. Stir in barbecue sauce. Bring to a boil. Reduce heat; simmer for 1-2 minutes or until heated through.

Sprinkle cheese down the center of each tortilla; top with the chicken mixture. Fold sides and ends over the filling and roll up.

In a large skillet over medium heat, brown the burritos in the remaining oil on all sides. Serve burritos with lime wedges, sour cream, shredded lettuce and chopped tomatoes if desired. **Yield:** 4 servings.

Bake, uncovered, at 375° for 20-23 minutes or until fish flakes easily with a fork. Meanwhile, in a small bowl, combine the salsa ingredients. Serve with salmon. **Yield:** 4 servings.

Editor's Note: When cutting or seeding hot peppers, use rubber or plastic gloves to protect your hands. Avoid touching your face.

Savory Beer Pork Chops
Prep/Total Time: 30 min.

These tender chops are perfect for a hectic weeknight because they're so simple to prepare. —Jana Christian
Farson, Wyoming

    4 boneless pork loin chops (3/4 inch thick and
       4 ounces *each*)
1/2 teaspoon salt
1/2 teaspoon pepper
    1 tablespoon vegetable oil
3/4 cup beer *or* nonalcoholic beer
    3 tablespoons ketchup
    2 tablespoons brown sugar

Sprinkle both sides of the pork chops with the salt and pepper. In a large skillet, brown the pork chops in oil on both sides over medium heat.

Combine the beer, ketchup and brown sugar; pour over the pork chops. Bring to a boil. Reduce the heat; simmer, uncovered, for 18-20 minutes or until the meat is tender. **Yield:** 4 servings.

Sugar 'n' Spice Salmon

Sugar 'n' Spice Salmon
(Pictured above)
Prep/Total Time: 25 min.

Tropical fruit lends a summery taste to this easy salmon main course. Serve it with cellophane noodles or jasmine rice for a fast yet impressive dinner.
—Mary Beth Harris-Murphree, Tyler, Texas

    4 salmon fillets (5 ounces *each*)
1/4 to 1/3 cup packed brown sugar
    1 teaspoon ground mustard
1/2 teaspoon salt
1/2 teaspoon cayenne pepper
1/4 teaspoon ground ginger
    4 tablespoons cold butter, cut into small pieces
TRIPLE-FRUIT SALSA:
1/2 cup mandarin oranges
1/2 cup chopped peeled kiwifruit
1/2 cup chopped peeled mango
1/4 cup finely chopped red onion
    3 tablespoons minced fresh cilantro
    3 tablespoons lime juice
    1 tablespoon chopped jalapeno pepper

Place the salmon fillets in a greased 13-in. x 9-in. x 2-in. baking dish. Combine the brown sugar, mustard, salt, cayenne pepper and ginger; sprinkle over the salmon fillets. Top with the butter.

Tasty Taco Bake
Prep/Total Time: 25 min.

If you can open a can, you can fix this delicious south-of-the-border casserole. And it's out of the oven in just 10 minutes. —June Karres, Grawn, Michigan

1-1/2 cups crushed nacho tortilla chips, *divided*
    1 can (15 ounces) chili with beans
    1 can (4 ounces) chopped green chilies
    1 can (3.8 ounces) sliced ripe olives, drained,
       divided
1/2 cup sour cream
1/2 cup shredded cheddar cheese
1/2 cup shredded Monterey Jack cheese
    1 jar (4-1/2 ounces) sliced mushrooms,
       drained
    4 green onions, thinly sliced
    1 cup shredded lettuce

Spread 1 cup tortilla chips into an ungreased 8-in. square baking dish. In a small bowl, combine the chili, green chilies and 1/2 cup olives; spoon over chips. Spread sour cream over the top. Sprinkle with cheddar cheese, Monterey Jack cheese, mushrooms, onions, and remaining chips and olives.

Bake, uncovered, at 375° for 10-15 minutes or until heated through and cheese is melted. Top with lettuce. **Yield:** 4 servings.

Italian Chicken Noodle Skillet

(Pictured below)

Prep/Total Time: 25 min.

This dinner not only boasts authentic Italian flavor, but it also uses lighter ingredients. —*Mary Jones*
St. Louis, Missouri

☑ Uses less fat, sugar or salt. Includes Nutrition Facts and Diabetic Exchanges.

- 1-3/4 cups uncooked egg noodles
- 1/2 cup sliced fresh mushrooms
- 1 can (14-1/2 ounces) diced tomatoes in sauce
- 1 can (10-3/4 ounces) reduced-fat reduced-sodium condensed cream of chicken soup, undiluted
- 2 cups cubed cooked chicken breast
- 1/4 cup shredded Parmesan cheese
- 1 teaspoon Italian seasoning
- 1/3 cup shredded part-skim mozzarella cheese

Cook noodles according to package directions. Meanwhile, in a large nonstick skillet coated with nonstick cooking spray, saute mushrooms for 2-4 minutes or until tender. Stir in tomatoes and soup until blended. Stir in the chicken, Parmesan cheese and Italian seasoning.

Bring to a boil. Reduce heat; simmer, uncovered, for 5-8 minutes or until heated through. Drain noodles; stir into skillet. Sprinkle with mozzarella cheese; cover until cheese is melted. **Yield:** 4 servings.

Nutrition Facts: 1-1/2 cups equals 291 calories, 7 g fat (3 g saturated fat), 85 mg cholesterol, 834 mg sodium, 26 g carbohydrate, 1 g fiber, 28 g protein. **Diabetic Exchanges:** 3 lean meat, 1-1/2 starch.

Strip Steaks with Mango Salsa

Strip Steaks with Mango Salsa

(Pictured above)

Prep/Total Time: 30 min.

Carrots add beautiful color and texture to this wonderful mango salsa, served over well-seasoned New York strips. The mouth-watering main course, created by our Test Kitchen, will make you the star of any cookout!

- 1 cup diced carrots
- 1 cup chopped peeled mango
- 1 medium ripe avocado, peeled and diced
- 1/4 cup chopped sweet red pepper
- 5 teaspoons lime juice
- 2 tablespoons minced fresh cilantro
- 1/8 teaspoon salt
- 1/8 teaspoon ground cumin
- 1 tablespoon Mexican seasoning
- 4 New York strip steaks (8 ounces *each*)

Place 1/2 in. of water in a small saucepan; add carrots. Bring to a boil. Reduce heat; cover and simmer for 7-9 minutes or until crisp-tender. Drain and cool.

In a small bowl, combine the mango, avocado, red pepper, lime juice, cilantro, salt, cumin and carrots. Refrigerate until serving.

Sprinkle Mexican seasoning over both sides of steaks. Grill, covered, over medium-hot heat for 6-10 minutes on each side or until meat reaches desired doneness (for medium-rare, a meat thermometer should read 145°; medium, 160°; well-done, 170°). Serve with mango salsa. **Yield:** 4 servings.

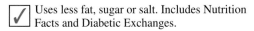

Italian Chicken Noodle Skillet

Chapter 14

WHAT'S BETTER than a rich, decadent, luscious dessert that delights your taste buds with every bite? A dessert that's quick to prepare, too!

The sweet treats in this chapter are twice as nice because they're not only taste-tempting favorites, but they're also done in a dash. So you can top off meals with Rocky Road Chocolate Cake, Apple Cream Cheese Pie, Chewy Caramel Bars and much more any time you like.

Whether you want to surprise your family with a special addition to a weeknight menu or you need an impressive dessert for a holiday dinner, you'll want to check this chapter for a treat everyone will love—including the time-crunched cook!

LUSCIOUS LAYERS. Blueberry Squares (p. 225).

Raspberry Truffle Brownies

for 2-3 minutes or until smooth, stirring twice. Transfer to a small mixing bowl; stir in vanilla. Place in a bowl of ice water; stir for 3-5 minutes. Beat on medium speed until soft peaks form.

Cut a small hole in a corner of a heavy-duty resealable plastic bag; insert #825 star tip. Fill with 1/2 cup frosting. Spread remaining frosting over brownies. Cut into 12 bars. Pipe a chocolate rosette in the center of each brownie; top with a raspberry. Cover and refrigerate for 30 minutes or until frosting is set. Refrigerate leftovers. **Yield:** 1 dozen.

Editor's Note: This recipe was tested in a 1,100-watt microwave.

Blond Butterscotch Brownies

Prep: 15 min. **Bake:** 20 min. + cooling

Toffee and chocolate dot the golden brown batter of my fudgy brownies. I often cook for the police officers I work with, and they'll get in line for these yummy bars.
—*Jennifer Ann Sopko, Battle Creek, Michigan*

✓ Uses less fat, sugar or salt. Includes Nutrition Facts and Diabetic Exchanges.

    2 cups all-purpose flour
    2 cups packed brown sugar
    2 teaspoons baking powder
1/4 teaspoon salt
1/2 cup butter, melted and cooled
    2 eggs
    1 teaspoon vanilla extract
    1 cup semisweet chocolate chunks
    4 Heath candy bars (1.4 ounces *each*), coarsely chopped

In a large bowl, combine the flour, brown sugar, baking powder and salt. In another bowl, beat the butter, eggs and vanilla until smooth. Stir into dry ingredients just until combined (batter will be thick).

Spread into a 13-in. x 9-in. x 2-in. baking pan coated with nonstick cooking spray. Sprinkle with chocolate chunks and candy bar pieces; press gently into batter.

Bake at 350° for 20-25 minutes or until a toothpick inserted near the center comes out clean. Cool on a wire rack. Cut into bars. **Yield:** 2 dozen.

Nutrition Facts: 1 brownie equals 218 calories, 9 g fat (5 g saturated fat), 29 mg cholesterol, 126 mg sodium, 35 g carbohydrate, 1 g fiber, 2 g protein. **Diabetic Exchanges:** 2 starch, 1-1/2 fat.

Raspberry Truffle Brownies

(Pictured above)

Prep: 30 min. **Bake:** 25 min. + chilling

This is a truly sophisticated dessert! Each rich, fudge-like brownie is bursting with fresh, plump red raspberries and topped with a dreamy, bittersweet ganache. It's the perfect treat for chocolate lovers of all ages.
—*Agnes Ward, Stratford, Ontario*

    6 squares (1 ounce *each*) bittersweet
       chocolate, chopped
1/2 cup butter, cubed
    2 eggs
    1 cup sugar
    1 teaspoon vanilla extract
    1 cup all-purpose flour
1/4 teaspoon baking soda
1/4 teaspoon salt
    1 cup fresh raspberries
FROSTING:
    6 squares (1 ounce *each*) bittersweet
       chocolate, chopped
3/4 cup heavy whipping cream
    2 tablespoons seedless raspberry jam
    1 teaspoon vanilla extract
   12 fresh raspberries

In a microwave-safe bowl, melt chocolate and butter; stir until smooth. In a large bowl, beat the eggs, sugar and vanilla. Stir in chocolate mixture. Combine the flour, baking soda and salt; gradually add to chocolate mixture until combined. Gently fold in raspberries.

Spread into a greased 9-in. square baking pan. Bake at 350° for 25-30 minutes or until a toothpick inserted near center comes out clean (do not overbake). Cool on a wire rack.

For frosting, in a microwave-safe bowl, combine the chocolate, cream and jam. Microwave at 50% power

Special Summer Berry Medley

(Pictured below)

Prep/Total Time: 25 min.

No matter how big the meal, folks always find room for this delightfully "special" dessert. With its hint of citrus and mint, the four-berry medley can even make a light side dish at casual cookouts or potlucks. Best of all, it's as fast and easy to make as it is to clean up!
—Nancy Whitford, Edwards, New York

✓ Uses less fat, sugar or salt. Includes Nutrition Facts and Diabetic Exchanges.

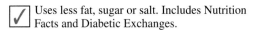

- 1 cup sparkling wine *or* white grape juice
- 1/2 cup sugar
- 1 tablespoon lemon juice
- 1-1/2 teaspoons grated lemon peel
- 1/2 teaspoon vanilla extract
- 1/8 teaspoon salt
- 3 cups sliced fresh strawberries
- 2 cups fresh blueberries
- 1 cup fresh raspberries
- 1 cup fresh blackberries
- 1 tablespoon minced fresh mint

In a small heavy saucepan, bring wine or grape juice and sugar to a boil. Cook, uncovered, until reduced to 1/2 cup, about 15 minutes, stirring occasionally. Cool slightly. Stir in the lemon juice and peel, vanilla and salt.

In a large bowl, combine the berries and mint. Add syrup and toss gently to coat. Cover and refrigerate until serving. **Yield:** 12 servings.

Nutrition Facts: 1/2 cup equals 85 calories, trace fat (trace saturated fat), 0 cholesterol, 26 mg sodium, 18 g carbohydrate, 3 g fiber, 1 g protein. **Diabetic Exchanges:** 1 fruit, 1/2 starch.

Special Summer Berry Medley

Strawberry Tart

Strawberry Tart

(Pictured above)

Prep: 20 min. **Bake:** 10 min. + chilling

Looking for the ideal ending to any summertime dinner? Here's a swift-to-fix, creamy tart that boasts a scrumptious chocolate layer on top of the crust. You could also make individual tartlets instead of a single large one.
—Dawn Tringali, Hamilton Square, New Jersey

- 1 sheet refrigerated pie pastry
- 3 ounces German sweet chocolate, melted
- 2 packages (8 ounces *each*) cream cheese, softened
- 3 tablespoons heavy whipping cream
- 2 teaspoons vanilla extract
- 1-3/4 cups confectioners' sugar
- 2-1/2 cups sliced fresh strawberries
- 1/4 cup red currant jelly

Press pastry onto the bottom and up the sides of an ungreased 9-in. fluted tart pan with a removable bottom. Place on a baking sheet. Bake at 450° for 10-12 minutes or until golden brown. Cool on a wire rack.

Spread melted chocolate over bottom of crust. Cover and refrigerate for 5-10 minutes or until almost set. Meanwhile, in a large mixing bowl, beat the cream cheese, cream and vanilla until smooth. Gradually beat in confectioners' sugar. Spread over chocolate layer.

Arrange strawberries over filling; brush with jelly. Cover and refrigerate for at least 2 hours. Remove sides of pan before serving. **Yield:** 6-8 servings.

Cherry-Chocolate Cream Puffs

(Pictured below)

Prep: 30 min. + cooling **Bake:** 30 min. + cooling

I recently came up with these fun chocolate-filled cream puffs. The chopped sweet cherries make them a little different.   —Christopher Fuso, Marysville, Ohio

    1 cup water
  1/3 cup butter, cubed
    1 tablespoon sugar
  1/8 teaspoon salt
    1 cup all-purpose flour
    4 eggs
FILLING:
    1 carton (8 ounces) frozen whipped topping, thawed
  1/2 cup sugar
  1/4 cup milk
    6 squares (1 ounce *each*) semisweet chocolate, chopped
  3/4 pound fresh *or* frozen sweet cherries, pitted and chopped
Confectioners' sugar

In a small saucepan over medium heat, bring water, butter, sugar and salt to a boil. Add flour all at once; stir until a smooth ball forms. Remove from the heat; let stand for 5 minutes. Add eggs, one at a time, beating well after each addition. Continue beating until mixture is smooth and shiny.

Drop by 2 rounded tablespoonfuls 3 in. apart onto

Apple Cream Cheese Pie

greased baking sheets. Bake at 400° for 30-35 minutes or until golden brown. Remove to wire racks. Immediately split puffs open; remove tops and set aside. Discard soft dough from inside. Cool puffs.

Let whipped topping stand at room temperature for 30 minutes. Meanwhile, in a small saucepan over medium heat, bring sugar and milk to a boil; cook and stir until sugar is dissolved. Reduce heat to low; stir in chocolate until melted. Transfer to a large bowl. Cool to room temperature, about 25 minutes, stirring occasionally. Fold in whipped topping.

Fill each cream puff with a heaping tablespoonful of cherries; top with chocolate filling. Replace tops. Dust with confectioners' sugar; serve immediately. Refrigerate leftovers. **Yield:** 13 servings.

Apple Cream Cheese Pie

(Pictured above)

Prep: 20 min. + chilling

With just a handful of ingredients and a topping of apples, this smooth and fluffy cream-cheese pie will put you at the head of the class with your family!
—Linda Duncan, Junction City, Oregon

    1 package (8 ounces) cream cheese, softened
  1/2 cup confectioners' sugar
    1 teaspoon vanilla extract
    1 carton (8 ounces) frozen whipped topping, thawed
    1 graham cracker crust (9 inches)
1-3/4 cups apple pie filling
Dash ground cinnamon

In a large mixing bowl, beat the cream cheese and confectioners' sugar until smooth. Add the vanilla. Fold in the whipped topping.

Pour into crust. Top with pie filling; sprinkle with cinnamon. Refrigerate for at least 2 hours before serving. **Yield:** 6-8 servings.

Cherry-Chocolate Cream Puffs

Deluxe Strawberry Shortcake

Prep: 25 min. **Bake:** 20 min. + cooling

Here's a yummy shortcake treat that's just perfect for the Fourth of July and other warm-weather holidays. I love the moist, from-scratch flavor of this very simple cake.
—Janet Fant, Denair, California

  1 package (18-1/4 ounces) yellow cake mix
  1 cup water
  1/2 cup sour cream
  1/3 cup vegetable oil
  3 eggs
  1 teaspoon vanilla extract
FILLING:
  1 package (8 ounces) cream cheese, softened
  1/3 cup sugar
  1 carton (8 ounces) frozen whipped topping, thawed
  3 cups chopped fresh strawberries

In a large mixing bowl, combine the first six ingredients; beat on low speed for 30 seconds. Beat on medium for 2 minutes. Pour into two greased and floured 9-in. round baking pans.

Bake at 350° for 20-25 minutes or until a toothpick inserted near the center comes out clean. Cool for 10 minutes before removing from pans to wire racks to cool completely.

In a small mixing bowl, beat cream cheese and sugar until smooth. Fold in whipped topping. Place one cake on a serving plate; top with half of the cream cheese mixture and strawberries. Repeat layers. Store in the refrigerator. **Yield:** 12 servings.

Banana-Chip Mini Cupcakes

Prep: 30 min. **Bake:** 15 min./batch + cooling

These cute little bites are packed with banana flavor and chocolate chips, then topped off with creamy frosting. They make a great, fast snack when the kids come home from school. *—Beverly Coyde, Gasport, New York*

  1 package (14 ounces) banana quick bread
    and muffin mix
  3/4 cup water
  1/3 cup sour cream
  1 egg
  1 cup miniature semisweet chocolate chips,
    divided
  1 tablespoon shortening

In a large bowl, combine the muffin mix, water, sour cream and egg; stir just until moistened. Fold in 1/2 cup chocolate chips.

Fill greased or paper-lined miniature muffin cups two-thirds full. Bake at 375° for 12-15 minutes or until a toothpick comes out clean. Cool for 10 minutes before removing from pans to wire racks to cool completely.

For frosting, in a small microwave-safe bowl, melt shortening and remaining chocolate chips; stir until smooth. Frost cupcakes. **Yield:** 3-1/2 dozen.

Caramel Cranberry Bars

(Pictured below)

Prep: 30 min. **Bake:** 30 min. + cooling

My mom created this wonderful dessert after tasting something similar. The sweet, tangy bars boast plenty of cranberry flavor. *—Debbie Kersh, Springtown, Texas*

  1 package (12 ounces) fresh *or* frozen
    cranberries, thawed
  1 package (8 ounces) chopped dates
  3/4 cup chopped pecans
  2 tablespoons plus 1/2 cup sugar, *divided*
2-1/3 cups all-purpose flour, *divided*
  2 cups old-fashioned oats
  1/2 cup packed brown sugar
  1/2 teaspoon baking soda
  1 cup butter, melted
  3/4 cup caramel ice cream topping

In a small bowl, combine the cranberries, dates, pecans and 2 tablespoons sugar; set aside.

In a large bowl, combine 2 cups flour, oats, brown sugar, baking soda and the remaining sugar. Stir in butter; set aside 1 cup for topping. Press the remaining crumb mixture into a greased 13-in. x 9-in. x 2-in. baking dish. Bake at 350° for 15 minutes.

Meanwhile, place the remaining flour in a small bowl. Stir in caramel topping until smooth; set aside. Sprinkle cranberry mixture over crust; drizzle with caramel mixture. Sprinkle with reserved crumb mixture.

Bake for 30-35 minutes or until golden brown and bubbly. Cool on a wire rack. Cut into bars. Store in the refrigerator. **Yield:** 2 dozen.

Caramel Cranberry Bars

Tastes Like Eggnog Cake

Lemon 'n' Lime Strawberry Ice

(Pictured below)

Prep: 30 min. + freezing

This bright, colorful and icy fruit treat has become a favorite summer dessert. It's so refreshing after dinner.
—Marie Rizzio, Interlochen, Michigan

✓ Uses less fat, sugar or salt. Includes Nutrition Facts.

     1 cup sugar
   3/4 cup water
     1 tablespoon shredded orange peel
     2 teaspoons shredded lemon peel
 1-1/2 teaspoons shredded lime peel
   1/3 cup orange juice
     3 tablespoons lemon juice
     2 tablespoons lime juice
     4 cups sliced fresh strawberries

In a small saucepan, combine the first five ingredients. Bring to a boil. Reduce heat; simmer, uncovered, for 5-6 minutes or until slightly thickened. Strain; discard peels. Add juices to the syrup; cool slightly.

Place half of the juice mixture and strawberries in a blender; cover and pulse until nearly smooth. Transfer to a 2-qt. freezer container. Repeat with remaining juice mixture and berries.

Cover and freeze mixture for 12 hours or overnight, stirring several times. Ice may be frozen for up to 3 months. Just before serving, break apart with a large spoon. **Yield:** 6 servings.

Nutrition Facts: 2/3 cup equals 173 calories, trace fat (trace saturated fat), 0 cholesterol, 2 mg sodium, 44 g carbohydrate, 3 g fiber, 1 g protein.

Tastes Like Eggnog Cake

(Pictured above)

Prep: 30 min. **Bake:** 25 min. + cooling

My holiday eggnog cake uses a convenient boxed mix and comes out perfect every time. It always gets compliments, and most people think that I spend hours in the kitchen working on it! My husband's colleagues at work ask for it every Christmas.
—Lisa Barrett
Durango, Colorado

     1 package (18-1/4 ounces) yellow cake mix
     1 teaspoon ground nutmeg
   1/4 teaspoon ground ginger
FROSTING:
 1-1/2 cups heavy whipping cream
     3 tablespoons confectioners' sugar
     1 teaspoon rum extract

Prepare cake batter according to package directions, adding nutmeg and ginger to dry ingredients. Pour into a greased 13-in. x 9-in. x 2-in. baking pan. Bake at 350° for 25-30 minutes or until a toothpick inserted near the center comes out clean. Cool on a wire rack.

For frosting, in a small mixing bowl, beat cream and confectioners' sugar until stiff peaks form. Fold in extract. Spread over cake. Store in the refrigerator. **Yield:** 12-15 servings.

Lemon 'n' Lime Strawberry Ice

Rhubarb Mallow Cobbler

Prep: 15 min. **Bake:** 50 min.

My mom used to make this yummy dessert regularly when I was growing up. Now we take fresh rhubarb to my son, who lives in Texas, so that he can share the lip-smacking recipe with his own family. —*Judy Kay Warwick Webster City, Iowa*

> 4 cups diced fresh *or* frozen rhubarb
> 2-1/2 cups sugar, *divided*
> 1 cup miniature marshmallows
> 1/2 cup butter, softened
> 1 teaspoon vanilla extract
> 1-3/4 cups all-purpose flour
> 3 teaspoons baking powder
> 1/2 teaspoon salt
> 1/2 cup milk

In a large bowl, combine rhubarb and 1-1/2 cups sugar. Transfer to a greased 11-in. x 7-in. x 2-in. baking dish. Sprinkle with marshmallows.

In a small mixing bowl, cream the butter, vanilla and remaining sugar. Combine the flour, baking powder and salt; add to creamed mixture alternately with milk. Beat just until moistened; spoon over rhubarb.

Bake at 350° for 50-55 minutes or until topping is golden brown. Serve warm. **Yield:** 10-12 servings.

Editor's Note: If using frozen rhubarb, measure rhubarb while still frozen, then thaw completely. Drain in a colander, but do not press liquid out.

Chocolate Coconut Candies

Prep: 30 min. + chilling

These candies disappear just as fast as I put them out. They're a snap to whip up and make a beautiful presentation on a holiday cookie plate. I mound them high and sprinkle on coconut...then watch them vanish! —*Mary Ann Marino, West Pittsburg, Pennsylvania*

✓ Uses less fat, sugar or salt. Includes Nutrition Facts and Diabetic Exchanges.

> 1-3/4 cups confectioners' sugar
> 1-3/4 cups flaked coconut
> 1 cup chopped almonds
> 1/2 cup sweetened condensed milk
> 2 cups (12 ounces) semisweet chocolate chips
> 2 tablespoons shortening

In a large bowl, combine the confectioners' sugar, coconut, almonds and milk. Shape into 1-in. balls. Refrigerate until firm, about 20 minutes.

In a microwave-safe bowl, melt the chocolate chips and shortening; stir until smooth. Dip the balls in the chocolate; allow the excess to drip off. Place on waxed paper; let stand until set. Store in an airtight container. **Yield:** 2-1/2 dozen.

Nutrition Facts: 1 piece equals 157 calories, 9 g fat (4 g saturated fat), 2 mg cholesterol, 22 mg sodium, 20 g carbohydrate, 1 g fiber, 2 g protein. **Diabetic Exchanges:** 1-1/2 starch, 1-1/2 fat.

Blueberry Squares

Blueberry Squares

(Pictured above and on page 218)

Prep: 25 min. **Bake:** 10 min. + chilling

I've made these easy berry squares for many years, and they never fail to bring raves from people of all ages. I'm always asked for the recipe! When things get really busy, I make this fuss-free dessert a day ahead of time. —*Barbara Robbins, Chandler, Arizona*

> 1 cup crushed vanilla wafers
> 2 tablespoons butter, melted
> 3/4 cup sugar
> 1/4 cup cornstarch
> 1/4 cup water
> 3 cups fresh blueberries, *divided*
> 3 tablespoons lemon juice
> 1 teaspoon grated lemon peel
> 1 cup heavy whipping cream
> 2 tablespoons confectioners' sugar
> 1-1/2 cups miniature marshmallows

In a small bowl, combine wafers and butter. Press into a greased 8-in. square baking dish. Bake at 350° for 8-10 minutes or until lightly browned. Cool on a wire rack.

In a small saucepan, combine sugar and cornstarch. Gradually whisk in water until smooth. Stir in 1-1/2 cups blueberries. Bring to a boil; cook and stir for 1-2 minutes or until thickened. Stir in the lemon juice, peel and remaining blueberries. Cool completely.

In a small mixing bowl, beat cream until it begins to thicken. Add confectioners' sugar; beat until soft peaks form. Fold in marshmallows. Spread over crust. Top with blueberry mixture. Cover and refrigerate until set, about 45 minutes. **Yield:** 9 servings.

Oatmeal Cookie Pizza

(Pictured below)

Prep: 20 min. **Bake:** 20 min. + cooling

When my son was 7, he used to love to make this pizza. It's great for days when you hear, "Mom, I'm bored!"
—Judi Brinegar, Liberty, North Carolina

> 1/2 cup butter, softened
> 3/4 cup packed brown sugar
> 1 egg
> 1-1/2 teaspoons vanilla extract
> 1 cup all-purpose flour
> 1 cup quick-cooking oats
> 1/2 teaspoon baking powder
> 1/2 teaspoon baking soda
> 1/4 teaspoon salt
> 1 package (12 ounces) M&M's miniature baking bits, *divided*
> 1/4 cup chopped walnuts *or* pecans
> 1/4 cup flaked coconut

In a small mixing bowl, cream butter and brown sugar. Beat in egg and vanilla. Combine the flour, oats, baking powder, baking soda and salt; add to creamed mixture and mix well. Stir in 1 cup baking bits.

Press onto a greased 12-in. pizza pan. Sprinkle with nuts, coconut and remaining baking bits; press lightly into dough. Bake at 350° for 18-22 minutes or until golden brown. Cool on a wire rack. Cut into wedges. **Yield:** 12 servings.

Oatmeal Cookie Pizza

Sweet Potato Pecan Pie

Prep: 30 min. **Bake:** 1 hour + cooling

This updated classic combines two Southern favorites in one luscious pie. —Glenda Conrad, Shelbyville, Indiana

> 1 sheet refrigerated pie pastry
> 2 cans (15-3/4 ounces *each*) sweet potatoes, drained
> 3 eggs
> 1 cup packed brown sugar, *divided*
> 1/2 teaspoon ground cinnamon
> 1/4 teaspoon ground ginger
> 2/3 cup light corn syrup
> 1 tablespoon butter, melted
> 1 teaspoon vanilla extract
> 1 cup pecan halves

On a lightly floured surface, roll out pastry to fit a 9-in. deep-dish pie plate. Transfer pastry to plate. Trim pastry to 1/2 in. beyond edge of plate; flute edges. Refrigerate.

In a small mixing bowl, mash the sweet potatoes. Add 1 egg, 1/3 cup brown sugar, cinnamon and ginger; mix well. Set aside.

In another small mixing bowl, combine remaining eggs and brown sugar. Add the corn syrup, butter and vanilla; mix well. Stir in the pecans. Pour the sweet potato mixture into the pastry shell; top with the pecan mixture.

Bake at 350° for 60-70 minutes or until a knife inserted near the center comes out clean. Cool on a wire rack. Refrigerate leftovers. **Yield:** 6-8 servings.

Kiwi Tiki Torches

Prep: 30 min. **Cook:** 10 min.

Kiwi, pineapple and strawberries taste wonderful with melted chocolate in this easy dessert. It can even make a sweet appetizer on a party buffet. —Elaine Sweet
Dallas, Texas

> 1 fresh pineapple, peeled and cut into 1-inch chunks
> 4 medium kiwifruit, peeled and cut into 3/4-inch chunks
> 2 cups fresh strawberries, halved
> **WHITE CHOCOLATE DIPPING SAUCE:**
> 1 cup heavy whipping cream
> 6 white chocolate Toblerone candy bars (3.52 ounces *each*), broken into pieces
> 1/4 cup finely chopped macadamia nuts
> 1 to 2 teaspoons rum extract
> 1/3 cup flaked coconut, toasted

Alternately thread the pineapple chunks, kiwi chunks and strawberry halves onto 12 metal or wooden skewers; set the skewers aside.

In a large saucepan over medium heat, bring cream to a boil. Remove from the heat; stir in candy bars until melted. Return to the heat. Stir in nuts and extract; heat through. Transfer to a fondue pot or 1-1/2-qt. slow cooker; keep warm. Sprinkle with coconut. Serve with fruit kabobs. **Yield:** 12 servings.

Chewy Caramel Bars

(Pictured at right)

Prep: 10 min. **Bake:** 40 min. + cooling

On many nights, I'd learn that one of my daughters had forgotten it was her turn to bring a treat to school the next day. These yummy bars were lifesavers!
—Debra Davidson-Cregeur, Harbor Beach, Michigan

✓ Uses less fat, sugar or salt. Includes Nutrition Facts and Diabetic Exchanges.

  1 package (18-1/4 ounces) yellow cake mix
  1 can (5 ounces) evaporated milk
1/2 cup chopped nuts
1/4 cup butter, melted
 36 Rolo candies, halved

In a large bowl, combine the cake mix, milk, nuts and butter. Spread half into a greased 13-in. x 9-in. x 2-in. baking pan. Bake at 350° for 13-15 minutes or until set.

Place candies, cut side down, over crust; top with remaining cake mixture. Bake 25-30 minutes longer or until golden brown. Cool on a wire rack. Cut into bars. **Yield:** 2 dozen.

Nutrition Facts: 1 bar equals 173 calories, 8 g fat (4 g saturated fat), 8 mg cholesterol, 177 mg sodium, 24 g carbohydrate, 1 g fiber, 2 g protein. **Diabetic Exchanges:** 1-1/2 starch, 1-1/2 fat.

Chocolate Cookie Cupcakes

(Pictured at right)

Prep: 20 min. **Bake:** 20 min. + cooling

I give basic white cake mix a kick start by adding chocolate cookie crumbs. —Mary Wiebe, Altona, Manitoba

✓ Uses less fat, sugar or salt. Includes Nutrition Facts and Diabetic Exchanges.

   1 package (18-1/4 ounces) white cake mix
1-1/4 cups water
 1/4 cup vegetable oil
   3 egg whites
   1 cup coarsely crushed cream-filled chocolate sandwich cookies (about 9 cookies)
   1 can (16 ounces) vanilla frosting
Additional crushed cream-filled chocolate sandwich cookies

In a large mixing bowl, combine the cake mix, water, oil and egg whites. Beat on low speed until moistened; beat on high for 2 minutes. Gently fold in cookie crumbs. Fill paper-lined muffin cups two-thirds full.

Bake at 350° for 18-22 minutes or until a toothpick comes out clean. Cool for 10 minutes before removing from pans to wire racks to cool completely. Frost cupcakes; sprinkle with additional cookie crumbs. **Yield:** 2 dozen.

Nutrition Facts: 1 cupcake equals 227 calories, 9 g fat (2 g saturated fat), 0 cholesterol, 214 mg sodium, 34 g carbohydrate, 1 g fiber, 2 g protein. **Diabetic Exchanges:** 2 starch, 1-1/2 fat.

Chewy Caramel Bars
Chocolate Cookie Cupcakes

Jumbleberry Crumble

Prep: 10 min. + standing **Bake:** 45 min.

A friend brought this down-home dessert to church and was kind enough to give out the recipe. It's especially wonderful served warm with a dollop of whipped topping.
—Mary Ann Dell, Phoenixville, Pennsylvania

   3 cups halved fresh strawberries
1-1/2 cups fresh raspberries
1-1/2 cups fresh blueberries
 2/3 cup sugar
   3 tablespoons quick-cooking tapioca
 1/2 cup all-purpose flour
 1/2 cup quick-cooking oats
 1/2 cup packed brown sugar
   1 teaspoon ground cinnamon
 1/3 cup butter, melted

In a large bowl, combine the strawberries, raspberries and blueberries. Combine sugar and tapioca; sprinkle over berries and toss gently. Pour into a greased 11-in. x 7-in. x 2-in. baking dish; let stand for 15 minutes.

Meanwhile, in a small bowl, combine the flour, oats, brown sugar and cinnamon. Stir in butter; sprinkle over berry mixture. Bake at 350° for 45-50 minutes or until filling is bubbly and topping is golden brown. Serve warm. **Yield:** 6-8 servings.

Rustic Apricot Tart

Strawberry Banana Squares

Prep: 15 min. **Bake:** 40 min. + cooling

When I combined the flavors of strawberry, banana and coconut in these squares, I knew I'd hit on a winner. This dessert has it all, and your kids will notice! Best of all, it only takes moments to assemble because it starts with a quick-bread mix.
—Lucille Mead, Ilion, New York

✓ Uses less fat, sugar or salt. Includes Nutrition Facts and Diabetic Exchanges.

1 package (14 ounces) banana quick bread and muffin mix
1/2 cup chopped walnuts
1/3 cup butter, softened
1 egg
1 can (14 ounces) sweetened condensed milk
1 can (20 ounces) strawberry pie filling
1/2 cup flaked coconut

In a small bowl, combine the bread mix, walnuts, butter and egg until crumbly. Press onto the bottom of a 13-in. x 9-in. x 2-in. baking dish coated with nonstick cooking spray. Bake at 350° for 8-10 minutes or until lightly browned.

Spread milk over crust; spoon pie filling over milk. Sprinkle with coconut. Bake 30-40 minutes longer or until golden brown. Cool on a wire rack. Cut into squares. **Yield:** 2 dozen.

Nutrition Facts: 1 piece equals 196 calories, 7 g fat (3 g saturated fat), 21 mg cholesterol, 158 mg sodium, 30 g carbohydrate, 1 g fiber, 3 g protein. **Diabetic Exchanges:** 2 starch, 1 fat.

Rustic Apricot Tart

(Pictured above)

Prep: 15 min. **Bake:** 35 min. + cooling

Apricots and pumpkin pie spice come together in this truly special tart from our Test Kitchen. Frozen, fat-free vanilla yogurt makes a perfect companion to the tart's warm fruit and wholesome goodness.

✓ Uses less fat, sugar or salt. Includes Nutrition Facts.

1/4 cup plus 1 teaspoon sugar, *divided*
2 tablespoons cornstarch
1/2 teaspoon pumpkin pie spice
3 cans (15 ounces *each*) reduced-sugar apricot halves, drained
Pastry for single-crust pie (9 inches)
1 egg white, beaten
2 tablespoons sliced almonds
1 tablespoon fat-free milk

In a large bowl, combine 1/4 cup sugar, cornstarch and pumpkin pie spice. Add apricots and toss to coat.

Place pastry on a parchment paper-lined 12-in. pizza pan. Brush with egg white to within 1-1/2 in. of edges. Spoon apricot mixture over egg white; sprinkle with almonds. Fold up edges of pastry over filling, leaving center uncovered. Brush folded pastry with milk; sprinkle with remaining sugar.

Bake at 375° for 35-40 minutes or until crust is golden and filling is bubbly. Use parchment paper to slide tart onto a wire rack to cool. **Yield:** 6 servings.

Nutrition Facts: 1 piece equals 278 calories, 11 g fat (4 g saturated fat), 7 mg cholesterol, 151 mg sodium, 43 g carbohydrate, 4 g fiber, 4 g protein.

Cherry Peach Cobbler

Prep: 15 min. **Bake:** 20 min.

This fuss-free cobbler has from-scratch taste but makes the most of convenience items. *—Sandra Pierce*
North Bonneville, Washington

1 can (21 ounces) cherry pie filling
1 can (8-1/2 ounces) sliced peaches, drained and halved
2 teaspoons lemon juice
1/2 teaspoon ground cinnamon
BISCUIT TOPPING:
1 cup biscuit/baking mix
4 teaspoons sugar, *divided*
3 tablespoons milk
2 tablespoons butter, melted
1 teaspoon grated lemon peel
1/8 teaspoon ground cinnamon
3 cups vanilla ice cream

In a greased microwave-safe 8-in. square baking dish, combine pie filling, peaches, lemon juice and cinnamon. Microwave, uncovered, on high for 3-4 minutes or until heated through, stirring once.

In a small bowl, combine the biscuit mix, 3 teaspoons sugar, milk, butter and lemon peel. Drop by rounded tablespoonfuls onto filling. Combine cinnamon and remaining sugar; sprinkle over topping. Bake at 400° for 17-19 minutes or until golden brown. Serve warm with ice cream. **Yield:** 6 servings.

Editor's Note: This recipe was tested in a 1,100-watt microwave.

Black 'n' Blue Berry Crumb Pie

(Pictured below)

Prep: 15 min. **Bake:** 55 min. + cooling

Here's a very simple recipe for a mouth-watering, fresh pie that features two kinds of berries. The crumb topping adds buttery, old-time crunchiness to this summery classic.
—Linda Palmer, Greenville, Ohio

    1 sheet refrigerated pie pastry
    3 cups fresh blackberries
    2 cups fresh blueberries
 3/4 cup sugar
 1/4 cup cornstarch
 1/8 teaspoon ground nutmeg
TOPPING:
 1/2 cup all-purpose flour
 1/4 cup packed brown sugar
 1/4 cup cold butter

Unroll pastry into a 9-in. pie plate. Trim pastry to 1/2 in. beyond edge of plate; flute edges. In a large bowl, combine blackberries and blueberries. Combine the sugar, cornstarch and nutmeg; sprinkle over berries and toss gently. Pour into crust.

In a small bowl, combine flour and brown sugar; cut in butter until crumbly. Sprinkle over filling. Bake at 375° for 55-60 minutes or until set (cover edges with

Black 'n' Blue Berry Crumb Pie

foil during the last 15 minutes to prevent overbrowning if necessary). Cool on a wire rack. **Yield:** 6-8 servings.

Caramel Cereal Treats

Prep: 20 min. + standing

I've received many compliments over the years for these sweet, crispy bars. The microwave treats make great after-school snacks with tall glasses of milk.
—Laurie Lingenfelter, Nevada, Iowa

    8 cups Sugar Smacks cereal
 1-3/4 cups dry roasted peanuts
    1 package (14 ounces) caramels
 1/2 cup sweetened condensed milk
    1 tablespoon butter
 1/2 cup milk chocolate chips, melted and cooled

In a large bowl, combine cereal and peanuts; set aside. In a large microwave-safe bowl, combine the caramels, milk and butter. Microwave, uncovered, on high for 1-2 minutes or until caramels are melted, stirring every 30 seconds.

Pour over cereal mixture; stir to coat. With greased hands, pat mixture into a greased 15-in. x 10-in. x 1-in. pan. Drizzle with chocolate. Let stand until set. Cut into bars. **Yield:** 3-1/2 dozen.

Editor's Note: This recipe was tested in a 1,100-watt microwave.

Butterfinger Delight

Prep: 30 min. + chilling

I got the recipe for this no-bake dessert from my mother-in-law because it's my husband's favorite.
—Linda Winter, Enid, Oklahoma

    1 cup crushed butter-flavored crackers (about 30 crackers)
    1 cup graham cracker crumbs
    4 Butterfinger candy bars (2.1 ounces *each*), crushed
 3/4 cup butter, melted
 1-1/2 cups cold milk
    2 packages (3.4 ounces *each*) instant vanilla pudding mix
    1 quart reduced-fat chocolate frozen yogurt, softened
    1 carton (12 ounces) frozen whipped topping, thawed, *divided*

In a large bowl, combine the first four ingredients; set aside 1/2 cup for topping. Press remaining crumb mixture into an ungreased 13-in. x 9-in. x 2-in. dish. Chill for 5 minutes.

Meanwhile, in a large bowl, whisk milk and pudding mixes for 2 minutes. Let stand for 2 minutes or until set (mixture will be thick). Stir in frozen yogurt and 1 cup whipped topping until smooth. Spread over crust. Top with remaining whipped topping. Sprinkle with reserved crumb mixture. Refrigerate for 8 hours or overnight. **Yield:** 12-15 servings.

Strawberry Dessert Soup

Prep: 20 min. + chilling

When I first prepared this change-of-pace soup for a party, everyone called it a hit!   —Sharon Delaney-Chronis
South Milwaukee, Wisconsin

✓ Uses less fat, sugar or salt. Includes Nutrition Facts.

   1 cup water, *divided*
   1 cup unsweetened apple juice
2/3 cup sugar
1/2 teaspoon ground cinnamon
1/8 teaspoon ground cloves
   2 cups fresh strawberries, hulled
   2 cups strawberry yogurt
   2 to 3 drops red food coloring, optional
1/4 cup sour cream
   2 tablespoons milk

In a large saucepan, combine 3/4 cup water, apple juice, sugar, cinnamon and cloves. Bring to a boil, stirring occasionally. Remove from the heat.

Place strawberries and remaining water in a blender; cover and process until smooth. Pour into apple juice mixture. Stir in yogurt and food coloring if desired. Cover and refrigerate for at least 2 hours or until chilled.

Ladle soup into bowls. Combine sour cream and milk; spoon about 2-1/2 teaspoons into the center of each bowl. Using a toothpick, pull mixture out, forming a flower or design of your choice. **Yield:** 7 servings.

Nutrition Facts: 3/4 cup equals 192 calories, 3 g fat (2 g saturated fat), 10 mg cholesterol, 45 mg sodium, 40 g carbohydrate, 1 g fiber, 3 g protein.

Rocky Road Chocolate Cake

Prep: 15 min. **Bake:** 40 min. + cooling

I combine the best of both worlds with this turtle-and-rocky-road cake. It's rich, chocolaty and irresistible.
   —Sherry Thompson, Seneca, South Carolina

   1 package (18-1/4 ounces) chocolate cake mix
   1 cup confectioners' sugar
   2 tablespoons baking cocoa
   6 tablespoons heavy whipping cream
1/2 teaspoon vanilla extract
   6 tablespoons caramel ice cream topping
   4 cups miniature marshmallows
   1 cup chopped pecans

Prepare and bake cake according to package directions, using a greased 13-in. x 9-in. x 2-in. baking pan.

Meanwhile, for frosting, combine confectioners' sugar and cocoa in a small bowl; whisk in cream and vanilla until smooth. While cake is still hot, drizzle with half of the caramel topping and half of the frosting. Sprinkle with marshmallows; return to the oven for 5 minutes or until marshmallows are softened.

Drizzle with remaining caramel topping; sprinkle with nuts. Drizzle with remaining frosting. Cool on a wire rack. **Yield:** 20 servings.

Heart Brownie Cookie

(Pictured above)

Prep: 25 min. **Bake:** 15 min. + cooling

My husband loves cookies, so I like to make this special heart for Valentine's Day...and, since that's my daughter's birthday, this treat is perfect for the whole family!
   —Angie Powell, Orem, Utah

1/3 cup butter-flavored shortening
3/4 cup packed brown sugar
1-1/2 teaspoons water
1/2 teaspoon vanilla extract
   1 egg
3/4 cup all-purpose flour
   3 tablespoons baking cocoa
1/4 teaspoon salt
1/8 teaspoon baking soda
   1 cup milk chocolate chips
FROSTING:
3-1/2 cups confectioners' sugar, *divided*
   3 tablespoons butter, softened
   1 tablespoon shortening
1/2 teaspoon vanilla extract
   3 to 4 tablespoons milk, *divided*
Red paste food coloring

In a large mixing bowl, cream the shortening, brown sugar, water and vanilla. Beat in egg. Combine the flour, cocoa, salt and baking soda; gradually add to creamed mixture until combined. Stir in chocolate chips. Pour into a greased and floured 9-in. heart-shaped baking pan.

Bake at 375° for 15-20 minutes or until center is set (do not overbake). Cool for 10 minutes before removing from pan to a wire rack.

In a large mixing bowl, combine 1-1/2 cups confectioners' sugar, butter, shortening, vanilla and 3 tablespoons milk; beat until smooth. Gradually add remaining confectioners' sugar; beat until light and fluffy, about 3 minutes. Add enough remaining milk to achieve a frosting consistency.

Frost the brownie with 3/4 cup frosting. Using the food coloring, tint the remaining frosting and decorate brownie as desired. **Yield:** 8-10 servings.

Frosted Snowmen

(Pictured below)

Prep: 25 min. **Bake:** 10 min./batch

I took these frosty fellows to my son's class, and everyone loved them. —Leah Gallington, Corona, California

1-1/2 cups butter (no substitutes), softened
2-1/4 cups sugar
  1 egg
  3 teaspoons vanilla extract
3-3/4 cups all-purpose flour
  1/2 teaspoon baking powder
  72 pretzel sticks
  1 can (16 ounces) vanilla frosting
Blue and red decorating icing

In a mixing bowl, cream butter and sugar. Gradually beat in egg and vanilla. Combine flour and baking powder; add to creamed mixture. Shape dough into 1-in., 5/8-in. and 1/4-in. balls. For each snowman, place one of each size ball 1/4 in. apart on ungreased baking sheets; place snowmen 2 in. apart. Break pretzel sticks in half; press into sides of middle balls.

Bake at 375° for 10-12 minutes or until bottoms are lightly browned. Cool 1 minute before removing to wire racks. Frost cooled cookies. Decorate with blue icing for eyes, mouths and buttons, and red for noses and scarves. **Yield:** 6 dozen.

Frosted Snowmen

Toffee-Almond Cookie Slices

Toffee-Almond Cookie Slices

(Pictured above)

Prep: 15 min. **Bake:** 40 min. + cooling

Make the Christmas season extra special for family and friends with these crispy cookies. Simply bake up a batch, wrap several slices in bright cellophane and add holiday stickers and curly ribbons for last-minute gifts.
—Julie Plummer, Sykesville, Maryland

✓ Uses less fat, sugar or salt. Includes Nutrition Facts and Diabetic Exchanges.

  1 package (17-1/2 ounces) sugar cookie mix
1/2 cup all-purpose flour
1/2 cup butter, softened
  1 egg
1/3 cup slivered almonds, toasted
1/3 cup miniature semisweet chocolate chips
1/3 cup English toffee bits *or* almond brickle chips

In a large mixing bowl, combine the sugar cookie mix, flour, butter and egg. Stir in the almonds, chocolate chips and toffee bits.

Divide dough in half. On an ungreased baking sheet, shape each portion into a 10-in. x 2-1/2-in. rectangle. Bake at 350° for 25-30 minutes or until lightly browned.

Carefully remove to wire racks; cool for 10 minutes. Transfer to a cutting board; with a serrated knife, cut each rectangle diagonally into 15 slices.

Place the slices cut side down on ungreased baking sheets. Bake for 15-20 minutes or until golden brown. Remove to wire racks to cool. Store in an airtight container. **Yield:** 2-1/2 dozen.

Nutrition Facts: 1 cookie equals 138 calories, 7 g fat (3 g saturated fat), 16 mg cholesterol, 87 mg sodium, 18 g carbohydrate, trace fiber, 1 g protein. **Diabetic Exchanges:** 1-1/2 fat, 1 starch.

Chapter 15

CLEVER COOKS know that a little bit of planning and preparation can go a long way toward saving precious time later. And this can't-miss chapter will help you do just that!

From mouth-watering main dishes such as Sweet Barbecued Pork Chops to Checkerboard Ice Cream Cake and other delectable desserts, these convenient recipes can be started in advance. On the day of your meal, you'll have little to do but sit down and enjoy dinner.

You'll find main courses you can freeze, grilled meats that marinate overnight, homemade mixes and much more. No matter which exceptional dish you choose, you'll be a step ahead!

FREEZER EASE. Pizza-Flavored Pasta Sauce (p. 236).

Sausage Pizza

Sausage Pizza

(Pictured above)

Prep: 20 min. **Bake:** 15 min.

Spicy sausage, onion, mushrooms and plenty of cheese make this pizza from our Test Kitchen a real keeper.

✓ Uses less fat, sugar or salt. Includes Nutrition Facts and Diabetic Exchanges.

  1 loaf (1 pound) frozen bread dough, thawed
3/4 pound bulk hot Italian sausage
1/2 cup sliced onion
1/2 cup sliced fresh mushrooms
1/2 cup chopped green pepper
1/2 cup pizza sauce
  2 cups (8 ounces) shredded part-skim
     mozzarella cheese

With greased fingers, pat dough onto an ungreased 12-in. pizza pan. Prick dough thoroughly with a fork. Bake at 400° for 10-12 minutes or until lightly browned. Meanwhile, in a large skillet, cook the sausage, onion, mushrooms and green pepper over medium heat until sausage is no longer pink; drain.

Spread pizza sauce over crust. Top with sausage mixture; sprinkle with cheese. Bake at 400° for 12-15 minutes or until golden brown. Or wrap pizza and freeze for up to 2 months.

To use frozen pizza: Unwrap and place on a pizza pan; thaw in the refrigerator. Bake at 400° for 18-22 minutes or until golden brown. **Yield:** 8 slices.

Nutrition Facts: 1 slice (prepared with turkey sausage and reduced-fat cheese) equals 311 calories, 11 g fat (4 g saturated fat), 39 mg cholesterol, 754 mg sodium, 33 g carbohydrate, 2 g fiber, 20 g protein. **Diabetic Exchanges:** 2 starch, 1-1/2 lean meat, 1-1/2 fat.

Southern Vegetable Soup

Prep/Total Time: 30 min.

I love this chunky, vegetable-filled soup. It features fresh or frozen okra, a popular fiber-filled veggie.
    —Christy Hinrichs, Parkville, Missouri

1/2 cup chopped onion
  2 teaspoons minced garlic
  2 teaspoons olive oil
  2 cans (14-1/2 ounces *each*) vegetable broth
  1 can (28 ounces) crushed tomatoes
  1 package (16 ounces) frozen mixed
     vegetables
  1 cup sliced fresh *or* frozen okra
  1 can (4 ounces) chopped green chilies
  2 teaspoons dried savory
  1 teaspoon sugar
1/2 teaspoon salt
1/2 teaspoon dried tarragon
1/8 teaspoon white pepper

In a Dutch oven, saute onion and garlic in oil for 3 minutes or until tender. Stir in the remaining ingredients. Bring to a boil. Reduce heat; cover and simmer for 15-20 minutes or until vegetables are crisp-tender.

Serve immediately or transfer to freezer containers. May be frozen for up to 3 months.

To use frozen soup: Thaw in the refrigerator overnight. Transfer to a saucepan. Cover and cook over medium heat until heated through. **Yield:** 6 servings (2-1/2 quarts).

Flavorful Southwestern Chili

Prep/Total Time: 30 min.

This hearty, freezer-friendly recipe comes from my grandmother. I top it with cheddar cheese and black olives.
    —Jenny Greear, Huntington, West Virginia

✓ Uses less fat, sugar or salt. Includes Nutrition Facts and Diabetic Exchanges.

  2 pounds ground beef
1-1/2 cups chopped onions
  2 cans (14-1/2 ounces *each*) diced tomatoes,
     undrained
  1 can (15 ounces) pinto beans, rinsed and
     drained
  1 can (15 ounces) tomato sauce
  1 package (10 ounces) frozen corn, thawed
  1 cup salsa
3/4 cup water
  1 can (4 ounces) chopped green chilies
  1 teaspoon ground cumin
1/2 teaspoon garlic powder

In a Dutch oven, cook beef and onions over medium heat until meat is no longer pink; drain. Stir in the remaining ingredients; simmer, uncovered, for 15 minutes.

Serve desired amount. Cool remaining chili; transfer to freezer containers. May be frozen for up to 3 months.

To use frozen chili: Thaw in the refrigerator. Place in a saucepan; heat through. **Yield:** 10 servings (2-1/2 quarts).

Nutrition Facts: 1 cup (prepared with lean ground beef) equals 245 calories, 7 g fat (3 g saturated fat), 44 mg cholesterol, 580 mg sodium, 22 g carbohydrate, 5 g fiber, 22 g protein. **Diabetic Exchanges:** 2 lean meat, 1 starch, 1 vegetable, 1 fat.

Marinated Ham Steaks

Prep: 10 min. + marinating **Grill:** 10 min.

These grilled steaks have become a mainstay. A friend shared the recipe, and I've won rave reviews at neighborhood barbecues. —*Judy Grimes, Brandon, Mississippi*

    1/2 cup ginger ale
    1/2 cup orange juice
    1/4 cup packed brown sugar
      1 tablespoon vegetable oil
  1-1/2 teaspoons white vinegar
      1 teaspoon ground mustard
    1/4 teaspoon ground ginger
    1/8 teaspoon ground cloves
      4 individual boneless fully cooked ham steaks
        (about 5 ounces *each*)

In a large resealable plastic bag, combine the first eight ingredients. Add ham steaks; seal bag and turn to coat. Refrigerate for 8 hours or overnight.

Prepare grill for indirect heat. Drain and discard marinade. Grill ham, covered, over indirect medium heat for 3-4 minutes on each side or until heated through. **Yield:** 4 servings.

Beef Enchiladas

Prep: 25 min. **Bake:** 30 min.

A variety of convenience products makes this spicy entree a snap to prepare. It's a good dish to feed a large group of people. —*Rosemary Gonser, Clay Center, Kansas*

  2-1/2 pounds ground beef
    2/3 cup chopped onion
      2 cans (15 ounces *each*) enchilada sauce
      1 can (10-3/4 ounces) condensed cream of
        mushroom soup, undiluted
      1 can (10-3/4 ounces) condensed tomato
        soup, undiluted
     20 flour tortillas (8 inches), room temperature
  2-1/2 cups (10 ounces) shredded cheddar cheese
  Additional shredded cheddar cheese

In a large skillet, cook beef and onion over medium heat until meat is no longer pink; drain. Combine sauce and soups; pour about 1 cup each into two ungreased 13-in. x 9-in. x 2-in. baking dishes. Stir 1-1/2 cups of sauce into beef mixture; set remaining sauce aside.

Spoon 1/4 cup beef mixture down the center of each tortilla; top with 2 tablespoons cheese. Roll up tightly; place 10 enchiladas seam side down in each prepared dish. Top with remaining sauce. Cover and freeze one pan for up to 3 months.

Cover and bake the remaining pan at 350° for 25-30

minutes. Uncover; sprinkle with additional cheese. Bake 5-10 minutes longer or until cheese is melted.

To use frozen enchiladas: Thaw in the refrigerator overnight. Bake as directed. **Yield:** 2 pans (10 enchiladas each).

Sweet Barbecued Pork Chops

(Pictured below)

Prep/Total Time: 30 min.

These tangy chops are sensational and require just a handful of everyday ingredients. They're so easy and taste so fresh, family and friends will never guess the extras were frozen! —*Susan Holderman, Fostoria, Ohio*

      8 boneless pork loin chops (3/4 inch thick and
        8 ounces *each*)
      2 tablespoons vegetable oil
    1/2 cup packed brown sugar
    1/2 cup chopped sweet onion
    1/2 cup *each* ketchup, barbecue sauce, French
        salad dressing and honey

In a large skillet, brown pork chops in oil in batches on both sides. Return all to the skillet. Combine the remaining ingredients; pour over chops. Bring to a boil. Reduce heat; cover and simmer for 12-14 minutes or until meat is tender.

Serve immediately, or cool before placing in a freezer container. Cover and freeze for up to 3 months.

To use frozen pork chops: Thaw in the refrigerator overnight. Place in a skillet; bring to a boil. Reduce heat; cover and simmer for 6-8 minutes or until heated through. **Yield:** 8 servings.

Sweet Barbecued Pork Chops

Pizza-Flavored Pasta Sauce

(Pictured below and on page 232)

Prep/Total Time: 30 min.

This chunky, "jazzed-up" spaghetti sauce with pasta is sure to please hungry kids...and busy moms, too. Served with garlic bread, it really hits the spot when you crave Italian food. —Angelina Falzarano, Midlothian, Texas

- 1 pound bulk Italian sausage
- 1/2 pound sliced fresh mushrooms
- 2 packages (3-1/2 ounces *each*) sliced pepperoni
- 3/4 cup chopped green pepper
- 1/2 cup chopped onion
- 2 jars (28 ounces *each*) meatless spaghetti sauce
- 1 can (3.8 ounces) sliced ripe olives, drained, *divided*
- 2 tablespoons Italian seasoning

Hot cooked pasta

In a large skillet, cook the sausage, mushrooms, pepperoni, green pepper and onion over medium heat until sausage is no longer pink; drain. Stir in the spaghetti sauce, olives and Italian seasoning.

Bring to a boil. Reduce heat; simmer, uncovered, for 10-12 minutes or until heated through. Serve desired amount over pasta. Cool remaining sauce; transfer to freezer containers. Freeze for up to 3 months.

To use frozen sauce: Thaw in the refrigerator overnight. Place in a saucepan and heat through. **Yield:** 9 servings (about 2 quarts).

Pizza-Flavored Pasta Sauce

Chicken Potato Casserole

Prep: 20 min. Bake: 45 min.

Need some comfort food? This savory, satisfying casserole fills the bill, and it freezes well, too.
—Kersten Campbell, Pullman, Washington

- 6 large baking potatoes, peeled and cubed
- 1-1/2 cups water
- 2 pounds boneless skinless chicken breasts, cut into 1-inch cubes
- 2 cups (16 ounces) sour cream
- 3/4 cup shredded cheddar cheese
- 1/2 cup butter, softened
- 1/4 cup shredded Parmesan cheese
- 1 envelope onion soup mix
- 1/4 cup finely chopped fresh spinach
- 1/4 cup shredded carrot
- 1/4 teaspoon salt
- 1/4 teaspoon garlic powder
- 1/4 teaspoon pepper
- 1/4 cup dry bread crumbs

Place potatoes and water in a 3-qt. microwave-safe dish. Cover and microwave on high for 12-15 minutes or until tender. Meanwhile, divide chicken between two greased 8-in. square baking dishes.

Drain potatoes and place in a large mixing bowl. Add sour cream, cheddar cheese, butter, Parmesan cheese, soup mix, spinach, carrot, salt, garlic powder and pepper; mash until smooth. Spoon over chicken; sprinkle with bread crumbs.

Bake one casserole, uncovered, at 350° for 45-50 minutes or until chicken juices run clear. Cover and freeze the remaining casserole for up to 3 months.

To use frozen casserole: Thaw in the refrigerator overnight. Remove from the refrigerator 30 minutes before baking. Bake as directed. **Yield:** 2 casseroles.

Creamy Chicken 'n' Mushrooms

Prep: 20 min. Bake: 20 min.

The convenience of canned soup makes this main dish a fast, easy option. Cook rice or noodles to go with it, and dinner's done. —Donna Brockett, Kingfisher, Oklahoma

- 8 boneless skinless chicken breast halves (6 ounces *each*)
- 4 tablespoons butter, *divided*
- 3 cups sliced fresh mushrooms
- 1/2 cup chopped onion
- 1/2 teaspoon garlic powder
- 2 cans (10-3/4 ounces *each*) condensed cream of mushroom soup, undiluted
- 1 cup milk
- 1/2 teaspoon pepper

Hot cooked rice *or* noodles

In a large skillet, brown chicken in batches in 2 tablespoons butter. Transfer to two ungreased 8-in. square baking dishes. Cover and bake at 350° for 20-25 minutes or until juices run clear.

Checkerboard Ice Cream Cake

Meanwhile, in the same skillet, saute mushrooms, onion and garlic powder in remaining butter until tender. Add the soup, milk and pepper. Bring to a boil. Reduce heat; simmer, uncovered, for 5-6 minutes or until heated through.

Drain chicken; top with soup mixture. Serve one casserole immediately with rice or noodles. Cover and freeze the remaining casserole for up to 3 months.

To use frozen casserole: Thaw in the refrigerator overnight. Cover and microwave on high for 8-10 minutes or until heated through, stirring once. Serve with rice or noodles. **Yield:** 2 casseroles (4 servings each).

Checkerboard Ice Cream Cake

(Pictured above and on the front cover)

Prep: 30 min. + freezing

I love fixing this special dessert for guests because it's so impressive. Everyone always wants to know the secret to making it. —*Erica Hunt, Gouverneur, New York*

  3 cups cream-filled chocolate sandwich cookie
    crumbs
1/2 cup sugar
1/2 cup butter, melted
  5 cups vanilla ice cream, softened
  4 cups chocolate ice cream, softened

In a large bowl, combine cookie crumbs, sugar and butter; set aside 1 cup for topping. Press remaining crumb mixture onto the bottom and 1-1/2 in. up the sides of an ungreased 10-in. springform pan.

Drop 1-3/4 cups vanilla ice cream by tablespoonfuls around the edge of the pan; flatten and smooth with a spatula into a 1-1/2-in.-wide ring. Drop 1 cup chocolate ice cream by tablespoonfuls next to the vanilla ring; flatten and smooth with a spatula into a 1-1/2-in.-wide ring. Fill in the center with 1/4 cup vanilla ice cream. Freeze for 30 minutes.

Drop 1-3/4 cups chocolate ice cream by tablespoonfuls over vanilla ice cream around edge of pan; smooth with a spatula into a 1-1/2-in.-wide ring. Drop 1 cup vanilla ice cream by tablespoonfuls next to the chocolate ring; smooth with a spatula into a 1-1/2-in.-wide ring. Fill in center with 1/4 cup chocolate ice cream. Freeze for 30 minutes.

Repeat pattern of first layer of ice cream. Sprinkle with reserved crumb mixture. Cover and freeze until firm. May be frozen for up to 2 months. Remove from the freezer 10 minutes before serving. **Yield:** 10-12 servings.

Frosty Lemon-Strawberry Dessert

(Pictured below)

Prep: 15 min. + freezing

This fun, frosty treat came from a dear elderly friend of mine who was a wonderful cook. I think of her whenever I make it. —*Gail Marshall, Fort Lauderdale, Florida*

✓ Uses less fat, sugar or salt. Includes Nutrition Facts and Diabetic Exchanges.

  1 quart fresh strawberries, hulled
1/2 gallon vanilla ice cream, softened
  1 can (12 ounces) frozen lemonade
    concentrate, thawed
  2 teaspoons grated lemon peel

Place berries in a food processor; cover and process until pureed. Transfer to a large mixing bowl; add ice cream, concentrate and lemon peel. Beat until blended.

Pour into an ungreased 13-in. x 9-in. x 2-in. dish. Cover and freeze overnight. Remove from the freezer 15 minutes before serving. **Yield:** 12 servings.

Nutrition Facts: 1 piece equals 194 calories, 8 g fat (5 g saturated fat), 31 mg cholesterol, 58 mg sodium, 30 g carbohydrate, 1 g fiber, 3 g protein. **Diabetic Exchanges:** 2 starch, 1-1/2 fat.

Frosty Lemon-Strawberry Dessert

Herb Mix for Rice
Cornflake Coating for Chicken

9 cups cornflakes, crushed
1 envelope onion soup mix
1 tablespoon garlic powder
1 tablespoon dried parsley flakes
2 teaspoons rubbed sage
1 teaspoon seasoned salt
1 teaspoon paprika
1 teaspoon pepper
ADDITIONAL INGREDIENT (for each batch):
4 boneless skinless chicken breast halves
(4 ounces *each*)

In an airtight container, combine the first eight ingredients. Store in a cool dry place for up to 6 months. **Yield:** 8 batches (about 4 cups total).

To prepare chicken: Place 1/2 cup cornflake coating in a shallow dish; coat the chicken on both sides. Place in a greased 11-in. x 7-in. x 2-in. baking dish. Bake, uncovered, at 350° for 30-35 minutes or until the chicken juices run clear. **Yield:** 4 servings.

Spaghetti Casserole

Prep: 20 min. **Bake:** 55 min.

This is a wonderful dish to prepare ahead of time, refrigerate and pop in the oven just before your company arrives. Canned mushroom soup makes this rave-winning casserole creamy, but it still cuts well for serving.
—*Kim Rocker, LaGrange, Georgia*

1 package (16 ounces) angel hair pasta
1-1/2 pounds ground beef
1 jar (26 ounces) spaghetti sauce
2 cans (8 ounces *each*) tomato sauce
1 can (10-3/4 ounces) condensed cream of
mushroom soup, undiluted
1 cup (8 ounces) sour cream
2 cups (8 ounces) shredded Colby-Monterey
Jack cheese

Cook pasta according to package directions. Meanwhile, in a large skillet, cook beef over medium heat until no longer pink; drain. Stir in spaghetti sauce and tomato sauce. Remove from the heat.

Drain the pasta. Combine cream of mushroom soup and sour cream. In two 8-in. square baking dishes, layer half of the meat sauce, pasta, soup mixture and cheese. Repeat the layers.

Cover and freeze one casserole for up to 3 months. Cover and bake the remaining casserole at 350° for 55-65 minutes or until cheese is melted.

To use frozen casserole: Thaw the casserole in the refrigerator overnight. Remove the casserole from the refrigerator 30 minutes before baking. Bake as directed. **Yield:** 2 casseroles (6 servings each).

Herb Mix for Rice

(Pictured above)
Prep/Total Time: 25 min.

This flavorful herb mix for rice is a great recipe to serve as a side with baked chicken or pork chops.
—*Arlene Haupt, Madison, Wisconsin*

5 tablespoons beef bouillon granules
3 tablespoons dried parsley flakes
2 tablespoons dried minced onion
4 teaspoons dried basil
2 teaspoons dried thyme
1 teaspoon garlic powder
ADDITIONAL INGREDIENTS (for each batch):
2 cups water
1 cup uncooked long grain rice

In an airtight container, combine the first six ingredients. Store in a cool dry place for up to 1 year. **Yield:** 4 batches (about 3/4 cup total).

To prepare rice: In a saucepan, bring water and 3 tablespoons herb mix to a boil. Stir in rice. Reduce heat; cover and simmer for 15 minutes or until rice is tender and liquid is absorbed. **Yield:** 4 servings.

Cornflake Coating for Chicken

(Pictured above)
Prep: 5 min. **Bake:** 30 min.

I always keep this mix on hand. It makes chicken crispy and so delicious! —*Denise Elder, Hanover, Ontario*

Chicken Stuffing Casserole

Prep: 15 min. **Bake:** 30 min.

Use up leftover cooked chicken in this tasty casserole that's chock-full of homey, comforting flavor. The recipe is very quick to prepare. —*Cathy Smith, Wyoming, Michigan*

2 packages (6 ounces *each*) chicken stuffing mix
2 cans (10-3/4 ounces *each*) condensed cream of mushroom soup, undiluted
1 cup milk
4 cups cubed cooked chicken
2 cups frozen corn
2 cans (8 ounces *each*) mushroom stems and pieces, drained
4 cups (1 pound) shredded cheddar cheese

Prepare stuffing mixes according to package directions. Meanwhile, in a large bowl, combine soup and milk; set aside. Spread the stuffing into two greased 8-in. square baking dishes. Layer with chicken, corn, mushrooms, soup mixture and cheese.

Cover and freeze one casserole for up to 3 months. Cover and bake the second casserole at 350° for 30-35 minutes or until cheese is melted.

To use frozen casserole: Remove from the freezer 30 minutes before baking (do not thaw). Bake at 350° for 1-1/2 hours. Uncover; bake 10-15 minutes or until heated through. **Yield:** 2 casseroles (6 servings each).

Breakfast Wraps

(Pictured below)

Prep/Total Time: 15 min.

We like quick and simple morning meals during the week, and these hearty wraps are great when they're fixed in advance. With just a minute in the microwave, your breakfast is ready! —Betty Kleberger, Florissant, Missouri

Breakfast Wraps

6 eggs
2 tablespoons milk
1/4 teaspoon pepper
1 tablespoon vegetable oil
1 cup (4 ounces) shredded cheddar cheese
3/4 cup diced fully cooked ham
4 flour tortillas (8 inches), warmed

In a small bowl, whisk the eggs, milk and pepper. In a large skillet, heat oil. Add the egg mixture; cook and stir over medium heat until the eggs are completely set. Stir in the cheese and ham.

Spoon egg mixture down the center of each tortilla; roll up. Serve immediately, or wrap in plastic wrap and freeze in a resealable plastic bag.

To use frozen wraps: Thaw in the refrigerator overnight. Remove plastic wrap; wrap tortilla in a moist microwave-safe paper towel. Microwave on high for 30-60 seconds or until heated through. Serve immediately. **Yield:** 4 servings.

Mini Shepherd's Pies

Prep: 30 min. **Bake:** 20 min.

Convenient potato flakes and refrigerated biscuits hurry along these tasty meat-and-potato pies. I'm as confident serving them to last-minute company as to my husband and three boys. —Ellen Osborne, Clarksville, Tennessee

1 pound ground beef
3 tablespoons chopped onion
1/2 teaspoon minced garlic
1/3 cup chili sauce *or* ketchup
1 tablespoon cider vinegar
1/2 teaspoon salt
1-1/4 cups water
3 tablespoons butter
1-1/4 cups mashed potato flakes
1 package (3 ounces) cream cheese, cubed
1 tube (12 ounces) refrigerated buttermilk biscuits
1/2 cup crushed potato chips
Paprika, optional

In a large skillet, cook beef, onion and garlic over medium heat until meat is no longer pink; drain. Stir in the chili sauce, vinegar and salt; set aside.

In a small saucepan, bring the water and butter to a boil. Pour into a small mixing bowl. Whisk in the mashed potato flakes until blended. Beat in the cubed cream cheese until smooth.

Press biscuits onto the bottom and up the sides of 10 greased muffin cups. Fill with beef mixture. Spread potato mixture over beef. Sprinkle with potato chips; press down lightly.

Bake at 375° for 20-25 minutes or until golden brown. Sprinkle with paprika if desired. Serve immediately, or cool before placing in a single layer in a freezer container. Cover and freeze for up to 2 months.

To use frozen pies: Thaw in the refrigerator for 8 hours. Place on a greased baking sheet. Bake at 375° for 15-18 minutes or until heated through. **Yield:** 5 servings.

Spinach Lasagna Roll-Ups

Spinach Lasagna Roll-Ups

(Pictured above and on the front cover)

Prep: 25 min. + chilling **Bake:** 35 min.

These Italian-inspired roll-ups are fast and fun to fix. With their elegant look, they're perfect for family meals and special-occasion dinners alike. —*Cindy Romberg Mississauga, Ontario*

✓ Uses less fat, sugar or salt. Includes Nutrition Facts and Diabetic Exchanges.

- 1 package (10 ounces) frozen chopped spinach, thawed and squeezed dry
- 1 cup (4 ounces) shredded part-skim mozzarella cheese
- 1 cup (8 ounces) small-curd 2% cottage cheese
- 3/4 cup grated Parmesan cheese, *divided*
- 1 egg, lightly beaten
- 6 lasagna noodles, cooked and drained
- 2 cans (15 ounces *each*) seasoned tomato sauce for lasagna

In a bowl, combine spinach, mozzarella, cottage cheese, 1/2 cup Parmesan and egg. Spread a heaping 1/3 cupful over each noodle. Roll up; secure with toothpicks.

Place seam side down in an 11-in. x 7-in. x 2-in. baking dish coated with nonstick cooking spray. Cover and refrigerate overnight.

Remove from the refrigerator 30 minutes before baking. Pour the tomato sauce over the roll-ups. Cover and bake at 350° for 33-38 minutes or until bubbly. Sprinkle with the remaining Parmesan cheese. Discard the toothpicks. **Yield:** 6 servings.

Editor's Note: This recipe was tested with Hunt's seasoned tomato sauce for lasagna.

Nutrition Facts: 1 roll-up equals 307 calories, 8 g fat (5 g saturated fat), 59 mg cholesterol, 1,205 mg sodium, 37 g carbohydrate, 4 g fiber, 21 g protein. **Diabetic Exchanges:** 2 starch, 2 lean meat, 1 vegetable.

Wild Rice Chicken Dinner

Prep/Total Time: 30 min.

With crunchy water chestnuts and nuts, this casserole is sure to please. —*Lorraine Hanson, Independence, Iowa*

- 2 packages (8.8 ounces *each*) ready-to-serve long grain and wild rice
- 2 packages (16 ounces *each*) frozen French-style green beans, thawed
- 2 cans (10-3/4 ounces *each*) condensed cream of celery soup, undiluted
- 2 cans (8 ounces *each*) sliced water chestnuts, drained
- 2/3 cup chopped onion
- 2 jars (4 ounces *each*) sliced pimientos, drained
- 1 cup mayonnaise
- 1/2 cup milk
- 1 teaspoon pepper
- 6 cups cubed cooked chicken
- 1 cup slivered almonds, *divided*

Heat rice according to package directions. Meanwhile, in a Dutch oven, combine the green beans, soup, water chestnuts, onion, pimientos, mayonnaise, milk and pepper. Bring to a boil. Reduce heat; cover and simmer for 5 minutes. Stir in chicken and rice; cook 3-4 minutes longer or until chicken is heated through.

Transfer half of the mixture to a serving dish; sprinkle with 1/2 cup almonds. Serve immediately. Pour the remaining mixture into a greased 13-in. x 9-in. x 2-in. baking dish; cool. Sprinkle with remaining almonds. Cover and freeze for up to 3 months.

To use frozen casserole: Thaw in the refrigerator overnight. Cover; bake at 350° for 40-45 minutes or until heated through. **Yield:** 2 casseroles (6-8 servings each).

Editor's Note: Reduced-fat or fat-free mayonnaise is not recommended for this recipe.

Chicken and Bows

Prep/Total Time: 25 min.

I first made this recipe when I was a professional nanny. It comes together quickly when the kids are hungry for dinner. —*Danette Forbes, Overland Park, Kansas*

✓ Uses less fat, sugar or salt. Includes Nutrition Facts and Diabetic Exchanges.

- 1 package (16 ounces) bow tie pasta
- 2 pounds boneless skinless chicken breasts, cut into strips
- 1 cup chopped sweet red pepper
- 1/4 cup butter, cubed
- 2 cans (10-3/4 ounces *each*) condensed cream of chicken soup, undiluted
- 2 cups frozen peas
- 1-1/2 cups milk
- 1 teaspoon garlic powder
- 1/4 to 1/2 teaspoon salt
- 1/4 teaspoon pepper
- 2/3 cup grated Parmesan cheese

Cook pasta according to package directions. Meanwhile, in a Dutch oven, cook chicken and red pepper in butter over medium heat for 5-6 minutes or until chicken juices run clear.

Stir in soup, peas, milk, garlic powder, salt and pepper. Bring to a boil. Reduce heat; simmer, uncovered, for 1-2 minutes or until heated through. Stir in Parmesan cheese. Drain pasta; add to chicken mixture. Toss to coat.

Serve half of the mixture immediately. Cool remaining mixture; transfer to a freezer container. Cover and freeze for up to 3 months.

To use frozen casserole: Thaw in the refrigerator overnight. Transfer to an ungreased shallow 3-qt. microwave-safe dish. Cover and microwave on high for 8-10 minutes or until heated through, stirring once. **Yield:** 2 casseroles (6 servings each).

Editor's Note: This recipe was tested in a 1,100-watt microwave.

Nutrition Facts: 1-1/3 cups equals 357 calories, 12 g fat (5 g saturated fat), 64 mg cholesterol, 636 mg sodium, 37 g carbohydrate, 3 g fiber, 26 g protein. **Diabetic Exchanges:** 3 very lean meat, 2 starch, 2 fat.

Three-Cheese Kielbasa Bake

Prep: 55 min. **Bake:** 30 min.

This hearty casserole takes advantage of garden-fresh vegetables and handy convenience items. My aunt originally served this for family gatherings, but it's so easy, you can fix it any night of the week. —Kate Beckman
Hemet, California

- 12 ounces uncooked elbow macaroni
- 2 pounds kielbasa *or* Polish sausage, halved lengthwise and sliced
- 1 tablespoon olive oil
- 2 medium onions, chopped
- 2 medium zucchini, quartered and sliced
- 2 medium carrots, grated
- 1/2 teaspoon minced garlic
- 1 jar (26 ounces) spaghetti sauce
- 1 can (14-1/2 ounces) stewed tomatoes
- 1 egg, lightly beaten
- 1 carton (15 ounces) ricotta cheese
- 2 cups (8 ounces) shredded cheddar cheese
- 2 cups (8 ounces) shredded part-skim mozzarella cheese
- 2 green onions, chopped

Cook the macaroni according to the package directions. Meanwhile, in a large skillet, brown the sausage in oil over medium heat. Add the onions, zucchini, carrots and garlic; cook and stir for 5-6 minutes or until crisp-tender. Stir in the spaghetti sauce and tomatoes. Bring to a boil. Reduce heat; simmer, uncovered, for 15 minutes. Drain the macaroni.

In each of two greased 13-in. x 9-in. x 2-in. baking dishes, layer a fourth of the macaroni and meat sauce. Combine egg and ricotta cheese; spoon a fourth over sauce. Sprinkle with a fourth of the cheddar and mozzarella. Repeat layers. Top with green onions.

Cool one casserole; cover and freeze for up to 2 months. Cover and bake the remaining casserole at 350° for 15 minutes. Uncover; bake 15 minutes longer or until cheese is melted.

To use frozen casserole: Thaw in the refrigerator for 24 hours. Remove from the refrigerator 30 minutes before baking. Cover and bake at 350° for 35-40 minutes or until heated through. **Yield:** 2 casseroles (8-10 servings each).

Frosty Pistachio Delight

(Pictured below)

Prep: 25 min. + freezing

I love the simple make-ahead convenience of this refreshing treat drizzled with fudge topping. Being able to make the dessert the night before and then freeze it gives me time to work on all of my last-minute dinner details!
—Sandie Davenport, Farmer City, Illinois

- 2-1/2 cups chocolate graham cracker crumbs
- 2/3 cup butter, melted
- 1 carton (1-3/4 quarts) vanilla ice cream, softened
- 2 packages (3.4 ounces *each*) instant pistachio pudding mix
- 1 cup plus 2 tablespoons pistachios, chopped, *divided*
- 3 drops green food coloring, optional
- 1 carton (8 ounces) frozen whipped topping, thawed
- 1 jar (11-3/4 ounces) hot fudge ice cream topping, warmed

In a small bowl, combine cracker crumbs and butter. Press into a greased 13-in. x 9-in. x 2-in. baking dish. Bake at 350° for 7-9 minutes or until set. Cool on a wire rack.

In a large bowl, combine the ice cream, pudding mixes, 1 cup pistachios and food coloring if desired. Fold in whipped topping. Spread over crust. Cover and freeze for at least 4 hours.

Remove from the freezer 10 minutes before serving. Drizzle with fudge topping; sprinkle with remaining pistachios. **Yield:** 15 servings.

Frosty Pistachio Delight

Chapter 16

Casseroles and Stovetop Suppers

PUTTING a winning dinner on the table pronto can be as easy as popping a quick casserole in the oven...or stirring up speedy fare on the stovetop.

To take advantage of these fast cooking strategies, turn to this chapter. You'll find an entire section of comforting casseroles, including Creamy Macaroni and Cheese, Sloppy Joe Hot Dish and Coq Au Vin.

Then turn the page for a sensational selection of dishes that come together in a jiffy on the range. Enjoy Teriyaki Mushroom Chicken, Scalloped Potato Skillet, Pizza Pasta Dinner and much more.

Just pull out a baking pan or grab a skillet...it's that simple!

STOVETOP SUPPER. Sweet-and-Sour Beef with Broccoli (p. 251).

243

Broccoli Chicken Casserole

Catchall Casseroles

WHEN it comes to family-pleasing fare, it's hard to beat a hearty, piping-hot, bubbling casserole straight from the oven. And you're sure to get smiles all around when you dish out big helpings of the comforting creations here.

Just toss together a green salad while the casserole bakes, and you'll soon have a satisfying supper your family will request time and again.

Broccoli Chicken Casserole

(Pictured above)

Prep: 15 min. **Bake:** 30 min.

All ages really seem to go for this heartwarming meal-in-one. The recipe requires just a handful of ingredients and minutes to put together. Sometimes I add dried cranberries to the stuffing mix for extra flavor and color.
—Jenn Schlachter, Big Rock, Illinois

1-1/2 cups water
   1 package (6 ounces) chicken stuffing mix
   2 cups cubed cooked chicken

   1 cup frozen broccoli florets, thawed
   1 can (10-3/4 ounces) condensed broccoli cheese soup, undiluted
   1 cup (4 ounces) shredded cheddar cheese

In a small saucepan, bring water to a boil. Stir in stuffing mix. Remove from the heat; cover and let stand for 5 minutes.

Meanwhile, layer chicken and broccoli in a greased 11-in. x 7-in. x 2-in. baking dish. Top with soup. Fluff stuffing with a fork; spoon over soup. Sprinkle with cheese.

Bake, uncovered, at 350° for 30-35 minutes or until heated through. **Yield:** 6 servings.

Sloppy Joe Hot Dish

Prep: 15 min. **Bake:** 20 min.

Dinner is served in a flash when you choose this kid-friendly meal. —Marlene Harguth, Maynard, Minnesota

   1 package (8 ounces) refrigerated crescent rolls
   1 pound ground beef
   1 can (15 ounces) tomato sauce
   1 envelope sloppy joe mix
   1 cup (4 ounces) shredded part-skim mozzarella cheese

Unroll crescent dough into two rectangles; seal seams and perforations. Roll out each rectangle between two pieces of waxed paper to fit an 11-in. x 7-in. x 2-in. baking dish. Grease the dish and place one rectangle inside. Bake at 425° for 5 minutes or until golden brown.

Meanwhile, in a large skillet, cook beef over medium heat until no longer pink; drain. Stir in the tomato sauce and sloppy joe mix; spoon over crust. Sprinkle with cheese; top with remaining dough. Bake 15-20 minutes longer or until golden brown. **Yield:** 6 servings.

Italian Meat and Potatoes

Prep: 25 min. **Bake:** 1-1/2 hours

My mom used to call this delicious dish "Potato Pizza." It was always a treat for us when she served it, and it's still one of my favorites for a cold winter day.
—Kaci Koltz, Cassville, Wisconsin

   1 pound ground beef
   1 pound bulk pork sausage
1/2 cup chopped onion
1/4 teaspoon pepper
1/8 teaspoon salt
   1 can (10-3/4 ounces) condensed cheddar cheese soup, undiluted
1-1/4 cups milk
   1 can (8 ounces) tomato sauce
   1 teaspoon garlic powder
   1 teaspoon dried oregano
1/2 teaspoon sugar
   6 medium potatoes, peeled and thinly sliced
   2 cups (8 ounces) shredded part-skim mozzarella cheese

In a large skillet, cook the beef, sausage, onion, pepper and salt over medium heat until meat is no longer pink. Meanwhile, in a small saucepan, combine the soup, milk, tomato sauce, garlic powder, oregano and sugar. Bring to a boil. Reduce heat; simmer, uncovered, for 5 minutes or until heated through.

Drain meat mixture; spoon half into a greased 13-in. x 9-in. x 2-in. baking dish. Layer with half of the potatoes. Repeat layers. Top with soup mixture.

Cover and bake at 350° for 1-1/4 hours or until the potatoes are tender. Uncover casserole; sprinkle with cheese. Bake 15 minutes longer or until the cheese is melted. **Yield:** 10-12 servings.

Polenta Chili Casserole

(Pictured below)

Prep: 20 min. **Bake:** 35 min. + standing

Our Test Kitchen whipped up a tasty bean-and-polenta bake with spicy chili and mixed vegetables.

> ✓ Uses less fat, sugar or salt. Includes Nutrition Facts.

- 1-1/4 cups yellow cornmeal
- 1/2 teaspoon salt
- 4 cups boiling water
- 2 cups (8 ounces) shredded cheddar cheese, *divided*
- 3 cartons (14.3 ounces *each*) fat-free vegetarian chili
- 1 package (16 ounces) frozen mixed vegetables, thawed and well drained

In a large saucepan, combine cornmeal and salt. Gradually whisk in boiling water. Cook and stir over medium heat for 5 minutes or until thickened. Remove from the heat. Stir in 1/4 cup cheddar cheese.

Spread into a 13-in. x 9-in. x 2-in. baking dish coated

Chicken Vegetable Casserole

with nonstick cooking spray. Bake, uncovered, at 350° for 20 minutes. Meanwhile, heat chili according to package directions.

Spread vegetables over polenta; top with chili. Sprinkle with remaining cheese. Bake 12-15 minutes longer or until cheese is melted. Let stand for 10 minutes before serving. **Yield:** 8 servings.

Nutrition Facts: 1 serving (prepared with reduced-fat cheese) equals 344 calories, 6 g fat (4 g saturated fat), 20 mg cholesterol, 551 mg sodium, 44 g carbohydrate, 13 g fiber, 19 g protein.

Chicken Vegetable Casserole

(Pictured above)

Prep: 20 min. **Bake:** 35 min.

This fuss-free recipe works wonders with leftover turkey or chicken. —*Genia McClinchey, Lakeview, Michigan*

- 1/2 cup butter, softened
- 1 cup (8 ounces) sour cream
- 1 egg
- 1 cup all-purpose flour
- 1 teaspoon baking powder
- 1 teaspoon salt
- 1/2 teaspoon rubbed sage
- 1 package (16 ounces) frozen mixed vegetables, thawed
- 2 cups cubed cooked chicken *or* turkey
- 1 can (10-3/4 ounces) condensed cream of mushroom soup, undiluted
- 1/2 cup chopped onion
- 1/2 cup shredded cheddar cheese

In a small mixing bowl, cream butter and sour cream. Add egg; beat well. Combine the flour, baking powder, salt and sage; add to creamed mixture. Spread into a greased 3-qt. baking dish.

In a large bowl, combine the vegetables, chicken, soup and onion. Pour over crust; sprinkle with cheese. Bake, uncovered, at 400° for 35-40 minutes or until heated through. **Yield:** 6 servings.

Polenta Chili Casserole

Crab 'n' Penne Casserole

(Pictured below)

Prep: 20 min. **Bake:** 40 min.

Purchased Alfredo sauce makes this casserole creamy, while red pepper flakes kick up the taste. The comforting dish also gets garden-fresh goodness from zucchini and summer squash. —*Bernadette Bennett, Waco, Texas*

```
1-1/2  cups uncooked penne pasta
    1  jar (17 ounces) Alfredo sauce
1-1/2  cups imitation crabmeat, chopped
    1  medium yellow summer squash, sliced
    1  medium zucchini, sliced
    1  tablespoon dried parsley flakes
  1/8 to 1/4 teaspoon crushed red pepper flakes
1-1/2  cups (6 ounces) shredded part-skim
         mozzarella cheese
    2  tablespoons dry bread crumbs
    2  teaspoons butter, melted
```

Cook pasta according to package directions. Meanwhile, in a large bowl, combine the Alfredo sauce, crab, yellow squash, zucchini, parsley and pepper flakes. Drain pasta; add to sauce mixture and toss to coat.

Transfer to a greased 13-in. x 9-in. x 2-in. baking dish. Sprinkle with cheese. Cover and bake at 325° for 35 minutes.

Toss bread crumbs and butter; sprinkle over casserole. Bake, uncovered, 5-6 minutes longer or until browned. **Yield:** 6 servings.

Crab 'n' Penne Casserole

Corn Tortilla Lasagna

Prep: 20 min. **Bake:** 30 min. + standing

Popular at office luncheons and potluck dinners, this simple lasagna has a terrific twist—it's packed with Southwestern flavor. —*Jo Terwilliger, Oneonta, New York*

```
1-1/2  pounds ground beef
  1/3  cup chopped onion
  1/2  teaspoon minced garlic
    1  jar (16 ounces) picante sauce
    1  package (10 ounces) frozen chopped
         spinach, thawed and squeezed dry
    2  medium tomatoes, seeded and chopped
    1  large sweet red pepper, chopped
    1  can (8 ounces) tomato sauce
    1  tablespoon lime juice
   12  corn tortillas
  3/4  cup shredded Monterey Jack cheese
    2  cups (16 ounces) sour cream
Additional picante sauce, optional
```

In a large skillet, cook the beef, onion and garlic over medium heat until meat is no longer pink; drain. Stir in the picante sauce, spinach, tomatoes, red pepper, tomato sauce and lime juice.

Arrange six tortillas in a greased 13-in. x 9-in. x 2-in. baking dish. Top with half of the meat mixture, 1/4 cup cheese and remaining tortillas. Spread with sour cream. Top with the remaining meat mixture and cheese.

Bake, uncovered, at 350° for 30-40 minutes or until heated through. Let stand for 10 minutes. Serve with additional picante sauce if desired. **Yield:** 10-12 servings.

Creamy Macaroni and Cheese

Prep: 20 min. **Bake:** 35 min.

This is the ultimate mac and cheese. It's creamy, thick and very rich. Once you try it, you'll definitely be hooked! —*Cindy Hartley, Chesapeake, Virginia*

```
    2  cups uncooked elbow macaroni
  1/2  cup butter, cubed
  1/2  cup all-purpose flour
1-1/2  cups milk
    1  cup (8 ounces) sour cream
    8  ounces process cheese (Velveeta), cubed
  1/4  cup grated Parmesan cheese
  1/2  teaspoon salt
  1/2  teaspoon ground mustard
  1/2  teaspoon pepper
    2  cups (8 ounces) shredded cheddar cheese
```

Cook macaroni according to package directions. Meanwhile, in a large saucepan, melt butter. Stir in flour until smooth. Gradually add milk. Bring to a boil; cook and stir for 2 minutes.

Reduce heat; stir in the sour cream, process cheese, Parmesan cheese, salt, mustard and pepper until cheese is melted and smooth.

Drain macaroni; toss with cheddar cheese. Transfer to a greased 3-qt. baking dish. Add cream sauce and mix

Hearty Turkey Casserole

Ham Broccoli Bake

Prep: 15 min. **Bake:** 20 min.

To use up some leftover cooked broccoli, I adapted this recipe from a friend. —Jennifer Shiew, Jetmore, Kansas

- 1-1/4 cups uncooked elbow macaroni
- 1-1/2 cups chopped fresh broccoli
- 1 can (10-3/4 ounces) condensed cream of mushroom soup, undiluted
- 1 cup cubed fully cooked ham
- 1 cup (4 ounces) shredded cheddar cheese
- 1/2 cup shredded part-skim mozzarella cheese
- 1/2 cup milk
- 1 tablespoon dried minced onion
- 1/4 teaspoon pepper
- 1 cup crushed potato chips

Cook macaroni according to package directions. Meanwhile, in a large bowl, combine the broccoli, soup, ham, cheeses, milk, onion and pepper. Drain macaroni; add to ham mixture.

Transfer to a greased 8-in. square baking dish; sprinkle with potato chips. Bake, uncovered, at 350° for 20-25 minutes or until bubbly. **Yield:** 4 servings.

Coq Au Vin

Prep: 20 min. **Bake:** 50 min.

Don't let the name fool you; this upscale dish is deliciously home-style. —Linda Clark, Stoney Creek, Ontario

- 6 medium red potatoes, quartered
- 1/2 cup water
- 2 medium carrots, sliced
- 1 can (10-3/4 ounces) condensed cream of mushroom soup, undiluted
- 1/2 cup white wine *or* chicken broth
- 1-1/2 teaspoons chicken bouillon granules
- 1 teaspoon minced garlic
- 1/2 teaspoon dried parsley flakes
- 1/4 teaspoon dried thyme
- 1/4 teaspoon pepper
- 4 boneless skinless chicken breast halves (6 ounces *each*)
- 1/2 pound sliced fresh mushrooms
- 4 bacon strips, cooked and crumbled
- 1/3 cup chopped green onions

Place potatoes and water in a microwave-safe dish; cover and microwave on high for 3 minutes. Add carrots; cook 4 minutes longer or until vegetables are tender. Drain.

In a large bowl, combine the soup, wine or broth, bouillon, garlic, parsley, thyme and pepper. Cut each chicken breast half into three pieces. Add the chicken, potato mixture, mushrooms, bacon and onions to soup mixture; stir to coat.

Transfer to a greased 13-in. x 9-in. x 2-in. baking dish. Cover and bake at 350° for 50-55 minutes or until chicken juices run clear. **Yield:** 6 servings.

Editor's Note: This recipe was tested in a 1,100-watt microwave.

well. Bake, uncovered, at 350° for 35-40 minutes or until golden brown and bubbly. **Yield:** 6 servings.

Hearty Turkey Casserole

(Pictured above)

Prep: 20 min. **Bake:** 35 min.

You can make this creamy pasta a day ahead and refrigerate it overnight. The next day, all you have to do is pop it in the oven. —Eunice Holmberg, Willmar, Minnesota

- 2 cups uncooked elbow macaroni
- 2 cups cubed cooked turkey breast
- 2 cups milk
- 1 can (10-3/4 ounces) condensed cream of mushroom soup, undiluted
- 1 can (10-3/4 ounces) condensed cream of celery soup, undiluted
- 1 can (8 ounces) sliced water chestnuts, drained
- 1/2 pound process cheese (Velveeta), cubed
- 3 hard-cooked eggs, chopped
- 1 jar (2 ounces) diced pimientos, drained
- 1 teaspoon grated onion

Cook macaroni according to package directions; drain and place in a large bowl. Add the remaining ingredients; mix well.

Transfer to a greased 13-in. x 9-in. x 2-in. baking dish. Bake, uncovered, at 350° for 35-40 minutes or until bubbly. **Yield:** 9 servings.

Golden Pork 'n' Noodles

Stovetop Suppers

GET A HANDLE on mealtime the easy way—grab a saucepan or skillet! This section of family-favorite recipes will let you do just that.

You'll find pleasing pasta dinners, a standout stir-fry and much more. So go ahead—rely on your range. Your family will be glad you did!

Golden Pork 'n' Noodles

(Pictured above)

Prep/Total Time: 30 min.

This hearty pork-and-noodle meal has lots of family-pleasing flavor. A vegetable side dish is the perfect accompaniment. —Nicole Werner, Roseville, Minnesota

 4 cups uncooked egg noodles
 1 pound ground pork
1/2 pound sliced fresh mushrooms
 1 cup chopped green pepper
1/2 cup chopped onion
 2 tablespoons vegetable oil
 1 can (10-3/4 ounces) condensed golden mushroom soup, undiluted
1/2 cup milk
 1 package (3 ounces) cream cheese, cubed
 1 jar (4 ounces) sliced pimientos, drained
1-1/2 teaspoons dried marjoram
3/4 teaspoon salt
1/2 teaspoon pepper

Cook the egg noodles according to the package directions. Meanwhile, in a large skillet, cook the ground pork over medium heat until no longer pink; drain. Keep the pork warm.

In the same skillet, saute the mushrooms, green pepper and onion in oil until crisp-tender. Stir in the soup, milk, cream cheese, pimientos, marjoram, salt and pepper.

Bring to a boil; cook and stir for 2 minutes or until cheese is melted. Drain noodles; stir into skillet. Add pork; heat through. **Yield:** 6 servings.

Skillet Franks

Prep/Total Time: 30 min.

Kids will have as much fun helping to make this all-in-one supper as they will eating it! Plus, cleanup is a cinch because everything goes in a single skillet. The recipe has been in my collection for decades. —Ruth Noland San Jose, California

 1 medium green pepper, julienned
1/2 cup chopped onion
 2 tablespoons butter
 1 pound hot dogs, halved lengthwise and cut into bite-size pieces
 1 can (14-1/2 ounces) diced tomatoes, undrained
 1 cup tomato juice
 1 teaspoon salt
1/2 teaspoon dried marjoram
1/2 teaspoon minced garlic
1/4 teaspoon dried basil
1/8 teaspoon pepper
 3 cups uncooked egg noodles

In a large skillet, saute green pepper and onion in butter until tender. Add the hot dogs, tomatoes, tomato juice, salt, marjoram, garlic, basil and pepper. Bring to a boil; add the noodles. Reduce heat; cover and simmer for 10-12 minutes or until noodles are tender. **Yield:** 6 servings.

Apple-Onion Pork Chops

Prep/Total Time: 30 min.

Everyday ingredients come together in moments for these homey pork chops. I combine apple juice and onion for a delicious main dish. —Lisa Bleich, Flagstaff, Arizona

1/4 cup all-purpose flour
1/2 teaspoon plus 1/8 teaspoon salt, *divided*
1/4 teaspoon plus 1/8 teaspoon pepper, *divided*
 4 boneless pork loin chops (1/2 inch thick and 6 ounces *each*)
 2 tablespoons butter

1 small onion, sliced and separated into rings
1 cup apple juice
1 tablespoon cornstarch
1 tablespoon cold water
1/4 teaspoon browning sauce, optional

In a large resealable plastic bag, combine the flour, 1/2 teaspoon salt and 1/4 teaspoon pepper. Add pork chops and shake to coat. In a large skillet, brown chops on both sides in butter.

Add onion and apple juice. Bring to a boil. Reduce heat; cover and simmer for 7-10 minutes or until the meat juices run clear.

Remove pork chops and keep warm. Combine cornstarch and water until smooth; stir into skillet. Bring to a boil; cook and stir for 1 minute or until thickened. Stir in remaining salt and pepper and browning sauce if desired. Serve with pork chops. **Yield:** 4 servings.

Ravioli Carbonara

Prep/Total Time: 25 min.

Creamy Alfredo sauce tops ravioli in this savory main course. I give it extra appeal with a topping of crisp bacon crumbles. This taste-tempting meal is just five ingredients and a little pepper away! —Ronda Weirich
Liberal, Kansas

1 package (16 ounces) frozen cheese ravioli
8 bacon strips, diced
1 cup prepared Alfredo sauce
1/4 cup milk
2 to 3 teaspoons dried basil
Pepper to taste

Cook ravioli according to package directions. Meanwhile, in a large skillet, cook bacon over medium heat until crisp. Remove to paper towels; drain, reserving 2 teaspoons drippings.

Stir the Alfredo sauce, milk and basil into drippings; cook and stir until heated through. Drain ravioli; add to sauce and toss to coat. Sprinkle with bacon and pepper. **Yield:** 3 servings.

Teriyaki Mushroom Chicken

Prep/Total Time: 25 min.

Fresh mushrooms and onion complement this savory skillet chicken with a rich, teriyaki-flavored sauce. It makes a pretty presentation for friends and family.
—Cheri Casolari, Rinard, Illinois

4 boneless skinless chicken breast halves
   (6 ounces *each*)
5 tablespoons butter, *divided*
4 cups sliced fresh mushrooms
1 cup sliced onion
1/4 cup water
1/4 cup honey teriyaki marinade

In a large skillet over medium heat, cook chicken in 1 tablespoon butter for 5-7 minutes on each side or until juices run clear. Remove and keep warm.

In the same skillet, saute the mushrooms and onion in remaining butter until tender, adding the water and marinade during the last 2 minutes. Return the chicken to the pan; heat through. **Yield:** 4 servings.

Prosciutto Pasta Toss

(Pictured below)

Prep/Total Time: 20 min.

I can't get enough of simple-but-delicious pasta dishes, and this is one of my all-time favorites. I toss together a green salad while the linguine is cooking, then serve up a homemade supper in minutes. To me, dinner doesn't get much better than that! —Laura Murphy-Ogden
Charlotte, North Carolina

1 package (16 ounces) linguine
1/2 cup frozen peas
2 tablespoons minced garlic
1 tablespoon Italian seasoning
1 teaspoon pepper
1/4 cup olive oil
1/2 pound thinly sliced prosciutto *or* deli ham,
   chopped
1/4 cup shredded Parmesan cheese

Cook linguine according to package directions, adding peas during the last 3 minutes. Meanwhile, in a large skillet, saute the garlic, Italian seasoning and pepper in oil for 2-3 minutes or until garlic is tender. Stir in prosciutto.

Drain linguine; add to skillet and toss to coat. Sprinkle with Parmesan cheese. **Yield:** 6 servings.

Prosciutto Pasta Toss

Shrimp Scampi With Lemon Couscous

(Pictured below)

Prep/Total Time: 20 min.

Just a few minutes of prep will get this tasty shrimp dish to the table.   —Diana Santospago, Isle au Haut, Maine

- 1 cup chicken broth
- 3 tablespoons lemon juice, *divided*
- 1 cup uncooked couscous
- 5 tablespoons butter, *divided*
- 3 tablespoons minced fresh parsley, *divided*
- 1 teaspoon grated lemon peel
- 2 tablespoons olive oil
- 1-1/2 teaspoons minced garlic
- 2 pounds cooked jumbo shrimp, peeled and deveined
- 1/3 cup white wine *or* additional chicken broth
- 1/4 teaspoon salt
- 1/8 teaspoon pepper
- 1/4 cup shredded Asiago cheese

In a small saucepan, bring broth and 1 tablespoon lemon juice to a boil. Stir in couscous, 1 tablespoon butter, 1 tablespoon parsley and lemon peel. Cover and remove from the heat; let stand for 5 minutes or until liquid is absorbed.

Meanwhile, in a large skillet, stir oil and remaining butter over medium-high heat until butter is melted.

Add the garlic; cook and stir until tender. Add the shrimp; cook for 1 minute on each side.

Add wine or additional broth, salt, pepper and remaining lemon juice; cook 2-3 minutes longer or until heated through. Serve with couscous. Sprinkle with cheese and remaining parsley. **Yield:** 6 servings.

Pizza Pasta Dinner

Pizza Pasta Dinner

(Pictured above)

Prep/Total Time: 25 min.

With the ever-popular flavor of pizza, this hearty dish can't miss. Plus, it's loaded with fun spiral pasta, veggies, mozzarella and three kinds of meat. No one will leave the table hungry—and they might just be too full for dessert!   —Claudia Malone, Louisville, Kentucky

- 2 cups uncooked spiral pasta
- 1/2 pound ground beef
- 1/2 pound bulk Italian sausage
- 1 small green pepper, chopped
- 1 small onion, chopped
- 1 cup sliced pepperoni
- 1 can (14-1/2 ounces) diced tomatoes, undrained
- 1 jar (14 ounces) spaghetti sauce
- 1 jar (4-1/2 ounces) sliced mushrooms
- 1 can (2-1/4 ounces) chopped ripe olives, drained
- 1 cup (4 ounces) shredded part-skim mozzarella cheese

Cook pasta according to package directions. Meanwhile, in a large skillet, cook the beef, sausage, green pepper and onion until meat is no longer pink; drain. Add the pepperoni, tomatoes, spaghetti sauce, mushrooms and olives; cook and stir for 5 minutes.

Drain pasta; stir into meat mixture. Heat through. Sprinkle with mozzarella cheese. Remove from the heat; cover and let stand until cheese is melted. **Yield:** 6 servings.

Scalloped Potato Skillet

Prep/Total Time: 30 min.

Here's a family-favorite recipe. It cooks in one pan, so cleanup's a snap.   —Barbara Heile, Fortuna, California

Shrimp Scampi with Lemon Couscous

1 tablespoon butter
1 tablespoon brown sugar
1 bone-in fully cooked ham steak (1 pound)
3 cups refrigerated sliced potatoes
1 can (10-3/4 ounces) condensed cream of
   mushroom soup, undiluted
1 cup frozen sliced carrots
2/3 cup milk
1/3 cup water
1/4 cup chopped onion
1/4 teaspoon coarsely ground pepper

In a large skillet, melt butter and brown sugar. Cut ham into four serving-size portions; discard bone. Add ham to skillet; cook over medium-high heat for 2-3 minutes or until browned. Remove and keep warm.

In the same skillet, combine the potatoes, soup, carrots, milk, water, onion and pepper. Cover and cook over medium heat for 10-12 minutes or until vegetables are tender. Return ham to the pan; cover and cook for 5 minutes or until heated through. **Yield:** 4 servings.

Mandarin Chicken

Prep/Total Time: 30 min.

This tropical medley was one of my mother-in-law's specialties. Now it's a mainstay in our household as well.
—Lynda Heminger, Yankton, South Dakota

☑ Uses less fat, sugar or salt. Includes Nutrition Facts and Diabetic Exchanges.

6 boneless skinless chicken breast halves
   (6 ounces *each*)
1 tablespoon olive oil
2 tablespoons all-purpose flour
1/2 cup chicken broth
1-1/2 cups orange juice
1 medium green pepper, chopped
1 medium sweet red pepper, chopped
1 can (11 ounces) mandarin oranges, drained
1 cup pineapple chunks
1/3 cup golden raisins
1/8 to 1/4 teaspoon crushed red pepper flakes
1/8 teaspoon salt
1/8 teaspoon pepper
Hot cooked rice, optional

Flatten chicken to 1/2-in. thickness. In a large skillet, cook chicken in oil for 4-5 minutes on each side or until juices run clear. Remove chicken and keep warm.

In a small bowl, combine flour and broth until smooth; stir into skillet. Add the orange juice, peppers, oranges, pineapple, raisins, pepper flakes, salt and pepper. Bring to a boil; cook and stir for 2 minutes or until thickened. Return chicken to the pan; heat through. Serve with rice if desired. **Yield:** 6 servings.

Nutrition Facts: 1 chicken breast half with 2/3 cup pineapple mixture (calculated without rice) equals 320 calories, 6 g fat (1 g saturated fat), 94 mg cholesterol, 213 mg sodium, 29 g carbohydrate, 2 g fiber, 36 g protein. **Diabetic Exchanges:** 5 very lean meat, 1-1/2 fruit, 1/2 starch, 1/2 fat.

Sweet-and-Sour Beef With Broccoli

(Pictured below and on page 242)

Prep/Total Time: 30 min.

Our Test Kitchen re-created this classic Chinese dish using a variety of veggies and inexpensive ground beef.

☑ Uses less fat, sugar or salt. Includes Nutrition Facts.

1 can (20 ounces) unsweetened pineapple
   tidbits
2 tablespoons cornstarch
1 cup reduced-sodium beef broth
1/4 cup reduced-sodium soy sauce
2 teaspoons minced fresh gingerroot
1 teaspoon minced garlic
2-1/2 cups uncooked instant rice
2 cups fresh broccoli florets
1/2 pound sliced fresh mushrooms
1 medium sweet red pepper, julienned
1 can (8 ounces) sliced water chestnuts,
   drained
1 tablespoon sesame oil
1 pound lean ground beef

Drain pineapple, reserving juice; set pineapple aside. In a small bowl, combine the cornstarch, broth, soy sauce, ginger, garlic and reserved juice until blended; set aside.

Cook rice according to package directions. Meanwhile, in a large skillet, stir-fry the broccoli, mushrooms, red pepper and water chestnuts in oil for 3-5 minutes or until crisp-tender; remove and set aside. In the same pan, cook beef over medium heat until no longer pink; drain.

Stir cornstarch mixture and add to the skillet. Bring to a boil; cook and stir for 1-2 minutes or until thickened. Stir in the reserved vegetable mixture and pineapple; heat through. Serve over rice. **Yield:** 6 servings.

Nutrition Facts: 1-1/3 cups beef mixture with 3/4 cup rice equals 386 calories, 8 g fat (3 g saturated fat), 37 mg cholesterol, 822 mg sodium, 57 g carbohydrate, 4 g fiber, 21 g protein.

Sweet-and-Sour Beef with Broccoli

Chapter 17

Fast, Delicious...and Nutritious

CAN DISHES as delicious as Bean 'n' Rice Burritos, Barbecued Potato Wedges, Chocolate Cherry Trifle and Tasty Blueberry Muffins really be quick to prepare and lighter, too? This chapter proves it's true!

Each mouth-watering recipe includes complete Nutrition Facts, and most have Diabetic Exchanges as well. So you can see at a glance that every dish is lower in fat, sugar and salt.

But your family will never guess they're eating lightened-up fare when they sample these scrumptious main dishes, sides, desserts and snacks. (All of the good-for-you foods throughout this book are flagged with a red checkmark in the indexes beginning on page 316.)

LIGHT AND LIVELY. Vegetable Curried Rice and Crumb-Coated Red Snapper (recipes on p. 261).

Parmesan Vegetable Saute
Chicken with Mustard Sauce

 All recipes in this chapter use less fat, sugar or salt and include Nutrition Facts and Diabetic Exchanges.

Parmesan Vegetable Saute

(Pictured above)

Prep/Total Time: 20 min.

One evening when I didn't have enough time to make pasta primavera, I came up with this recipe. It makes a savory and hearty veggie dish. —*Caroline Sperry*
Shelby Township, Michigan

 2 medium zucchini, cut into 1/4-inch slices
1-1/4 cups sliced fresh mushrooms
 1/2 cup chopped green onions
  1 teaspoon minced garlic
 1/2 teaspoon salt
 1/4 teaspoon pepper
  2 tablespoons olive oil
  1 medium tomato, chopped
  2 tablespoons shredded Parmesan cheese

In a large skillet, saute the zucchini, mushrooms, onions, garlic, salt and pepper in oil for 6-8 minutes or until tender. Remove from the heat; stir in tomato. Sprinkle with Parmesan cheese. **Yield:** 4 servings.

 Nutrition Facts: 3/4 cup equals 104 calories, 8 g fat (1 g saturated fat), 2 mg cholesterol, 347 mg sodium, 7 g carbohydrate, 2 g fiber, 4 g protein. **Diabetic Exchanges:** 1-1/2 vegetable, 1-1/2 fat.

Chicken with Mustard Sauce

(Pictured above)

Prep: 15 min. **Cook:** 25 min.

This luscious chicken entree is truly something special. Dijon mustard and lemon peel add a tangy taste to the perfectly seasoned sauce—and it all goes together in minutes!
—*Coleen Deon, Dover Plains, New York*

  3 tablespoons all-purpose flour
 1/2 teaspoon dried marjoram
 1/2 teaspoon dried thyme
 1/2 teaspoon pepper
  4 boneless skinless chicken breast halves
   (4 ounces *each*)
  2 teaspoons olive oil
 1/2 cup white wine *or* reduced-sodium chicken broth
  1 cup reduced-sodium chicken broth
  2 tablespoons Dijon mustard
 1/4 teaspoon grated lemon peel
  3 tablespoons fat-free milk

In a large resealable plastic bag, combine the flour, marjoram, thyme and pepper; set aside 1 tablespoon flour mixture. Add chicken to the bag, a few pieces at a time, and shake to coat.

In a large skillet, cook chicken in oil over medium heat for 5-7 minutes on each side or until juices run clear. Remove and keep warm. Stir wine or chicken broth into the pan. Bring to a boil. Reduce heat; simmer, uncovered, for 6-8 minutes or until reduced by half. Stir in the chicken broth, mustard and lemon peel.

Place reserved flour mixture in a small bowl; stir in milk until smooth. Stir into broth mixture. Bring to a boil. Reduce heat; simmer, uncovered, for 2-3 minutes or until thickened. Return chicken to skillet; cook for 5 minutes or until heated through. **Yield:** 4 servings.

Nutrition Facts: 1 chicken breast half with 1/4 cup sauce equals 202 calories, 6 g fat (1 g saturated fat), 63 mg cholesterol, 407 mg sodium, 7 g carbohydrate, trace fiber, 25 g protein. **Diabetic Exchanges:** 3 lean meat, 1/2 starch.

Three-Fruit Smoothies

Prep/Total Time: 10 min.

Blend some ice cubes into a mix of fruits, yogurt and honey, and you'll have these super 10-minute smoothies. They're terrific as a quick breakfast or afternoon pick-me-up, but you'll want to make them even when you're not short on time. —Sarah Hulslander, Arlington, Texas

>   2 cartons (6 ounces *each*) fat-free
>   reduced-sugar cherry-vanilla yogurt
>   1 small banana, halved
>   3/4 cup fresh *or* frozen blueberries
>   1 tablespoon honey
>   15 ice cubes

In a blender, combine the yogurt, banana, blueberries and honey; cover and process until smooth. While processing, add a few ice cubes at a time until mixture achieves desired thickness. Pour into chilled glasses; serve immediately. **Yield:** 3 servings.

Nutrition Facts: 1 cup equals 130 calories, trace fat (trace saturated fat), 2 mg cholesterol, 69 mg sodium, 28 g carbohydrate, 2 g fiber, 6 g protein. **Diabetic Exchange:** 2 fruit.

Lemon Feta Chicken

Prep/Total Time: 25 min.

Just four ingredients give this moist chicken loads of flavor. My husband and I prepare this entree often, and we never tire of it.   —Ann Cain, Morrill, Nebraska

>   4 boneless skinless chicken breast halves
>   (4 ounces *each*)
>   2 to 3 tablespoons lemon juice
>   1/4 cup crumbled feta cheese
>   1 teaspoon dried oregano
>   1/4 to 1/2 teaspoon pepper

Place chicken in a 13-in. x 9-in. x 2-in. baking dish coated with nonstick cooking spray. Pour lemon juice over chicken; sprinkle with feta cheese, oregano and pepper.

Bake, uncovered, at 400° for 20-25 minutes or until chicken juices run clear. **Yield:** 4 servings.

Nutrition Facts: 1 chicken breast half equals 143 calories, 4 g fat (1 g saturated fat), 66 mg cholesterol, 122 mg sodium, 1 g carbohydrate, trace fiber, 24 g protein. **Diabetic Exchanges:** 3-1/2 very lean meat, 1/2 fat.

Gingered Beef Stir-Fry

(Pictured below)

Prep/Total Time: 20 min.

Stir-fry is popular in our household. My oldest son especially likes this beef recipe featuring fresh ginger, sweet red peppers and bright-green snap peas. —Debbie Williams Ashland, Ohio

> 1-1/2 teaspoons sugar
>   1 teaspoon cornstarch
>   1/4 cup cold water
>   3 tablespoons reduced-sodium soy sauce
>   2 teaspoons sesame oil, *divided*
>   1 beef flank steak (1 pound), cut into thin
>   strips
>   1 jar (8 ounces) whole baby corn, drained
>   1/4 cup julienned sweet red pepper
>   2 teaspoons minced fresh gingerroot
>   2 teaspoons minced garlic
>   1/4 pound fresh sugar snap peas
>   3 cups hot cooked rice

In a small bowl, combine sugar and cornstarch. Stir in the water, soy sauce and 1 teaspoon oil until smooth; set aside. In a large nonstick skillet or wok, stir-fry beef in remaining oil for 4-5 minutes or until no longer pink.

Add the corn, red pepper, ginger and garlic; stir-fry for 2-3 minutes or until the vegetables are crisp-tender. Add the peas; stir-fry 30 seconds longer. Stir the soy sauce mixture and add to the pan. Bring to a boil; cook and stir for 2 minutes or until thickened. Serve with rice. **Yield:** 4 servings.

Nutrition Facts: 1 cup beef mixture with 3/4 cup rice equals 377 calories, 12 g fat (4 g saturated fat), 48 mg cholesterol, 618 mg sodium, 41 g carbohydrate, 2 g fiber, 25 g protein. **Diabetic Exchanges:** 3 lean meat, 2 starch, 1 vegetable, 1/2 fat.

Gingered Beef Stir-Fry

Strawberry Shortcake Dessert

(3 g saturated fat), 11 mg cholesterol, 192 mg sodium, 29 g carbohydrate, 1 g fiber, 2 g protein. **Diabetic Exchanges:** 2 starch, 1/2 fat.

Pork 'n' Potato Skillet

(Pictured below)

Prep/Total Time: 30 min.

This scrumptious skillet dinner makes the ideal hurry-up entree for a hungry family. Round out the meal with steamed vegetables or a crisp green salad.
—*Mary Tallman, Arbor Vitae, Wisconsin*

    4 **boneless pork loin chops (1 inch thick and 4 ounces *each*)**
 1/4 **teaspoon pepper**
    1 **tablespoon olive oil**
    4 **medium red potatoes, thinly sliced**
    1 **medium onion, sliced**
    1 **teaspoon dried oregano**
    1 **cup chicken broth**
 1/2 **cup diced roasted sweet red peppers**

Sprinkle the pork chops with pepper. In a large skillet, brown the chops in oil on both sides; drain. Remove and keep warm.

In the same skillet, saute the potatoes, onion and oregano for 6-8 minutes or until potatoes are almost tender. Stir in broth and red peppers; bring to a boil.

Top with pork chops. Reduce heat; cover and simmer for 10-15 minutes or until potatoes are tender and meat juices run clear, stirring occasionally. **Yield:** 4 servings.

Nutrition Facts: 1 serving (prepared with reduced-sodium broth) equals 292 calories, 10 g fat (3 g saturated fat), 55 mg cholesterol, 297 mg sodium, 24 g carbohydrate, 3 g fiber, 26 g protein. **Diabetic Exchanges:** 3 lean meat, 1 starch, 1 vegetable.

Strawberry Shortcake Dessert

(Pictured above)

Prep: 10 min. **Bake:** 30 min. + chilling

A co-worker gave me this rave-winning recipe. I've tried it with other fruits, including blueberries, cherries and peaches. —*Michele Trachier, Pasadena, Texas*

    1 **package (18-1/4 ounces) white cake mix**
1-1/3 **cups water**
 1/4 **cup unsweetened applesauce**
    2 **egg whites**
    1 **egg**
    1 **package (.6 ounce) sugar-free strawberry gelatin**
    2 **cups boiling water**
    1 **package (16 ounces) frozen unsweetened whole strawberries, thawed, drained and sliced**
    1 **carton (16 ounces) frozen reduced-fat whipped topping, thawed**
 10 **fresh strawberries, halved**

In a large mixing bowl, combine the dry cake mix, water, applesauce, egg whites and egg; beat on low speed for 30 seconds. Beat on medium for 2 minutes.

Pour into a 13-in. x 9-in. x 2-in. baking dish coated with nonstick cooking spray. Bake at 350° for 30-35 minutes or until a toothpick inserted near the center comes out clean.

In a large bowl, dissolve gelatin in boiling water. Stir in strawberries. Using a sharp knife, make a diamond pattern in the top of the hot cake; immediately pour gelatin mixture over cake. Cool on a wire rack. Refrigerate for at least 6 hours. Spread with whipped topping. Garnish with fresh strawberries. **Yield:** 20 servings.

Nutrition Facts: 1 piece equals 179 calories, 5 g fat

Pork 'n' Potato Skillet

Roasted Vegetables with Orzo
Barbecued Potato Wedges

Roasted Vegetables with Orzo

(Pictured at left)

Prep/Total Time: 30 min.

What's great about this delicious and versatile dish is that once you get it started, it's relatively hands-free. I often substitute a variety of seasonal vegetables.
—Sam Stusek, Annapolis, Maryland

```
    1 cup uncooked orzo pasta
    1 cup cherry tomatoes
  1/2 cup each chopped green and sweet red
        pepper
  1/4 cup chopped onion
    2 tablespoons olive oil
1-3/4 teaspoons minced garlic
  1/2 teaspoon salt
  1/4 to 1/2 teaspoon pepper
```

Cook orzo according to package directions. Meanwhile, in an ungreased 2-qt. baking dish, combine the remaining ingredients. Bake, uncovered, at 450° for 15-20 minutes or until vegetables are tender, stirring occasionally. Drain orzo; stir into vegetable mixture. **Yield:** 6 servings.

Nutrition Facts: 2/3 cup equals 178 calories, 5 g fat (1 g saturated fat), 0 cholesterol, 202 mg sodium, 28 g carbohydrate, 2 g fiber, 5 g protein. **Diabetic Exchanges:** 2 starch, 1/2 fat.

Spinach Feta Frittata

Prep/Total Time: 30 min.

When I want something special and substantial for breakfast, I rely on this full-flavored egg entree for a family-pleasing meal. —Laura Fall-Sutton, Buhl, Idaho

```
    6 egg whites
    3 eggs
    2 tablespoons water
  1/2 teaspoon coarsely ground pepper
  1/4 teaspoon salt
  1/2 cup chopped onion
  1/2 teaspoon minced garlic
    2 tablespoons olive oil
    2 medium red potatoes, cut into 1/4-inch cubes
    1 package (10 ounces) frozen chopped
        spinach, thawed and squeezed dry
  3/4 cup crumbled feta cheese
    2 tablespoons minced fresh basil
```

In a bowl, whisk the egg whites, eggs, water, pepper and salt; set aside. In a 10-in. ovenproof skillet, saute onion and garlic in oil for 2 minutes. Add potatoes; cook and stir until almost tender, about 10 minutes. Reduce heat; sprinkle with spinach, feta cheese and basil.

Top with egg mixture. Cover and cook for 4-6 minutes or until nearly set. Uncover; broil 3-4 in. from the heat for 2-3 minutes or until eggs are completely set. Let stand for 5 minutes. Cut into wedges. **Yield:** 6 servings.

Nutrition Facts: 1 wedge equals 178 calories, 9 g fat (3 g saturated fat), 114 mg cholesterol, 358 mg sodium, 12 g carbohydrate, 3 g fiber, 12 g protein. **Diabetic Exchanges:** 2 vegetable, 1-1/2 fat, 1 lean meat.

Barbecued Potato Wedges

(Pictured above)

Prep: 10 min. **Bake:** 25 min.

So easy to prepare, these toasty roasted potato wedges go well with just about any meat entree. They are a year-round favorite at our house. —Karen McRowe, Avon, Ohio

```
  2 pounds small red potatoes, cut into wedges
  2 tablespoons butter, melted
  1 tablespoon honey
  3 teaspoons chili powder
1/2 teaspoon salt
1/4 teaspoon garlic powder
1/4 teaspoon pepper
```

Place the potatoes in a 15-in. x 10-in. x 1-in. baking pan coated with nonstick cooking spray. Drizzle with butter and honey. Sprinkle with chili powder, salt, garlic powder and pepper; toss to coat.

Bake, uncovered, at 450° for 25-30 minutes or until potatoes are tender and golden brown, stirring once. **Yield:** 6 servings.

Nutrition Facts: 1 cup equals 158 calories, 4 g fat (2 g saturated fat), 10 mg cholesterol, 258 mg sodium, 28 g carbohydrate, 3 g fiber, 3 g protein. **Diabetic Exchange:** 2 starch.

Fun Fruit Dessert

(Pictured below)

Prep/Total Time: 20 min.

Our Test Kitchen staff created this colorful, refreshing dish that's welcome anytime. Served with a touch of chocolate, it makes an elegant yet kid-friendly treat.

> 1 cup vanilla yogurt
> 1 tablespoon honey
> 1 to 2 tablespoons minced fresh mint
> 3/4 cup chopped peeled peaches *or* nectarines
> 1-1/2 teaspoons orange juice
> 3/4 cup chopped fresh strawberries
> 3/4 cup fresh raspberries
> 3/4 cup fresh blueberries
> 1 tablespoon sugar
> 1 package (3.78 ounces) curved chocolate slices (Swoops)

In a small bowl, combine yogurt, honey and mint. Cover; refrigerate until serving.

Just before serving, place peaches in a large bowl; sprinkle with orange juice. Add the berries. Sprinkle with sugar; toss gently. Using a slotted spoon, transfer fruit to a serving bowl. Serve with yogurt sauce and chocolate slices. **Yield:** 6 servings.

Nutrition Facts: 1/2 cup fruit with 2 tablespoons yogurt sauce and 3 chocolate slices equals 191 calories, 7 g fat (4 g saturated fat), 4 mg cholesterol, 93 mg sodium, 29 g carbohydrate, 3 g fiber, 4 g protein. **Diabetic Exchanges:** 1 starch, 1 fruit, 1 fat.

Colorful Lentil Salad

Prep: 30 min. + chilling

You'll love the refreshing color and taste of this versatile salad...and the fact that it's on the healthier side, too. Store any leftover dried lentils in an airtight container for up to 1 year, then use them to simmer up soups, stews and more.
—Martha Pollock, Oregonia, Ohio

> 5 cups plus 2 tablespoons water, *divided*
> 1 cup dried lentils, rinsed
> 3 tablespoons olive oil
> 2 tablespoons balsamic vinegar
> 1 teaspoon Dijon mustard
> 1/2 teaspoon salt
> 1/2 teaspoon sugar
> 1/2 teaspoon dried basil
> 1/2 teaspoon dried oregano
> 1/4 teaspoon minced garlic
> 1/4 teaspoon pepper
> 1 small cucumber, chopped
> 1/2 cup shredded carrot
> 1/2 cup finely chopped sweet red pepper
> 1/4 cup chopped sweet onion
> 1/4 cup minced fresh cilantro

In a large saucepan, bring 5 cups water and lentils to a boil. Reduce heat; cover and simmer for 20-25 minutes or until tender. Drain and rinse in cold water. Place lentils in a large bowl; cool.

Fun Fruit Dessert

Meanwhile, in a jar with a tight-fitting lid, combine the oil, vinegar, mustard, salt, sugar, basil, oregano, garlic, pepper and remaining water; shake well.

Add the cucumber, carrot, red pepper, onion and cilantro to lentils; toss to combine. Add dressing; gently toss to coat. Cover and refrigerate for 2 hours before serving. **Yield:** 6 servings.

Nutrition Facts: 2/3 cup equals 188 calories, 7 g fat (1 g saturated fat), 0 cholesterol, 227 mg sodium, 23 g carbohydrate, 11 g fiber, 10 g protein. **Diabetic Exchanges:** 1-1/2 fat, 1 starch, 1 vegetable.

Chipotle Apricot Chicken

Prep/Total Time: 30 min.

Although chipotle peppers may be unfamiliar to some home cooks, these peppers are worth exploring—especially when you have a recipe like this one! Their warm, smoky flavor really complements the apricots in this absolutely wonderful entree.
—Trisha Kruse, Eagle, Idaho

   4 boneless skinless chicken breast halves
     (6 ounces *each*)
   2 tablespoons butter
   2 fresh apricots, thinly sliced
 1/2 cup chicken broth
 1/3 cup apricot preserves
   2 tablespoons chopped chipotle pepper in
     adobo sauce
 1/2 teaspoon salt
Hot cooked rice, optional

In a large skillet, brown chicken in butter on both sides. Combine the apricots, broth, preserves, chipotle pepper and salt; pour over chicken.

Bring to a boil. Reduce heat; simmer, uncovered, for 15-20 minutes or until chicken juices run clear and sauce is thickened. Serve with rice if desired. **Yield:** 4 servings.

Nutrition Facts: 1 chicken breast half (calculated without rice) equals 312 calories, 10 g fat (5 g saturated fat), 109 mg cholesterol, 612 mg sodium, 20 g carbohydrate, 1 g fiber, 35 g protein. **Diabetic Exchanges:** 5 very lean meat, 1 starch, 1 fat.

About Apricots

EATEN ALONE as a snack and used in recipes such as Chipotle Apricot Chicken (above), apricots are a dense, sweet fruit with a smooth skin. They are generally available from May through August.

Select apricots that are plump and fairly firm, not hard, and are orange-yellow to orange in color. Avoid apricots that have blemishes or soft spots...or that have a pale-yellow or greenish-yellow color.

Firm apricots should be stored at room temperature. Once an apricot begins to yield to gentle pressure, store it in your refrigerator for 2-3 days.

Chocolate Chip Cookies

Chocolate Chip Cookies

(Pictured above)

Prep: 15 min. **Bake:** 10 min./batch

After trying several low-fat chocolate chip cookie recipes that were puffy and cake-like, I experimented and came up with these. I don't let anyone know they're light, and no one can tell!   —Bethany Thayer, Troutville, Virginia

 1/2 cup reduced-fat margarine
 3/4 cup sugar
 3/4 cup packed brown sugar
   2 eggs
 1/4 cup fat-free plain yogurt
   2 teaspoons vanilla extract
2-1/2 cups all-purpose flour
   1 teaspoon baking soda
   1 teaspoon salt
1-1/2 cups miniature semisweet chocolate chips
 1/2 cup chopped walnuts, toasted

In a large mixing bowl, lightly cream the margarine and sugars. Add eggs, one at a time, beating well after each addition. Beat in yogurt and vanilla. Combine the flour, baking soda and salt; gradually add to creamed mixture. Stir in chocolate chips and walnuts.

Drop by heaping tablespoonfuls 2 in. apart onto baking sheets coated with nonstick cooking spray. Bake at 375° for 8-10 minutes or until golden brown. Remove to wire racks. **Yield:** 4 dozen.

Editor's Note: This recipe was tested with Parkay Light stick margarine.

Nutrition Facts: 2 cookies equals 190 calories, 7 g fat (2 g saturated fat), 18 mg cholesterol, 187 mg sodium, 30 g carbohydrate, 1 g fiber, 3 g protein. **Diabetic Exchanges:** 2 starch, 1/2 fat.

Veggie Chowder

Baby Carrots with Almonds

Prep/Total Time: 10 min.

I often prepare these not-so-candied carrots for my husband, who is diabetic. The simple side dish is not only a great choice for him, but it's also one that everyone enjoys because of the toasted almonds and slight sweetness. —Jane Kittle
Columbia Cross Roads, Pennsylvania

1 package (16 ounces) fresh baby carrots
2 tablespoons water
2 tablespoons slivered almonds, toasted
1 tablespoon sugar
1 tablespoon butter
1/8 teaspoon salt

Place the carrots and water in a microwave-safe bowl. Cover and microwave on high for 4-6 minutes or until tender; drain. Stir in the remaining ingredients. **Yield:** 4 servings.

Editor's Note: This recipe was tested in a 1,100-watt microwave.

Nutrition Facts: 3/4 cup equals 96 calories, 5 g fat (2 g saturated fat), 8 mg cholesterol, 191 mg sodium, 13 g carbohydrate, 2 g fiber, 1 g protein. **Diabetic Exchanges:** 2 vegetable, 1 fat.

Apple Bran Muffins

Prep: 15 min. **Bake:** 20 min.

A hint of vanilla and apple sweetens these moist and tender muffins. I can bake up a batch in no time flat for a hearty morning treat. —Tony Flores, Edinburg, Texas

2-1/2 cups bran flakes, crushed
1-1/4 cups all-purpose flour
2 tablespoons sugar
1 teaspoon baking powder
1/4 teaspoon baking soda
1/2 teaspoon salt
1 egg
3/4 cup 1% buttermilk
1/4 cup canola oil
1/4 cup maple syrup
1/2 teaspoon vanilla extract
1 medium McIntosh apple, peeled and shredded

In a large bowl, combine the bran flakes, flour, sugar, baking powder, baking soda and salt. In another bowl, whisk the egg, buttermilk, oil, syrup and vanilla. Stir into dry ingredients just until moistened. Fold in apple.

Coat muffin cups with nonstick cooking spray or use paper liners; fill three-fourths full with batter. Bake at 375° for 20-25 minutes or until a toothpick comes out clean. Cool for 5 minutes before removing from pan to a wire rack. Serve warm. **Yield:** 1 dozen.

Nutrition Facts: 1 muffin equals 160 calories, 6 g fat (1 g saturated fat), 18 mg cholesterol, 241 mg sodium, 26 g carbohydrate, 2 g fiber, 3 g protein. **Diabetic Exchanges:** 1-1/2 starch, 1 fat.

Veggie Chowder

(Pictured above)

Prep/Total Time: 30 min.

This brothy soup makes for a veggie-filled delight. Serve the fast-to-fix chowder alongside sandwiches for a satisfying light meal. —Vicki Kerr, Portland, Maine

2 cups reduced-sodium chicken broth
2 cups cubed peeled potatoes
1 cup chopped carrots
1/2 cup chopped onion
1 can (14-3/4 ounces) cream-style corn
1 can (12 ounces) fat-free evaporated milk
3/4 cup shredded reduced-fat cheddar cheese
1/2 cup sliced fresh mushrooms
1/4 teaspoon pepper
2 tablespoons real bacon bits

In a large saucepan, combine the chicken broth, potatoes, carrots and onion. Bring to a boil. Reduce the heat; simmer, uncovered, for 10-15 minutes or until the vegetables are tender.

Add the corn, milk, cheese, mushrooms and pepper. Cook and stir 4-6 minutes longer or until heated through. Sprinkle with bacon. **Yield:** 7 servings.

Nutrition Facts: 1 cup equals 178 calories, 3 g fat (2 g saturated fat), 12 mg cholesterol, 554 mg sodium, 29 g carbohydrate, 2 g fiber, 11 g protein. **Diabetic Exchanges:** 2 starch, 1/2 fat.

Crumb-Coated Red Snapper

(Pictured below and on page 252)

Prep/Total Time: 30 min.

I reel in compliments with these moist, crispy fish fillets whenever I serve them. The effortless bread-crumb coating gets jazzed up with Parmesan cheese and lemon-pepper seasoning. It's a wonderful treatment for the red snapper.
—Charlotte Elliott, Neenah, Wisconsin

1/2 cup dry bread crumbs
  2 tablespoons grated Parmesan cheese
  1 teaspoon lemon-pepper seasoning
1/4 teaspoon salt
  4 red snapper fillets (6 ounces *each*)
  2 tablespoons olive oil

In a shallow bowl, combine the dry bread crumbs, grated Parmesan cheese, lemon-pepper seasoning and salt; add the red snapper fillets to the mixture, one at a time, and turn to coat.

In a heavy skillet over medium heat, cook fillets in oil in batches for 4-5 minutes on each side or until fish flakes easily with a fork. **Yield:** 4 servings.

Nutrition Facts: 1 fillet equals 288 calories, 10 g fat (2 g saturated fat), 62 mg cholesterol, 498 mg sodium, 10 g carbohydrate, trace fiber, 36 g protein. **Diabetic Exchanges:** 5 very lean meat, 1 fat, 1/2 starch.

Vegetable Curried Rice

(Pictured below and on page 252)

Prep/Total Time: 30 min.

With mild curry flavor, this colorful side complements a range of entrees. *—Frances Easton, Warrenton, Virginia*

1/2 cup uncooked long grain rice
1/3 cup chopped onion
  1 tablespoon olive oil
  1 cup reduced-sodium chicken broth *or* vegetable broth
1/2 teaspoon curry powder
1/4 teaspoon salt
1/8 teaspoon ground turmeric
1/3 cup frozen corn, thawed
1/3 cup frozen peas, thawed
1/4 cup slivered almonds, toasted

In a small saucepan, cook rice and onion in oil until rice is lightly browned and onion is tender. Stir in the broth, curry powder, salt and turmeric. Bring to a boil. Reduce heat; cover and simmer for 12 minutes.

Stir in corn and peas. Cover and simmer 3-6 minutes longer or until rice and vegetables are tender. Sprinkle with almonds. **Yield:** 4 servings.

Nutrition Facts: 1/2 cup equals 184 calories, 7 g fat (1 g saturated fat), 0 cholesterol, 318 mg sodium, 26 g carbohydrate, 2 g fiber, 5 g protein. **Diabetic Exchanges:** 1-1/2 starch, 1-1/2 fat.

Crumb-Coated Red Snapper
Vegetable Curried Rice

Bean 'n' Rice Burritos

(Pictured below)

Prep/Total Time: 25 min.

These hearty burritos can be assembled in a jiffy. With brown rice and beans, the satisfying sandwiches are sure to fill you up. —Kim Hardison, Maitland, Florida

1-1/2 cups water
1-1/2 cups uncooked instant brown rice
   1 medium green pepper, diced
  1/2 cup chopped onion
   1 teaspoon minced garlic
   1 tablespoon olive oil
   1 tablespoon chili powder
   1 teaspoon ground cumin
  1/8 teaspoon crushed red pepper flakes
   1 can (15 ounces) black beans, rinsed and drained
   8 flour tortillas (8 inches), warmed
   1 cup salsa
Reduced-fat shredded cheddar cheese and reduced-fat sour cream, optional

In a small saucepan, bring water to a boil. Add rice. Return to a boil. Reduce heat; cover and simmer for 5 minutes. Remove from the heat. Let stand for 5 minutes or until water is absorbed.

Meanwhile, in a large skillet, saute the green pepper, onion and garlic in oil for 3-4 minutes or until tender. Stir in the chili powder, cumin and pepper flakes until combined. Add beans and rice; cook and stir for 4-6 minutes or until heated through.

Spoon about 1/2 cup of filling off-center on each tortilla; top with 2 tablespoons salsa. Fold sides and ends over filling and roll up. Serve with cheese and sour cream if desired. **Yield:** 8 servings.

Nutrition Facts: 1 burrito (calculated without cheese and sour cream) equals 290 calories, 6 g fat (1 g saturated fat), 0 cholesterol, 504 mg sodium, 51 g carbohydrate, 6 g fiber, 11 g protein.

Bean 'n' Rice Burritos

Fresh Fruit Parfaits

Prep/Total Time: 30 min.

I fix this simple recipe when I want to prepare something impressive for guests. It's a low-calorie breakfast that seems indulgent. —Karin Christian, Plano, Texas

   4 ounces reduced-fat mixed berry yogurt
  3/4 cup reduced-fat whipped topping
   1 cup sliced ripe banana
   1 cup sliced fresh strawberries
   1 cup cubed fresh pineapple
   1 cup fresh blueberries
   4 whole strawberries

In a small bowl, combine yogurt and whipped topping; set aside 4 teaspoons for topping. Spoon half of the remaining yogurt mixture into four parfait glasses; layer with half of the banana, sliced strawberries, pineapple and blueberries. Repeat layers.

Top each parfait with reserved yogurt mixture and a whole strawberry. Chill until serving. **Yield:** 4 servings.

Nutrition Facts: 1 parfait equals 149 calories, 2 g fat (2 g saturated fat), 2 mg cholesterol, 22 mg sodium, 31 g carbohydrate, 4 g fiber, 2 g protein. **Diabetic Exchanges:** 2 fruit, 1/2 fat.

Cherry-Almond Drop Scones

Prep/Total Time: 30 min.

Studded with dried cherries and crunchy almonds, these golden brown goodies are surprisingly easy to whip up. Pair them with mugs of steaming hot chocolate, coffee or tea for a cold-weather treat that'll warm you heart and soul.

—Helen Phillips, Eaton, Colorado

2-1/4 cups all-purpose flour
   2 tablespoons sugar
2-1/4 teaspoons baking powder
  1/2 teaspoon baking soda
  1/2 teaspoon salt
   1 cup reduced-fat vanilla yogurt
  1/4 cup butter, melted
   1 egg, lightly beaten
  1/4 teaspoon almond extract
  1/2 cup dried cherries, chopped
  1/2 cup slivered almonds

In a large bowl, combine the flour, sugar, baking powder, baking soda and salt. In another bowl, combine the yogurt, butter, egg and extract. Stir into dry ingredients just until moistened. Fold in cherries and almonds.

Drop by heaping tablespoonfuls 2 in. apart onto a baking sheet coated with nonstick cooking spray. Bake at 400° for 15-18 minutes or until lightly browned. Remove to wire racks. Serve warm. **Yield:** 14 scones.

Nutrition Facts: 1 scone equals 166 calories, 6 g fat (2 g saturated fat), 25 mg cholesterol, 243 mg sodium, 24 g carbohydrate, 1 g fiber, 4 g protein. **Diabetic Exchanges:** 1 starch, 1 fat, 1/2 fruit.

Tasty Blueberry Muffins

Prep: 15 min. **Bake:** 20 min.

This is a wonderful recipe that can be mixed in minutes the night before or in the morning for a speedy breakfast. The oats and orange juice give the muffins unique flavor, and the applesauce makes them a bit lighter.
—Beth Oliver, Waterford, Wisconsin

```
1-1/2 cups all-purpose flour
  1/2 cup quick-cooking oats
  1/2 cup sugar
1-1/4 teaspoons baking powder
  1/2 teaspoon salt
  1/4 teaspoon baking soda
  1/2 cup orange juice
  1/4 cup egg substitute
  1/4 cup unsweetened applesauce
  1/4 cup canola oil
    1 cup fresh blueberries
```

In a large bowl, combine the first six ingredients. Combine the orange juice, egg substitute, applesauce and oil; stir into dry ingredients just until moistened. Fold in blueberries.

Coat muffin cups with nonstick cooking spray; fill half full with batter. Bake at 400° for 18-22 minutes or until a toothpick comes out clean. Cool for 5 minutes before removing from pan to a wire rack. Serve warm. **Yield:** 1 dozen.

Nutrition Facts: 1 muffin equals 159 calories, 5 g fat (trace saturated fat), 0 cholesterol, 177 mg sodium, 26 g carbohydrate, 1 g fiber, 3 g protein. **Diabetic Exchanges:** 1 starch, 1 fat, 1/2 fruit.

Oven-Barbecued Pork Tenderloins

Prep: 5 min. **Bake:** 35 min.

These lean but luscious tenderloins are popular with my friends and family. Featuring a cayenne-spiced barbecue sauce, the pork has great taste and doesn't seem "light."
—Ruby Williams, Bogalusa, Louisiana

```
  3 tablespoons ketchup
  2 tablespoons cider vinegar
  1 tablespoon maple syrup
  2 teaspoons Dijon mustard
  1 teaspoon Worcestershire sauce
1/8 teaspoon cayenne pepper
  2 pork tenderloins (3/4 pound each)
```

In a bowl, combine the first six ingredients. Place tenderloins on a rack in a roasting pan; brush with some of the sauce.

Bake, uncovered, at 425° for 35-40 minutes or until a meat thermometer reads 160°, basting occasionally with remaining sauce. Let stand for 5 minutes before slicing. **Yield:** 6 servings.

Nutrition Facts: 3 ounces cooked pork equals 151 calories, 4 g fat (1 g saturated fat), 63 mg cholesterol, 185 mg sodium, 5 g carbohydrate, trace fiber, 23 g protein. **Diabetic Exchange:** 3 lean meat.

Orange Fruit Slaw

Orange Fruit Slaw

(Pictured above)

Prep/Total Time: 20 min.

I just love this tangy, refreshing coleslaw that makes the most of winter fruits. The basic recipe combines orange sections, red grapes and chopped apple for a tongue-tingling medley. Try it in place of your usual coleslaw—you'll be pleasantly surprised! —Cynthia France, Murray, Utah

```
  3 cups shredded cabbage
  1 medium navel orange, peeled and sectioned
  1 cup seedless red grapes, halved
  1 medium apple, chopped
1/2 cup finely chopped celery
  1 carton (6 ounces) reduced-fat orange yogurt
1/4 teaspoon salt
1/8 teaspoon pepper
1/4 cup slivered almonds, toasted
```

In a large bowl, combine cabbage, orange, grapes, apple and celery. Stir in yogurt, salt and pepper; toss until well coated. Cover; refrigerate until serving. Sprinkle with almonds just before serving. **Yield:** 6 servings.

Nutrition Facts: 3/4 cup equals 104 calories, 3 g fat (trace saturated fat), 1 mg cholesterol, 133 mg sodium, 18 g carbohydrate, 3 g fiber, 3 g protein. **Diabetic Exchanges:** 1 starch, 1/2 fat.

Using Egg Substitute

LOOK in the refrigerated or frozen food area of stores for egg substitutes in cartons. Egg substitutes use egg whites and contain no cholesterol and little or no fat. One-fourth cup of substitute is equal to one egg.

Chocolate Chocolate Chip Muffins

Chocolate Chocolate Chip Muffins

(Pictured above)

Prep: 20 min. Bake: 20 min./batch

The name says it all! These extra-chocolaty muffins use nutritious whole wheat flour and applesauce to make them lighter without sacrificing flavor. —*Theresa Harrington Sheridan, Wyoming*

2-1/2 cups all-purpose flour
1-3/4 cups whole wheat flour
1-3/4 cups packed brown sugar
  1/2 cup baking cocoa
1-1/4 teaspoons salt
   1 teaspoon baking powder
   1 teaspoon baking soda
   2 egg whites
   1 egg
   2 cups unsweetened applesauce
1-3/4 cups fat-free milk
   2 tablespoons canola oil
2-1/2 teaspoons vanilla extract
1-1/4 cups semisweet chocolate chips

In a large bowl, combine the flours, brown sugar, cocoa, salt, baking powder and baking soda. In another bowl, whisk the egg whites, egg, applesauce, milk, oil and vanilla. Stir into dry ingredients just until moistened. Fold in chocolate chips.

Coat muffin cups with nonstick cooking spray; fill three-fourths full with batter. Bake at 350° for 18-20 minutes or until a toothpick comes out clean. Cool for 5 minutes before removing from pans to wire racks. Serve warm. **Yield:** 32 muffins.

Nutrition Facts: 1 muffin equals 161 calories, 3 g fat (1 g saturated fat), 7 mg cholesterol, 150 mg sodium, 31 g carbohydrate, 2 g fiber, 3 g protein. **Diabetic Exchanges:** 2 starch, 1 fat.

Chocolate Cherry Trifle

Prep/Total Time: 20 min.

With pineapple, cherries and pudding, this creamy dessert has luscious layers. It's a frequently requested treat for church gatherings because it's light yet so good.
—*Angela Oelschlaeger, Tonganoxie, Kansas*

   3 cups cold fat-free milk
   2 packages (1.4 ounces *each*) sugar-free instant chocolate fudge pudding mix
   1 prepared angel food cake (9 ounces), cut into 1-inch cubes
   2 cans (20 ounces *each*) reduced-sugar cherry pie filling
   2 cans (20 ounces *each*) unsweetened crushed pineapple, drained
   1 carton (16 ounces) frozen reduced-fat whipped topping, thawed
 1/4 cup chopped pecans

In a large bowl, whisk milk and pudding mixes for 2 minutes. Let stand for 2 minutes or until soft-set.

Place half of the cake cubes in a 4-qt. trifle or glass bowl. Top with half of the pudding, pie filling, pineapple and whipped topping. Repeat layers. Sprinkle with pecans. Refrigerate leftovers. **Yield:** 18 servings.

Nutrition Facts: 1 cup equals 221 calories, 5 g fat (3 g saturated fat), 1 mg cholesterol, 266 mg sodium, 41 g carbohydrate, 1 g fiber, 3 g protein.

Creamy Chicken Dish

Prep/Total Time: 15 min.

A creamy sauce coats moist chicken and garden-fresh vegetables in this wholesome main course. Best of all, the recipe requires just 15 minutes from start to finish. Who knew something so good could be ready to enjoy so quickly?
—*Margery Bryan, Moses Lake, Washington*

   2 cups cubed cooked chicken
   1 can (10-3/4 ounces) condensed cream of mushroom soup, undiluted
   1 cup chopped cauliflower
   1 cup chopped fresh broccoli
 1/4 cup sliced water chestnuts
   2 tablespoons diced pimientos
 1/4 teaspoon dried thyme
 1/4 teaspoon pepper
Hot cooked rice

In a microwave-safe dish, combine the first eight ingredients. Cover and microwave on high for 5-7 minutes or until bubbly and vegetables are tender, stirring twice. Serve with rice. **Yield:** 4 servings.

Editor's Note: This recipe was tested in a 1,100-watt microwave.

Nutrition Facts: 1 cup equals 212 calories, 9 g fat (3 g saturated fat), 65 mg cholesterol, 609 mg sodium, 10 g carbohydrate, 2 g fiber, 23 g protein. **Diabetic Exchanges:** 3 lean meat, 1/2 starch.

Lemon-Basil Snow Peas

Prep/Total Time: 10 min.

My family loves the taste of this crunchy, lemon-flavored side dish. —Mitzi Sentiff, Alexandria, Virginia

- 1/2 teaspoon minced garlic
- 2 teaspoons olive oil
- 1-1/2 pounds fresh snow peas
- 1 cup chopped sweet yellow pepper
- 1/3 cup minced fresh basil
- 2 tablespoons lemon juice
- 1/2 teaspoon sugar
- 1/2 teaspoon grated lemon peel
- 1/4 teaspoon salt
- 1/4 teaspoon pepper

In a large skillet, saute garlic in oil for 30 seconds. Add snow peas and yellow pepper; saute for 2-3 minutes or until crisp-tender. Stir in the remaining ingredients; saute 1 minute longer. Serve immediately. **Yield:** 6 servings.

Nutrition Facts: 3/4 cup equals 71 calories, 2 g fat (trace saturated fat), 0 cholesterol, 104 mg sodium, 11 g carbohydrate, 4 g fiber, 4 g protein. **Diabetic Exchange:** 2 vegetable, 1/2 fat.

Warm Fruit Kabobs

Prep/Total Time: 30 min.

For a refreshing summer snack or dessert, try this impressive treat. —Janet Schroeder, Strawberry Point, Iowa

- 1 medium apple
- 1 medium banana
- 1 medium fresh peach *or* nectarine
- 1 medium pear
- 2 slices fresh pineapple (1 inch thick)
- 2 tablespoons brown sugar
- 2 tablespoons lemon juice
- 2 tablespoons canola oil
- 1 teaspoon ground cinnamon

Cut all of the fruit into 1-in. chunks. Alternately thread onto 16 soaked wooden skewers (using two skewers side by side for each kabob so the fruit doesn't turn). In a small bowl, combine the brown sugar, lemon juice, oil and cinnamon. Grill kabobs, uncovered, over medium heat for 6 minutes or until heated through, turning often and basting frequently with brown sugar mixture. **Yield:** 8 servings.

Nutrition Facts: 1 kabob equals 144 calories, 4 g fat (1 g saturated fat), 0 cholesterol, 3 mg sodium, 29 g carbohydrate, 3 g fiber, 1 g protein. **Diabetic Exchanges:** 2 fruit, 1/2 fat.

Blueberry Oatmeal Pancakes

(Pictured at right)

Prep: 20 min. **Cook:** 5 min./batch

These thick, moist pancakes are bursting with juicy blueberries. —Amy Spainhoward, Bowling Green, Kentucky

- 2 cups all-purpose flour
- 2 packets (1.51 ounces *each*) instant maple and brown sugar oatmeal mix
- 2 tablespoons sugar
- 2 teaspoons baking powder
- 1/8 teaspoon salt
- 2 egg whites
- 1 egg
- 1-1/2 cups fat-free milk
- 1/2 cup reduced-fat sour cream
- 2 cups fresh *or* frozen blueberries

BLUEBERRY SYRUP:
- 1-1/2 cups fresh *or* frozen blueberries
- 1/2 cup sugar

In a large bowl, combine the first five ingredients. In another bowl, whisk the egg whites, egg, milk and sour cream. Stir into dry ingredients just until moistened. Fold in blueberries.

Spoon batter by 1/4 cupfuls onto a hot griddle coated with nonstick cooking spray. Turn when bubbles form on top of pancake; cook until the second side is golden brown.

In a microwave-safe bowl, combine the syrup ingredients. Microwave, uncovered, on high for 1 minute; stir. Microwave 1-2 minutes longer or until hot and bubbly. Serve warm with pancakes. **Yield:** 14 pancakes (1-1/4 cups syrup).

Editor's Note: If using frozen blueberries, do not thaw before adding to batter. This recipe was tested in a 1,100-watt microwave.

Nutrition Facts: 1 pancake with 1 tablespoon syrup equals 171 calories, 2 g fat (1 g saturated fat), 19 mg cholesterol, 145 mg sodium, 34 g carbohydrate, 2 g fiber, 5 g protein.

Blueberry Oatmeal Pancakes

Zucchini Red Pepper Lasagna

(Pictured below)

Prep: 20 min. **Bake:** 55 min. + standing

Pesto adds zip to this lasagna that's simply overflowing with vegetables and cheese. With sliced portobello mushrooms in every bite, the hearty main dish from our Test Kitchen is perfect for company.

- 1 carton (15 ounces) ricotta cheese
- 1-1/2 cups (6 ounces) shredded part-skim mozzarella cheese, *divided*
- 2 eggs
- 3 tablespoons prepared pesto
- 2 cups sliced zucchini
- 2 cups sliced baby portobello mushrooms
- 2 tablespoons canola oil
- 2 jars (one 26 ounces, one 14 ounces) meatless spaghetti sauce
- 9 no-cook lasagna noodles
- 1 jar (12 ounces) roasted sweet red peppers, drained

In a small bowl, combine the ricotta cheese, 1/2 cup mozzarella cheese, eggs and pesto; set aside. In a large skillet, saute zucchini and mushrooms in oil for 5 minutes or until crisp-tender; set aside.

Spread 1 cup spaghetti sauce in a 13-in. x 9-in. x 2-in. baking dish coated with nonstick cooking spray. Top with three noodles; spread 1 cup sauce to edges of noodles. Layer with half of the zucchini mixture, red peppers and cheese mixture. Top with three more noodles and another cup of sauce. Layer with remaining zucchini mixture, peppers, cheese mixture, noodles and sauce.

Cover and bake at 375° for 45 minutes. Uncover; sprinkle with remaining mozzarella. Bake 10 minutes longer or until cheese is melted. Let lasagna stand for 15 minutes before cutting. **Yield:** 12 servings.

Nutrition Facts: 1 piece equals 241 calories, 11 g fat (5 g saturated fat), 59 mg cholesterol, 651 mg sodium, 23 g carbohydrate, 3 g fiber, 13 g protein. **Diabetic Exchanges:** 2 vegetable, 1 starch, 1 lean meat, 1 fat.

Zucchini Red Pepper Lasagna

Broccoli Parmesan

Prep/Total Time: 20 min.

This oh-so-easy, cheesy side dish goes well with just about any entree.   —Jessie Sarrazin, Livingston, Montana

- 1 medium bunch broccoli (1-1/2 pounds), cut into spears
- 1 can (14-1/2 ounces) reduced-sodium chicken broth
- 1/2 cup chopped onion
- 3 teaspoons minced garlic
- 1 tablespoon butter
- 1/4 to 1/2 teaspoon dried basil
- 1/4 teaspoon pepper
- 2 teaspoons shredded Parmesan cheese

In a large saucepan, bring broccoli and broth to a boil. Reduce heat; cover and simmer for 5-8 minutes or until crisp-tender.

Meanwhile, in a small skillet, saute onion and garlic in butter until tender. Stir in basil and pepper. Drain broccoli and place in a serving bowl; add onion mixture. Sprinkle with Parmesan cheese. **Yield:** 6 servings.

Nutrition Facts: 2/3 cup equals 61 calories, 2 g fat (1 g saturated fat), 6 mg cholesterol, 109 mg sodium, 8 g carbohydrate, 4 g fiber, 4 g protein. **Diabetic Exchanges:** 1-1/2 vegetable, 1/2 fat.

Hot Fruit Compote

Prep: 15 min. **Bake:** 40 min.

This sweet and colorful fruit compote pairs nicely with an egg casserole for a holiday brunch. It can bake right alongside the eggs, so everything is conveniently done at the same time.   —Joyce Moynihan, Lakeville, Minnesota

- 2 cans (15-1/4 ounces *each*) sliced pears, drained
- 1 can (29 ounces) sliced peaches, drained
- 1 can (20 ounces) unsweetened pineapple chunks, drained
- 1 package (20 ounces) pitted dried plums
- 1 jar (16 ounces) unsweetened applesauce
- 1 can (21 ounces) cherry pie filling
- 1/4 cup packed brown sugar

In a large bowl, combine the first five ingredients. Pour into a 13-in. x 9-in. x 2-in. baking dish coated with nonstick cooking spray. Spread pie filling over fruit mixture; sprinkle with brown sugar.

Cover and bake at 350° for 40-45 minutes or until bubbly. Serve warm. **Yield:** 20 servings.

Nutrition Facts: 1/2 cup equals 187 calories, trace fat (trace saturated fat), 0 cholesterol, 15mg sodium, 46 g carbohydrate, 3 g fiber, 2 g protein.

Yellow Squash and Peppers

Yellow Squash and Peppers

(Pictured above)

Prep/Total Time: 20 min.

To perk up just about any dinner, try this quick veggie side dish. We usually have lots of squash and peppers from the garden, and this is a tasty way to use them up.
—Anna Stodolak, Volant, Pennsylvania

   3 cups sliced yellow summer squash
1/2 cup sliced onion
1/2 cup *each* julienned green and sweet red
     peppers
   1 tablespoon canola oil
1/4 cup water
1-1/2 teaspoons minced garlic
1/4 teaspoon salt
1/4 teaspoon pepper

In a large skillet, saute the squash, onion and peppers in oil for 4-5 minutes or until crisp-tender. Add the remaining ingredients. Reduce heat to medium. Cook, uncovered, for 3-4 minutes or until vegetables are tender, stirring occasionally. Serve with a slotted spoon. **Yield:** 4 servings.

Nutrition Facts: 3/4 cup equals 62 calories, 4 g fat (trace saturated fat), 0 cholesterol, 151 mg sodium, 7 g carbohydrate, 3 g fiber, 1 g protein. **Diabetic Exchanges:** 2 vegetable, 1/2 fat.

Ranch Chicken Salad Sandwiches

Prep/Total Time: 15 min.

A creamy dressing mixture gives these sandwiches terrific taste. They feature tender chicken and crunchy vegetables.
—Bobbie Scroggie, Scott Depot, West Virginia

1/4 cup reduced-fat mayonnaise
   3 tablespoons fat-free ranch salad dressing
   3 tablespoons fat-free sour cream
   1 tablespoon lemon juice
1/8 teaspoon pepper
   2 cups cubed cooked chicken breast
1/2 cup thinly sliced celery
   2 tablespoons diced sweet red pepper
   1 tablespoon chopped green onion
   6 hamburger buns, split
   6 lettuce leaves
   6 slices tomato

In a small bowl, combine the mayonnaise, ranch dressing, sour cream, lemon juice and pepper. Stir in the chicken, celery, red pepper and onion until combined. Spoon 1/3 cup onto each bun bottom; top with lettuce and tomato. Replace bun tops. **Yield:** 6 servings.

Nutrition Facts: 1 sandwich equals 257 calories, 7 g fat (1 g saturated fat), 41 mg cholesterol, 456 mg sodium, 29 g carbohydrate, 2 g fiber, 18 g protein. **Diabetic Exchanges:** 2 starch, 2 very lean meat, 1/2 fat.

Colorful Crab Stir-Fry

let or wok, stir-fry carrots in oil. Add the peas, red pepper, ginger and garlic; stir-fry 2 minutes longer or until vegetables are crisp-tender.

Stir the cornstarch mixture and add to the pan. Bring to a boil; cook and stir for 2 minutes or until thickened. Add the crab; heat through. Serve with rice if desired. **Yield:** 4 servings.

Nutrition Facts: 3/4 cup (calculated without rice) equals 126 calories, 4 g fat (trace saturated fat), 7 mg cholesterol, 562 mg sodium, 16 g carbohydrate, 2 g fiber, 7 g protein. **Diabetic Exchanges:** 3 vegetable, 1 lean meat.

Blueberry Chutney For Grilled Chicken

Prep: 30 min. + marinating **Grill:** 10 min.

Fresh blueberries and dried apricots are tossed with brown sugar, fresh ginger and more, then lightly simmered to create a delectable chutney. Serve this treat from our Test Kitchen warm or at room temperature.

2 cups fresh *or* frozen blueberries
1/2 cup chopped dried apricots
1/3 cup packed brown sugar
1/3 cup finely chopped onion
3 tablespoons cider vinegar
3 teaspoons minced fresh gingerroot
1/2 teaspoon minced garlic
1/4 teaspoon ground coriander
1/2 cup Italian salad dressing
6 boneless skinless chicken breast halves
  (6 ounces *each*)

For chutney, in a large saucepan, combine the first eight ingredients. Bring to a boil. Reduce heat to medium-low; cook, uncovered, for 20-25 minutes or until thickened, stirring occasionally.

Meanwhile, pour salad dressing into a large resealable plastic bag; add the chicken. Seal bag and turn to coat; refrigerate for 20 minutes.

Cool chutney to room temperature. Drain and discard marinade. Grill chicken, covered, over medium heat for 5-6 minutes on each side or until juices run clear. Serve with chutney. **Yield:** 6 servings.

Nutrition Facts: 1 chicken breast half with 3 tablespoons chutney equals 344 calories, 10 g fat (2 g saturated fat), 94 mg cholesterol, 348 mg sodium, 29 g carbohydrate, 2 g fiber, 35 g protein. **Diabetic Exchanges:** 5 very lean meat, 1 starch, 1 fruit, 1 fat.

Colorful Crab Stir-Fry

(Pictured above)

Prep/Total Time: 30 min.

My love for seafood has carried over from childhood, when we used to fish together as a family. So I was happy to find this change-of-pace recipe that combines stir-fry with seafood. It tastes like a special treat but is a breeze to prepare.
—Lee Deneau, Lansing, Michigan

2 teaspoons cornstarch
1 teaspoon chicken bouillon granules
3/4 cup water
1/2 teaspoon reduced-sodium soy sauce
1 cup sliced fresh carrots
1 tablespoon canola oil
1 cup fresh *or* frozen snow peas
1/2 cup julienned sweet red pepper
1 teaspoon minced fresh gingerroot
1 teaspoon minced garlic
1 package (8 ounces) imitation crabmeat
Hot cooked rice, optional

In a small bowl, combine the cornstarch, bouillon, water and soy sauce until smooth; set aside. In a large skil-

Rice Rerun

When I have leftover cooked rice from a stir-fry or other dish, I brown bulk sausage in a skillet and stir in the rice. Then I scramble a few eggs into the mixture and add chopped green onion. Spooned into flour tortillas and topped with shredded cheese, it's a great breakfast. —*Kay Myers, Lawton, Oklahoma*

Sunflower Beet Salad

Prep/Total Time: 5 min.

With just five ingredients, this super salad comes together in a flash. —*Shirley Glaab, Hattiesburg, Mississippi*

  2 cups torn romaine
  1 can (14-1/2 ounces) sliced beets, drained
  1 medium red onion, thinly sliced
  1/2 cup unsalted sunflower kernels, toasted
  1/4 cup prepared fat-free French salad dressing

Divide the romaine among four salad plates; top with beets, onion and sunflower kernels. Drizzle with dressing. Serve immediately. **Yield:** 4 servings.

  Nutrition Facts: 1 serving equals 159 calories, 8 g fat (1 g saturated fat), 0 cholesterol, 336 mg sodium, 19 g carbohydrate, 5 g fiber, 5 g protein. **Diabetic Exchanges:** 1 starch, 1 vegetable, 1 fat.

Frosted Fruit Salad

Prep/Total Time: 10 min.

This breakfast recipe uses up the bananas and apples I always have on hand. —*Ann Fox, Austin, Texas*

  2 large apples, cut into 3/4-inch cubes
  2 medium firm bananas, sliced
  2 teaspoons lemon juice
  1 carton (6 ounces) fat-free reduced-sugar
    raspberry yogurt
  1/4 cup raisins
  1 tablespoon sunflower kernels

In a large bowl, combine apples and bananas. Sprinkle with lemon juice; toss to coat. Stir in the yogurt, raisins and sunflower kernels. Serve immediately. **Yield:** 6 servings.

  Nutrition Facts: 3/4 cup equals 124 calories, 1 g fat (trace saturated fat), 1 mg cholesterol, 31 mg sodium, 28 g carbohydrate, 3 g fiber, 3 g protein. **Diabetic Exchanges:** 2 fruit.

Sole Fillets in Lemon Butter

(Pictured below)

Prep/Total Time: 20 min.

Here's a fast, easy and tasty way to serve fish. Try it, and you'll agree! —*Barbara Sharon, Plymouth, Wisconsin*

  4 sole fillets (4 ounces *each*)
  1/4 teaspoon salt
  1/8 teaspoon pepper
  3 tablespoons butter, melted
  1/2 cup minced fresh parsley
  1 tablespoon lemon juice
  1/4 cup crushed butter-flavored crackers
  1/2 teaspoon paprika

Place the sole in an ungreased microwave-safe 11-in. x 7-in. x 2-in. dish; sprinkle with salt and pepper. Cover and microwave on high for 3-4 minutes.

  In a small bowl, combine butter, parsley and juice; pour over fillets. Sprinkle with cracker crumbs. Microwave, uncovered, for 3-4 minutes or until fish flakes easily with a fork. Sprinkle with paprika. **Yield:** 4 servings.

  Editor's Note: This recipe was tested in a 1,100-watt microwave.

  Nutrition Facts: 1 fillet equals 213 calories, 11 g fat (6 g saturated fat), 77 mg cholesterol, 377 mg sodium, 5 g carbohydrate, trace fiber, 22 g protein. **Diabetic Exchanges:** 3 very lean meat, 2 fat.

Sole Fillets in Lemon Butter

YOU'LL feel like celebrating when you page through this festive chapter! It makes throwing a party so quick and easy, even the busiest cooks will have time to host a fun-filled event for family and friends.

You're sure to get in the spirit when you see the exciting themes we've gathered together. Invite guests to a midwinter escape…a "stone soup" event for kids…a playful pool party… even a bountiful buffet of summertime appetizers.

Just choose which delightful bash suits your mood, then revel in the surprisingly easy recipes featured here. You'll have an unforgettable party put together before you know it!

DIVE INTO DESSERT. Pool Party Cake (p. 276).

Get Away for a Midwinter Escape

IF AN ISLAND VACATION isn't in your budget, a simple spread of tropical delights might be the ticket for curing a family-size case of cabin fever.

Pick a free night and invite everyone to wear summer T-shirts or swimsuits and flip-flops. Then whip up the following snacks, crank up the heat and bask in relaxing, seaside thoughts.

Lemon-Lime Punch

(Pictured at far right)

Prep: 10 min. + chilling

This frothy, citrusy refresher topped with lime sherbet is a longtime family favorite and truly the best punch I've ever had. —*Mary Ray, Raccoon, Kentucky*

- 2 quarts water
- 2 cups sugar
- 2 envelopes unsweetened lemon-lime soft drink mix
- 1 can (46 ounces) unsweetened pineapple juice
- 1 liter ginger ale, chilled
- 1 quart lime sherbet

In a bowl, combine water, sugar and soft drink mix; stir until dissolved. Stir in pineapple juice. Refrigerate until chilled. Just before serving, stir in ginger ale and top with scoops of sherbet. **Yield:** 6 quarts.

Pineapple-Pecan Cheese Spread

(Pictured at far right)

Prep/Total Time: 20 min.

Here's a smooth, creamy cheese spread that's always a hit in my home. —*Cynde Sonnier, Mont Belvieu, Texas*

- 2 packages (8 ounces *each*) cream cheese, softened
- 1-1/2 cups (6 ounces) shredded cheddar cheese
- 1 cup chopped pecans, toasted, *divided*
- 3/4 cup crushed pineapple, drained
- 1 can (4 ounces) chopped green chilies, drained
- 2 tablespoons chopped roasted sweet red pepper
- 1/2 teaspoon garlic powder
- Assorted fresh vegetables

In a large mixing bowl, the beat cream cheese until smooth. Add the cheddar cheese, 3/4 cup pecans, pineapple, green chilies, red pepper and garlic powder; mix well. Transfer the spread to a serving dish. Cover and refrigerate until serving.

Sprinkle with remaining pecans just before serving. Serve with fresh vegetables. **Yield:** 3-3/4 cups.

Fruit Salsa with Cinnamon Chips

(Pictured at right)

Prep/Total Time: 30 min.

I first prepared this fresh, fruity salsa and sweet chips for a family baby shower. Everyone wanted the recipe!
—*Jessica Robinson, Indian Trail, North Carolina*

- 1 cup finely chopped fresh strawberries
- 1 medium navel orange, peeled and finely chopped
- 3 medium kiwifruit, peeled and finely chopped
- 1 can (8 ounces) unsweetened crushed pineapple, drained
- 1 tablespoon lemon juice
- 1-1/2 teaspoons sugar
- CINNAMON CHIPS:
- 10 flour tortillas (8 inches)
- 1/4 cup butter, melted
- 1/3 cup sugar
- 1 teaspoon ground cinnamon

In a small bowl, combine the first six ingredients. Cover; refrigerate until serving.

For chips, brush tortillas with butter; cut each into eight wedges. Combine sugar and cinnamon; sprinkle over tortillas. Place on ungreased baking sheets. Bake at 350° for 5-10 minutes or just until crisp. Serve with fruit salsa. **Yield:** 2-1/2 cups salsa (80 chips).

Mini Chicken Salad Croissants

Prep/Total Time: 25 min.

Over the years I've tried many versions of chicken salad, but this one served on mini croissants is still tops.
—*Andrea Donofrio, Walpole, Massachusetts*

- 2 cups cubed cooked chicken
- 12 seedless red *or* green grapes, halved
- 1 medium apple, chopped
- 1/2 cup mayonnaise
- 1/3 cup chopped walnuts, toasted
- 1/4 cup plain yogurt
- 3 tablespoons cider vinegar
- 1/8 teaspoon salt
- Dash pepper
- 16 miniature croissants *or* rolls, split
- 4 to 6 lettuce leaves, torn
- 16 frilled toothpicks, optional

In a small bowl, combine the first nine ingredients. Spoon about 1/4 cup chicken salad onto the bottom of each miniature croissant; top with lettuce. Replace the croissant tops. Insert toothpicks into the sandwiches if desired. **Yield:** 16 appetizers.

Lemon-Lime Punch
Pineapple-Pecan Cheese Spread
Fruit Salsa with Cinnamon Chips

Serve Up Some Stone Soup

CHILDREN need books in order to learn and grow, and they also need opportunities to grasp the importance of community giving. Why not meet those needs in a fun-filled way with a neighborhood "stone soup" party? Everyone will have a great time...and enjoy a terrific meal, too!

Stone Soup is a wonderful folktale about a hungry traveler who outwits some tightfisted villagers into making him a meal. Setting out to make soup from water and a stone, he tricks the curious folks into contributing just an onion...or a carrot...or whatever they can spare—resulting in a wonderful soup for all. It's an easy lesson in how much people can accomplish if they work together and share what they have...and it's an economical party idea!

Invite each of the children to bring two favorite, gently used books, as well as one specific ingredient for the "stone soup." From the collected books, each child can select one that is new to them to take home. Give the remainder to your school's library. From the donated veggies and soup ingredients, dinner is served!

We've provided a basic recipe for "stone soup," as well as some simple and delicious snack foods to go with it. So go ahead, get some friends together and host your own "souper" party!

Stone Soup

(Pictured below)

Prep: 15 min. **Cook:** 40 min.

After reading the story Stone Soup, our Test Kitchen enjoyed creating this version of the folktale classic. It's chock-full of vegetables and many more ingredients...enough for everyone to bring something to add to the flavor and fun!

4 cans (14-1/2 ounces *each*) chicken broth
4 medium red potatoes, cut into eighths
1 yellow summer squash, chopped
2 medium carrots, chopped
1 medium onion, chopped
2 celery ribs, chopped
1 teaspoon dried thyme
1/2 teaspoon pepper
4 cups cubed cooked chicken
1 cup frozen cut green beans
1/2 cup quick-cooking barley
1 can (14-1/2 ounces) diced tomatoes, undrained
4 cups salad croutons
1 cup shredded Parmesan cheese

Stone Soup
Go-Go Garlic Bread

In a Dutch oven or soup kettle, combine the first eight ingredients. Bring to a boil. Reduce heat; cover and simmer for 10-15 minutes or until vegetables are crisp-tender.

Stir in the chicken, beans and barley. Bring to a boil. Reduce heat; cover and simmer for 10-12 minutes or until vegetables and barley are tender. Add tomatoes; heat through. Serve with croutons and Parmesan cheese. **Yield:** 12 servings.

Go-Go Garlic Bread

(Pictured below left)

Prep/Total Time: 25 min.

I call this "go-go" bread because it's always gone before I know it! —Dolores Brigham, Inglewood, California

    1/2 cup butter, softened
    1/2 cup mayonnaise
      1 tablespoon grated Parmesan cheese
      2 teaspoons minced garlic
    1/2 teaspoon Italian seasoning
    1/8 teaspoon seasoned salt
    1/2 cup shredded Monterey Jack cheese
      1 loaf French bread (about 20 inches), halved
        lengthwise

In a small mixing bowl, beat butter and mayonnaise until smooth. Beat in the Parmesan cheese, garlic, Italian seasoning and seasoned salt. Stir in Monterey Jack cheese. Spread over cut sides of bread.

Place on an ungreased baking sheet. Bake at 350° for 10-15 minutes or until cheese is melted. Slice and serve warm. **Yield:** 12 servings.

Editor's Note: Reduced-fat or fat-free mayonnaise is not recommended for this recipe.

Orange-Cola Chocolate Cake

(Pictured above right)

Prep: 25 min. **Bake:** 30 min. + cooling

Most people are shocked to learn this moist and luscious cake starts with a mix. Substituting cola for water, adding a hint of citrus and serving each slice with a dipped strawberry turns the mix into a spectacular dessert people love.
—Stephanie Vogel, Lincoln, Nebraska

      1 package (18-1/4 ounces) devil's food cake mix
      3 eggs
  1-1/3 cups cola
    1/2 cup vegetable oil
      1 tablespoon orange extract
CHOCOLATE-COVERED STRAWBERRIES:
    1/2 cup semisweet chocolate chips
      1 teaspoon shortening
     12 fresh strawberries
FROSTING:
    1/2 cup butter, softened
  3-3/4 cups confectioners' sugar
      3 tablespoons instant chocolate drink mix
    1/4 cup cola
    1/2 teaspoon orange extract

Orange-Cola Chocolate Cake

In a large mixing bowl, combine the cake mix, eggs, cola, oil and extract. Beat on low speed for 30 seconds; beat on medium for 2 minutes. Pour into a greased 13-in. x 9-in. x 2-in. baking pan. Bake at 350° for 30-35 minutes or until a toothpick inserted near the center comes out clean. Cool on a wire rack.

In a small microwave-safe bowl, melt chocolate chips and shortening; stir until smooth. Wash strawberries and pat dry. Dip each strawberry into chocolate; allow excess to drip off. Place on a waxed paper-lined baking sheet; refrigerate until set, about 30 minutes.

In a small mixing bowl, combine the frosting ingredients; beat until smooth. Frost the cake. Garnish each serving with a chocolate-covered strawberry. **Yield:** 12 servings.

Editor's Note: Diet colas are not recommended for this recipe.

Pineapple-Lime Gelatin Mold

Prep: 10 min. + chilling

Jolly, jiggly gelatin comes in a rainbow of colors and fits any party mold. This tangy, lime-green salad makes a refreshing and fun side dish. —Christine Arter
Crestline, Ohio

      2 packages (3 ounces *each*) lime gelatin
      2 cups boiling water
      1 can (20 ounces) crushed pineapple,
        undrained
      1 cup (8 ounces) sour cream
    1/2 cup chopped pecans

In a large bowl, dissolve gelatin in water. Stir in pineapple; cover and refrigerate until syrupy.

Whisk in sour cream; add pecans. Transfer to a 6-cup ring mold coated with nonstick cooking spray. Cover and refrigerate until firm. Unmold onto a serving plate. **Yield:** 12 servings.

Dip into a Playful Pool Party

IF YOU'RE LOOKING to throw a "cool" pool party for the neighborhood kids, it's simpler than you think to take the plunge! We've planned a menu that's both kid- and mom-friendly.

The fish-shaped sandwiches are so quick to fix, they're a great way to set the scene for your poolside bash. Plus, the easy beans and fruit dip make delicious sides everyone will love. And guests will be lining up to dive into the pretty pool cake!

Fun Fish Sandwiches

(Pictured below)

Prep/Total Time: 30 min.

Children will love these cute fish sandwiches, which are a cinch to assemble using a fish-shaped cookie cutter. If some of your party guests are picky eaters, cut out fish-shaped peanut butter and jelly sandwiches instead.
—Carolyn Schmeling, Brookfield, Wisconsin

> 1 package (21 ounces) frozen crunchy breaded fish fillets
> 1/2 cup mayonnaise
> 1/4 cup ranch salad dressing
> 2 tablespoons sweet pickle relish
> 1/4 teaspoon garlic powder
> 12 slices white bread
> 6 slices process American cheese
> 6 lettuce leaves

Fun Fish Sandwiches

Prepare fish fillets according to package directions. Meanwhile, in a small bowl, combine the mayonnaise, ranch dressing, relish and garlic powder; spread over six slices of bread. Place two fillets on each slice.

Top with cheese, lettuce and remaining bread. Using a 3-1/2-in. fish-shaped cookie cutter, cut two fish shapes from each sandwich. Serve immediately. **Yield:** 6 servings.

Editor's Note: This recipe was tested with Van de Kamp's frozen crunchy breaded fish fillets.

Kids' Baked Beans

Prep/Total Time: 20 min.

Grape jelly is the "secret ingredient" that sweetens these versatile beans. —*Jessie Sarrazin, Livingston, Montana*

> 2 cans (16 ounces *each*) baked beans
> 3/4 cup grape jelly
> 1/2 cup chopped onion
> 2 tablespoons prepared mustard
> 1 teaspoon Worcestershire sauce

In a large saucepan, combine all ingredients. Bring to a boil. Reduce heat; simmer, uncovered, for 15-20 minutes or until thickened. **Yield:** 6 servings.

Marshmallow Fruit Dip

Prep/Total Time: 10 min.

You can whip up this creamy dip in a mere 10 minutes! I like to serve it with fresh-picked strawberries at spring and summer brunches or luncheons. —*Cindy Steffen Cedarburg, Wisconsin*

> 1 package (8 ounces) cream cheese, softened
> 1 carton (6 ounces) cherry yogurt
> 1 carton (8 ounces) frozen whipped topping, thawed
> 1 jar (7 ounces) marshmallow creme
> Assorted fresh fruit

In a small mixing bowl, beat cream cheese and yogurt until blended. Fold in whipped topping and marshmallow creme. Serve with fruit. **Yield:** 5 cups.

Pool Party Cake

(Pictured above right and on page 270)

Prep: 45 min. + chilling **Bake:** 25 min. + chilling

This cleverly decorated cake with its "pool" of cool blue gelatin will steal the show at any gathering! Our Test Kitchen staff dipped into their imaginations to come up with this whimsical party cake that doubles as a festive centerpiece.

 1 package (18-1/4 ounces) white cake mix
 1 package (3 ounces) berry blue gelatin
 3/4 cup boiling water
 1/2 cup cold water
Ice cubes
 1 package (8 ounces) cream cheese, softened
 1/4 cup butter, softened
 1 teaspoon vanilla extract
 1/8 teaspoon salt
 4 cups confectioners' sugar
 1 piece red shoestring licorice
 14 Swedish Fish candies
 5 Peachie-O's candies
 5 Necco wafer candies, divided
 2 Air Head candies
 8 Runts candies
 1 lollipop stick
 2 Now and Later candies
 1 stick spearmint chewing gum
 1 Life Savers Gummy
 98 Smarties candies
 1 Sour Brite Octopus candy

Grease two 9-in. round baking pans and line with waxed paper; grease and flour the paper. Prepare cake batter according to package directions. Pour into prepared pans. Bake at 350° for 21-26 minutes or until a toothpick comes out clean. Cool for 10 minutes; remove from pans to wire racks to cool completely.

In a small bowl, dissolve gelatin in boiling water. Pour cold water into a 2-cup measuring cup; add enough ice cubes to measure 1-1/4 cups. Add to gelatin; stir until slightly thickened. Discard any remaining ice. Refrigerate for 30 minutes or until soft-set.

For frosting, in a large mixing bowl, beat cream cheese and butter until smooth. Add vanilla and salt. Beat in confectioners' sugar until smooth and fluffy. Set aside 2 tablespoons frosting for decorating. Place one cake on a glass or plastic board. Frost top of cake with 2/3 cup frosting.

For pool, cut a 5-in. circle (1 in. deep) in the center of second cake (save removed cake for another use). Place over frosted cake. Slowly pour gelatin into circle. Frost top and sides of cake.

For ladder, cut licorice into two 4-in. pieces; gently press 1-1/4 in. apart into frosting, looping top ends for handles. Cut three 1-1/4-in. pieces of licorice for ladder steps; press into frosting. Decorate sides of cake with Swedish Fish and Peachie-O's.

For steps to pool, use a small amount of reserved frosting to attach four wafer candies to board. Trim two Air Head candies and bend into chair shapes; with frosting, attach Runts to chairs for legs. For table, attach remaining wafer candy to lollipop stick; push into cake. Place chairs and table on cake and board.

For diving board, spread frosting between two Now and Later candies; attach gum to top of candies with frosting. Cut Life Savers Gummy in half; attach to sides of gum. Place on cake.

Arrange Smarties on cake for pool tile. Place a line of Smarties on gelatin to form a buoy rope. Place octopus candy in pool. Refrigerate for 1-2 hours or until gelatin is set. **Yield:** 12-16 servings.

Bask in a Summer Snack Buffet

WHEN the weather heats up, welcome summer fun with family and friends...and a buffet of outstanding appetizers! Your guests won't be able to resist this finger-licking lineup.

Start the party with a tray of Pesto Cheese Tarts. The savory nibbles are impressive but are assembled in a pinch with prepared pesto and frozen tart shells.

You can't go wrong when warm Spinach Artichoke Dip appears on your buffet table. Loaded with flavor, this dip is made in the microwave.

Taco-Flavored Chicken Wings and unique Fried Asparagus are sure to turn heads at your summer soiree. Best of all, each of these party favorites comes together in only 30 minutes...or less!

Pesto Cheese Tarts

(Pictured below)
Prep/Total Time: 20 min.

These little bites are perfect for parties. Whether I serve the tarts at a family gathering or another event, they always get raves. —Jean Kern, Charlotte, North Carolina

Pesto Cheese Tarts

2/3 cup chopped tomatoes
1/3 cup mayonnaise
1/4 cup shredded part-skim mozzarella cheese
3 tablespoons shredded Parmesan cheese
2 teaspoons prepared pesto
1/8 teaspoon pepper
1 package (2.1 ounces) frozen miniature phyllo tart shells

In a small bowl, combine the tomatoes, mayonnaise, mozzarella cheese, Parmesan cheese, pesto and pepper. Spoon heaping teaspoonfuls of the mixture into the phyllo tart shells. Place on an ungreased baking sheet. Bake at 350° for 8-12 minutes or until lightly browned. **Yield:** 15 appetizers.

Spinach Artichoke Dip

Prep/Total Time: 25 min.

I entertain a lot, and this crowd-pleasing dip is fast and fabulous! With its thick, cheesy texture and wonderfully rich flavor, no one ever guesses that it was made in the microwave. —Suzanne Zick, Maiden, North Carolina

1 package (10 ounces) frozen chopped spinach
1/4 cup chopped onion
1 tablespoon butter
4 ounces cream cheese, softened
1/4 cup heavy whipping cream
1 can (14 ounces) water-packed artichoke hearts, rinsed, drained and chopped
1 cup (4 ounces) shredded Monterey Jack cheese
1/2 cup shredded part-skim mozzarella cheese
1/2 cup shredded Swiss cheese
1/4 teaspoon cayenne pepper
1/8 teaspoon pepper
1/2 cup shredded Parmesan cheese
Assorted crackers

Cook spinach according to package directions for microwave; drain and squeeze dry. Set aside. Place onion and butter in a small microwave-safe bowl. Cover and microwave at 70% power for 2-3 minutes or until onion is tender, stirring once; set aside.

In a large mixing bowl, beat cream cheese and whipping cream until smooth. Fold in the spinach, artichokes, cheeses, cayenne, pepper and onion mixture.

Transfer to a greased 9-in. microwave-safe pie plate. Sprinkle with Parmesan cheese. Microwave, uncovered, on high for 4-5 minutes or until bubbly. Serve with crackers. **Yield:** about 3-1/2 cups.

Editor's Note: This recipe was tested in a 1,100-watt microwave.

Taco-Flavored Chicken Wings
Fried Asparagus

Taco-Flavored Chicken Wings

(Pictured above)

Prep/Total Time: 20 min.

Want a sure hit at your next summertime event? Dress up chicken wings with this lively marinade to create a fantastic appetizer. I like these grilled wings spicy, so I often give them a kick with extra hot sauce. —Deb Keslar
Utica, Nebraska

  1 **envelope taco seasoning**
  3 **tablespoons vegetable oil**
  2 **tablespoons red wine vinegar**
  2 **teaspoons hot pepper sauce,** *divided*
  4 **pounds fresh** *or* **frozen chicken wingettes, thawed**
  1 **cup ranch salad dressing**

In a large resealable plastic bag, combine the taco seasoning, oil, vinegar and 1 teaspoon hot pepper sauce; add chicken. Seal bag and turn to coat.

Grill chicken, covered, over medium heat for 5 minutes. Grill 10-15 minutes longer or until juices run clear, turning occasionally.

In a small bowl, combine ranch dressing and remaining hot pepper sauce. Serve with chicken. **Yield:** about 2-1/2 dozen.

Fried Asparagus

(Pictured above)

Prep/Total Time: 30 min.

This battered asparagus recipe is a favorite at parties. It's fun to eat with a side of ranch dressing for dipping.
—Lori Kimble, Montgomery, Alabama

    1 **cup all-purpose flour**
  3/4 **cup cornstarch**
1-1/4 **teaspoons salt**
1-1/4 **teaspoons baking powder**
  3/4 **teaspoon baking soda**
  3/4 **teaspoon garlic salt**
  1/2 **teaspoon pepper**
    1 **cup beer** *or* **nonalcoholic beer**
    3 **egg whites**
2-1/2 **pounds fresh asparagus, trimmed**
Oil for deep-fat frying
Ranch salad dressing

In a large bowl, combine the first seven ingredients. Combine beer and egg whites; stir into dry ingredients just until moistened. Dip asparagus into batter.

In an electric skillet, heat 1-1/2 in. of oil to 375°. Fry asparagus in batches for 2-3 minutes on each side or until golden brown. Drain on paper towels. Serve immediately with ranch dressing. **Yield:** 2-1/2 dozen.

Chapter 19

INSTEAD of grabbing a candy bar from the vending machine when you need a snack...or relying on ho-hum chips and dip from the store when you have a party...look to the inspiring hors d'oeuvres and satisfying snacks here. You might be pleasantly surprised!

That's because each impressive, tasty appetizer requires just minutes to fix—even specialties such as Spicy Breaded Chicken Wings, Sausage Wonton Cups, Jalapenos with Olive Cream Filling and Antipasto Bread.

So whether you want elegant finger foods for holiday guests or just need a bite to tide you over before dinnertime, this chapter is the one for you!

SPECIAL SNACKING. Chutney-Topped Brie (recipe on p. 287).

281

Sausage Wonton Cups

(*Pictured below*)

Prep/Total Time: 30 min.

Here's a hot, tasty appetizer that's ideal when you want fun finger foods and quick bites for a party. I've prepared this fuss-free recipe several times, and the meaty little wonton cups always disappear before I know it.
—*Shirley Van Allen, High Point, North Carolina*

✓ Uses less fat, sugar or salt. Includes Nutrition Facts and Diabetic Exchanges.

  4 Italian turkey sausage links (4 ounces *each*), casings removed
  1 can (15 ounces) tomato sauce
1/2 teaspoon garlic powder
1/2 teaspoon dried basil
 24 wonton wrappers
  1 cup (4 ounces) shredded Italian cheese blend

In a large skillet, cook sausage over medium heat until no longer pink; drain. Stir in tomato sauce, garlic powder and basil. Bring to a boil. Reduce heat; simmer, uncovered, for 8-10 minutes or until thickened.

Meanwhile, press wonton wrappers into miniature muffin cups coated with nonstick cooking spray. Bake at 350° for 8-9 minutes or until lightly browned.

Spoon sausage mixture into cups. Sprinkle with cheese. Bake 5-7 minutes longer or until cheese is melted. Serve warm. **Yield:** 2 dozen.

Nutrition Facts: 1 wonton cup equals 68 calories, 3 g fat (1 g saturated fat), 15 mg cholesterol, 270 mg sodium, 6 g carbohydrate, trace fiber, 5 g protein. **Diabetic Exchanges:** 1/2 starch, 1/2 fat.

Spicy Breaded Chicken Wings

Spicy Breaded Chicken Wings

(*Pictured above*)

Prep: 25 min. **Bake:** 25 min.

Everyone really loves these spicy chicken wings. They taste just like fried chicken, but they're baked and are wonderful even without the dipping sauce. You can also make them with bags of drumettes instead of whole wings.
—*Barbara White, Katy, Texas*

  1 egg
  1 tablespoon water
2/3 cup dry bread crumbs
  1 teaspoon onion powder
  1 teaspoon dried basil
  1 teaspoon cayenne pepper
1/2 teaspoon garlic salt
1/2 teaspoon paprika
 10 whole chicken wings
DIPPING SAUCE:
  2 tablespoons ketchup
  2 tablespoons honey
  1 tablespoon Worcestershire sauce
1/2 teaspoon hot pepper sauce

In a shallow bowl, beat egg and water. In another shallow bowl, combine the bread crumbs, onion powder, basil, cayenne, garlic salt and paprika.

Cut chicken wings into three sections; discard wing tip sections. Dip chicken wings into egg mixture, then coat with crumb mixture. Place in a greased 15-in. x 10-in. x 1-in. baking pan. Bake at 425° for 25-30 minutes or until juices run clear, turning every 10 minutes.

In a small bowl, combine the sauce ingredients. Serve with chicken wings. **Yield:** 6 servings.

Sausage Wonton Cups

King Crab Puffs

(Pictured below)

Prep: 30 min. **Bake:** 20 min./batch

My mother loved entertaining when I was growing up, and she often served these delectable puffs at her parties.
—Krisann Anderson, Forest Lake, Minnesota

✓ Uses less fat, sugar or salt. Includes Nutrition Facts and Diabetic Exchanges.

- 2 cans (6 ounces *each*) crabmeat, drained, flaked and cartilage removed
- 3 green onions, chopped
- 1/2 cup shredded sharp cheddar cheese
- 2 teaspoons Worcestershire sauce
- 1 teaspoon ground mustard
- 1 cup water
- 1/2 cup butter, cubed
- 1/4 teaspoon salt
- 1 cup all-purpose flour
- 4 eggs

In a small bowl, combine the crab, onions, cheese, Worcestershire sauce and mustard; set aside. In a large saucepan, bring water, butter and salt to a boil. Add flour all at once and stir until a smooth ball forms. Remove from the heat; let stand for 5 minutes.

Add eggs, one at a time, beating well after each addition. Continue beating until mixture is smooth and shiny. Stir in crab mixture.

Drop by tablespoonfuls 2 in. apart onto ungreased baking sheets. Bake at 400° for 20-25 minutes or until golden brown. Remove to wire racks. Serve warm. **Yield:** 4 dozen.

Nutrition Facts: 1 crab puff equals 44 calories, 3 g fat (2 g saturated fat), 30 mg cholesterol, 70 mg sodium, 2 g carbohydrate, trace fiber, 3 g protein. **Diabetic Exchanges:** 1/2 lean meat, 1/2 fat.

Marinated Mozzarella

Marinated Mozzarella

(Pictured above)

Prep: 15 min. + marinating

I come home with an empty dish whenever I take these cheese cubes to an event. Serve them with pretty party picks for a fun look. —Peggy Cairo, Kenosha, Wisconsin

- 1/3 cup olive oil
- 1 tablespoon chopped oil-packed sun-dried tomatoes
- 1 tablespoon minced fresh parsley
- 1 teaspoon crushed red pepper flakes
- 1 teaspoon dried basil
- 1 teaspoon minced chives
- 1/4 teaspoon garlic powder
- 1 pound mozzarella cheese, cut into 1-inch cubes

In a large resealable plastic bag, combine the first seven ingredients; add cheese cubes. Seal bag and turn to coat; refrigerate for at least 30 minutes. Transfer to a serving dish; serve with toothpicks. **Yield:** 8-10 servings.

King Crab Puffs

Appetizer Party Pointers

HOSTING an appetizer buffet with no set seating? To make it more manageable for guests to mingle while munching, make note of these key tips:

- Choose some foods that can be picked up and eaten without a plate, such as cubed sausage and cheese, skewered meatballs and cut-up vegetables.
- Offer guests small, sturdy plates that are easy to handle. Consider making simple-to-carry bundles of cutlery and napkins.
- Set out bowls of nuts and snack mixes in other rooms, away from the buffet table. Make extra napkins readily available in these areas.

Black-Eyed Pea Salsa

Black-Eyed Pea Salsa

(Pictured above)

Prep/Total Time: 25 min.

This tongue-tingling salsa is full of possibilities. Colorful and mouth-watering, it's the perfect choice for your family's favorite tortilla chips. But it's also a wonderful accompaniment for pork chops and other main-course meats.
—Peg Wilson, Elm Creek, Nebraska

✓ Uses less fat, sugar or salt. Includes Nutrition Facts and Diabetic Exchanges.

- 4 large tomatoes, seeded and chopped
- 1 package (16 ounces) frozen corn, thawed
- 1 can (15-1/2 ounces) black-eyed peas, rinsed and drained
- 1/2 cup chopped green pepper
- 3 green onions, sliced
- 2 tablespoons minced fresh cilantro
- 1 cup Italian salad dressing
- Assorted tortilla chips
- Pork chops

In a large bowl, combine the first six ingredients. Drizzle with dressing and toss to coat. Serve with a slotted spoon as a salad, with tortilla chips or over pork chops. Refrigerate leftovers. **Yield:** 6 cups.

Nutrition Facts: 1/4 cup equals 74 calories, 4 g fat (trace saturated fat), 0 cholesterol, 208 mg sodium, 9 g carbohydrate, 1 g fiber, 2 g protein. **Diabetic Exchanges:** 1/2 starch, 1/2 fat.

Antipasto Bread

Prep/Total Time: 30 min.

Sauteed vegetables add a fresh, robust taste to these Italian bread slices. For a change of pace, use prosciutto or shaved deli ham instead of salami. —Genise Krause
Sturgeon Bay, Wisconsin

- 1 loaf (1 pound) unsliced Italian bread
- 3 tablespoons olive oil, *divided*
- 1 large carrot, chopped
- 1 medium green pepper, chopped
- 1 medium celery rib, chopped
- 1 medium onion, chopped
- 1 teaspoon minced garlic
- 1/2 cup prepared pesto
- 8 thin slices hard salami
- 4 plum tomatoes, sliced
- 1/2 cup chopped pitted green olives
- 2 cups (8 ounces) shredded Italian cheese blend

Cut bread in half lengthwise, then in half widthwise. Place cut side up in a foil-lined 15-in. x 10-in. x 1-in. baking pan. Brush with 2 tablespoons oil. Bake at 450° for 5-8 minutes or until lightly browned.

Meanwhile, in a small skillet, saute the carrot, green pepper, celery, onion and garlic in remaining oil for 5 minutes or until tender.

Spread the pesto over the bread. Top with the salami, tomatoes, carrot mixture and green olives. Sprinkle with the cheese. Bake for 8-10 minutes or until the cheese is melted. Cut each piece of bread in half to serve. **Yield:** 8 servings.

Spicy Stuffed Mushrooms

Prep: 30 min. **Bake:** 25 min.

These savory stuffed mushrooms have been a huge hit with family and friends. For a little less heat, substitute a milder sausage and different cheese for the pepper Jack.
—Amy Derkos, Escanaba, Michigan

  1/2 pound bulk spicy pork sausage
   24 large fresh mushrooms
  1/2 cup chopped green onions
  1/4 cup minced garlic
  1/4 cup butter
    1 cup seasoned bread crumbs
    1 cup (4 ounces) shredded pepper Jack cheese, *divided*

In a small skillet, cook sausage over medium heat for 5-6 minutes or until no longer pink; drain.

Remove stems from mushrooms and finely chop; set caps aside. In a large skillet, saute the stems, onions and garlic in butter for 4-5 minutes or until crisp-tender. Stir in the sausage, bread crumbs and 1/2 cup cheese.

Spoon about 2 tablespoons into each mushroom cap. Place on a foil-lined baking sheet; sprinkle with remaining cheese. Bake at 350° for 22-25 minutes or until mushrooms are tender. **Yield:** 2 dozen.

Smoked Trout Cucumber Canapes

(Pictured below)

Prep/Total Time: 20 min.

When I served these elegant appetizers at my last party, guests thought I'd had them catered! Everyone loved the warm and creamy seafood spread on the cool cucumber slices. —*Debora Ross, Hamilton, Ohio*

Smoked Trout Cucumber Canapes

Onion Veggie Dip

✓ Uses less fat, sugar or salt. Includes Nutrition Facts and Diabetic Exchanges.

4-1/2 ounces smoked trout *or* salmon fillets, flaked
    1 package (3 ounces) cream cheese, softened
    2 tablespoons finely chopped red onion
    2 teaspoons minced fresh dill
    2 teaspoons lemon juice
1-1/2 teaspoons prepared horseradish
    1 teaspoon grated lemon peel
   24 cucumber slices (1/4 inch thick)

In a small bowl, combine the trout, cream cheese, onion, dill, lemon juice, horseradish and lemon peel. Spread over each cucumber slice. Refrigerate until serving. **Yield:** 2 dozen.

Nutrition Facts: 1 appetizer equals 24 calories, 2 g fat (1 g saturated fat), 8 mg cholesterol, 118 mg sodium, trace carbohydrate, trace fiber, 2 g protein. **Diabetic Exchange:** 1/2 fat.

Onion Veggie Dip

(Pictured above)

Prep: 10 min. + chilling

With just four ingredients and only 10 minutes of prep, this zippy dip is perfect with veggies or crackers.
—Ruthie Pomeroy, Mt. Angel, Oregon

    2 cups (16 ounces) sour cream
    3 tablespoons dried minced onion
    3 tablespoons dried parsley flakes
    1 teaspoon seasoned salt
Assorted fresh vegetables *or* crackers

In a small bowl, combine the first four ingredients. Cover and chill for at least 1 hour. Serve with vegetables or crackers. **Yield:** 2 cups.

1/4 cup minced fresh cilantro
2 tablespoons lime juice
1/8 teaspoon salt

Place corn in a small saucepan and cover with water. Bring to a boil; cover and cook for 1-2 minutes or until crisp-tender. Drain and rinse in cold water.

Place the corn in a large bowl; stir in the remaining ingredients. Serve the salsa immediately or refrigerate. **Yield:** 4 cups.

Editor's Note: When cutting or seeding hot peppers, use rubber or plastic gloves to protect your hands. Avoid touching your face.

Nutrition Facts: 1/4 cup equals 28 calories, trace fat (trace saturated fat), 0 cholesterol, 22 mg sodium, 6 g carbohydrate, 1 g fiber, 1 g protein. **Diabetic Exchange:** 1/2 starch.

Ranch Popcorn

(Pictured above)
Prep/Total Time: 20 min.

What's a movie without a bowl of popcorn? The next time your family gathers around the TV for movie night at home, try a big tub of our Test Kitchen's buttery, show-stopping blend. It's easy, cheesy and finger-lickin' good!

3 quarts popped popcorn
1/3 cup butter, melted
1/4 cup grated Parmesan cheese
2 tablespoons ranch salad dressing mix
1 teaspoon dried parsley flakes
1/4 teaspoon onion powder

Place the popcorn in an ungreased 13-in. x 9-in. x 2-in. baking pan. Combine the remaining ingredients; pour over popcorn and toss to coat.

Bake, uncovered, at 350° for 10 minutes or until lightly browned. Serve warm. **Yield:** 8 servings.

Watermelon Salsa

Prep/Total Time: 25 min.

Shake things up at summer parties with our Test Kitchen's fruity take on classic salsa. This chip dip combines traditional corn and hot jalapenos with cool chopped watermelon and fresh blueberries.

☑ Uses less fat, sugar or salt. Includes Nutrition Facts and Diabetic Exchanges.

1-1/2 cups fresh corn
3 cups chopped seedless watermelon
1 cup fresh blueberries
1 jalapeno pepper, seeded and chopped
2 green onions, chopped

Tomato Guacamole Dip

(Pictured below)
Prep/Total Time: 15 min.

So light and fresh, this colorful dip is the perfect way to start off your dinner. —Jill Perez, Racine, Wisconsin

2 medium ripe avocados, peeled and chopped
1 tablespoon lime juice
1 small tomato, seeded and chopped
3 tablespoons sour cream
1/2 teaspoon salt
1/2 teaspoon minced garlic
Tortilla chips

In a small bowl, mash avocados and lime juice with a fork. Stir in the tomato, sour cream, salt and garlic. Cover and refrigerate for 5 minutes. Serve with tortilla chips. **Yield:** 2-1/3 cups.

Tomato Guacamole Dip

Pesto Chili Peanuts
Chutney-Topped Brie

Pesto Chili Peanuts

(Pictured above)

Prep/Total Time: 25 min.

Who'd ever dream of teaming pesto with peanuts? I did! And the result is a can't-stop-eating-it snack that's salty, savory and sure to be in "hot" demand with your friends and family...just try it and see.
—*Dennis Dahlin*
Bolingbrook, Illinois

  1 envelope pesto sauce mix
  3 tablespoons olive oil
  1 teaspoon chili powder
1/4 teaspoon cayenne pepper
  5 cups salted dry roasted peanuts

In a small bowl, whisk the pesto mix, oil, chili powder and cayenne. Pour into a large resealable plastic bag; add peanuts. Seal bag and shake to coat. Transfer to a greased 13-in. x 9-in. x 2-in. baking pan.

Bake, uncovered, at 350° for 15-20 minutes, stirring once. Spread on waxed paper to cool. Store in an airtight container. **Yield:** 5 cups.

Chutney-Topped Brie

(Pictured above and on page 280)

Prep/Total Time: 15 min.

This appetizer couldn't be much simpler—it has only four ingredients! I created it after trying something similar at a cheese shop. —*Rebecca Irons, Lubbock, Texas*

  1 round (8 ounces) **Brie** *or* **Camembert cheese**
1/4 cup chutney
  2 tablespoons real bacon bits
Assorted crackers

Place cheese in an ungreased ovenproof serving dish. Top with chutney and bacon. Bake, uncovered, at 400° for 10-12 minutes or until cheese is softened. Serve with crackers. **Yield:** 8 servings.

Deluxe Nachos

Deluxe Nachos

(Pictured above)

Prep/Total Time: 30 min.

Packed with fresh-veggie goodness and topped with sour cream, these delicious nachos always delight family and friends. It's convenient to keep the ingredients on hand so I can serve up a platter whenever hunger hits. —Jennifer Parham
Browns Summit, North Carolina

2 cans (10-3/4 ounces *each*) condensed
 cheddar cheese soup, undiluted
1 cup salsa
2 packages (10 ounces *each*) tortilla chips
2 to 4 plum tomatoes, chopped
1 medium green pepper, chopped
1 medium sweet red pepper, chopped
4 to 6 green onions, sliced
2 cans (2-1/4 ounces *each*) sliced ripe olives,
 drained
1 cup (8 ounces) sour cream

In a saucepan, combine soup and salsa; heat through. Arrange tortilla chips on two serving platters; top with soup mixture. Sprinkle with tomatoes, peppers, onions and olives. Top with sour cream. Serve immediately. **Yield:** 8 servings.

Onion Rings

Prep/Total Time: 25 min.

These mouth-watering bites will keep everyone wondering what's different about the recipe...and they'll never guess it's the apple juice! The rings make a terrific snack or side dish when time is of the essence. —Joan Hallford
North Richland Hills, Texas

2 large sweet onions
1-1/4 cups all-purpose flour
1 teaspoon salt
3/4 teaspoon baking powder

1/4 teaspoon pepper
1 egg, lightly beaten
1 cup apple juice
1 tablespoon vegetable oil
Additional oil for frying

Cut onions into 1/4-in. slices and separate into rings. In a shallow bowl, combine the flour, salt, baking powder and pepper. In a small bowl, combine the egg, apple juice and oil; stir into dry ingredients just until moistened.

In an electric skillet or deep-fat fryer, heat 1 in. of oil to 375°. Dip onion rings into batter. Fry, a few at a time, for 2-3 minutes on each side or until golden brown. Drain on paper towels. **Yield:** 4 servings.

Healthy House

(Pictured below)

Prep/Total Time: 10 min.

When my daughter Jessica was in the third grade, she had an extra-credit assignment dealing with nutrition. While I was combing through cookbooks, Jessica came up with this! Everyone at school loved it, and since then, she's been eager to help in the kitchen and try new recipes.
—Mary Wollensak, Brookfield, Wisconsin

1 slice whole wheat bread, crust removed
1 tablespoon peanut butter
1 thin slice deli turkey
1 raisin
5 pieces Rice Chex
1 slice American cheese
1 celery stick

Spread bread with peanut butter. For door, cut turkey into a 1-1/2-in. x 1-1/4-in. rectangle; position on bread. Add raisin for doorknob and cereal for windows.

Cut the cheese slice in half diagonally; place one piece above bread for roof (save remaining piece for another use). Add celery stick for chimney. **Yield:** 1 serving.

Healthy House

Jalapenos with Olive-Cream Filling

In a shallow bowl, beat eggs. In a large resealable plastic bag, combine the cornflakes, chili powder and garlic salt. Dip potato wedges into eggs, then place in bag, a few at a time, and shake to coat.

Place potatoes in a single layer in two greased 15-in. x 10-in. x 1-in. baking pans. Drizzle with oil. Bake, uncovered, at 400° for 20 minutes. Turn; bake 10-15 minutes longer or until crisp outside and tender inside.

In a small bowl, combine sour cream and salsa. Serve with potatoes for dipping. **Yield:** 8 servings.

Mini Veggie Wagon

(Pictured below)

Prep/Total Time: 15 min.

I assembled these wagons for our farm-themed family reunion and received a lot of compliments on them. Even the youngsters were delighted and enthusiastically ate up their vegetables—right down to the cucumber-slice wagon wheels!
—*Nella Parker, Hersey, Michigan*

   2 celery ribs
   1 medium cucumber
   2 wooden skewers (6 inches)
**Fresh baby carrots and green and purple broccoli
   florets *or* vegetables of your choice**
Vegetable dill dip

Cut celery ribs in half lengthwise and then into 6-in. pieces. Cut cucumber into 1/2-in. slices. Place one cucumber slice on the end of each skewer; place celery pieces lengthwise across skewers to form wagon frame.

Pile carrots, broccoli and remaining cucumber on wagon. Serve with dip. **Yield:** 4-6 servings.

Jalapenos with Olive-Cream Filling

(Pictured above)

Prep/Total Time: 25 min.

One word describes these jalapenos—great! I take them to just about every get-together and potluck I attend.
—*Krystal Peterson, Walker, Louisiana*

   1 package (8 ounces) cream cheese, softened
1/4 cup chopped pimiento-stuffed olives
   2 tablespoons olive juice
   **16 large jalapeno peppers, halved lengthwise
   and seeded**

In a small mixing bowl, combine the cream cheese, olives and olive juice. Spoon about 2 teaspoons into each jalapeno half. Serve immediately or refrigerate. **Yield:** 32 appetizers.

   Editor's Note: When cutting or seeding hot peppers, use rubber or plastic gloves to protect your hands. Avoid touching your face.

Hot Potato Dippers

Prep: 20 min. **Bake:** 30 min.

These crunchy fries go over big. For variety, substitute Parmesan cheese and Italian herb seasoning for the chili powder and garlic salt. —*Ray Luoma, Mansfield, Ohio*

   2 eggs
1-1/2 cups crushed cornflakes
   3 tablespoons chili powder
   1 tablespoon garlic salt
   **8 medium unpeeled potatoes, cut into
   1/4-inch-thick wedges**
1/4 cup vegetable oil
2/3 cup sour cream
   6 tablespoons salsa

Mini Veggie Wagon

DO SOME RECIPES turn you off because they appear too complicated and time-consuming to fit your hectic schedule? Here, our Test Kitchen pros have shared their secrets to creating fancy-looking, homemade specialties your family will think you spent hours preparing.

Discover shortcuts and helpful hints for making impressive chicken rolls...using fresh melon...assembling gourmet-style ice cream sandwiches...roasting veggies...and whipping up perfect crumb crusts for pies.

You'll likely be amazed at the restaurant-worthy recipes you'll be able to fix in minutes in your own kitchen. Just let our home economists show you how!

SPEEDY BUT SPECIAL. Pesto Shrimp Pasta Toss (p. 301).

Left to right:
Mushroom-Stuffed Chicken Breasts
Southwest Chicken Kiev
Mashed Potato Chicken Roll-Ups

Roll Out Special Chicken

LOOKING for something new for supper? It's simpler than you might think to create stuffed chicken roll-ups. With some hints from our Test Kitchen cooks, you'll soon be rolling along, turning chicken into delicious breaded specialties. And once you get the hang of it, you may want to experiment with other stuffing and breading ideas (see the tip box below right).

Southwest Chicken Kiev

(Pictured above)

Prep: 25 min. **Cook:** 15 min.

This updated version of chicken Kiev uses taco seasoning and green chilies to add Southwestern flavor. I cook the roll-ups in the microwave for a fast, stress-free meal.
—Lesley Tragesser, Charleston, Missouri

  1 **cup miniature cheese crackers, crushed**
1-1/2 **teaspoons taco seasoning**
  5 **tablespoons butter, softened,** *divided*
  3 **tablespoons shredded cheddar cheese**
  2 **tablespoons canned chopped green chilies**
  2 **teaspoons dried minced onion**
1/2 **teaspoon salt**
  6 **boneless skinless chicken breast halves**
    (6 ounces *each***)**

In a shallow bowl, combine cracker crumbs and taco seasoning; set aside. In another bowl, combine 3 tablespoons butter, cheese, chilies, onion and salt. Shape mixture into six balls.

Flatten chicken to 1/4-in. thickness. Place a butter ball in the center of each. Roll up and secure with toothpicks. In a shallow microwave-safe bowl, melt remaining butter. Dip chicken in butter, then coat evenly with cracker mixture.

Place seam side down in a greased shallow round 3-qt. microwave-safe dish. Microwave, uncovered, on high for 12-14 minutes or until chicken juices run clear. Discard toothpicks. **Yield:** 6 servings.

Editor's Note: This recipe was tested in a 1,100-watt microwave.

More Choices for Chicken

FEEL FREE to experiment with these coatings:
• Crushed cornflakes
• Crushed saltines
• Panko (Japanese bread crumbs)
• Bread crumbs tossed with taco or fajita seasoning
• Bread crumbs with Parmesan cheese

You could also try these possibilities for stuffing:
• Cream cheese with herbs
• Feta cheese and kalamata olives
• Sauteed garlic and mushrooms
• Ham and mozzarella
• Cooked sausage

Mashed Potato Chicken Roll-Ups

(Pictured at left)

Prep: 25 min. **Bake:** 40 min.

My grandchildren always help me in the kitchen, and I try to encourage their interest in cooking. My granddaughter, Nicole, loves to help combine and layer the ingredients for casseroles. This wonderful, potato-stuffed chicken was invented by my grandson, Joey. —Rosemary Gisin
Putnam Valley, New York

  6 **boneless skinless chicken breast halves**
     (6 ounces *each*)
  1 **tub (24 ounces) refrigerated cheddar**
     mashed potatoes, *divided*
  1 **package (10 ounces) frozen chopped**
     spinach, thawed and squeezed dry
  1 **cup all-purpose flour**
  2 **eggs**
  2 **tablespoons water**
1-1/2 **cups seasoned bread crumbs**
  1 **can (10-3/4 ounces) condensed cream of**
     mushroom soup, undiluted
  1/2 **cup milk**

Flatten the chicken to 1/2-in. thickness. Spread 2 tablespoons of mashed potatoes down the center of each; top with the spinach. Roll up the chicken and secure with toothpicks.

Place the flour in a shallow bowl. In another bowl, whisk the eggs and water. Place the bread crumbs in a third bowl. Coat the chicken with flour, dip in egg mixture, then roll in crumbs.

Place each chicken roll-up seam side down in a greased 11-in. x 7-in. x 2-in. baking dish. Bake, uncovered, at 375° for 40-45 minutes or until the chicken juices run clear.

In a small saucepan, combine the cream of mushroom soup and milk; cook over medium-high heat for 5-7 minutes or until heated through. Heat the remaining mashed potatoes according to the package directions. Discard the toothpicks from the chicken; serve with sauce and potatoes. **Yield:** 6 servings.

Mushroom-Stuffed Chicken Breasts

(Pictured at top left)

Prep: 20 min. **Bake:** 30 min.

Stuffing mix provides a deliciously crisp coating and pleasant filling for these chicken breasts. The moist and satisfying main course looks time-consuming, but it requires just 20 minutes of prep work before I pop it in the oven.
—Edie DeSpain, Logan, Utah

1-1/2 **cups chopped fresh mushrooms**
  1/4 **cup chopped celery**
  1/4 **cup chopped green onions**
  1/4 **teaspoon dried marjoram**

Making Elegant Chicken Roll-Ups

1. Place a chicken breast inside a resealable plastic bag or under plastic wrap. Lightly pound chicken with a meat mallet to flatten evenly.

2. Place the desired filling (about 2-3 tablespoons) in the center and roll up.

3. Secure with toothpicks. Then dip in egg mixture or butter.

4. Coat all sides of each chicken roll-up with the coating of your choice.

  1/4 **cup butter, *divided***
  1 **package (6 ounces) chicken-flavored stuffing**
     mix, coarsely crushed, *divided*
  4 **boneless skinless chicken breast halves**
     (6 ounces *each*)
  1 **egg**
  2 **tablespoons milk**
  1 **teaspoon paprika**

In a small skillet, saute the mushrooms, celery, green onions and marjoram in 2 tablespoons butter for 3-4 minutes or until the vegetables are tender. Stir in 1/2 cup stuffing mix.

Flatten chicken to 1/4-in. thickness. Spoon mushroom mixture down the center of each. Roll up and secure with toothpicks.

In a shallow bowl, whisk the egg and milk. Place the remaining stuffing mix in another bowl; stir in the paprika. Dip the chicken in egg mixture, then coat with crumb mixture. Place seam side down in a greased 8-in. square baking dish.

Melt the remaining butter and drizzle over the chicken. Bake, uncovered, at 375° for 30-35 minutes or until the chicken juices run clear. Discard the toothpicks. **Yield:** 4 servings.

Fiesta Fruit Cups

Meanwhile, in a large bowl, combine the strawberries, melons and orange. Stir in preserves. Using a slotted spoon, spoon into dessert cups. Serve with tortilla chips. Garnish with whipped topping and additional strawberries if desired. **Yield:** 6 servings.

Nutrition Facts: 2/3 cup fruit with 6 tortilla chips (calculated without optional ingredients) equals 280 calories, 9 g fat (4 g saturated fat), 15 mg cholesterol, 288 mg sodium, 49 g carbohydrate, 2 g fiber, 4 g protein.

Mint Watermelon Sorbet

Prep: 20 min. + freezing

Looking for something fruity and sweet to cool off a hot day? Whip up this fun sorbet from our Test Kitchen.

☑ Uses less fat, sugar or salt. Includes Nutrition Facts and Diabetic Exchanges.

  1/2 cup sugar
  1/2 cup water
    4 cups cubed seedless watermelon
    2 tablespoons orange juice
    1 tablespoon minced fresh mint
    1 tablespoon honey
    2 teaspoons lime juice

In a small saucepan, bring sugar and water to a boil, stirring constantly until sugar is dissolved; set aside. In a blender, process watermelon in batches until smooth. Transfer to a large bowl; stir in the sugar syrup, orange juice, mint, honey and lime juice.

Pour into a 13-in. x 9-in. x 2-in. dish; cover and freeze for 8 hours or until firm. Just before serving, transfer to a food processor; cover and process in batches until smooth. **Yield:** 7 servings.

Nutrition Facts: 1/2 cup equals 90 calories, trace fat (0 saturated fat), 0 cholesterol, 3 mg sodium, 25 g carbohydrate, 1 g fiber, trace protein. **Diabetic Exchanges:** 1 starch, 1/2 fruit.

Melons Bring a Slice of Summer

JUICY, sweet and bursting with flavor, there's nothing like fresh melon in the summertime. Here, our Test Kitchen pros offer cantaloupe cutting hints. Plus, you'll see delightful recipes featuring not only cantaloupe, but also watermelon and honeydew, too.

Fiesta Fruit Cups

(Pictured above)

Prep/Total Time: 25 min.

These colorful fruit bowls are nice to serve for brunch...or even as a snack. —*Karen Ann Bland, Gove, Kansas*

☑ Uses less fat, sugar or salt. Includes Nutrition Facts.

  6 flour tortillas (6 inches)
  3 tablespoons butter, melted
  3 tablespoons cinnamon-sugar
  2 cups halved fresh strawberries
  1 cup cubed cantaloupe
  1 cup cubed honeydew
  1 large navel orange, peeled and sectioned
1/2 cup peach preserves
Whipped topping and additional strawberries, optional

Place tortillas on ungreased baking sheets. Brush with butter; sprinkle with cinnamon-sugar. Cut each tortilla into six wedges. Bake at 350° for 12-15 minutes or until lightly browned. Cool on wire racks.

Cutting Cantaloupe Like a Pro

1. Place the cantaloupe on a cutting board and cut off the ends of the melon with a sharp knife.

2. Stand the cantaloupe on one end and gently cut away the rind, leaving as much of the tender flesh intact as possible.

Chicken Breasts with Melon Relish

(Pictured above)

Prep/Total Time: 30 min.

For a quick but attractive entree, try this recipe. Each grilled chicken breast is topped with a tropical, sweet relish. Rubbing the chicken with spices enhances the flavor in a flash. —Roxanne Chan, Albany, California

✓ Uses less fat, sugar or salt. Includes Nutrition Facts and Diabetic Exchanges.

    1/4 teaspoon salt
    1/4 teaspoon ground ginger
    1/4 teaspoon ground nutmeg
    1/4 teaspoon pepper
      4 boneless skinless chicken breast halves
        (6 ounces *each*)
      1 tablespoon canola oil
RELISH:
      1 cup diced cantaloupe
    1/4 cup finely chopped celery
      1 green onion, chopped
      2 tablespoons minced fresh mint
      1 tablespoon chopped candied ginger
      1 tablespoon lime juice
      1 tablespoon honey
    1/2 teaspoon grated lime peel

In a small bowl, combine the salt, ginger, nutmeg and pepper. Rub over both sides of chicken. In a large skillet, cook chicken in oil over medium heat for 8-10 min-utes on each side or until juices run clear. Meanwhile, in a small bowl, combine the relish ingredients. Serve with chicken. **Yield:** 4 servings.

Nutrition Facts: 1 chicken breast half with 1/4 cup relish equals 260 calories, 8 g fat (2 g saturated fat), 94 mg cholesterol, 243 mg sodium, 12 g carbohydrate, 1 g fiber, 35 g protein. **Diabetic Exchanges:** 5 very lean meat, 1 starch, 1/2 fat.

Cantaloupe-Orange Milk Shakes

Prep/Total Time: 10 min.

These irresistible thirst-quenchers are a cinch to fix with just a handful of ingredients. In fact, you'll need to spend only 10 minutes in the kitchen! It's a special treat to sit down and relax with one of these shakes on a hot summer day. —Carol Mead, Los Alamos, New Mexico

    3/4 cup cubed cantaloupe
    4-1/2 teaspoons orange juice concentrate
      1 cup vanilla ice cream *or* frozen yogurt
    3/4 cup milk
      3 tablespoons sugar

In a blender, combine cantaloupe and orange juice concentrate; cover and process for 30 seconds or until smooth. Add ice cream, milk and sugar; cover and process until blended. Pour into chilled glasses; serve immediately. **Yield:** 2 servings.

Try Ice Cream Sandwiches

NO MATTER what your age may be, you likely have fond summer memories of racing to eat all of your ice cream before it could drip away. Why not relive some of that fun with the hassle-free treats here? They're sure to delight young and old alike.

In this section, you'll discover the secret to creating an assortment of sensational ice cream sandwiches. Begin with the basic brownie recipe on this page, then choose any of the accompanying recipes to turn the brownie into a scrumptious ice cream specialty. You'll find a variety of lip-smacking flavors, from caramel-coffee to double peanut butter.

Store these sandwiches in the freezer as a sweet surprise for your family and friends on a hot summer day. We guarantee that these treats will disappear before even a single drip can appear!

Brownie for Ice Cream Sandwiches

Prep: 10 min. **Bake:** 10 min. + cooling

This fast-to-fix brownie recipe offers just the right chocolaty complement to all sorts of yummy ice cream sandwich variations. Baked in a sheet pan, the big brownie gives you enough to create a dozen or more sweet sandwiches.
—*Lucie Fitzgerald, Spring Hill, Florida*

1/2 cup butter, cubed
  4 squares (1 ounce *each*) semisweet chocolate
  2 eggs
  1 cup sugar
  1 teaspoon vanilla extract
3/4 cup all-purpose flour
1/4 teaspoon salt

In a microwave-safe bowl or heavy saucepan, melt butter and chocolate; stir until smooth. Cool slightly. In a large mixing bowl, beat eggs and sugar. Stir in vanilla and chocolate mixture. Combine flour and salt; gradually add to chocolate mixture.

Pour into a parchment paper-lined 15-in. x 10-in. x 1-in. baking pan. Bake at 400° for 10-12 minutes or until center is set (do not overbake). Cool completely on a wire rack. Invert brownie onto a work surface and remove parchment paper.

Prepare according to recipe directions for Candy Bar Ice Cream Sandwiches, Banana Split Ice Cream Sandwiches, Raspberry-Orange Ice Cream Sandwiches, S'more Ice Cream Sandwiches, Caramel-Coffee Ice Cream Sandwiches or Double Peanut Butter Ice Cream Sandwiches (recipes on this page and pages 298-299). **Yield:** enough to make 12-15 ice cream sandwiches.

S'more Ice Cream Sandwiches

(Pictured at left)

Prep: 35 min. + freezing

From our Test Kitchen staff, these cool treats deliver the same classic taste as a toasty s'more...but you don't need a bonfire or roasting stick to enjoy it!

Brownie for Ice Cream Sandwiches (recipe on page 296)
    4 cups chocolate ice cream, softened
    1 cup marshmallow creme
Graham cracker crumbs

Prepare, bake and cool Brownie for Ice Cream Sandwiches according to recipe directions. Cut brownie in half widthwise. Spread ice cream over one brownie half. Spread marshmallow creme over remaining brownie; place over ice cream, marshmallow side down. Cover and freeze for 2 hours or until firm.

Cut into bars, squares or desired shapes. Dip sides of ice cream sandwiches in graham cracker crumbs. Wrap in plastic wrap. Freeze until serving. **Yield:** 12-15 servings.

Caramel-Coffee Ice Cream Sandwiches

(Pictured above left)

Prep: 25 min. **Bake:** 10 min. + freezing

Coffee lends grown-up appeal to this luscious combination. With caramel and chocolate, the tempting dessert created by our home economists will cool you off but leave your taste buds wanting more!

Brownie for Ice Cream Sandwiches (recipe on page 296)
    1 teaspoon instant coffee granules
    4 cups dulce de leche caramel
      ice cream, softened
Chocolate-covered coffee beans, chopped

Prepare batter for Brownie for Ice Cream Sandwiches; stir in coffee granules. Bake and cool according to recipe directions. Cut brownie in half widthwise. Spread ice cream over one brownie half. Turn over remaining brownie half; place over ice cream. Cover and freeze for 2 hours or until firm.

Cut into bars, squares or desired shapes. Dip sides of ice cream sandwiches in coffee beans. Wrap in plastic wrap. Freeze until serving. **Yield:** 12-15 servings.

1. Cut brownie sheet in half widthwise.

2. Cut open the quart-sized carton of softened ice cream. Cut the ice cream into four slices to make it easier to spread. Using a spatula, spread the ice cream slices onto the brownie sheet.

3. To create dipped ice cream sandwiches, cut the large brownie sandwich into smaller pieces. Dip one end of the sandwich into the coating, letting the excess drip off. Place dipped brownie sandwiches on a waxed paper-lined baking sheet; let stand until set. Wrap in plastic wrap and freeze until serving.

Banana Split Ice Cream Sandwiches
Candy Bar Ice Cream Sandwiches
Raspberry-Orange Ice Cream Sandwiches
Double Peanut Butter Ice Cream Sandwiches

Candy Bar Ice Cream Sandwiches

(Pictured at left)

Prep: 25 min. **Bake:** 10 min. + freezing

Our Test Kitchen staff assembled this out-of-this-world dessert in minutes. With such decadent ingredients, who wouldn't love these bars?

Brownie for Ice Cream Sandwiches (recipe on page 296)
    4 cups Snickers ice cream, softened
    1 bottle (7-1/4 ounces) chocolate hard-shell ice cream topping

Prepare, bake and cool Brownie for Ice Cream Sandwiches according to recipe directions. Cut brownie in half widthwise. Spread ice cream over one brownie half. Turn over remaining brownie half; place over ice cream. Cover and freeze for 2 hours or until firm.

Cut into bars, squares or desired shapes. Drizzle with ice cream topping; let stand for 1-2 minutes or until topping is set. Wrap in plastic wrap. Freeze until serving. **Yield:** 12-15 servings.

Raspberry-Orange Ice Cream Sandwiches

(Pictured at left)

Prep: 25 min. **Bake:** 10 min. + freezing

Orange adds a surprisingly fresh and fruity flavor to this elegant sorbet sandwich from our home economists.

Brownie for Ice Cream Sandwiches (recipe on page 296)
    1/2 to 1 teaspoon grated orange peel
    4 cups raspberry sorbet, softened
White chocolate curls

Prepare batter for Brownie for Ice Cream Sandwiches; stir in orange peel. Bake and cool according to recipe directions. Cut brownie in half widthwise. Spread sorbet over one brownie half. Turn over remaining brownie half; place over sorbet. Cover and freeze for 2 hours or until firm.

Cut into bars, squares or desired shapes. Dip sides of ice cream sandwiches in chocolate curls. Wrap in plastic wrap. Freeze until serving. **Yield:** 12-15 servings.

Double Peanut Butter Ice Cream Sandwiches

(Pictured at left)

Prep: 25 min. **Bake:** 10 min. + freezing

Chocolate and peanut butter...that popular combo was our Test Kitchen's starting point for these luscious bars. They're also dipped in a creamy candy coating. Yum!

Brownie for Ice Cream Sandwiches (recipe on page 296)
    4 cups peanut butter ice cream with peanut butter cup pieces, softened

    8 ounces white candy coating, coarsely chopped
    1 tablespoon creamy peanut butter
    1 teaspoon shortening

Prepare, bake and cool Brownie for Ice Cream Sandwiches according to recipe directions. Cut brownie in half widthwise. Spread ice cream over one brownie half. Turn over remaining brownie half; place over ice cream. Cover and freeze for 2 hours or until firm.

In a microwave-safe bowl, melt the candy coating, peanut butter and shortening at 70% power for 1-2 minutes; stir until smooth.

Cut ice cream sandwich into bars, squares or desired shapes. Dip into coating mixture, letting excess drip off. Place on waxed paper; let stand until set. Wrap in plastic wrap. Freeze until serving. **Yield:** 12-15 servings.

Banana Split Ice Cream Sandwiches

(Pictured at far left)

Prep: 25 min. **Bake:** 10 min. + freezing

Enjoy a banana split without the spoon! Our home economists captured the flavors of that favorite ice cream sundae, serving it up sandwich-style.

Brownie for Ice Cream Sandwiches (recipe on page 296)
    1/2 cup chopped pecans
    1/2 cup hot fudge ice cream topping, warmed
    4 cups strawberry ice cream, softened
    1 medium firm banana, thinly sliced

Prepare batter for Brownie for Ice Cream Sandwiches. Pour into prepared pan; sprinkle with pecans. Bake and cool according to recipe directions. Cut brownie in half widthwise. Spread hot fudge topping over one brownie half; spread with ice cream and layer with banana slices. Turn over remaining brownie half; place over bananas. Cover and freeze for 2 hours or until firm.

Cut into bars, squares or desired shapes. Wrap in plastic wrap. Freeze until serving. **Yield:** 12-15 servings.

Ice Cream Variety

FOR a fun change of pace, try dipping the sides of your ice cream sandwiches into any of the following yummy options:
- Chopped nuts
- Chocolate jimmies
- Colored sprinkles
- Cookie crumbs
- Toasted flaked coconut
- Chopped candy bars
- Cereal crumbs
- Crushed peppermint candies or candy canes

Zippy Potato Chunks

sauce; drizzle over potatoes.

Bake, uncovered, at 450° for 45-50 minutes or until tender, stirring occasionally. Serve with salad dressing. **Yield:** 6 servings.

Veggie Bruschetta

Prep: 30 min. **Bake:** 20 min.

This scrumptious appetizer from our Test Kitchen is worth every minute it takes to make! You're sure to love the vegetable combination on crisp baguettes and the sprinkling of mozzarella cheese on top.

☑ Uses less fat, sugar or salt. Includes Nutrition Facts and Diabetic Exchanges.

    1 **medium zucchini, cut into 1/2-inch pieces**
    1 **cup chopped sweet red pepper**
    1 **cup chopped sweet yellow pepper**
 3/4 **cup chopped fresh mushrooms**
4-1/2 **teaspoons olive oil**
    1 **teaspoon Italian seasoning**
    1 **teaspoon minced garlic**
 1/4 **teaspoon salt**
 1/4 **teaspoon pepper**
    2 **French bread baguettes (10-1/2 ounces**
     each)
1-1/2 **teaspoons capers, drained**
    1 **cup (4 ounces) shredded part-skim**
     mozzarella cheese

In a small bowl, combine the first nine ingredients. Transfer to a 15-in. x 10-in. x 1-in. baking pan coated with nonstick cooking spray. Bake, uncovered, at 425° for 20-25 minutes or until vegetables are crisp-tender.

Cut each baguette into 16 slices. Stir capers into vegetable mixture; spoon 1 tablespoon onto each slice of bread. Sprinkle with cheese. Broil 3-4 in. from the heat for 3-4 minutes or until golden brown. **Yield:** 32 appetizers.

Nutrition Facts: 1 piece equals 98 calories, 3 g fat (1 g saturated fat), 2 mg cholesterol, 151 mg sodium, 15 g carbohydrate, 1 g fiber, 3 g protein. **Diabetic Exchanges:** 1 starch, 1/2 fat.

Get the Most Out of Roasting

SURE, IT'S EASY to steam or microwave some vegetables and serve them with tonight's dinner. But why do that when you can fix some terrific recipes? On these 2 pages, our Test Kitchen shares tips for creating special dishes big on flavor. Each one features veggies cooked at high oven temperatures, caramelizing the ingredients for a rich, intense taste. Enjoy!

Zippy Potato Chunks

(Pictured above)

Prep: 5 min. **Bake:** 45 min.

I took my cue from chicken wing recipes and gave these roasted potatoes a dash of hot sauce and a creamy dip. It's a side dish my friends and family can't resist.
   —Priscilla Gilbert, Indian Harbour Beach, Florida

    4 **medium baking potatoes, peeled and cut**
     into chunks
 1/3 **cup butter, melted**
    1 **envelope herb and garlic soup mix**
    1 **tablespoon hot pepper sauce**
Blue cheese *or* **ranch salad dressing**

Place the potatoes in a greased 13-in. x 9-in. x 2-in. baking dish. Combine the butter, soup mix and pepper

Helpful Hints for Roasting

- Get that oven hot! Suggested roasting temperatures range between 400 to 450 degrees.
- Cut vegetables into uniform sizes to cook them evenly. If you're working with a mixture of different vegetables, cut denser varieties, such as carrots and potatoes, into smaller pieces so they'll be done with everything else.
- Toss your vegetables with olive oil before roasting to add flavor and moisture and to prevent them from sticking to the pan.
- Spread vegetables in a single layer in a heavy, shallow-sided roasting pan. If the vegetables are crowded, they will steam instead of becoming crisp.

Rosemary Root Vegetables

(Pictured below)

Prep: 20 min. **Bake:** 20 min.

The ingredient list for this colorful fall medley may seem to be on the longer side, but our home economists made the recipe a snap to prepare.

☑ Uses less fat, sugar or salt. Includes Nutrition Facts and Diabetic Exchanges.

  1 small rutabaga, peeled and chopped
  1 medium sweet potato, peeled and chopped
  2 medium parsnips, peeled and chopped
  1 medium turnip, peeled and chopped
1/4 pound fresh brussels sprouts, halved
  2 tablespoons olive oil
  2 tablespoons minced fresh rosemary *or*
    2 teaspoons dried rosemary, crushed
  1 teaspoon minced garlic
1/2 teaspoon salt
1/2 teaspoon pepper

Place the vegetables in a large resealable plastic bag. Add the oil, rosemary, garlic, salt and pepper; seal bag and shake to coat.

Arrange vegetables in a single layer in two 15-in. x 10-in. x 1-in. baking pans coated with nonstick cooking spray. Bake, uncovered, at 425° for 20-25 minutes or until tender, stirring once. **Yield:** 10 servings.

Nutrition Facts: 3/4 cup equals 78 calories, 3 g fat (trace saturated fat), 0 cholesterol, 137 mg sodium, 13 g carbohydrate, 3 g fiber, 1 g protein. **Diabetic Exchanges:** 1 starch, 1/2 fat.

Rosemary Root Vegetables

Pesto Shrimp Pasta Toss

Pesto Shrimp Pasta Toss

(Pictured above and on page 290)

Prep/Total Time: 30 min.

I can whip up this elegant entree in just 30 minutes. Coated in pesto and topped with walnuts and Parmesan, the blend of pasta, shrimp and vegetables adds a dressed-up touch to any weeknight meal.
        —Fran Scott
        Birmingham, Michigan

  9 ounces uncooked linguine
  1 pound deveined peeled cooked medium
    shrimp
  1 pound fresh asparagus, trimmed and cut
    into 2-inch pieces
  1 medium yellow summer squash, sliced
  1 cup fresh baby carrots, halved lengthwise
  1 tablespoon butter, melted
1/2 teaspoon lemon-pepper seasoning
1/4 teaspoon salt
1/2 cup prepared pesto
1/2 cup shredded Parmesan cheese
1/2 cup chopped walnuts, toasted, optional

Cook the linguine according to the package directions, adding the shrimp during the last minute. Meanwhile, in a greased 15-in. x 10-in. x 1-in. baking pan, combine the asparagus, squash and carrots. Drizzle with butter; sprinkle with lemon-pepper and salt. Bake, uncovered, at 450° for 15-20 minutes or until vegetables are tender, stirring once.

Drain linguine and shrimp; transfer to a serving bowl. Add the vegetable mixture and pesto; toss gently. Sprinkle with Parmesan cheese and walnuts if desired. **Yield:** 6 servings.

Cran-Raspberry Pie

In a large bowl, dissolve gelatin in boiling water. Stir in cranberry sauce and pineapple. Chill until partially set. Pour into crust. Refrigerate until set.

Meanwhile, in a heavy saucepan, combine marshmallows and milk. Cook and stir over medium-low heat until marshmallows are melted. Remove from the heat. Stir in vanilla. Transfer to a large bowl. Cover and let stand until cooled to room temperature.

Whisk in a third of the whipped cream until smooth (mixture will be stringy at first). Fold in the remaining whipped cream. Spread over gelatin layer. Refrigerate until set. **Yield:** 6-8 servings.

Grasshopper Pie

(Pictured below)

Prep: 15 min. + chilling

With a refreshing combination of chocolate and mint, this dessert has become a must-have at Christmastime for our family. Just follow the directions for a cream-filled chocolate crust (see tip box below right) to prepare the crust yourself. —*Melissa Sokasits, Warrenville, Illinois*

> 1-1/2 cups cold milk
> 1 package (3.9 ounces) instant chocolate pudding mix
> 2-3/4 cups whipped topping, *divided*
> 1 package (4.67 ounces) mint Andes candies, chopped, *divided*
> 1 chocolate crumb crust (9 inches)
> 1/4 teaspoon mint extract
> 2 drops green food coloring, optional

In a small bowl, whisk milk and pudding mix for 2 minutes. Let stand for 2 minutes or until soft-set. Fold in

Make a Perfect Crumb Crust

WHO HAS TIME during the holiday season to make homemade pie crusts? You do! In just minutes, you can put together a wonderful crumb crust your family and friends will think you slaved over. But you don't have to tell them how simple it was to follow the helpful chart and hints from our Test Kitchen staff (see the tip boxes on the next page).

Cran-Raspberry Pie

(Pictured above)

Prep: 20 min. + chilling

Sweet raspberry gelatin and ruby-red cranberries really brighten up this Christmasy pie. Use a store-bought crust if you're short on time, or make a simple graham cracker crust at home. —*Eddie Stott, Mt. Juliet, Tennessee*

> 1 package (3 ounces) raspberry gelatin
> 1 cup boiling water
> 1 cup whole-berry cranberry sauce
> 1 can (8 ounces) unsweetened crushed pineapple, drained
> 1 graham cracker crust (9 inches)
> 2 cups miniature marshmallows
> 1/4 cup sweetened condensed milk
> 1/2 teaspoon vanilla extract
> 1 cup heavy whipping cream, whipped

Grasshopper Pie

Gingersnap Pumpkin Pie

4 ounces cream cheese, softened
1 tablespoon sugar
1-1/2 cups whipped topping
1 cup cold milk
2 packages (3.4 ounces *each*) instant butterscotch pudding mix
1/2 cup canned pumpkin
1/2 teaspoon pumpkin pie spice
1/2 teaspoon vanilla extract
1/4 teaspoon ground cinnamon
Additional whipped topping, optional

In a small bowl, combine cookie crumbs and butter. Press onto the bottom and up the sides of an ungreased 9-in. pie plate. Bake at 375° for 8-10 minutes or until crust is lightly browned. Cool on a wire rack.

For filling, in a small mixing bowl, beat cream cheese and sugar until smooth. Fold in whipped topping. Spread over crust.

In a small bowl, whisk milk and pudding mixes for 2 minutes. Let stand for 2 minutes or until soft-set. Stir in the pumpkin, pie spice, vanilla and cinnamon. Spread over cream cheese layer. Cover and refrigerate overnight. Garnish with additional whipped topping if desired. **Yield:** 6-8 servings.

3/4 cup whipped topping. Fold in 3/4 cup candies. Spoon into crust.

In another bowl, combine extract and remaining whipped topping; add food coloring if desired. Spread over pudding layer; sprinkle with remaining candies. Cover and refrigerate for 4 hours or until set. **Yield:** 8 servings.

Gingersnap Pumpkin Pie

(Pictured above)

Prep: 30 min. + chilling

Give pumpkin pie some pizzazz with a gingersnap crust and cream cheese.   —*Liz Raisig, New York, New York*

1-1/2 cups finely crushed gingersnaps (about 32 cookies)
1/4 cup butter, melted

Taking Shape

TO SHAPE your pie crust, press the crumb mixture onto the bottom and up the sides of a 9-inch pie plate. Pressing with a measuring cup will keep your hands clean.

Chart and Directions for Different Crumb Crusts

TO MAKE a crumb crust, follow the chart below. Just combine the necessary ingredients for the type of crust you want, then press the mixture onto the bottom and up the sides of an ungreased 9-inch pie plate. Before filling the crust, either chill it for 30 minutes or bake it at 375° for 8-10 minutes or until lightly browned, then cool.

Type of Crust	Amount of Crumbs	Sugar	Butter or Margarine, Melted
Graham Cracker	1-1/2 cups (24 squares)	1/4 cup	1/3 cup
Chocolate Wafer	1-1/4 cups (20 wafers)	1/4 cup	1/4 cup
Vanilla Wafer	1-1/2 cups (30 wafers)	none	1/4 cup
Cream-Filled Chocolate	1-1/2 cups (15 cookies)	none	1/4 cup
Gingersnap	1-1/2 cups (24 cookies)	none	1/4 cup

Chapter 21

HAVE A HARVEST of garden-fresh produce to use up? Want something new for a backyard barbecue, or your family's weekly pizza night? Maybe you're looking ahead to Christmastime and need some great gift ideas.

You'll find foods that fit all of those categories in this themed chapter. Enjoy favorite recipes featuring juicy tomatoes, sweet corn, deliciously different ideas for pizza, grilled specialties and gifts-from-the-kitchen that are perfect for the holiday season.

Similar dishes are grouped together, so you can easily locate the types you're looking for—whether it's a summertime refresher such as Chicken Salad in Tomato Cups or a merry treat such as Pecan Candy Clusters.

FRESH-AIR FARE. Sausage Veggie Grill (recipe on p. 310).

Pizza Pleasers

NEED A DINNER IDEA that's quick, easy and sure to satisfy family and friends? Make pizza new again with these simple-to-fix favorites. Each of the following recipes starts with a prebaked Italian bread shell crust and features an assortment of toppings that'll suit every mood. No matter whose taste buds you aim to please, there's definitely something here for you!

Bacon-Olive Tomato Pizza

(Pictured at far right)

Prep/Total Time: 30 min.

Bacon and tomatoes bring the taste of a BLT to this hearty and delicious pizza. I call this "championship pizza" because it always gives our team the winning edge!
—*Cindy Clement, Colorado Springs, Colorado*

  1 prebaked Italian bread shell crust (14 ounces)
1/3 cup ranch salad dressing
  1 pound sliced bacon, cooked and crumbled
  4 plum tomatoes, sliced
  1 cup sliced fresh mushrooms
  1 can (2-1/4 ounces) sliced ripe olives, drained
  2 cups (8 ounces) shredded part-skim mozzarella cheese

Place crust on an ungreased 12-in. pizza pan. Top with dressing, bacon, tomatoes, mushrooms, olives and cheese. Bake at 450° for 10-12 minutes or until cheese is melted. **Yield:** 8 slices.

Thai Chicken Pizza

(Pictured at far right)

Prep/Total Time: 25 min.

I came up with this recipe after trying a similar appetizer pizza at a restaurant. This Thai-style pie is a delightfully different way to use up leftover grilled or baked chicken.
—*Cheryl Taylor, Ortonville, Michigan*

  1 prebaked Italian bread shell crust (14 ounces)
  1 tablespoon olive oil
  4 ounces ready-to-serve roasted chicken breast strips
  2 to 3 large fresh mushrooms, thinly sliced
1/4 cup plus 2 tablespoons Oriental peanut sauce, *divided*
  2 cups (8 ounces) shredded part-skim mozzarella cheese, *divided*
1/4 cup thinly sliced red onion
1/2 cup fresh snow peas, halved
1/4 cup chopped sweet red pepper

1/4 cup julienned carrot
  2 green onions, sliced
1/2 cup salted peanuts

Place crust on an ungreased 12-in. pizza pan; brush with oil. In a small bowl, combine the chicken, mushrooms and 1/4 cup peanut sauce; spread over crust. Sprinkle with 1 cup cheese.
  Layer with red onion, snow peas, red pepper and carrot. Sprinkle with remaining cheese. Top with green onions and peanuts. Drizzle with remaining peanut sauce. Bake at 450° for 10-12 minutes or until cheese is melted. **Yield:** 8 slices.

Mexican Pizza

(Pictured at right)

Prep/Total Time: 30 min.

I love the ease and versatility of this crowd-pleasing pizza that features Southwestern flavors. You can add shredded chicken and taco seasoning for meat lovers or leave the meat off for a quick vegetarian meal.
—*Kathleen Hall, Irmo, South Carolina*

  1 large onion
  1 prebaked Italian bread shell crust (14 ounces)
  1 can (16 ounces) refried beans
  2 cups (8 ounces) shredded cheddar cheese
  3 cups shredded lettuce
  1 cup (4 ounces) shredded Mexican cheese blend
1/3 cup chopped seeded tomato
  2 tablespoons sliced ripe olives
1/2 cup coarsely chopped ranch-flavored tortilla chips

Slice half of the onion and chop the rest; set aside. Place crust on an ungreased 12-in. pizza pan. Spread beans over crust to within 1/2 in. of edges. Top with cheddar cheese and sliced onion.
  Bake at 450° for 10-12 minutes or until cheese is melted. Top with lettuce, Mexican cheese, chopped onion, tomato, olives and tortilla chips. **Yield:** 8 slices.

Caramelized Onion 'n' Pear Pizza

(Pictured at right)

Prep/Total Time: 30 min.

Get your knife and fork ready for this one! The home economists in our Test Kitchen used delectable layers to create a mouth-watering, eye-appealing main course that eats like a meal. This savory pie with pears and two kinds of cheese is sure to get rave reviews.

  1 large red onion, sliced and separated into rings
  3 tablespoons butter
  3 tablespoons sugar
  1 prebaked Italian bread shell crust (14 ounces)

Clockwise from top:
Mexican Pizza
Caramelized Onion 'n' Pear Pizza
Thai Chicken Pizza
Bacon-Olive Tomato Pizza

   2 medium pears, peeled and sliced
   1 cup (4 ounces) shredded part-skim
      mozzarella cheese
1/4 cup crumbled Gorgonzola cheese
   2 cups ready-to-serve salad greens
   1 large tomato, sliced
1/3 cup blue cheese salad dressing
1/4 cup chopped hazelnuts

In a large skillet, saute onion in butter until tender. Add sugar; cook and stir over medium heat for 5-10 minutes or until onions are caramelized.

Place crust on an ungreased 12-in. pizza pan; spread with onion to within 1 in. of edges. Layer with pears and cheeses. Bake at 450° for 5-8 minutes or until cheese is melted. Top with greens and tomato. Drizzle with dressing. Sprinkle with hazelnuts. **Yield:** 8 slices.

Grape Tomato Mozzarella Salad

Tasty Tomatoes

FOR JUICY, fresh-off-the-vine flavor, you just can't beat the taste of a sun-warmed tomato. The versatile veggie offers a bounty of opportunities. And the crop of reader recipes here will help you make the most of them—whether you choose beefsteak, cherry or plum—and their all-too-short season in the sun.

Grape Tomato Mozzarella Salad

(Pictured above)

Prep/Total Time: 15 min.

I created this recipe after enjoying something similar on a cruise. —Linda Haas, Tenmile, Oregon

✓ Uses less fat, sugar or salt. Includes Nutrition Facts and Diabetic Exchanges.

- 1/2 large sweet onion, thinly sliced
- 1 medium cucumber, sliced
- 2 cups grape tomatoes
- 1/2 cup loosely packed fresh basil leaves, sliced
- 4 ounces fresh mozzarella cheese, sliced
- 1/3 cup prepared Italian salad dressing

Arrange the onion, cucumber, tomatoes, basil and mozzarella on salad plates. Drizzle with dressing. Serve immediately. **Yield:** 6 servings.

Nutrition Facts: 1 serving (prepared with fat-free dressing) equals 85 calories, 4 g fat (3 g saturated fat), 15 mg cholesterol, 224 mg sodium, 7 g carbohydrate, 1 g fiber, 5 g protein. **Diabetic Exchanges:** 1 lean meat, 1 vegetable.

Italian Chicken and Squash

Prep/Total Time: 30 min.

We love Mediterranean food, so I decided to try making it at home. I was surprised that so much flavor came from so little effort! —Lisa Leavitt, Chubbuck, Idaho

- 1 pound boneless skinless chicken breasts, cut into strips
- 3 tablespoons butter
- 1 medium yellow summer squash, halved lengthwise and thinly sliced
- 1 medium zucchini, halved lengthwise and thinly sliced
- 8 ounces uncooked angel hair pasta
- 1/4 cup chicken broth
- 3 tablespoons lemon juice
- 20 cherry tomatoes, halved
- 3/4 cup grated Parmesan cheese
- 3/4 cup crumbled tomato and basil feta cheese

In a large skillet, cook chicken in butter over medium heat until no longer pink. Add yellow squash and zucchini; cook for 3-4 minutes or until tender. Meanwhile, cook the pasta according to package directions.

Stir broth and lemon juice into chicken mixture. Bring to a boil. Reduce heat; cover and simmer for 5 minutes or until heated through, stirring occasionally. Drain pasta; toss with chicken mixture and tomatoes. Sprinkle with cheeses. **Yield:** 5 servings.

Beef Ragu with Ravioli

(Pictured below)

Prep: 15 min. **Cook:** 40 min.

This sweet and easy sauce from our Test Kitchen tastes like it was simmering all day! Serve it with store-bought ravioli for a simple, last-minute meal.

  1 pound ground beef
1/2 cup chopped onion
  1 pound plum tomatoes, diced
  1 cup beef broth
1/2 cup red wine *or* additional beef broth
  1 can (6 ounces) tomato paste
  2 teaspoons minced fresh rosemary
  1 teaspoon sugar
  1 teaspoon minced garlic
1/2 teaspoon salt
  1 package (20 ounces) refrigerated cheese
    ravioli
Grated Parmesan cheese, optional

In a large skillet, cook beef and onion over medium heat until no longer pink; drain. Add the tomatoes, broth, wine or additional broth, tomato paste, rosemary, sugar, garlic and salt. Bring to a boil. Reduce heat; simmer, uncovered, for 30 minutes.

Cook ravioli according to package directions; drain. Top with meat sauce. Sprinkle with Parmesan cheese if desired. **Yield:** 4 servings.

Chicken Salad in Tomato Cups

Chicken Salad in Tomato Cups

(Pictured above)

Prep/Total Time: 25 min.

Garden-fresh tomatoes make this a real treat. My family loves it! —*Judy Robertson, Russell Springs, Kentucky*

  4 large tomatoes
  2 cups finely chopped cooked chicken
3/4 cup mayonnaise
1/2 cup chopped pecans
1/4 cup chopped celery
  1 tablespoon diced pimientos
  1 tablespoon lime juice
1/8 teaspoon salt
1/8 teaspoon pepper

Cut a thin slice off the top of each tomato. Scoop out the pulp, leaving 1/2-in. shells. Invert onto paper towels to drain. In a large bowl, combine the remaining ingredients. Spoon into the tomatoes. Serve immediately. **Yield:** 4 servings.

Rapid Ripening

To ripen green garden tomatoes, put them inside brown paper bags. Don't stack too many tomatoes in one bag, or they might get bruised. Check them every few days and remove the ripe ones.
—*Delia Kennedy, Deer Park, Washington*

Beef Ragu with Ravioli

Sausage Veggie Grill

until meat is no longer pink and vegetables are tender. Open foil carefully to allow steam to escape. **Yield:** 4 servings.

Monterey Chicken

(Pictured below)

Prep: 15 min. + marinating **Grill:** 20 min.

Try this chicken from the grill served in a refreshingly different way. Although the ingredient list may appear long, the cheesy main dish is really a cinch to make.
—Sherri Gordon, Pickerington, Ohio

  6 bacon strips, halved
  6 boneless skinless chicken breast halves
    (4 ounces *each*)
1/2 cup olive oil
1/4 cup red wine vinegar
1/4 cup soy sauce
  1 teaspoon minced garlic
1/2 teaspoon salt
1/2 teaspoon dried oregano
1/4 teaspoon pepper
  6 thin slices sweet onion
  6 thin slices tomato
  6 thin slices avocado
  6 thin slices Monterey Jack cheese

Cook the bacon according to the package directions; drain. Meanwhile, flatten the chicken to an even thickness. In a large resealable plastic bag, combine the oil, vinegar, soy sauce, garlic, salt, oregano and pepper; add the chicken. Seal the bag and turn to coat; refrigerate for at least 30 minutes.

Drain and discard marinade. Grill chicken, uncovered, over medium heat for 6 minutes on each side. Move chicken to edges of grill. Top each with two bacon pieces and one slice of onion, tomato, avocado and cheese. Cover and grill 4-6 minutes longer or until cheese is melted. **Yield:** 6 servings.

Great Grilling

IN THE SUMMERTIME, you can't beat spending time outdoors. So give your oven some time off and fire up the grill! Just grab a glass of lemonade, then let these grilled recipes be your ticket to fresh-air fare.

Sausage Veggie Grill

(Pictured above and on page 304)

Prep: 10 min. **Grill:** 25 min.

This is great for a party on the patio. With sausage, veggies and herbs, the pouch of summer favorites is as colorful as it is tasty. —Laura Hillyer, Bayfield, Colorado

  1 pound Italian sausage links, cut into 1/2-inch
    slices
  1 medium zucchini, cut into 1-inch slices
  1 medium yellow summer squash, cut into
    1-inch slices
  1 medium sweet red pepper, sliced
  1 medium onion, cut into wedges
  1 cup quartered fresh mushrooms
1/4 cup olive oil
  1 tablespoon dried oregano
  1 tablespoon dried parsley flakes
  1 teaspoon garlic salt
  1 teaspoon paprika

In a large bowl, combine the first six ingredients. In a small bowl, combine the oil, oregano, parsley, garlic salt and paprika. Pour over sausage mixture; toss to coat. Divide between two pieces of heavy-duty foil (about 14 in. x 12 in.). Fold foil around sausage mixture and seal tightly.

Grill, covered, over medium heat for 25-30 minutes or

Monterey Chicken

Ham Kabobs

(Pictured at right)

Prep: 20 min. + marinating **Grill:** 10 min.

These kabobs with two kinds of meats and plenty of vegetables are one of our family's favorite dishes. They're so simple to fix...and even simpler to clean up!
—Trudy Gernert, Seymour, Indiana

✓ Uses less fat, sugar or salt. Includes Nutrition Facts and Diabetic Exchanges.

Ham Kabobs

       1 cup white vinegar
   1/2 cup packed brown sugar
       1 pound cubed fully cooked lean ham (2 cups)
       4 Italian turkey sausage links, cut into 1-inch slices
       2 medium sweet potatoes, peeled and cut into 1-inch cubes
       1 tablespoon water
       2 medium green peppers, cut into 1-inch pieces
       1 medium onion, cut into wedges
     16 cherry tomatoes
1-1/2 cups pineapple chunks

In a small bowl, combine vinegar and brown sugar. Pour half of the marinade into a large resealable plastic bag; add ham and sausage. Seal bag and turn to coat; refrigerate for at least 2 hours. Refrigerate remaining marinade for basting.

Place sweet potatoes and water in a microwave-safe dish. Cover and microwave on high for 4 minutes or until tender; drain.

Drain and discard marinade. Alternately thread the ham, sausage, sweet potatoes, green peppers, onion, tomatoes and pineapple onto eight metal or soaked wooden skewers.

Grill, covered, over medium heat or broil 4-6 in. from the heat for 8-10 minutes or until sausage is no longer pink and vegetables are tender, turning and basting occasionally with reserved marinade. **Yield:** 8 servings.

Editor's Note: This recipe was tested in a 1,100-watt microwave.

Nutrition Facts: 1 kabob equals 281 calories, 8 g fat (3 g saturated fat), 52 mg cholesterol, 1,074 mg sodium, 31 g carbohydrate, 3 g fiber, 21 g protein. **Diabetic Exchanges:** 3 very lean meat, 1 starch, 1 vegetable, 1 fat, 1/2 fruit.

Lemony Grilled Salmon

Prep: 10 min. + marinating **Grill:** 15 min.

Here's a no-fail idea that's really tasty: Grilling salmon directly on lemon slices! It leaves the salmon moist, flaky and extremely aromatic. Our Test Kitchen created this delectable combination.

1/2 cup honey
1/4 cup lemon juice
1/4 cup unsweetened pineapple juice
   2 teaspoons teriyaki sauce
   1 teaspoon grated lemon peel

1/2 teaspoon minced garlic
1/4 teaspoon crushed red pepper flakes
   4 salmon fillets (6 ounces *each*), skin removed
   8 lemon slices (3/4 inch thick)

In a small bowl, combine the first seven ingredients. Pour 2/3 cup into a large resealable plastic bag; add salmon. Seal bag and turn to coat; refrigerate for at least 2 hours. Cover and refrigerate remaining marinade for basting.

Coat grill rack with nonstick cooking spray before starting the grill. Arrange lemon slices on rack. Drain and discard marinade. Place each salmon fillet over two lemon slices.

Grill, covered, over medium heat for 5 minutes. Brush with some of the reserved marinade. Grill 10-15 minutes longer or until fish flakes easily with a fork, basting occasionally with remaining marinade. **Yield:** 4 servings.

Salsa Zucchini

Prep/Total Time: 30 min.

It took just three ingredients to make this extra-easy side dish. It's great on the grill, but the best part is there's no cleanup. —Terri Wolfson, Knoxville, Tennessee

✓ Uses less fat, sugar or salt. Includes Nutrition Facts and Diabetic Exchanges.

   2 small zucchini, cut into 1/2-inch slices
   1 cup salsa
1/2 cup shredded Monterey Jack cheese

Place zucchini on a double thickness of heavy-duty foil (about 18 in. x 12 in.). Top with salsa. Fold foil around zucchini and seal tightly.

Grill, covered, over medium heat for 25-30 minutes or until zucchini is crisp-tender. Open foil carefully to allow steam to escape. Transfer zucchini to a serving bowl; sprinkle with cheese. **Yield:** 4 servings.

Nutrition Facts: 3/4 cup equals 81 calories, 4 g fat (3 g saturated fat), 13 mg cholesterol, 357 mg sodium, 4 g carbohydrate, 3 g fiber, 4 g protein. **Diabetic Exchanges:** 1 lean meat, 1 vegetable.

Carefully peel back cornhusks to within 1 in. of bottoms; remove silk. Brush with remaining butter mixture. Rewrap corn in husks and secure with kitchen string.

Grill corn, covered, over medium heat for 25-30 minutes or until tender, turning occasionally. Cut string and peel back husks. Drizzle corn with reserved butter mixture; sprinkle with Parmesan cheese. **Yield:** 8 servings.

Creative Corn

DOES anything capture the spirit of summer like sweet corn? Pick up some extra ears from the farmers market or grocery store tonight, then savor the delicious salad, entree and side-dish recipes here.

Garlic-Butter Parmesan Corn

(Pictured above)

Prep: 15 min. + soaking **Grill:** 25 min.

This is the best grilled corn I've ever tasted! The butter, garlic and cheese perk up the flavor and make it hard to resist. —*Mitzi Sentiff, Alexandria, Virginia*

  8 medium ears sweet corn in husks
1/3 cup butter, cubed
1/2 teaspoon minced garlic
1/4 teaspoon salt
1/4 cup grated Parmesan cheese

Soak corn in cold water for 20 minutes. Meanwhile, in a small saucepan, combine the butter, garlic and salt. Cook and stir over medium heat until butter is melted; set aside 2 tablespoons.

Veggie Steak Salad

Prep/Total Time: 30 min.

Here's a salad that really satisfies as a main dish. What's more, it's quick to prepare and tastes delicious.
  —*Tiffany Martinez, Aliso Viejo, California*

  2 medium ears sweet corn, husks and silk removed
  1 beef flank steak (1 pound)
1/4 teaspoon salt
1/4 teaspoon pepper
1/4 cup olive oil, *divided*
  2 tablespoons balsamic vinegar
  1 teaspoon garlic powder
  1 teaspoon capers, drained
  1 teaspoon Dijon mustard
  1 package (5 ounces) spring mix salad greens
  1 large tomato, chopped
  4 slices red onion, separated into rings
1/4 cup minced fresh parsley
1/4 cup shredded Parmesan cheese

In a Dutch oven, bring 8 cups of water to a boil. Add corn; boil 5-7 minutes or until tender. Drain and immediately place corn in ice water for about 10 minutes. Drain and pat dry; cut the kernels from the cobs.

Meanwhile, rub the steak with salt and pepper. In a large skillet, cook the steak in 2 tablespoons oil for 6-8 minutes on each side or until meat reaches desired doneness (for medium-rare, a meat thermometer should read 145°; medium, 160°; well-done, 170°).

For dressing, combine the vinegar, garlic powder, capers, mustard and remaining oil in a jar with a tight-fitting lid; shake well.

Thinly slice beef across the grain. In a large bowl, combine the salad greens, tomato, onion, parsley, corn and beef. Drizzle with dressing; toss to coat. Sprinkle with Parmesan cheese. **Yield:** 5 servings.

Cilantro Corn Saute

(Pictured below)

Prep/Total Time: 15 min.

This simple side goes with almost anything. The cilantro and cumin give it just the right amount of Southwestern flavor. —Lisa Langston, Conroe, Texas

☑ Uses less fat, sugar or salt. Includes Nutrition Facts and Diabetic Exchanges.

3-1/3 **cups fresh** *or* **frozen corn, thawed**
   1 **medium green pepper, chopped**
   1 **tablespoon finely chopped onion**
   2 **tablespoons butter**
1/2 **cup minced fresh cilantro**
1-1/2 **teaspoons ground cumin**

In a large skillet, saute the corn, green pepper and onion in the butter until tender. Stir in the cilantro and cumin; saute 1-2 minutes longer or until heated through. **Yield:** 4 servings.

Nutrition Facts: 3/4 cup equals 173 calories, 7 g fat (4 g saturated fat), 15 mg cholesterol, 80 mg sodium, 27 g carbohydrate, 4 g fiber, 5 g protein. **Diabetic Exchanges:** 1-1/2 starch, 1 fat.

Cilantro Corn Saute

Wild Rice Chicken Skillet

Prep/Total Time: 25 min.

It's hard to believe that this scrumptious meal-in-one requires less than half an hour in the kitchen. But it's true! Featuring plenty of rice, corn and cheddar cheese, the fast chicken entree is popular with my family.
—Deborah Webb, Kalispell, Montana

☑ Uses less fat, sugar or salt. Includes Nutrition Facts and Diabetic Exchanges.

   4 **boneless skinless chicken breast halves**
     (4 ounces *each***)**
   1 **tablespoon olive oil**
1/2 **teaspoon salt**
1/4 **teaspoon pepper**
1-1/2 **cups fresh** *or* **frozen corn, thawed**
   1 **package (8.8 ounces) ready-to-serve long grain and wild rice**
1/2 **cup shredded cheddar cheese**

In a large skillet, brown the chicken in oil over medium heat. Sprinkle with salt and pepper. Reduce the heat to low; cover and cook for 10-15 minutes or until the juices run clear.

Stir in the corn and rice; sprinkle with cheese. Cover and cook 3-4 minutes longer or until heated through and cheese is melted. **Yield:** 4 servings.

Nutrition Facts: 1 chicken breast half with 3/4 cup rice mixture equals 341 calories, 12 g fat (4 g saturated fat), 78 mg cholesterol, 763 mg sodium, 30 g carbohydrate, 3 g fiber, 30 g protein. **Diabetic Exchanges:** 4 very lean meat, 2 starch, 1 fat.

Cooking with Corn

• **For no-fuss grilling...**
Soak corn in cold water for 20 minutes. Carefully peel back husks from each ear to within 1 in. of bottom; remove silk. Rewrap corn in husks and secure with kitchen string. Grill, covered, over medium heat for 25-30 minutes or until tender, turning occasionally.

• **For stress-free blanching...**
Boil corn in 6-8 quarts of water in a Dutch oven or kettle for 5-7 minutes or until tender. If the corn is larger than 2 inches in diameter, cook it a few minutes longer. Place the cooked corn in ice water for about 10 minutes. Drain and pat dry.

• **For easy boiling...**
Place corn in a Dutch oven or kettle; cover with water. Bring to a boil. Reduce heat; cover and cook for 3-5 minutes or until tender.

• **For fast trimming...**
Stand corn on a cutting board. Starting at the top, run a sharp knife down the cob, cutting deeply to remove whole kernels.

Spiced Rum-Nut Brittle
Pecan Candy Clusters

Festive Gifts

TOO TIRED to shop crowded malls for all the names on your Christmas list? For gifts that are always in good taste, think presents from the pantry! They're simple, economical and can be personalized for any age or taste. Best of all, the merry munchies featured here go together quick as a wink.

You'll even find directions for making a fun paper holder for your treats (see the tip box on p. 315).

Pecan Candy Clusters

(Pictured above)

Prep: 30 min. + standing

My grandchildren and the kids in my neighborhood love helping me fix—and eat—these yummy four-ingredient treats. —Flo Burtnetther, Gage, Oklahoma

- **2 cups milk chocolate chips, *divided***
- **64 pecan halves (about 1-1/2 cups)**
- **28 caramels**
- **2 tablespoons heavy whipping cream**

Line a baking sheet with waxed paper; set aside. In a microwave-safe bowl, melt 1 cup chocolate chips; stir until smooth. Drop the chocolate by tablespoonfuls onto the prepared baking sheet. Immediately place four pecans on top of each chocolate drop.

Place the caramels in a 1-qt. microwave-safe dish; add cream. Microwave, uncovered, on high for 2 minutes, stirring once. Spoon onto the middle of each cluster.

Melt the remaining chocolate chips; stir until smooth.

Spread over caramel. Let stand until set. **Yield:** 16 candies.

Editor's Note: This recipe was tested in a 1,100-watt microwave.

Spiced Rum-Nut Brittle

(Pictured above)

Prep: 25 min. + cooling

Seasoned with cayenne and cinnamon, this microwave brittle warms up holiday visitors…and makes a delicious stocking stuffer. —Terri McKitrick, Delafield, Wisconsin

- **1 cup sugar**
- **1/2 cup light corn syrup**
- **1/2 cup chopped cashews**
- **1/2 cup chopped pecans**
- **1 teaspoon butter**
- **1/2 teaspoon ground cinnamon**
- **1/4 teaspoon cayenne pepper**
- **1/8 teaspoon salt**
- **Pinch ground nutmeg**
- **1 teaspoon baking soda**
- **1/2 teaspoon rum extract**
- **1/2 teaspoon vanilla extract**

Butter a 15-in. x 10-in. x 1-in. pan; set aside. In a 2-qt. microwave-safe bowl, combine sugar and corn syrup. Microwave, uncovered, on high for 3 minutes; stir. Microwave 2-1/2 minutes longer. Stir in cashews, pecans, butter, cinnamon, cayenne, salt and nutmeg.

Microwave, uncovered, on high for 2 minutes or until mixture turns a light amber color (mixture will be very hot). Quickly stir in baking soda and extracts until light and foamy. Immediately pour into prepared pan; spread with a metal spatula. Cool completely. Break into pieces; store in an airtight container. **Yield:** 1 pound.

Editor's Note: This recipe was tested in a 1,100-watt microwave.

Peanut Butter Popcorn Crunch

(Pictured at right)

Prep: 20 min. **Bake:** 1 hour + cooling

This sweet, crunchy mix is a delightful snack to give loved ones or to munch while watching Christmas movies. To craft the fun treat holder shown at right, see the tip box below. —LaVonne Smith, Kennebec, South Dakota

    12 cups popped popcorn
     4 cups miniature pretzels
    2/3 cup sugar
    1/2 cup honey
    1/2 cup light corn syrup
    2/3 cup creamy peanut butter
     1 teaspoon vanilla extract
     4 cups chocolate-covered peanuts

In a large bowl, combine popcorn and pretzels; set aside. In a small saucepan, combine the sugar, honey and corn syrup. Bring to a boil; cook and stir for 2 minutes or until sugar is dissolved.

Remove from heat. Stir in peanut butter and vanilla. Pour over popcorn mixture and toss to coat. Pour into two greased 15-in. x 10-in. x 1-in. baking pans.

Bake, uncovered, at 250° for 1 hour, stirring every 15 minutes. Cool for 10 minutes. Break into clusters; place in a large bowl. Add chocolate-covered peanuts; mix well. Cool completely. **Yield:** about 4 quarts.

Peanut Butter Popcorn Crunch

Oatmeal Pecan Cookie Mix

Prep/Total Time: 15 min.

Layered in pretty bow-tied jars, this cookie mix looks as good as it tastes! Include the prep instructions with your gift tag. —Beverly Woodcock, Kingston, Ontario

     1 cup all-purpose flour
    1/2 cup sugar
    1/2 teaspoon baking soda
    1/2 teaspoon baking powder
    1/2 cup packed brown sugar
    3/4 cup old-fashioned oats
    1/2 cup chopped pecans
     1 cup crisp rice cereal

ADDITIONAL INGREDIENTS:
    1/2 cup butter, softened
     1 egg
     1 teaspoon vanilla extract

In a small bowl, combine the flour, sugar, baking soda and baking powder. In a 1-qt. glass jar, layer the flour mixture, brown sugar, oats, pecans and rice cereal, packing well between each layer. Cover and store the mix in a cool dry place for up to 6 months. **Yield:** 1 batch (about 4 cups total).

To prepare: In a large mixing bowl, cream butter until light and fluffy. Beat in egg and vanilla. Gradually add cookie mix. Drop by rounded teaspoonfuls 2 in. apart onto greased baking sheets. Bake at 350° for 8-10 minutes or until golden brown. Cool for 2 minutes before removing from pans to wire racks. **Yield:** about 3 dozen.

A Holiday Treat Holder in 3 Easy Steps

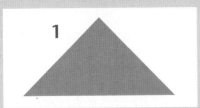

Fold a 12-inch square of double-sided paper in half diagonally to make a triangle.

Fold opposite sides in as shown, making sure the top edges are parallel with the bottom edge.

Fold the top layer down and place treats inside the pocket.

General Recipe Index

This handy index lists every recipe by food category, major ingredient and/or cooking method, so you can easily locate recipes to suit your needs.

✓Recipe includes Nutrition Facts and Diabetic Exchanges

✓*Recipe includes Nutrition Facts and Diabetic Exchanges*

✓*Recipe includes Nutrition Facts and Diabetic Exchanges*

✓Recipe includes Nutrition Facts and Diabetic Exchanges

✓Recipe includes Nutrition Facts and Diabetic Exchanges

✓Recipe includes Nutrition Facts and Diabetic Exchanges

✓Recipe includes Nutrition Facts and Diabetic Exchanges

✓*Recipe includes Nutrition Facts and Diabetic Exchanges*

✓Recipe includes Nutrition Facts and Diabetic Exchanges

✓Recipe includes Nutrition Facts and Diabetic Exchanges

✓Recipe includes Nutrition Facts and Diabetic Exchanges

✓Recipe includes Nutrition Facts and Diabetic Exchanges

✓Recipe includes Nutrition Facts and Diabetic Exchanges

✓*Recipe includes Nutrition Facts and Diabetic Exchanges*

✓Recipe includes Nutrition Facts and Diabetic Exchanges

✓Recipe includes Nutrition Facts and Diabetic Exchanges

Alphabetical Index

This handy index lists every recipe in alphabetical order, so you can easily find your favorite recipes.

✓Recipe includes Nutrition Facts and Diabetic Exchanges

✓Recipe includes Nutrition Facts and Diabetic Exchanges

✓*Recipe includes Nutrition Facts and Diabetic Exchanges*

✓Recipe includes Nutrition Facts and Diabetic Exchanges

✓Recipe includes Nutrition Facts and Diabetic Exchanges